BHAKTI IN CURRENT RESEARCH

SOUTH ASIA INSTITUTE, NEW DELHI BRANCH
HEIDELBERG UNIVERSITY
SOUTH ASIAN STUDIES NO. XLIV

Bhakti in Current Research, 2001-2003

Proceedings of the Ninth International Conference on Early Devotional Literature in New Indo-Aryan Languages, Heidelberg, 23-26 July 2003

edited by

MONIKA HORSTMANN

With a DVD by DANIEL GOLD

MANOHAR
2006

First published 2006

ISBN 81-7304-694-8

Published by
Ajay Kumar Jain *for*
Manohar Publishers & Distributors
4753/23 Ansari Road, Daryaganj
New Delhi 110 002

Printed at
Lordson Publishers Pvt. Ltd.
Delhi 110 007

Distributed in South Asia by
FOUNDATION BOOKS
4381/4, Ansari Road
Daryaganj, New Delhi 110 002
and its branches at Mumbai, Hyderabad,
Bangalore, Chennai, Kolkata

Contents

Preface

The present volume forms the ninth in a series of proceedings of the triennial International Conference on Early Devotional Literature in New Indo-Aryan Languages. The first conference of its kind was organized by Winand M. Callewaert in Leuven in 1979. The subsequent conferences took place in St. Augustin/Bonn (1982), Leiden (1985), Cambridge (1988), Paris (1991), Seattle (1994), Venice (1997), once again Leuven (2000), and finally Heidelberg (2003). In 2006, the tenth conference is scheduled to take place in India, as has been long overdue.

These proceedings unite twenty contributions which reflect original research carried out by their authors in the period under review. A number of the papers read at the conference have not found their way into this volume.

The contributions did not lend themselves naturally to an arrangement by thematic clusters. For all their diversity, many of them bring to mind that the term Bhakti is a locus where various concepts and often composite religious identities meet. While the focus of the conference was on the northern vernacular traditions, with no Sanskrit and little Dravidian material being discussed, the contributions represent facets of a broader South Asian religious and literary complex, of which Indic and Islamicate traditions as well as a whole gamut of literary languages is constitutive.

The conference was sponsored by the Deutsche Forschungsgemeinschaft and the Stiftung Universität Heidelberg. Ulrike Stark co-organized the conference and my historian colleague, Professor Volker Sellin, inaugurated it. Ingrid Schuhmann and Susanne Kempe helped with the preparation of the camerea-ready copy of the book, and Quoc-Bao Do with its layout. I wish to thank all of them sincerely.

MONIKA HORSTMANN

Note on Transcription

It was not attempted to impose a uniform system of transliteration on the contributions united in this volume. Consistency was, however, sought to be established for each individual paper. For pre-modern names, diacritic marks have normally been given; for modern names, this has been left to the authors' discretion. Names and words current in English generally appear in their English spelling.

Political Contextualization, Individualism and Search for a New Style in Late Brajbhāṣā Court Poetry:

The Quatrains of Ṭhākur from Bundelkhand*

Imre Bangha

On my trip to India in March 2003 I met an elderly scholar, who described how in his childhood he saw a court poet in Mirzapur. The future intellectual was deeply impressed by the poet's attire, his voluminous turban and dhoti, the sword at his side and by his ability to produce a quatrain on a given rhyme or a phrase, a *samasyā*, within a few minutes. Hearing this description I felt that the ambience and appreciation of court poetry were present almost at a tangible distance.

This is all the more interesting since in the first half of the last century such knowledge was still a part of living tradition, but the personalities of similar court poets have virtually disappeared from our horizon since then. In the 1920s Lala Bhagavandin, the head of the Hindi Department at Benares Hindu University, was not only able to collect several legends on a court poet in Bundelkhand who died a hundred years earlier but also met his descendants. In 2001 another scholar, Ganga Prasad 'Barsainya,' visited the places connected with the same poet but was not able to find people who knew about him.

The poet in question signed his quatrains as *Ṭhākur*, 'Lord,' however in spite of such a pen-name he was not a Bundela Rajput but a Kayastha as claimed by Bhagavandin, who had met his descendants. Ṭhākur was one of the last pre-modern Brajbhāṣā authors, who along with Padmākar, his more celebrated contemporary, was amongst the favourites of nineteenth-century anthologists. In the twentieth century he would become known as one of the few representatives of a personal voice in the highly stylised *Rītikāl*, the 'Era of Convention.' He became celebrated as a 'true love poet' for whose poetic work the expression of personal sentiments was a driving force and not the illustration of poetic conventions, as considered usual in his times. His love for independence and self-assertion, present in the few poems speaking about himself, are more often than not put into the mouth of the *gopīs*, the cowherd girls of the Krishna-lore. His poetry usually followed conventional

* I am grateful to Prof: Govind Sharma for helping me to interpret the difficulties of the Braj texts and to Dr Allison Busch for her comments on the article.

Krishna-themes in Brajbhāṣā but his style is peculiar to him not simply because of his sporadic use of Bundelkhandī themes, vocabulary and morphology, but rather because of an almost obsessive inclination to put proverbs into his poems. Scholars often refer to him informally as the 'Ṭhākur of the proverbs' *(muhāvrāvālā Ṭhākur)*.

This article will show on the example of Ṭhākur how creative forces were at work in content and style in the literature of an era which has been denounced as 'frozen' and 'derivative' by almost all twentieth-century scholars. I will also demonstrate that innovations associated with modern poets, such as Hariaudh's political contextualization of the Krishna myth in the first modern Hindi *mahākāvya*, the *Priya-pravās* (1914), an increased sense of individuality so closely connected to the *Chāyāvādī* poets of the 1920s and 1930s, or a search for simple post-mannerist style was already present in Ṭhākur.

Mythological contextualization of history

Tradition recorded as early as 1878[1] and the legends collected by Bhagavandin in the 1920s[2] or earlier relate Ṭhākur (*c.*1766–1827)[3] to the Bundelkhand of the late eighteenth and early nineteenth centuries which at that time was ruled by Bundela Rajputs, who were descendants of Chatrasāl, the founder of Chatarpur. As opposed to the *bādśāhī* 'royalist' Bundelas they were called *daṅgāhī* 'quarrelsome' Bundelas because of their resistance to the Mughals. The history of this region was particularly troubled in the eighteenth century with the constant emergence and dissolution of political entities, fragile alliances, intrigue, small princely states, petty chieftains, adventurers and a warlord of naked ascetics with an army of twenty thousand, Himmat Bahādur.

Already in 1878 Śivsiṃh Seṃgar mentioned Ṭhākur's connection with the Gosvāmī warlord Anūpgiri (*c.* 1734–1804) alias Himmat Bahādur, who established himself in Bundelkhand in 1792 by defeating the Bundela Rajput Arjun Singh.[4] A Bundelkhandi poet recounted to Śivsiṃh Seṃgar how Ṭhākur received a reward from Himmat Bahādur by dissuading the disgruntled Bundelas assembled in Chatarpur from attempting to kill the

---

1. Kishorilal Gupta, *Saroj sarvekṣaṇ*, Allahabad: Hindustānī Ekeḍemī, 1967, p. 328.
2. Lala Bhagavandin, *Ṭhākur ṭhasak*, Benares: Sāhitya Sevak Kāryālay, 1924, 'Ṭhākur kavi kā jīvancarit,' pp. 5-18.
3. The dates have been established by Lala Bhagavandin 1924 on the basis of family lore. See Bhagavandin, *Ṭhākur ṭhasak*, 'Ṭhākur kavi kā jīvancarit' pp. 6 and 23.
4. William Pinch, 'Who was Himmat Bahadur? Gosains, Rajputs and the British in Bundelkhand ca. 1800', *The Indian Economic and Social History Review*, vol. 35, 3 (1998), p. 313.

warlord and exhorting them to accept the situation. The means of this political action was a quatrain apparently about the cowherd girls' distress, who have been abandoned by Krishna and denigrated by gossipers,

कहिबे सुनिबे की कछू न इहाँ न लटी भली को दुख पावनौ है।
इनकी मरजी मैं सदा रहियै अपने मन कों समझावनौ है।
कबि ठाकुर कान्ह के देखिबे कौं अब मंत्र यही ठहरावनौ है।
इन चौंचँदहाइन मैं परिकै समयौ यह बीर बरावनौ है ॥166॥[5]

There is nothing left to say or hear in this case; there is no distress from good or bad.
We must convince ourselves to remain always according to his wishes.
The poet Ṭhākur says, this is the counsel to be followed in order to see Krishna:
Having fallen amongst these troublemakers, my friends/heroes, we have to get through this time.

There are similar legends that link Ṭhākur[6] to the political setting of smaller centres in Eastern Bundelkhand such as Jaitpur, Bijawar, Panna and Banda. Connection with so many minor courts points towards the life-style of court poets in those precarious times, when with the weakening of one patron the poet needed to move on to another one. Although the idea of a troubled Bundelkhand prior to the British conquest as well as the image of a court poet constantly changing patrons fit well into the colonial conception of Indian history, it should not be forgotten that the mere presence of mannerist or post-mannerist court poets indicates that there were also peaceful and creative periods between military campaigns.

While investigating Ṭhākur's political engagement, it is possible to observe that Krishna-poetry was not limited to describing amorous situations and was not so much alienated from the world as later critics of the Era of Convention suggest. This literature was also a forceful vehicle of political ideas; and in this respect it does not really matter whether Ṭhākur actually sent this poem to the Bundelas in Chatarpur or not. Tradition perceived it as a political message maybe, though less likely, even without the intention of the poet.

The fact that the tight framework of mannerist poetry served political purposes is not exceptional. There are already famous examples of political contextualization in Bihārī's couplets. The following *dohā* by Ṭhākur's time,

5. Quotations of Ṭhākur, if not indicated otherwise, are taken from Chandrashekhar Mishra, *Ṭhākur Granthāvalī*, Benares: Nāgarī Pracāriṇī Sabhā, 1973.

6. The dates have been established by Lala Bhagavandin 1924 on the basis of family lore. See Bhagavandin, *Ṭhākur ṭhasak*, 'Ṭhākur kavi kā jīvancarit,' pp. 6 and 23.

as attested by Lallū Lāl (1763-1825), was conceived as political advice to Mirzā Rājā Jaisingh, the commander of Aurangzeb's army, not to attack Śivaji, his fellow Hindu,

> स्वारथ सुकृत न स्रम बृथा देखि बिहंग बिचार।
> बाज पराए पानि परि तू पछीहि न मार ॥६३६॥[7]

> Your aim is not virtuous and your effort is useless—reflect on it, o bird;
> Falcon, you are in the hands of others, do not attack the fowl!

The same Lallū Lāl considered this device under the aesthetic rubric of 'saying something else,' *anyokti.*[8] Anyokti was conceived as an *alaṃkāra* 'figure of speech' by the Kashmirian Rudrata and later it has been connected either to the *alaṃkāras* such as *aprastuta-praśaṃsā, samāsokti, rūpakātiśayokti, prastutāṃkura* or to *dhvani* 'suggestion'. The practice of anyokti has a long tradition in Sanskrit with works such as the *Śataka*[9] of the ninth-century Kashmirian poet *Bhallata* and other authors[10] upto Paṇḍitarāja Jagannātha's *Bhāminīvilāsa*, which is also called *Anyoktivilāsa.*[11] In Hindi literature, apart from Bihārī, Rahīm and Vṛnd, some minor poets also used this device, which became the organizing force of the poetry of 'Bābā' Dīndayāl Giri (1802–65), who for example wrote about virtues such as knowledge, renunciation etc. in the framework of the description of seasons. The tradition continued to be popular well into the twentieth century with Badrinatha (Jha) Sharma's *Anyoktisāhasrī*,[12] Mathura Prasad Dikshit's *Anyokti-taraṃgiṇī*[13] in Sanskrit or Surendra Jha Suman's *Anyoktikā: mukraka*

---

7. Pandey, *Bihārī Satsaī:Lālcandrikā ṭīkā sahit*, Benares: Nāgarī Pracāriṇī Sabhā, 1977, p. 347.

8. Another example of *anyokti* in Bihārī quoted by Lallū Lāl (Pandey, *Bihārī Satsaī*, p. 346) is a poem addressed to Jaisingh when he was infatuated with a young girl: *nahī parāga nahī madhura madhu, nahī bikāsa ihi kāla; alī, kalī hī te bandhyo, āge kauna havāla.* (630) No pollen, no sweet nectar, no blossoming yet; if the bee is caught up with the bud even, what will happen later [when it blooms]? (Translation by R. Snell: Rupert Snell, *The Hindi Classical Tradition: A Braj Bhāṣā Reader*, London: School of Oriental and African Studies, 1991, p. 135).

9. Ramapratapa Vedakumari Ghai, *Bhallaṭaśataka: Māheśvarī saṃskṛta ṭīkā, hindī evam angrejī anuvāda sahita ālocanātmaka saṃskaraṇa,* New Delhi: Meharacanda Lachamanadāsa, 1985.

10. Just to mention a few other works: Śambhu kavi's *Anyoktimuktakalatā,* Rudra's *Bhāvavilāsa*, Madhusūdana's *Anyūpadeśaśataka* and Hansavijaya Gani's *Anyoktimuktāvalī.*

11. Paṇḍitarāja Jagannātha, *Bhāminī vilāsaḥ: Anyokti vilāsaḥ: Saṃskṛta hindī vyākhyā ṭippaṇyādayaḥ*, Gorakhpur: Vaiśālī Prakāśana, 1998.

12. Badrinatha (Jha) Sharma, *Anyoktisāhasrī*, Benares: Māsṭara Khelārīlāla, 1938.

13. Mathura Prasad Dikshit, *Anyoktitaraṃgiṇī,* Benares?, VS 2023 [1966 or 1967].

dohā-kāvya[14] in Maithili. Modern Indian critics can interpret even Jāysī's *Padmāvat* or Spencer's *Faeree Queene* as *anyokti*.[15]

Notwithstanding classical categories a love poem could be contextualized on the spot and interpreted as *anyokti*, as was the case with Nizām-ul Mulk in 1737 entreating Nādīr Śāh to stop his massacre of Delhi by reciting the following couplet about a cruel beloved in Persian,

> *Lay down your sword of pride, for none is left for you to slay*
> *—Except you raise the dead to life that you may slay again.*[16]

Ṭhākur's poem quoted above with the force of political contextualization was not an isolated example as seem to have been the case with the few couplets of Bihārī. There are many other stories about when and where a poem of his was born. Some of them may even represent different political settings. The stories collected by Bhagavandin from Ṭhākur's descendants show rather the poet's opposition to Himmat Bahādur and do not mention the one cited above through which he earned a reward from the warlord. However, even Bhagavandin's stories admit that Ṭhākur had also been present in Himmat Bahdādur's court and indicate the privileged status of a court poet to criticise his master. According to one story he saved Maharaja Parīksit of Jaitpur from the trap of Himmat Bahādur by recounting another plight of the forsaken cowherd-girls against the slanderers,

> कैसे सुचित भए निकसौ नहिँ दैबो करौ सब के गलबाहीं।
> जे छल छिद्रन के छल ताकती हैं कपटी हित की अवगाहीं।
> ठाकुर वे जुरि एक भईं रचिहैं परपंच कछू ब्रज माहीं।
> हाल चबाइन को दहुचाल सु लाल तुम्हैं है दिखात कि नाहीं
> ॥169॥

> *How carelessly you are setting off! Do not keep putting your arm on others' shoulders!*
> *Those who watch you through the clefts of deceit and fraud are malicious although they look with love.*
> *Ṭhākur says, they have gathered together and are about to make some plot in Braj.*
> *My friend, can you see the recent wicked conduct of the slanderers or not?*

---

14. Surendra Jha 'Sumaṅa', *Anyoktikā: mukraka dohā-kāvya*, Darbhanga: Maithilī-Mandira, 1969.

15. Ramsvarup Tripathi: *Anyoktikār Jāysī aur Spensar: 'Padmāvata' aur 'Pheyrīkvīn': ek tulnātmak samīkṣā*, Agra: Bāṅkebihārī Prakāśan, 1992.

16. Khurshidul Islam and Ralph Raussell, *Three Mughal Poets: Mir, Sauda, Mir Hasan*, Delhi: Oxford University Press, 1969 (1998 impression), p. 230 (note).

The story here reveals that the covert messages were not necessarily so easily understood. In this case the prince missed the meaning and Ṭhākur had to recite another quatrain to make his point clear.

A similar poem on the quandary of the forsaken *gopī*s allegedly recited at the court of Kiśorī Singh of Panna laments a state of affairs that had changed for the worse,

चाल न वा चरचा न वा चातुरी वा रस रीति न प्रीति को ढौर है।
साँच घटो बढ़ो झूँठ जहान मैं लोभ के लाने जहाँ तहाँ दौर है।
ठाकुर वेई गोपाल वही हम वोही चबाउ बनो इक ठौर है।
मेरेइ देखत मेरी भटू सिगरो ब्रज ह्वै गयो और को और है ॥174॥

No longer the same manners, the same talk, not the same dexterity, not the same emotional manner and flow of love.
Truth decreased and falsity increased in the world, there is rush everywhere out of greed.
Ṭhākur says, Krishna is the same, we are the same — slander arose in the same place.
The whole Braj has changed into something different, my companion, in front of my eyes.

A relatively simple pattern of contextualization can be observed in these poems. The setting is Braj, the geographical sphere of the activities of the speaker and the addressed person, while the absence of Krishna refers to the absence of favourable times. The speaker, a cowherd girl abandoned by Krishna, addresses one or more girls of her community who share the same fate: they have to cope with both these unfavourable times and the enemies, the slanderers. Bearing all this in mind one would read even those poems in which no explicit political context is mentioned with an eye to contextualization. There are for example poems that strongly suggest moral attitudes that transcend the framework of the Krishna-mythology, rather than a *bhakti* context as is the case with the following quatrain,

पिय मोहन कौ वह मौंहनौं रूप निहारे बिना नहिं जीजतु है।
तिहि ते जु लटी भली या जग मैं सिख मानि सबै सुनि लीजतु है।

कहि ठाकुर लाल के देखिबे कै लियै ज्वाब न काहुवे दीजतु है।
अब का कहियै अपने उरझैं सबही की खुसामद कीजतु है॥ 17[१७]

I cannot live without seeing that enchanting face of the dear Enchanter.
Therefore, I listen to everything, good and bad in this world, and consider it as teaching.
Ṭhākur says, in order to see Krishna I do not reply back to anyone.
What can I say when I have been entangled? I flatter all the people.

In a similar vein, the following poem laments the unpredictable behaviour of the lords apparently in connection with Krishna, but with the adverb *sadā* 'always' and with the emphatic progressive verbal form of *hotaī āe* 'have been (till the present)' the poet makes it explicit that his statement also refers to the lords of his times,

मेवा बई घनी काबुल मैं बिंद्राबन आनि करील जमाए।
राधिका सी सुभ बाम बिहाय कै कूबरी संग सनेह बढाए।
मेवा तजी दुरजोधन की बिदुराइन के घर छोकल खाए।
ठाकुर ठाकुर की का कहौं सदा ठाकुर बावरे होतई आए ॥49॥

He planted nuts in plenty in Kabul, but when he came to Vrindaban he sew caperbush.
He abandoned a shining woman like Radha and grew his love with the hunchback woman.
He disposed of Duryodhana's dry fruits and ate the peels in the house of Vidura's wife.
Ṭhākur asks: what shall I say of my Lord? Lords have always been crazy.

These poems present two attitudes of people who are subject to a lord but still expose their independent thinking. The first one about flattering also implies that the subjugation of sentiments and flattering those in power is done involuntarily and only with the prospect of acquiring incomparable benefit through it. The second one does not present inimical superiors: although criticising the lords of all times, it accepts their eccentricity. Both of them suggest the policy of rational compromise.

[17] *Sudhāsar (Pañcam taraṃg)*. MS preserved at the Vrindaban Research Institute, nr. 6773, fol. 11r.

'The Pride of Ṭhākur'

It is not only the covert political message that makes Ṭhākur's poems interesting. The above idea about rational compromise as well as the fact that he was a Kayastha in the service of other lords may seem to contradict it, nevertheless, Ṭhākur possessed an independent soldier's standing and assertiveness. According to Bundelkhandi lore he recited the following *kavitt* with unsheathed sword in front of an infuriated Himmat Bahādur,

सेवक सिपाही हम उन रजपूतन के
दान जुद्ध जुरिबे मैं नेकु जे न मुरके।
नीति देनवारे हैं मही के महिपालन कौं
कवि उनहीं के जे सनेही साँचे उर के।
ठाकुर कहत हम बैरी बेवकूफन के
जालिम दमाद हैं अदानिया ससुर के।
चोजन के चोर रस मोजन के पातसाहि
ठाकुर कहावत पै चाकर चतुर के ॥5॥

I serve as soldier those Rajputs who do not turn the least away from donations and battles.
I give prudent counsel to the kings of the earth; I am the poet of those who love the true heart.
Ṭhākur says, I am the enemy of the stupid, the cruel son-in-law of the miser father-in-law.
I am the thief of wonders and the emperor of the surges of emotion; I am called Lord but I am the servant of the intelligent one.

It is not without reason that Bhagavandin published the collection of his poems under the name of *Ṭhākur-ṭhasak* 'The pride of Ṭhākur'. Ṭhākur's standing and independence was usually channelled through traditional subject matters such as the cowherd girls' passionate plight against Uddhava, Krishna's messenger, propagating the doctrine of discipline, 'yoga.' Another favourite theme was adulterous love disregarding all bonds, another example of independent standing. While the Uddhava-poems had been a favourite theme of the *bhakti* poets since the sixteenth century, the time of poets like Sūrdās and Nandadās, devotional or mannerist poets barely emphasised the theme of explicit adulterous love. In these poems Ṭhākur uses almost no veneer of the Krishna legend although the situation might remind the listener or the reader that in many legends Radha, the beloved par excellence, was also the wife of someone else and not of Krishna. Since this theme was easily inserted into the classical framework of the 'classification of heroines,' the *nāyika-bheda*, there was no subversiveness found in it and indeed in some anthologies such poems are introduced as examples of the category *parakīyā nāyikā*, 'the heroine who belongs to someone else.' Moreover, the *parakīyā nāyikā* class was not the only possibility of inserting these poems into a *nāyika-bheda* framework. For example the following poem in the anthology *Sudhāsar* was given as an illustration of *prītopālambha* 'complaint against love,'[18]

जानत ही अपने नहीं होत पराए पिया यह बेदन गाई।
सो परहेलि कै प्रीति करी गुरु लोगन की कुलकानि गँवाई।
ठाकुर ते न भए अपने अब कौन को दोस लगाइयै माई।
दूध की माखी उजागर बीर सु हाइ मैं आँखिन देखत खाई ॥88॥

I knew that the beloved is not my own but of someone else—this is sung in the Vedas.
Neglecting this, I fell in love and discarded the family honour of the elders.
That lord has not become mine. Whom shall I blame for this, my sister?
A bee is visible in the milk, my friend, I have drunk it though it was right before my eyes.

The presentation of 'adulterous' poems in these conventional categories illustrate that in the same vein as Krishna mythology, the *nāyikā-bheda* could also be exploited to express the individual attitudes of the poet.

Style and Self-reflection of the Art

With the powerful last line of the above poem we reach the most striking peculiarity of Ṭhākur, the style of his quatrains. Although *lokokti*, the insertion of proverbs into the poem, has been classified as an *alaṃkāra* in the Sanskrit *Kuvalyānanda*, a sixteenth-century treatise on rhetoric, it was rarely used in poetry. Proverbs in the last line are a defining feature of Ṭhākur's poetry, setting him apart from all other Brajbhāṣā poets. They render his already relatively simple language even more down-to-earth and thus evoke the simplicity of the pastoral life. As wonderful examples of the use of proverbs, in the following two poems the forsaken cowherd girls of Braj speak to Krishna's messenger, Uddhava,

18. This is a rubric within the different types of complaint and is opposed to the categories of *virahopālambha* 'complaint against separation,' *nāyak prati upālambha* 'complaint against the lover' and *kāmopālambha* 'complaint against erotic desire' in the same work.

कूबरी कान्हर कों इकलास कियो सबही बिधि खूब है अल्ला।
का करिये, रिस लागति है चुप ह्वै रहिये बसि प्रेम के तल्ला।
ऊधो सँदेस पठायो पठायहै पै न डरै हम जोग के हल्ला।
जैसे को तैसो ही जाय मिलै उतै फूटी मसीद को आँधरो मुल्ला
॥48॥

The hunchback woman made Krishna join her: God is wonderful in every aspect.
What shall we do when we are angry? Let us remain silent staying at the foot of love.
He sent and will be sending messages through Uddhava, but we are not afraid of the fuss of discipline.
A person gets what he deserves: the broken mosque there has a blind mullah.

रस रीति की प्रीति कौं चीनौ नहीं कपटी चटसार की पाटी पढे।
हम वै प्रभु छोडि कै जात रहे उंत कूबरी के सँगवाति चढे।
तब चौरे मैं चौरी बखानत ते अब काम परै बहु घाती गढे।
हम जानि कछू पिय मोह मढे नकटे हरि चैतुवा मीत कढे॥[19]

He did not appreciate the proper ways of emotions, but studied from a slate of the school of trickery.
The Lord has abandoned us, went away, and there he entered into relationship with a hunchback.
Once he spoke openly about his theft but now love has become our powerful destroyer.
We thought that our beloved was somewhat coated with infatuation but the brazen Krishna turned out to be a friend only at the spring harvest.

It is not only the use of proverbs in a simple language that revitalises the centuries-old theme of the cowherd-girls but also the occasional use of Bundeli pronouns *(tauna, jauna)*, verbal forms and vocabulary. Even in his choice of theme Ṭhākur may link himself to Bundelkhand and describes in many poems the typically Bundelkhandi festival of *Akṣay Tṛtīyā* on the third day of the bright half in the month of *Vaiśākha*.

The use of Bundeli words and other features not only evokes the language of the people but also emphasises Bundela identity and creates a situation reminiscent of the Rajput painting traditions. In miniature painting the Rajput courts developed their own styles and the miniatures served almost like banners to a state, so the use of Bundeli features may have shown

19. *Sudhāsar (Pañcam taraṃg)*. MS preserved at the Vrindaban Research Institute, nr. 6773, fol. 60r.

that the poem originated from Bundelkhand, increasing the prestige of the Bundela ruler. This pride in Bundelkhand can also be evinced from the fact that two of the best poets of the time, Ṭhākur and Padmākar worked mostly in Eastern Bundelkhand. According to the family lore collected by Bhagavandin, Ṭhākur was born in Orcha but moved to Jaitpur in his childhood with his family. This move also hints at a shift of Brajbhāṣā poetic activities towards the East.

Ṭhākur's simplicity and (to a certain extent) regionalizing impulses should not simply be glossed over as the stuff of mere folk tradition. It is rather a possible progression from the highly ornate poetry of his predecessors like Keśavdās, Dev and Ānandghan. Simplicity is a common feature of both Ṭhākur and Padmākar. While on the one hand Padmākar combines this simplicity with conventionalism, on the other hand Ṭhākur does it with *anyokti* and proverbs. Behind this move in Ṭhākur lies an increased poetic consciousness in searching for an individual style and ridiculing age-old conventions,

सीख लीन्हो मीन मृग खंजन कमल नैन
सीख लीन्हो जस औ प्रताप को कहानो है।
सीख लीन्हो कल्पबृक्ष कामधेनु चिंतामनि
सीख लीन्हो मेर औ कुबेर गिर आनो है।
ठाकुर कहत याकी बड़ी है कठिन बात
बाकी नहीं भूलि कहूं बाँधियत बानो है।
डेल सो बनाय आय मेलत सभा के बीच
लोगन कबित्त कीबो खेल कर जानो है ॥7॥

They have learnt 'eyes like fish,' 'antelope,' 'wagtail' or 'lotus,'
They have learnt 'a story of fame and valour,'
They have learnt 'Tree of Desires,' 'Cow of Wishes,' 'Jewel of Thought;'
they have learnt 'Meru' and 'Mountain of Kuvera:'
But Ṭhākur says: poetry is a most difficult matter
words can never, not even accidentally confine it;
Still they churn it out and introduce it to the assembly:
people think writing poetry is an easy game.

This poem is often quoted as one of the fundaments of the idea of poetry free from the convention (*rītimukt*) and is interpreted as a refutation of *rīti*-poetry in favour of a more individualised literature. The idea of *rītimukt* poetry is a twentieth-century concept that developed parallel with the literary movement of *Chāyāvād*. Some critics grouped together Ālam, Ānandghan, Ṭhākur, Dvijdev and others and presented them as poets who wrote to express their individual love rather than to describe poetic emotions in a romantic opposition to the classicist *rīti*-poetry.[20]

It is easy to see that the *sīkha līnho* repetition in each of the first four lines is a kind of dramatic stylistic reinforcement of the point of repeated learning tradition itself. It should, however, be born in mind that in some places convention is as important to the *rītimukt* poets as to the other *Rīti*-authors. What Ṭhākur has done is not to get stuck in poetic customs for their own sake. He breathed new life into them and, therefore, he did not really condemn literary conventions per se.

To overcome the unquestionable presence of conventions in Ṭhākur's poetry modern Indian scholarship distinguished one or two other poets called Ṭhākur. A Brahmin Ṭhākur who is claimed to have preceded our author lived not in Bundelkhand but in Asnī near Benares.[21] Scholars like Lala Bhagavandin and Vishvanathprasad Mishra referred to him as *Rītibaddh*, 'conventionalist,' Ṭhākur and made desperate efforts in sorting out which quatrain might belong to which Ṭhākur. (To maintain the clear concept of *rītimukt* literature Vishvanathprasad Mishra proposed a similar separation in the case of Ānandghan and Ghanānand, where he artificially attributed the bhakti-poetry of a '*rītimukt*' author to an earlier devotional poet.[22] Facing more recent manuscript evidence, however, he rejected his earlier idea.[23])

The 'most recent' edition, the *Ṭhākur Granthāvalī* edited by Chandrashekhar Mishra, noticeably under the influence of his father, Vishvanathprasad Mishra, in 1973 presented 219 and 51 poems under the conception of two different Ṭhākurs. Manuscript material, however, does not support this separation. No anthology gives the slightest hint that these poems are not of one but two Ṭhākurs. Moreover, if there had been two poets of the same name distant neither in time nor in space, it could have been easy to refer to at least one of them with an adjective to distinguish him from the other.

Conclusion

In the twentieth century Ṭhākur was viewed among the *rītimukt* poets. Although unlike Ālam-Śekh, Ānandghan, Bodhā (and even Raskhān), there

---

20. About the development of the concept of *rītimukt* poetry see my article 'The idea of "rītimukt" poetry,' *South Asia Research* 25 (2005): 13-30.

21. A third poet called Ṭhākur wrote in 1804 the 'Devakīnandan commentary' to the *Satsaiyā* of Bihārī in Benares. He seems to be clearly distinct from the author(s) of the quatrains.

22. Vishvanathprasad Mishra, *Ghanānand aur Ānandghan (granthāvalī)*, Benares: Vāṇī Vitān, 1945, 'Introduction,' pp. 6-14.

23. Vishvanathprasad Mishra, *Ghanānand (granthāvalī)*, Benares: Vāṇī Vitān, 1952, '*Vāṅmukh*', pp. 51-79, especially pp. 67-8.

is no significant love story attached to his name as an inspirational force behind his poems he struck a more personal note in many of his quatrains than most of his contemporaries. Behind the rather thin surface of the Krishna myths and classification of heroes and heroines one can feel the proud standing and love for independence, even with the price of confrontation, or on the contrary, the realism of political compromise of someone who lived in the troubled years of Bundelkhand.

The importance of Ṭhākur lies not in the fact that he was an innovative poet shifting the emphasis from one aspect of already existing conventions to others but rather in his not being an isolated phenomenon. In the expression of individual sentiments he may well be indebted to Ānandghan while many of his innovations foreshadow twentieth-century developments.

His era, the turn of the nineteenth century, is very little studied by Hindi literary historians who consider the poetic output of this period as largely normative and derivative expression of a literature frozen into mannerist rules. According to them this 'dead' Hindi poetry will only be revitalised by western influence from the middle of the nineteenth century. A study of this concept with the help of post-colonial theories may radically change our perception of the transition from traditional to modern.

Thakur's poetry is present in innumerable nineteenth-century anthologies both handwritten and printed. His popularity at that time may well suggest that his move away from the ornamented Brajbhāṣā of Ānandghan and Dev towards simplicity as well as his poetic self-assertion prepared the aesthetic sensibilities of Hindi audiences and readers for the acceptance of a more straightforward and more individualistic western literature. In this way the appearance of these western ideas was not a radically new phenomenon in an otherwise dead literary tradition but rather the confirmation of already existing developments.

Social Practice of Bhakti in the Śiv Nārāyaṇ *Saṃpradāya*

Maren Bellwinkel-Schempp

There have been several attempts by scholars to frame heterodox *nirguṇ* Bhakti as a religion of the oppressed. It has been argued that those poet-saints attacked the caste system.[1] This is the uniform and unequivocal opinion of Dalit authors, foremost and first formulated by Dr. Ambedkar.[2] Gail Omvedt stresses 'the radicalism of the Sants against traditional Brahmanical interpretations.'[3] Caste is the proofstone in the assessment of Bhakti.

That women, Śūdras or untouchables could become Sants and disciples of Sants was a 'minor social revolution.'[4] It did not last long, the heyday of Bhakti between the fifteenth and seventeenth century gave way to a Brahmanical appropriation of Bhakti.[5] This was twofold: On the one hand, it spread Brahmanical values. 'But paradoxical as it may seem, in spite of its anti-caste, anti-Sanskrit and anti-elitist stance, the Bhakti movement spread values such as vegetarianism and teetotalism–both characteristic of the highest castes–and the importance of religion and spirituality, among the people at large.'[6] On the other hand, for untouchables Bhakti became the prerequisite of exclusive sects, castes or both, as in the case of the Satnāmīs.[7]

---

1. Unfortunately Oliver Mendelsohn and Marika Viscziany fail to point out who considered 'Bhakti to be a systematic attack on the caste system' in their co-edited volume *The Untouchables: Subordination, Poverty and the State in Modern India,* Cambridge: Cambridge University Press, 1998, p. 22.
2. Bhimrao Ambedkar, 'Annihilation of Caste,' in *Dr. Babasaheb Ambedkar, Writings and Speeches,* vol. I, Bombay: Government of Maharashtra, 1936, p. 74.
3. Gail Omvedt, *Buddhism in India: Challenging Brahmanism and Caste,* New Delhi: Sage Publications, 2003, p. 187.
4. Richard Burghart, 'The Founding of the Ramanandi Sect,' *Ethnohistory* 25.2 (1978), pp. 121-39, p. 121.
5. Walter Fernandes, *The Emerging Dalit Identity: The Reassertion of the Subalterns*, New Delhi: Indian Social Institute, 1996, p. 4.
6. M. N. Srinivas, 'Introduction,' in *Caste, Its Twentieth-Century Avatar,* ed. by M. N. Srinivas, New Delhi: Penguin Publ., 1997, p. XV.
7. Pumendu Rajan, 'Kabirpanth and Politics in Mithila,' in *Dalits and Peasants: The Emerging Caste-Class Dynamics,* ed. by Ashish Ghosh, Delhi: Gyan Sagar Publication,

The social practice of Bhakti contradicted the egalitarian religious teaching. Caste has been derogated, but has never been overcome.[8]

Another way to argue starts from the point of view of political religiosity. For Ranajit Guha, Bhakti is a precolonial mode of submission and subordination. It replaced mere force by religious devotion and inwardly asceticism. 'Bhakti, in other words, is an ideology of subordination par excellence. All the inferior terms in any relationship of power structured as Dominance or Subordination within the Indian tradition, can be derived from it.'[9]

This subaltern argument is modified by Nandini Gooptu and applied by her to her study of the urban poor in the major towns of Uttar Pradesh. She differentiates between the Dalit and Śūdra poor who are characterised by different modes of religiosity: The Dalits are adherents of *nirguṇ* Bhakti and follow Sant Raidās, Kabīr and Śiv Nārāyaṇ. She concedes that Bhakti has an assertive quality, but on the whole it stands for a docile mode in juxtaposition to that of the Śūdras who pursue *saguṇ* devotionalism which is combined with a militant Hindu *sanātana dharma* orientation.[10] As she draws most of her material from Kanpur, I would like to qualify and contextualise her argument in respect to the Śiv Nārāyaṇ *saṃpradāya*.

Svāmī Śiv Nārāyaṇ (1716-90) was a Kṣatriya from Candravār in Ballia District in eastern Uttar Pradesh. He founded a rather large *nirguṇ* Bhakti sect of now approximately 300,000 members. They are spread over eastern Uttar Pradesh, western Bihar, Nepal and Bengal. Most of the followers are Dalits, although their founder was a Rājpūt. They mainly belong to the Dhūsiyā and Jaisvārā subcastes of the Camār. They were landless labourers, some of them worked as leatherworkers and masons.[11] The Dhūsiyā served in the army and the Jaisvārā worked in the mills in Kolkata, Mumbai and Kanpur but also in the coal mines of Dhanbad district. Eastern Uttar Pradesh and western Bihar is the poorhouse of India, and labour migration was a necessity to eke out a living. Usually single men worked in the major towns of northern India, with their wives and children left behind in the village.[12] Besides, quite a substantial number were

---

1999, pp. 145-65; Saurabh Dube, *Untouchable Pasts: Religion, Identity and Power Among a Central Indian Community,* New York: State University of New York Press, 1998.

8. Robert Deliege, *The Untouchables of India,* Oxford: Berg Publishers, 1999, p. 148.

9. Ranajit Guha, *Dominance Without Hegemony: History and Power in Colonial India,* Cambridge, Mass.: Harvard University Press, 1997, p. 50.

10. Nandini Gooptu, *The Politics of the Urban Poor in Early Twentieth-Century India*, Cambridge: Cambridge University Press, 2001, pp. 150, 197.

11. Briggs mentioned Jaisvārā and Dusadhs as main members of the sect. To my knowledge Dusadh and Dhūsiyā are the same. George Weston Briggs, *The Chamars,* Calcutta: Associated Press, 1920, p. 211.

12. Nowadays the Śiv Nārāyaṇ *panth* has members in Gorakhpur, Ghazipur, Jaunpur, Allahabad, Varanasi, Raibareilly, Chandauli, Bareilly, Lucknow, Kanpur, Jhansi, Mathura,

recruited as indentured labourers from the 1830s onwards.[13] They migrated to Mauritius, South Africa and the Caribbean.[14] Quite a number of them are to be found in England and the United States, although among the diaspora Sant *saṃpradāyas* they do not play a prominent role.[15]

Among the Bhakti Sants, Svāmī Śiv Nārāyaṇ is a latecomer. Most of the sects trace their origin to Rāmānanda (traditionally dated 14th century, but probably later) who is credited for having brought South Indian Vaishnavism to northern India and having opened it for a non-Twice-Born constituency. He is the alleged guru of low caste saints like Kabīr and Raidās who drew a fairly large following.[16] Although there exists a substantial body of literature on Kabīr and Raidās, references to Śiv Nārāyaṇ are rather scanty.

There are only few comprehensive accounts on Svāmī Śiv Nārāyaṇ.[17] Paraśurām Caturvedī's *Uttarī bhārat kī sant-paramparā* gives a detailed account of Svāmī Śiv Nārāyaṇ and mentions the vast number of Non-Resident Indians in the Śiv Nārāyaṇ *panth*. Although Karine Schomer refers to Paraśurām Caturvedī's book, she surprisingly does not include the Śiv Nārāyaṇīs into her rather detailed description of the various Sant *saṃpradāyas*.[18]

Agra, Nainital, Dehradun, Bhagalpur, Ara, Sivan, Chapra, Sonpur, Muzaffarpur, Patna, Khagol, Samsthipur, Barauni, Mokama, Vachvara, Gangajhali, Ariya, Purnia, Koshanganj, Champaran, Raksaul, Ghatshila, Katiyar, Vardvan, Dhanbad, Betiya, Jamalpur, Bhabhua, Chindvara, Sinhbhumi, Bokaro, Tata Jamshedpur, Virbhumi, Dinajpur, Howrah and Kolkata, Asam, Naida, Dibugarh, Orissa, Hazaribagh, Jharkhand, Purliya, Chakradharpur, Ratlam, Indore, Jabalpur, Nimadh Khandva, Baitul, Mahu Chavani, Manmarh, Nasik, Ahmedabad, Jaipur, Puna in Maharashtra, Mumbai, Delhi, Jalandhar, Nepal, Sikkim, Dhaka, Mauritius, London, South Africa, Natal, America.' This list is derived from the invitation letter for the Guru Granth Jayantī Samāroh on 6th December 2003.

13. Marina Carter, *Voices from Indenture. Experiences of Indian Migrants in the British Empire,* London and New York: Leicester University Press, 1996, p. 21.

14. Steven Vertovic, 'Hinduism in Diaspora,' in *Hinduism Reconsidered,* ed. by Günther-Dietz Sontheimer and Hermann Kulke, New Delhi: Manohar, 1997, p. 288.

15. I owe this information to Sita Ram, a Canadian Dalit activist. He had just come back from the First Dalit World Congress in Malaysia to attend the Buddh Mahotsav in Sarnath and Bodh Gaya. He supplied me with an exhaustive overview of the Kabīrpanthī and Raidāsī diaspora congregation in the form of visiting cards. Most of them he had collected during the congress. Two of them belonged to Śiv Nārāyaṇīs. Communication of 5th December 1998.

16. George A. Grierson, 'Rāmānandīs,' in *Encyclopaedia of Religion and Ethics,* vol. 10, 1919, pp. 569-72.

17. George A. Grierson, 'Śiva Nārāyaṇīs', in *Encyclopaedia of Religion and Ethics*, vol. 11, 1921 and J. N. Farquhar, *An Outline of the Religious Literature of India,* Delhi: Motilal Banarsidass, 1966.

18. Karine Schomer, 'Introduction. The Sant Tradition in Perspective,' in *The Sants: Studies in a Devotional Tradition,* ed. by Karine Schomer and W. H. McLeod, Delhi: Motilal Banarsidass, 1987, p. 5.

The Śiv Nārāyāṇīs are a 'textual community,'[19] insofar as the fifteen books which Svāmī Śiv Nārāyaṇ wrote play a prominent role in teaching, ritual, and symbolism of the sect.[20] The most important book, the *Gurū anyās* (variant of *nyās*, 'deposit, trust, endowment') is also called *Gurū Granth Sāhib* like the holy book of the Sikhs, and *Gyān dīpak*. The great importance of the book becomes also obvious in the fact that the main festival of the Śiv Nārāyaṇīs is the Gurū Granth Sāhib Divas on the thirteenth day of the lunar month of Agahan (November/December). It is celebrated to commemorate the divine revelation of the book. On that occasion all *mahānts* and sadhus of the *panth* assemble in Candravār Dhām, the birthplace of Svāmī Śiv Nārāyaṇ.

The book is placed in the centre of the altar (*gaddī*) which is usually an elevated stool, sometimes under a canopy. This altar resembles very much the altar in a Sikh temple (*gurdvārā*), with only the martial insignia missing. The *Guru anyās* is the iconic representation of God, the focus of devotion and the basic text for preaching. Although it has the rank of a canonical text, it is mostly used as an icon. Every *mahānt* had to own the book which does not mean that he was able to read it. It was prestigious to copy the *Gurū anyās* by hand although that was left to experienced scribes. This holy book as icon gave legitimacy to the *saṃpradāya*.

Most of the members of the sect were illiterate which made oral transmission of its teachings especially important. Literacy, though much desired, never replaced oral teaching. This allowed for the flexibility and contextual adaptability of the interpretation of the text. The words of Svāmī Śiv Nārāyaṇ or the guru were considered to be identical. The isomorphism between God and guru gave a higher legitimacy to the spoken work than to the written text.[21] As the written text only became alive through the charismatic preaching of the respective *mahānt* or *ācārya*, his interpretation of the written text was authoritative.

Besides, the language of the books could not be understood easily. Some guessed that it was originally written in *gurmukhī*, the script of the *Ādī granth*. Others pointed to the Muṛiyā or to the Kaithī script, which was used

---

19. Harjot Oberoi, *The Construction of Religious Boundaries: Culture, Identity and Diversity in the Sikh Tradition*, New Delhi: Oxford University Press, 1995, p. 89.
20. These are 1. *Lava granth*, 2. *Sant vilās*, 3. *Sant o jān granth*, 4. *Santsundar*, 5. *Gurū anyās*, 6. *Sant ācāri*, 7. *Santopadeś*, 8. *Śabdāvali*, 9. *Sant parvānā*, 10. *Sant mahimā*, 11. *Sant sāgar*, 12. *Baṛā stotra*, 13. *Baṛā parvānā*, 14. *Pati parvānā*, 15. *Baṛi Bāṇī*. The sixteenth book still has to be revealed. George A. Grierson, 'Śiva Nārāyaṇīs,' o.c., p. 579.
21. Heinrich von Stietencron, 'Charisma and Canon: The Dynamics of Legitimization and Innovation in Indian Religions,' in *Charisma and Canon. Essays on the Religious History of the Indian Subcontinent,* ed. by Vasudha Dalmia, Angelika Malinar and Martin Christoph-Füchsle, New Delhi: Oxford University Press, 2001, p. 24.

by accountants and traders.[22] The confusion between script and language illustrates the widespread ignorance of the written text. This was partially overcome by printed editions with a commentary in Hindi. They go back to the Lahore edition of 1920 with a Hindi commentary of the original Awadhi text.[23]

The second book of importance is the *Sant vilās* which is recited and preached upon on the occasion of death. Like in most Sant *saṃpradāyas*, in the Śiv Nārāyaṇ *saṃpradāya* death is considered to be the ultimate liberation of man from the cycle of rebirth. The procession to the grave is accompanied by music. The Dalit members of the sect bury their dead, the Kṣatriya members burn them. Both of them construct graves *(samādhis)* for important members of the *panth.*

On initiation *(dīkṣā)* which takes place on Vasant Pañcamī, the spring festival, the new disciple is given a small booklet instead of a the holy thread *(janeū)* as in Brahmanical Hinduism or a necklace of beads *(kaṇṭhī)* as in some Sant groups. The book is called *Lau parvānā*. *Parvānā* means 'order, warrant, passport.' It is also called *Hukm nāmā* which means 'divine order.'[24] The term is rather misleading as the booklet does not contain any orders, rules or commandments. It is neither a catechism nor a code of conduct. Instead it teaches the message of an inwardly oriented religiosity. Only those who internalize the spiritual meaning will be able to escape the cycle of rebirth (*saṃsāra*), only they are able to get access to the heavenly abode and attain eternal salvation. The *Lau parvānā* contains the essence of Svāmī Śiv Nārāyaṇ's teaching.

There are strong similarities with Udāsī Sikhism.[25] The Udāsīs follow the teachings of Gurū Nānak but they reject the dress code, initiation ritual, body culture and code of conduct of the Khālsā Sikhs.[26] *Udāsī* means 'detached' and signifies indifference to the world. In the seventeenth century Udāsīs spread all over northern India, and even after the establishment of the

---

22. This information I owe to Walter John, friend and mentor in my explorations into Dalit Bhakti. A fervent admirer of Kabīr, he did not feel comfortable with Svāmī Śiv Nārāyaṇ's teachings. His native village is right next to Candravār Dhām and much information concerning the Dhām I owe to him. He died unexpectedly in July 2003.

23. Communication by Benī Mādhav Sonkar in August 1977 in Kanpur. Other urban editions were published in Shimla, Lucknow, Allahabad, Kanpur and Mumbai. *Śrī 108 Svāmī Śiv Nārāyaṇī Gurū anyās, Gyān Dīpak*, Kānpur: Sant Samāj Prabandhak Samiti, 1964, p. 4.

24. W. H. McLeod, *Gurū Nānak and the Sikh Religion*, New Delhi: Oxford University Press, 1968, p. 150.

25. Udāsī Sikhs can be traced back to Sri Chand, the second son of Gurū Nānak, ibid., p. 79.

26. The Five Ks, each begins with the character 'k', are uncut hair *(keś);* wooden comb (*kaṅghā*); sword *(kirpan);* steel bracelet *(kaṛā);* and undershorts *(kach)*. Harjot Oberoi, *Construction*, p. 25.

Khālsā in 1699, they maintained their independence and inwardly oriented mode of worship.

The eighteenth century was marked by the decline of Mogul sovereignty, the rise of local powers, and the beginning of colonial penetration by the East India Company. It witnessed the assertion of Sikhism as a new religion in Northern India against Mogul hegemony. The Nawab of Awadh transformed his territory into an independent kingdom in Uttar Pradesh. It was a time of warfare, uncertainty, and famine. The Muslim and Christian influence is reflected in the hagiography of Svāmī Śiv Nārāyaṇ.

Svāmī Śiv Nārāyaṇ was a Bund-Niraunī Kṣatriya. His father Bāghrāy had to leave his native place due to a severe famine. He settled in Candravār in present day Ballia District.[27] Śiv Nārāyaṇ was born there in the year 1716. At the age of seven he had a mystical encounter with his inner guru. God is for him Viṣṇu and his inner guru Dukhharaṇ and God are identical. Dukhharaṇ, the Dispeller of Sorrow, borrows from Christian, Islamic and Buddhist conceptions of God.

When Svāmī Śiv Nārāyaṇ was sixteen there was a drought again. According to the sectarian tradition, he went to Delhi to meet Emperor Muḥammad Śāh (1719-48) and asked for tax exemption. He was put into jail instead where he had to grind cereals. The jail was full of other sadhus and Sants. Svāmī Śiv Nārāyaṇ stopped them from grinding the cereals and miraculously, the flour mills ran on their own. Svāmī Śiv Nārāyaṇ proved himself as wonder-worker which impressed Muḥammad Śāh deeply. Svāmī Śiv Nārāyaṇ was released from jail and the other holy men with him.

Muḥammad Śāh invited Svāmī Śiv Nārāyaṇ and the sadhus for a meal but the food was inappropriate.[28] Svāmī Śiv Nārāyaṇ argued that sadhus and Sants only eat pearls. The emperor ordered pearls to be served, but Svāmī Śiv Nārāyaṇ transformed the pearls into delicious food. From that day onwards the offering (*prasād*) of Svāmī Śiv Nārāyaṇ is called *motībhoj* or *mohanbhog*.[29] Muḥammad Śāh became his first disciple.

The peaceful compromise with the Muslim power is only one aspect of the hagiography. Among later disciples of esteem were the Rājā of Ayodhyā and one Mr. Brown, to balance the three major religions against each other. Svāmī Śiv Nārāyaṇ also had to compete with Kabīr and Gorakh

---

27. In 1878 Ghazipur District was divided and the new district of Ballia founded. Nowadays Candravār Dhām is situated in Ballia district. The *Ghazipur District Gazetteer* mentions famines in 1631, 1770, and after the introduction of the British Rāj, in 1783. H. R. Nevill, *Ghazipur District Gazetteer,* vol. 24, Allahabad: Government of India Press, 1908, p. 48.

28. The hagiography does not dwell on that but I assume the sadhus were served beef. *Svāmī Śiv Nārāyaṇ jīvan caritra,* ed. by Benī Mādhav Sonkar, Kanpur: Deepak Press, 1962, p. 36.

29. At the beginning of any major festival the *mohanbhog* has to be prepared and consecrated to Svāmī Śiv Nārāyaṇ before the religious ceremony (*pūjā*) begins. It consists of nourishing semolina with sugar and clarified butter (*ghī*), and it is cooked in milk.

Nāth. During a meeting (*goṣṭhī*) of all the three it had to be decided who could sit in the sky. Of course only Svāmī Śiv Nārāyaṇ could.

At last the episode of the fish eaters should be mentioned. As Svāmī Śiv Nārāyaṇ was outwardly not discernable as a sadhu, the Rājā of Ayodhyā neglected to invite him for a sacrifice (*yajña*). So Svāmī Śiv Nārāyaṇ fried fish next to the *yajña* which disturbed the ceremony. He was severely reprimanded for that. His response was that the other sadhus were fish eaters as well. The Rājā was puzzled but when he lifted the turbans of the sadhus and untied their hair the fish dropped from it.

This episode does not only refer to the Shaivite identity of Svāmī Śiv Nārāyaṇ looming in the background[30] but also to the tantric heritage represented by the five Ms.[31] It also repeats the common Sant motif of the futility of ritualism. Unless man performs the sacrifice within his own body in a purely esoteric manner, salvation can't be achieved.

His hagiography is very much in line with the *nirguṇ* Sants of northern India: Svāmī Śiv Nārāyaṇ is a non-Brahman, he adheres to Viṣṇu, he is reborn in each aeon (*yug*). God reveals himself to him at the early age of seven. He is a householder (*gṛhasth*) and has two children, a son and a daughter. He has encounters with the Muslim emperor, a Hindu king and a Brahman. His death is miraculous and his body is not found.[32] His final liberation (*samādhi*) leaves no trace on earth, a common motif in Sant hagiographies.

The *Gurū anyās* is written in verse form, with a metrical structure resembling that of the *Rāmcaritmānas* of Tulsīdās. *Caupāīs* give the narrative and *dohās* a thematical conclusion. The whole book is organised in twelve chapters (*khaṇḍ*).[33] It depicts a theological monism of Sant orientation. Upanishadic conceptions of the world as illusion (*māyā*) and of

---

30. This episode repeats the puranic legend how Śiva was not invited to the Vedic *yajña* of his father-in-law Dakṣa because he lived as an ascetic. Out of fury, he decapitated Dakṣa and thereby committed the mortal sin of murdering a Brahmin. Axel Michaels, *Der Hinduismus*, München: C. H. Beck, 1998, p. 240. The same motif has many variations. Raidās, the untouchable cobbler-saint, is not invited to a ritual meal when food is served to the Brahmans. Miraculously he multiplies and sits next to each Brahman, thereby punishing them for practising untouchability.

31. The five Ms are: liquor (*madya*), meat (*māṃsa)*, fish (*matsya*), parched grain or kidney beans (*mudrā*) and sexual union (*maithuna*), for which see Agehananda Bharati, *The Tantric Tradition*, London: Rider and Company, 1965, p. 242.

32. David Lorenzen, 'The Life of Nirguṇī Saints,' in *Bhakti Religion in Northern India: Community Identity and Political Action*, ed. by David Lorenzen, New Delhi: Manohar, 1996, pp. 186-7.

33. The chapters are called: 1. Introduction ('Ārambh khaṇḍ'), 2. Yoga, 3. The trader ('Sāhū khaṇḍ'), 4. The thief ('Cor khaṇḍ'), 5. Consummation of marriage ('Gavan khaṇḍ'), 6. The passionate woman ('Kāminī khaṇḍ'*)*, 7. Mortal sin ('Yam khaṇḍ'*)*, 8. Devotion ('Bhakti khaṇḍ'*)*, 9. Ten forms of Viṣṇu *(*'Das avatār khaṇḍ'*)*, 10. The four ages of the world ('Yug'), 11. Four heroines ('Cār nāyikā khaṇḍ'), 12. Devotee ('Bhakta khaṇḍ').

ultimate salvation (*samādhi*) from the cycle of rebirth through interior devotion prevail.

Only the guru, who is identical with God, can save from the ocean of existence. It is through the grace of God alone that the liberating insight of the ultimate union of individual soul and eternal soul can be achieved. God or the highest self is called Viṣṇu. There are the ten incarnations (*avatāras*) of Viṣṇu and Svāmī Śiv Nārāyaṇ is his tenth *avatāra*, replacing Kalkī. The Vedas are accepted, *karma* and *saṃsāra* are part of the theology. The world is an illusion (*māyā*). Man can achieve salvation by realising that only God is the ultimate reality. The *Gurū anyās* is a plea not to waste one's life in the entanglement of *māyā* but to search for the eternal truth and for liberation from *saṃsāra*.

Liberation is possible through meditation and yoga. The *Gurū anyās* is full of tantric images. The human body is depicted as the vessel for the eternal essence. The tantric notion of the rising *kuṇḍalinī* expresses man's ascent to unification with *paramātma*, the highest self. Bhakti is conceptualized in highly emotional, sensual images. Unification with God as the eternal man (*puruṣa)* is seen as the consummation of the sacred marriage between a loving, passionate woman and the divine. But a woman easily goes astray and gets entangled in the net of *māyā*. Only when she realizes the eternal truth she is able to cross the ocean of existence and unite with the embodied eternal *puruṣa*.

Elaborate typologies classify the mortal sinner, of whom there are fourteen categories, as well as the truthful devotee. Five devoted *bhaktas* and four heroines (*nāyikās*) are distinguished who represent the inner virtues and the nobility of heart in their devotion to the highest self. They are role models of piety, truthfulness, and devotion. Besides, there are heroes of Bhakti like Hanumān and the five Pāṇḍavas, as well as the Bhakti saints who are identified in the *Gurū anyās*. Svāmī Śiv Nārāyaṇ puts himself in one line with Rāmānanda, Tulsīdās, Kabīr and Gurū Nānak. The day of ultimate liberation (*mukti divas*) is celebrated on the seventh day of the waxing half of the lunar month of Śrāvaṇ (July/August) which is also Tulsīdās's birthday (*jayantī*). The Śiv Nārāyaṇ *panth* borrows from a wide range of traditions, Brahmanic-Sanskritic as well as Sant.

There is no 'rough rhetoric' as in Kabīr's oeuvre,[34] no challenge to the Brahmans as in Raidās's hagiography,[35] and no outright condemnation of caste as in Gurū Nānak's sayings.[36] The teaching of Svāmī Śiv Nārāyaṇ is

34. Linda Hess, 'Kabir's Rough Rhetoric', in *The Sants*, o.c., pp. 143-66. J. H. Farquhar claims that Svāmī Śiv Nārāyaṇ stands in the tradition of Kabīr, but there is no evidence of that. Farquhar, *Outline*, p. 334.

35. Winand M. Callewaert and Peter G. Friedlander, *The Life and Works of Raidās*, New Delhi: Manohar, 1992, p. 31.

36. W. H. McLeod, *Gurū Nānak*, p. 209.

rather moderate, inwardly oriented. Caste is not mentioned and Brahmanism is neither attacked nor ridiculed.

In Kanpur, the Śiv Nārāyaṇīs were the first to present themselves in public with the construction of a beautiful temple. This temple is even marked on the city map as *gurdvārā.* It was constructed in 1870 by Bihārī Lāl, a rich Khaṭik building contractor.

These were the 'golden days' for Kanpur's Dalits.[37] The British had not only decided to reconstruct Kanpur as a Civic Station after the devastation through the 'First Indian War of Independence,' but were also expanding on industrial lines. Kanpur was going to become India's first industrial town, the so called 'Manchester of the East.' The nascent industrial town needed coolies, labourers and mechanics (*mistries*) to set up and later on work in, the factories. This opened up unequalled opportunities for Dalits. The Khaṭiks are a Dalit caste (*jāti*).[38] In Kanpur they constitute two endogamous groups, each of them with a distinct settlement history, distinct profession and distinct religious orientation. The Khaṭiks in Colonelganj ward (*mohallā*) were experienced masons and followers of the Bhakti saint Śiv Nārāyaṇ, the Khaṭiks off Latoucheroad were pork butchers, bristle manufacturers and followers of devotional Hinduism, especially of the Goddess, Devī, in her many manifestations. Both profited from colonial power and became immensely rich. This is perhaps the reason why their Dalit identity became camouflaged, negated and blurred.

For Bihārī Lāl and his extended family, the veneration for Svāmī Śiv Nārāyaṇ was a matter of vocation, but for the Dhūsiyā and Jaisvārā a matter of tradition. Both came from eastern Uttar Pradesh and were Dalit. The Dhūsiyā blended their Sant Dharm with Ārya Samāj notions. For them, life reform was important. They actively practiced *śuddhi* (cleanliness and life reform) and abstained from meat and alcohol. Their weekly meetings (*satsaṃg*) took place in the Ārya Samāj Hall off Cooliebazaar under the photo of Dayānand Sarasvatī.

The Jaisvārā have a different tradition. Originally they worked for the British in the cantonments. Their military background is also reflected in the offices of the Śiv Nārāyaṇ *saṃpradāya*. They range from the *hukmī mahānt* over the *brigadier mahānt* to the *mahānt* proper. In the 1940s they were recruited in large numbers for the textile industry to break the Brahman

37. I am deliberately borrowing an expression from David Washbrook. He uses the term to describe the situation of the Dalits in the Madras Presidency in the eighteenth century. At that time they profited from colonial rule. David Washbrook, 'Land and Labour in Late Eighteenth Century South India: The Golden Age of the Pariah?' in *Dalit Movements and the Meaning of Labour in India*, ed. by Peter Robb, New Delhi: Oxford University Press, 1993.

38. Gooptu does not know of the difference between the two Khaṭik lineages and takes their claims for higher status for granted. For her, the Khaṭik are Śūdras and she builds her argument of Hindu militancy on them.

dominance in the trade union movement. Recruited as docile labourers, they became to be regarded as rebellious devotees (*bhagats*) because they neither abstained from meat nor from alcohol. Through their religious practice, the Śiv Nārāyaṇ *panth* became the epitome of untouchable culture.

This was vehemently brought forth against them by the Kabīrpanthīs. They also had established themselves in Kanpur at the beginnings of industrialization. Their membership was overwhelmingly Dalit as well with members from Korī (weaver) and Kurīl (Camār leatherworker) *jātis*. The Korīs were poor whereas among the Kurīl there were quite a number of rich patrons, most of them leather merchants.[39]

The Kabīrpanthīs belonged to the Dhamakhera branch which practiced an elitist *śuddhi* ideology with Brahmanical overtones.[40] Disputes between Kabīrpanthīs and Śiv Nārāyaṇīs arose on matters of purity and pollution.[41] Paradoxically, the, in the literal sense of the word, purist Kabīrpanthīs were pursuing a ritually polluting profession like tanning and work with leather, whereas the untouchable *(achūt)* Śiv Nārāyaṇīs were working in clean professions of textile industry and construction. Besides, the Śiv Nārāyaṇīs were accused of 'dirty' tantrism and secretiveness by the Kabīrpanthīs.

This melee became even more intriguing when the Raidāsīs from 1924 onwards became prominently visible with an annual procession (*julūs*). A new version of Dalit Bhakti emerged: After the 'untouchable' Bhakti of the Śiv Nārāyaṇīs and the purism of the Kabīrpanthīs, the Raidāsīs presented themselves as an assertive Dalit movement (*āndolan)*.[42]

This was an epistemological shift in the understanding of Bhakti. An inwardly oriented religiosity was turned outside and became a public arena

---

39. Maren Bellwinkel-Schempp, 'Kabīr-Panthīs in Kanpur: From *sampradāya* to Dalit Identity,' in *Images of Kabīr*, ed. by Monika Horstmann, New Delhi, Manohar, 2002, pp. 215-32.

40. The Dhamakhera branch is headed by a Vaiśya *ācārya* but the members are mostly Dalits. The spiritual essence of Satguru Kabīr runs through the hereditary line from his first disciple Dharmdās to the present *ācārya*. Their religious function, the *caukā,* enacts the revelation of the four Vedas through elaborate ritualism. They believe in *karma* and rebirth and represent within the different branches of the Kabīrpanth an orthodox orientation. See also Uma Thukral, 'The Avatar Doctrine in the Kabīr Panth,' in *Bhakti Religion,* o.c. pp. 221-30.

41. This is even recorded by George Herbert Westcott, an Anglican missionary from the Society of the Propagation of the Gospel who lived in Kanpur from 1890 till 1915. He wrote one of the first books on Kabīr. He quotes the Kabīrpanthīs saying that the lowest castes like sweepers and washermen should join the Śiv Nārāyaṇ *panth* and not be allowed to wear *kaṇṭhīs*. George Herbert Westcott, *The Kabir Panth,* Calcutta: Susil Gupta, 1953, p. 73.

42. In Uttar Pradesh the Raidāsīs do not constitute a *panth* as in Punjab. Marc Juergensmeyer, *Religion as Social Vision: The Movement Against Untouchability in 20th-Century Punjab,* Berkeley: University of California Press, 1982, p. 87.

activity and as such the leading model.[43] The Raidāsīs questioned the Śiv Nārāyaṇīs: Why follow a Ṭhākur saint when the Ṭhākurs have been the exploiters and oppressors for so long? Self-reliance and trust in God is embodied in Raidās. Why not follow one of their own brethren?[44]

The Śiv Nārāyaṇīs tried to gain ground. Fortunately, they gained a potent patron in Jagjīvan Rām (1908-86), the Harijan leader of the Congress and leading Congress politician during the era of Indira Gandhi. His wife was from Kanpur, therefore he kept close contact with the Dhūsiyās in Cooliebazaar and came for meetings and inaugurations. His father was a Śiv Nārāyaṇ *mahānt* from Bihār and Jagjīvan Rām got initiated into the Śiv Nārāyaṇ *panth* as well.[45] In his autobiography, however, there is no mention of that spiritual allegiance.[46] In 1945 however, he presided over an Akhil Bhāratīya Svāmī Śiv Nārāyaṇ Sammelan in Kanpur.

The 1950s and 1960s were a time of optimism, industrial expansion and intellectual fermentation in Kanpur. For the first generation of educated Dalits, there were new openings in Government service, education, and politics through reservation. The Raidās *julūs* became increasingly longer, more elaborate, and politically more pronounced.[47] The Śiv Nārāyaṇīs responded with a procession on Śiv Nārāyaṇ's commemoration day (*jayantī*) which was of course shorter.[48] Moreover, Benī Mādhav Sonkar, a descendent of Bihārī Lāl, undertook the enormous task to publish the fifteen books of Svāmī Śiv Nārāyaṇ with a Hindi commentary in the 1960s.[49] He was not

43. Sandria Freitag, *Collective Action and Community: Public Arenas and the Emergence of Communalism in North India,* Berkeley: University of California Press, 1989.

44. Maren Bellwinkel, *Die Kasten-Klassenproblematik im städtisch-industriellen Bereich. Historisch-empirische Fallstudie über die Industriestadt Kanpur in Uttar Pradesh, Indien,* Wiesbaden: Franz Steiner Verlag, 1980, p. 217.

45. His wife Indrāṇī gives a detailed description of the Śiv Nārāyaṇ *panth* in her autobiography: Indrāṇī Jagjīvan Rām, *Dekhī sunī bītī bātem̐ (Seen, Heard and Past Tales),* New Delhi: Jagjīvan Bhavan Press, 1994, p. 52.

46. He mentions Raidās, Kabīr, and Dayānand Sarasvatī as his spiritual fathers. Jagjivan Ram, *Caste Challenge in India,* New Delhi: Vision Books, 1980, p. 38.

47. Arthur Niehoff gives a detailed description of the Raidās procession in Kanpur but does not mention the Śiv Nārāyaṇīs at all. See his *Factory Workers in India,* Wisconsin: Milwaukee Public Museum, 1959, p. 73.

48. This procession left the temple (*maṭh*) in Colonelganj and went via Gwaltoli, the working class area, to Parade, the main meeting place right in the middle of Kanpur, and back. It lasted till 1961, the Indo-Pakistan War, when all public processions were prohibited. It was not resumed after the war.

49. They can't be easily compared with Grierson's compilation as some compilations contain more than one book. 1. *Gurū anyās bhāṣā ṭīkā sahit*, 2. *Śabd granth sant vilās*, 3. *Śabdāvalī bhajnāvalī*, 4. *Lav parvānā bhāṣā ṭīkā*, 5. *Santākṣarī*, 6. *Saral pūjan vidhi (mantrāvalī)*, 7. *Saṃgrah granth jis mem̐ Jajbulākī saṃvād tathā tīnom̐ vānī* , 8. *Pati parvāṇā*, 9. *Sant sundar granth*, 10. *Mūl granth (jīvan caritra)*, 11. *Saṃgrah granth (jis mem̐ do granth haiṃ).*

alone in this endeavour. Printed versions of these books were published in many towns of northern India.

When the Dalit movement finally turned Buddhist in the 1980s, the Śiv Nārāyaṇīs fell into oblivion. In the 1990s Navayāna Buddhism became a public arena activity with mass conversions and mass weddings. This did not tally well with the inner devotionalism of the Śiv Nārāyaṇīs. They withdrew. A few educated Śiv Nārāyaṇīs converted to Buddhism without renouncing the religion of their forefathers. When the mills closed in the 1990s, the Śiv Nārāyaṇīs lost their patrons as well as their followers. And the silver coins which Bihārī Lāl inserted into the Colonelganj temple (*maṭh*) have long been removed.

The least privileged of the Dalit in Kanpur, the Śiv Nārāyaṇīs in Candravār Dhām, presented themselves much more radical. Candravār Dhām is situated 7 km off Rasra, a small country town of approximately 6000 inhabitants in Ballia District. Rasra Tehsil is predominantly inhabited by Dalits and Other Backward Castes. An area of great poverty, it became the focus of activity of a Catholic order, namely, that of the 'Queen of the Apostles' which set up a mission station there in 1947.[50] It lies close to the Dhām. Its high school and health post served as a model for Candravār Dhām insofar as there is, beyond the boundary walls of the monastery proper, a Dr. Ambedkar Health Post and High School.

Crooke claims that the Śiv Nārāyaṇīs are susceptible to Christian influence which he attributes to the similarity between Dukhharaṇ, the Merciful, and Jesus Christ.[51] According to one narrative, the Catholic mission was invited to the area by a Dalit *mistry* out of a number of considerations. He had become quite wealthy and wanted to invest his money in land. He was originally from Azamgarh, but as there was land available in Rasra, he settled down there. He came under Christian influence in Varanasi. Although there was already an Anglican mission in Rasra, he nevertheless thought it better to ask the Catholic fathers for support. He feared that the Ṭhākurs would otherwise appropriate his land. For him, the celibate fathers were less susceptible to intimidation than the married Anglicans. It was his initiative which lead to the establishment of the Catholic mission station.[52]

---

50. M. Callista Panachickel, SRAP, *The Fall and Rise of a Grain of Wheat: Origin and Development of Missionary Sisters of 'Queen of Apostles,'* Vienna: Missionary Sisters of 'Queen of Apostles', 1995, p. 167.

51. Briggs, *Chamars*, p. 214.

52. He was Walter John's grandfather who settled in a village called Nimbu near Francispur. Walter John only disclosed his family history shortly before my first visit to Candravār Dhām from 28th February 2001 to 4th March 2001. Monika Horstmann and Martin Fuchs accompanied me. I am grateful for their company and help. I would also like to thank the sisters in St. Francispur, Walter John's relations in Nimbu and especially Mahānt Bholānāth and *bhajanīk* Śyām Sundar Dās in Candravār Dhām for their hospitality. Since that visit we

The exchange between Francispur and Candravār Dhām was amicable in the 1950s and 1960s. Even nowadays, there are vivid memories of the theological debates (*goṣṭhī*) between a Canadian Capuchian monk and the then Dalit *ācārya*.[53] These were the days of recognition and support. Jagjīvan Rām also extended his patronage to Candravār Dhām and visited it four times during his ministry. Once he even organised a Congress workshop on the premises of the Dhām. But still, the monastery is only known to insiders, and also in recent publications there is no mention of the monastery.[54] All this can be attributed to the inwardly oriented and secretive nature of Svāmī Śiv Nārāyaṇ's teachings and the fact that the *panth* was politically for a long time in the Congress fold.

Quite to the contrary of many other Sant *saṃpradāyas*, the genealogy of the *panth* shows openness and flexibility with regard to gender and caste.[55] Although there were in the past three times as many caste Hindu *ācāryas* as Dalit *ācāryas*, under the present Dalit *ācārya*, Sarjū Dās, the Dalit dominate. It is unknown to what extent Svāmī Śiv Nārāyaṇ's five disciples constituted different branches (*gharānās)* of their own.[56] Three *gharānās* were pointed out to me. In Sasna there is a Brahman *gharānā* which centres around the grave (*samādhi*) of Dukhharaṇ. They only accept Brahman disciples. There is a dispute over land.[57] In Nagra there has been a Kṣatriya *gaddī* for seven generations. Its followers burn their dead but build *samādhīs* for them. There are also women *mahānts* in that line. The third

---

have been reckoned as members of the *panth* and included into the annual invitation letter for the 'Guru Granth Jayantī Samāroh' as Prof. Dr. Monika, Dr. Maren and Dr. Martin.

53. The Capuchian monk was John Viani, a Canadian with an Italian name. He worked for forty years in the Banaras Diocese but only lived from 1952 till 1955 in St. Francispur. He left a lasting impression due to his spirituality, wisdom and ascetic living.

54. There is no mention of the Dhām, neither in the District Gazetteers, nor in more recent accounts on Ballia District. H. K. Nevill, *Ballia, A District Gazetteer*, Allahabad: Government of India Press, 1907; Anil K. Singh, *Ballia District: A Study in Rural Settlement Geography*, Varanasi: The National Geographical Society, 1985, and S. B. Singh, *Fairs and Festivals in Rural India: A Geospatial Study of Belief Systems*, Varanasi: Tara Book Agency, 1989.

55. 1. Śiv Nārāyaṇ, Rājpūt; 2. Lakhan Rām, Rājpūt; 3. Dāyal Rām, Camār; 4. Baudha Devī, f. Brahman; 5. Rajkalo Mai, f. Rājpūt; 6. Ajāheb Rām, Rājpūt; 7. Chetan Dās, Camār, 8. Raghunāth Singh, Rājpūt; 9. Muneshvar Singh, Rājpūt; 10. Jhandul Dās, Gareriā; 11. Bacho Devī, f. Brahman; 12. Gulāb Chand, son of Bacho Devī; 13. Sansāraṇ Dās, Camār; 14. Sarjū Dās, Camār.

56. These were (1) Rām Nāth from Parsia, a Kṣatriya; (2) Sadāśiv from Citraya in Ballia District; (3) Lekhrāj from Madhuban in Azamgarh District, a Bhatbramar; 4. his brother Jobrāj, 5. Lakhan Rām from Bharsari in Ghazipur District, a Rājpūt. Among Svāmī Śiv Nārāyaṇ's disciples, he was the only educated. Svāmī Śiv Nārāyaṇ's books are supposed to have been kept with Lakhan Rām.

57. Communication by Sukhdeo Singh on 4th March 2001 and discussion with Viśva Mahānt Sarjū Dās on 16th February 2002.

gharānā is in Ghazipur, with the *maṭh* nowadays dilapidated. This is a Dalit line. The Camār there call themselves Rāvat.

Since Viśva Mahānt Sarjū Dās got elected in 1982 to head Candravār Dhām, the *saṃpradāya* pursues a more assertive course. Although he is illiterate, only he is believed to have the power (*śakti*) to make an impact on Candravār Dhām and the Śiv Nārāyaṇīs in general. The present flourishing state of the monastery goes entirely to his credit. Svāmī Śiv Nārāyaṇ's *samādhi* was constructed in the form of an impressive two-cella temple in 1991. The translation of *samādhi* as 'grave' is misleading insofar as death is understood in the Sant tradition as the ultimate liberation of man from the cycle of rebirth. Besides, as already mentioned, nobody knows where Svāmī Śiv Nārāyaṇ actually died. The two cellas of the temple contain the iconic representations of two books. The *Gurū anyās* represents the spiritual birth and the *Sant vilāś* the spiritual liberation of Svāmī Śiv Nārāyaṇ. The temple is constructed in west-eastern direction, so that the symbolic representation of spiritual birth is facing north, death facing south. This is in line with Hindu cosmology of north as the abode of the gods and eternal life and south as the direction of decay and damnation.

Residential buildings, storerooms and working quarters followed. The *samādhis* of former *mahānts* were set up and decorated. Considerable land is connected with the Dhām which was appropriated from the Grām Pañcāyat and has been successfully defended against other claimants. This construction work was made possible through donations which were instigated through extensive promotion tours of Viśva Mahānt Sarjū Dās. Nowadays, the leading members of the *panth* are in Government positions or run Non-Governmental Organisations. Besides, there is a substantial number of Non-Resident Indians among the Śiv Nārāyaṇīs. Some have maintained their allegiance to the Dhām by high remittances. The cosmopolitan constituency of the *panth* made Sarjū Dās adopt the title of Viśva Mahānt. Although illiterate, he feels even at the age of eighty fully capable to run the Dhām, and his authority is unchallenged. However, his closest disciples have taken precaution for a smooth transition after his demise, and in 2003 Candravār Dhām got registered as a trust.

Viśva Mahānt Sarjū Dās, like the few high officials of the *panth,* is an ascetic. His biography combines misery and mysticism with a tremendous spiritual and social radicalism. Born into a family of landless labourers who had to perform forced labour (*begār),* his alienation from wordly life began when his father died and his mother left him behind. He joined the company of sadhus and Sants, and was a Nāgā monk for a long time. He grew up a radical and became, according to his own words, a revolutionary (*krāntikārī*). He was involved in several agricultural labour movements in the countryside. Out of compassion, he returned to the religion of his forefathers.

According to him, Svāmī Śiv Nārāyaṇ was born to abolish caste. The Kṣatriya origin of Svāmī Śiv Nārāyaṇ is reconciled with the Dalit membership of the *panth* through the inversion of the Aryan theory of race. The Camār were originally Kṣatriyas of the Sūryavaṃśī lineage, a theory which is widespread among the Camār. Svāmī Śiv Nārāyaṇ and his present-day followers are of the same stock. Not only that, for Viśva Mahānt Sarjū Dās the Dalits are morally superior to the *savarṇa*, because they embody equality as preached by Svāmī Śiv Nārāyaṇ. The dignity and equality of man are derived from the theological concept that every man partakes in the divine essence.

This does not mean that his Dalit brethren need no rectification and enlightenment. He fights a crusade against alcohol and intoxicants, the vices of untouchable culture. He does it with every means possible: Slogans condemning liquor are painted on the walls of the hostel (*dharmśālā*).[58] Drunkards are thrown out of the Dhām by him personally, and he preaches untiringly against the vice of drinking. Teetotalism and vegetarianism are integral parts of Viśva Mahānt Sarjū Dās's teaching. This is derived from the theology of Sant Dharm which relies on the mythical union of the individual soul (*ātma*) and the universal soul (*paramātma*). The divine essence has its equivalent in the human soul. The body is depicted as the vessel of divinity and therefore it should not be adulterated by impure substances. Only the divine bliss should intoxicate man, not alcohol. The mystical insight should light the fire within the human body, not the consumption of alcohol and meat.

Sant Dharm is juxtaposed to Hinduism, which for Viśva Mahānt Sarjū Dās is hollow ritualism. Outward ritualism and suppression through the caste system go together. Sant Dharm is inwardly oriented. It does not need the veneration of Devīs, as any mother, sister, and daughter by her inherent nature replaces the goddess. Bhakti as loving devotion should be directed towards the members of one's family. Children should be fed with healthy and good food. They should be clothed and educated. Husband and wife should lead a pure, pious life in devotion to each other. The inward purity should also be outwardly reflected and vice versa. Mere life reform as practiced and preached by Buddhism is not enough. The spiritual quest is not fulfilled by the five commandments (*pañcśīl*).[59] Navayāna Buddhism is for Viśva Mahānt Sarjū Dās a social and not a spiritual religion.

---

58. On our first visit in 2001 the slogans were freshly painted. In 2002 the monsoon had washed them away, and while whitewashing the walls they were not applied again.

59. These are: 'not to kill, not to steal, not to tell a lie, not to indulge in sexual immorality and not to indulge in drinking.' See Bhimrao Ambedkar, *The Buddha and His Dhamma: Dr. Babasaheb Ambedkar, Writings and Speeches*, vol. II, Bombay: Government of Maharashtra, 1957, p. 293.

Bhakti is for the Viśva Mahānt man's spiritual union with God as well as his decent living on earth. Bhakti is a life in dignity, equality and mutual help. The followers of the Śiv Nārāyaṇ *panth* should contribute their share in money, grain and clothing to the Dhām and Viśva Mahānt Sarjū Dās will provide them with spiritual guidance, food and shelter. Those who are not willing to give are not initiated. But the poor and pious are fed and clothed. His greatest concern is appropriate hospitality. As he set up *dharmśālās* already, he wants to improve the sanitary conditions. Within a global world, the foreign *panthīs* should be adequately housed. Good and tasty food he finds still badly missing. His storerooms are filled with grain and pulse, he owns plates and glasses, but there is no one to prepare tasty food.

The social wing of Candravār Dhām is the Dr. Ambedkar Health Centre and School. It was founded by Dr. Parasnāth, a Śiv Nārāyaṇī and homeopathic doctor, at the end of 1980s. He pursues Dr. Ambedkar's social tenets but disapproves of his conversion to Buddhism. Buddhism is for him a social gospel, not a spiritual religion. As already mentioned, the high school is built on a plot adjacent to the Dhām. On my visit in 2001, the school had around six hundred students and a staff of fifteen teachers. It put special emphasis on female education. Not only Dr. Ambedkar's three tenets, 'Educate, Organise, Unite', were preached but many of the burning social issues like atrocities against Dalits, dowry murder and rape as an instrument of subjugation and reglementation were mentioned.

On my visit a year later, the school buildings were barred.[60] The Dr. Ambedkar School had been hit by an intrigue between two Dalit factions which had led to the brutal interference of police and administration to close the school. Since more than a year, the students had been sitting outside in the open. The number of students and teachers had dwindled to half of its former size. Dr. Parasnāth has been fighting a courtcase before the Highcourt in Allahabad since then. Viśva Mahānt Sarjū Dās was disgruntled: He would have solved the problem directly with the persons concerned. But at the age of eighty, he does no longer feel fit for a retaliation in the Nāgā style.

On my third visit to Candravār Dhām, we discussed the matter extensively with Dr. Parasnāth.[61] For the last one and a half year he had been busy to get the school reopened again. He was so involved in those matters

---

60. Also during my second visit to Candravār Dhām from 15th to 19th February 2002, I was not alone. Pintoo Singh and Rajendranath Ahervar were kind enough to accompany me. I again enjoyed the hospitality of the sisters of St. Francispur. Pintoo and Rajendranath were kindly welcomed at the *maṭh.* For the hospitality extended to us I would like to thank Viśva Mahānt Sarjū Dās and Upmahānt Bholānāth.

61. I was accompanied by Raja Ram Jaisvar, a senior educational officer at the Jhansi Polytechnique. We enjoyed the hospitality of Candravār Dhām. A local medical practitioner, Dr. Srivastava, was kind enough to solve our transport problems. He gave us his car for the time of our stay.

so that he could neither attend the Gurū Granth Divas nor the Dr. Ambedkar Paranirvāṇ Divas. In 2003, both commemoration days fell on the 6th of December. The school organised a small function. The picture of Dr. Ambedkar was put up, garlanded and a light waved ritually before it (*āratī*). In marked contrast to Kanpur, no picture of Buddha was put up next to Dr. Ambedkar. This shows the different approach to the Dr. Ambedkar movement which clearly differs from Navayāna Buddhism.

This small meeting stood in stark contrast with the big gathering on the occasion of the Gurū Granth Jayantī Samāroh which was attended by 3000 Śiv Nārāyaṇīs. The celebrations took place under a huge tent which was put up in front of one of the lodges. The *gaddī* was set up there. It began in the afternoon at 5 pm with prayers and teaching by Viśva Mahānt Sarjū Dās. The night celebrations started with prayers, too, and then speeches by leading members of the *panth* expressed their opinions about the social and political discrimination of the Dalits. It had the character of a political meeting rather than a religious function. It was interrupted by a meal and closed with the main speech of Viśva Mahānt Sarjū Dās. Then the *mohanbhog* was brought but only offered to the *Gurū anyās*. Viśva Mahānt Sarjū Dās gave initiation to the new disciples by whispering the *mantra* into their ears. The meeting closed in the early morning by 2 am on 7th December with prayers and singing. Simultaneously worship was offered at the *samādhi* of Svāmī Śiv Nārāyaṇ.

Bhakti as a specific mode of religiosity can't be brought under one heading. Even among Dalits, it is too heterogeneous. Besides, and that holds true for all Dalit *jātis* and not only for the so called Śūdra poor, Bhakti was never practiced exclusively. It blended with *saguṇ* forms of devotionalism, especially in the veneration of the Devī. The Śiv Nārāyaṇīs, Kabīrpanthīs and Raidāsīs created their temples and iconic representations of their specific Sants although their founding fathers were iconoclasts. *Saguṇ* forms of devotionalism penetrated the *nirguṇ* understanding. The distinction between Hindu militancy and Bhakti devotionalism, between Śūdra and Dalit poor, as projected by Nandini Gooptu, does not hold true. There were wide variations in radicalism, lifestyle, public representations, and social practice among the different Bhakti *saṃpradāyas*.

There is a discrepancy between the esoteric teaching of Svāmī Śiv Nārāyaṇ which is very much in line with Upanishadic concepts of world denial and renunciation, and the social practice of the Śiv Nārāyanīs in Kanpur whose eating and drinking habits exhibit untouchable culture. Viśva Mahānt Sarjū Dās fights for a *śuddhi* lifestyle. This is for him at the core of Svāmī Śiv Nārāyaṇ's teachings. He combines a Brahmanical-Sanskritic transformation of lifestyle, in the sense of M. N. Srinivas, with Dalit assertiveness. Dr. Ambedkar's social gospel is fully accepted in the Dhām as well as in the school. In contrast with Kanpur, where Buddhism is an intrinsic part of the Dalit movement, in Candravār this is absent. Buddhism is not amalgamated with Sant Dharm, as in Kanpur among the educated Śiv Nārāyaṇīs. In Candravār Dhām, Buddhism is considered to be a social gospel, not a path to salvation.

The shifting meanings of a textual tradition within the realm of an oral tradition are obvious. Although the *Gurū anyās* does not mention caste at all, there is general agreement that Svāmī Śiv Nārāyaṇ was born to abolish caste. This is paradoxical insofar as even within the Śiv Nārāyaṇ *saṃpradāya,* there was neither connubium nor commensality between the different *jātis.* They only partook in the communion, the *mohanbhog*, of the sect.

Questioning the Tropes about *'Bhakti'* and *'Rīti'* in Hindi Literary Historiography

Allison Busch

'Early Indian Spirituality' *versus* 'Late Courtly Decadence'

This article probes the stigma that has come to be attached to Brajbhasha poets from the *rīti* period of Hindi literature, and the frequent (but frequently unwarranted) gulf in critical esteem that separates the treatment of *bhakti* and rīti literature in modern Hindi scholarship. I begin by briefly surveying the original conception behind the terms *bhaktikāl* (period of devotion) and *rītikāl* (period of high style) as they crystallized in Hindi literary historiography, querying whether the foundational poetic principles that these terms purport to encapsulate are reliable indexes of Brajbhasha textual history. The standard narratives about *bhakti* and *rīti* that have become entrenched in the field of Hindi studies recapitulate a number of colonial-period tropes about Indian spirituality and courtly decadence, and their survival long into the post-colonial period has not attracted the critique it merits. I am hardly the first person to register discontent with the concepts of *bhakti* and *rīti* as primary organizing categories for 'medieval' Hindi literature. Recently a number of Western scholars have stressed the overlapping *bhakti* and *rīti* personas of some prominent seventeenth- and eighteenth-century poets, and here I will be adding my voice to this emerging chorus with reference to the literary profiles of even earlier poets like Viṣṇudās (fl.1435), Kṛpārām (fl.1541), Nanddās (fl.1570) and Keśavdās (fl.1600), features of whose work challenge the very idea of literary history's traditional *bhakti-rīti* dividing line.[1] The terms *bhakti* and *rīti* have also been the object of occasional scrutiny by a range of Hindi critics, who have occasionally proposed alter-

1. For the inseparability of *bhakti* and *rīti* in the work of Bihārīlāl (b. early 1600s) see Rupert Snell, 'Bhakti versus Rīti? The Satsaī of Bihārīlāl,' *Journal of Vaishnava Studies* 3.1 (1994), pp. 153-70. New work by Imre Bangha, 'Lover and Saint: The Early History of Ānandghan's Reputation,' *Journal of the Royal Asiatic Society* 11.2 (2001), pp. 175-90, and Heidi Pauwels, 'Romancing Rādhā: Nāgarīdās' Royal Appropriations of *Bhakti* Themes,' *South Asia Research* 25.1 (2005), pp. 55-78, on Ānandghan and Nāgarīdās respectively, has encouraged a more complex analysis of *bhakti* and *rīti*, tending to view them as choices in a repertory of poetic voices rather than fixed identities.

natives for naming and periodizing the principal constituents of the Hindi corpus.[2] But these relatively minor adjustments do not go far enough in correcting the slant of the core ideological orientations that underpinned the creation of the categories in the first places, and my purpose here is to intensify this corrective process.

The question I am raising about the validity of these literary-historical categories is no simple matter of nomenclature. To query the logic behind the categories *bhakti* and *rīti* is simultaneously to engage a larger set of intellectual concerns about how India's precolonial literary past has been viewed and represented over the last two hundred years: what is valued (religious literature), and what is not (courtly literature), why this should be the case—particularly when it is not clear that watertight binaries like 'religious' and 'courtly' literature were invariably meaningful to premodern Hindi poets—and who has historically been empowered to decide such matters. For it's hardly news to declare that literary values are not naturally-existing universals but part of culturally-constructed interpretive regimes, which, under conditions of colonialism, generally enforced particular ideologies about 'native' literary modes or, under conditions of nationalism, demanded acute selectivity about the literary motifs that could be allowed to represent the modern Indian state.

There is not much about either colonial regimes or nationalistic projects that is conducive to an unproblematic appraisal of a region's cultural heritage. In the unequal interpretive milieu of late nineteenth-century India the literary prejudices of the British were often accepted without sufficient debate or rigorous critical analysis. In some cases Indians were actively indoctrinated into feeling a new sense of shame—or in more extreme situations hatred—for their formerly-prized literary heritage. Under pressure to conform to Western poetic regimes such as Romanticism, many traditions were reevaluated, found wanting, and then subjected to rehabilitation.[3] The perceived need for India's cultural rehabilitation fed directly into the stream of nationalist thought, and fostered the conditions for a modernizing literary ethos spearheaded in Hindi circles by reformers like Mahāvīr Prasād Dvivedī (1864-1938). During the heyday of early nationalism in the first decades of the twentieth century, when Hindi was increasingly being mobilized as the linguistic flagship of the Indian nation, creating socially useful literature for the changing conditions of modern India emerged as a compelling desideratum, and the many aspects of Hindi's literary past that were not in keeping with such modernizing aims were summarily dismissed. These

2. See note 16 below.

3. A valuable study of Urdu literature's (often unfortunate) encounters with 'Wordsworthian' aesthetics is Frances Pritchett, *Nets of Awareness*, Berkeley: University of California Press, 1994. Comparable processes in Hindi have not been as well documented or critiqued.

choices are directly reflected in the historiography of the period, a historiography that remains today substantively unchanged from the 1920s.

The bulk of what came to be rejected under the colonial and nationalist enterprises were the kinds of courtly writings now lumped together under the rubric of '*rīti* literature.' Traditional courtly litterateurs' predilection for erotic themes and Sanskrit-style literary taxonomies came to be newly viewed as the self-indulgent hallmarks of a tired and decadent feudal past, a past tha. he growing Hindi literary public became increasingly anxious to repudiate. Once esteemed as the gems of poetic craftsmanship that had commanded fame and fortune in the *samasyāpūrti* (poetry contest) culture of early-modern courtly life, *rīti* works were now reviled as baroque, showy, and stilted. It was not just the aesthetics of *rīti* that came under attack. The poetry became morally suspect because it seemed to lack any higher purpose and its *raison d'être* (or so it was often accused) was to please rich, undeserving patrons of a medieval social order rather than to edify the masses. In contrast, the religious (*bhakti*) features of the Indian poetic terrain were perceived to be more in accordance with the radical reformist values of the period, garnering prestige in the modernizing literary imagination. For instance, when Indian society had come under repeated attack for its treatment of women and the lower castes, premodern *bhakti* literature seemed creditable for an almost modern-style progressivism. With certain blinders on (one would have to ignore, for instance, Tulsī's infamous dictum that women and low castes, like drums, are especially suitable for beating[4]), *bhakti* religion and literature could be constructed as a potential answer to some of the social ills deemed to be plaguing Indian society.[5] *Bhakti* could even be deployed in the service of nationalist causes: a new coinage for patriotism (*deśbhakti*) gave an older term with limited parameters an expanded scope and a purposeful, topical ring.[6] In short, *bhakti* literature could be dressed up in new clothes and made to appear

---

4. *Rāmcaritmānas* of Tulsīdās, 96th ed., Gorakhpur: Gītā Press, 1993, v. 5.58.6.

5. Rāmcandra Śukla made the perceived connection between (nirguṇ) *bhakti* and colonial-period reformist values explicit when he stated, 'These religious mystics bestowed a great gift on illiterate and low-caste people. They made a commendable effort to uplift them, giving them some sense of higher things, emphasizing purity of conduct, rejecting religious ostentation, and instilling a sense of self-worth. When Westerners referred to them by the term "religious reformers" it was with this in mind.' Rāmcandra Śukla, *Hindī sāhitya kā itihās,* 29th ed., Varanasi: Nāgarī Pracāriṇī Sabhā, 1994, p. 39. (Translations from the Hindi here and elsewhere are my own.)

6. Maithilī Śaraṇ Gupta, one of the Hindi tradition's most celebrated Dvivedī-period poets, exhibited a striking blend of patriotism and *bhakti* in his famous poem *Sāket.* See Harish Trivedi, 'The Progress of Hindi, Part 2: Hindi and the Nation,' in *Literary Cultures in History,* ed. by Sheldon Pollock, Berkeley: University of California Press, 2003, p. 990. Hariaudh's *Priyāpravās* was a dramatic retooling of Kṛṣṇa-Rādhā themes for a modern reformist context. See Karine Schomer, *Mahadevi Varma and the Chhayavad Age of Modern Hindi Poetry*, 1983, repr. Berkeley: University of California Press, 1998, p. 10.

democratic, pragmatic, and morally exemplary, whereas *rīti* was constructed as its antithesis: it seemed feudal, frivolous, and morally suspect. It did not hurt *bhakti*'s case that it also had more in common with Western literary sensibilities like Romanticism, and Christian religious tenets like monotheism, which were of course the cultural preferences of India's colonial rulers.

The Origins of Modern Hindi Classificatory Systems

Decades of colonial and reformist thinking about Hindi were eventually distilled into definitive historiographical shape in 1929 with the publication of Rāmcandra Śukla's highly influential *Hindī sāhitya kā itihās* (History of Hindi literature). The cornerstone of Śukla's work was its fourfold periodization scheme (*kāl vibhāg*), which is worth laying out in full detail here because it remains, after much debate but ultimately with only minor modifications, the dominant system for conceptualizing Hindi literature:

1. **Ādikāl**	(Vīrgāthākāl)	{Vikram 1050-1375}
2. Pūrv madhyakāl	(**Bhaktikāl**)	{Vikram 1375-1700}
3. Uttar madhyakāl	(**Rītikāl**)	{Vikram 1700-1900}
4. **Ādhunik kāl**	(Gadyakāl)	{Vikram 1900-1984}

These Hindi categories and Hindu dates translate as follows:

1. Beginning period	(Period of heroic songs)	{CE 993-1318}
2. Early medieval period	(Period of devotion)	{CE 1318-1643}
3. Late medieval period	(Period of style)	{CE 1643-1843}
4. Modern period	(Period of prose)	{CE 1843-1927}[7]

At first glance these categories may seem utterly banal and hardly worthy of clamorous critique. But it is surely worth pausing to ask how Hindi literature ended up with a medieval period that extends all the way into the mid-nineteenth century, when—historians must universally agree—the expiration date for anything that could reasonably be called 'medieval' had long passed in the West. The idea that Hindi literature (like India) could only achieve modernity with the advent of the British seems upon closer scrutiny more

---

7. Śukla, *Itihās*, p. 1. The terms indicated in bold face are still standard in the field. This system did not just emerge *ex nihilo*. The works of earlier literary historians such as Śiv Singh Seṃgar, George Abraham Grierson, and the Miśra brothers all need to be factored into our understanding of how a literary past was first generated for Hindi. An overview of these matters is Allison Busch, 'The Courtly Vernacular: The Transformation of Braj Literary Culture (1590-1690),' Ph.D. diss., University of Chicago, 2003, pp. 55-76.

likely to be an unexamined relic of a paternalistic colonial worldview than a sound classificatory principle for literature.[8]

Of most critical importance to this discussion, however, is Śukla's surprising bifurcation of medieval literature into an earlier '*bhakti*' period and a later 'rīti' period. Śukla took two major trends in Hindi literature, the devotional and the courtly, trends that we will find to be far more logically distinguishable in terms of stylistic and patronage configurations, and accorded them a new temporal significance that no one had ever before attributed to them. Furthermore, the dates for these newly-posited historical epochs acquired a strangely arbitrary specificity: we are asked to believe that the early (*pūrv*) or '*bhakti*' portion of the proposed medieval period began precisely in CE 1318, and lasted just until the year 1643, at which point it supposedly underwent a shift, transitioning to a later (*uttar*) entity characterized by '*rīti*'.

Any careful reader of Śukla's *Itihās* soon discovers that new periods were not the only things being proposed. Inherent in the model (although its fullest instantiation would await a rash of post-Independence literary-histories) is a sense of pronounced hierarchy between *bhakti* and *rīti* in terms of their larger literary and socio-cultural merit. Whereas the category *bhakti*, pregnant with positive connotations of spirituality, betokens what is generally constructed as a hallowed Indian cultural trait, the very idea of 'rīti' suggests some kind of medieval excess. Frequently glossed in English by the regrettable term 'mannerist', *rīti* does not just innocently mean 'style', a literal translation of the Hindi word, but carries the derogatory implication of 'too much style'.

Aside from dissatisfaction with the names and the cultural assumptions that lurk behind them, Śukla's model sparks other pressing questions. Why was the category of medieval Hindi literature split into two at the particular point he proposed, and what were the historical grounds for seeing a split between *bhakti* and *rīti* in the first place? It is difficult to think of anything that happened in 1643 (1700 Vikram era) to make this year an important turning point for Hindi literature. No major political event occurred that year, nor was any epoch-making literary text produced. In fact, the 1640s were a decade of relative quiescence in the otherwise remarkably dynamic seventeenth century, where virtually nothing of significance seems

8. Śukla cannot be held fully responsible for the way he carved up Hindi literary production into beginning, medieval, and modern periods. The perception that Indians were static inhabitants of a long-enduring medieval realm prior to the arrival of the British is a well-attested part of colonial discourse. There was also a literary-historical precedent for some of this terminology in *Miśrabandhuvinod* (Delight of the Miśra brothers) by Ganeśbihārī Miśra, Śyāmbihārī Miśra, and Śukdevbihārī Miśra, vol. 1, Allahabad: Hindīgranth-prasārak Maṇḍalī, 1913, which featured the divisions 'early medieval Hindi' and 'advanced medieval Hindi,' although with dates substantially earlier and therefore less questionable than those proposed by Śukla. See Miśra et al., introduction to vol. 1, p. v.

to have occurred in the entire field of Hindi literature. Of course, literary historians can only sketch an approximate picture of literary trends, and they can hardly be expected to defend every periodization with absolute rigor. One surmises that for Śukla the sheer volume of 'medieval' texts rendered that category unwieldy, and the nice, round number of 1700 in the Hindu Vikram calendar presented itself as a convenient midpoint for dividing the material into two more manageable sections.

Was there a solid intellectual basis for the radical new concept that medieval Hindi literature consisted of two historically distinct phases?[9] This is where *bhakti* and *rīti* are supposed to come into play. For Śukla the four proposed eras of Hindi literature could be distinguished by their principal tendencies (*pravṛttiyāṁ*), such as the heroic (*vīra*) spirit of the *rāso* genres in the beginning period, or in some cases a major literary event (*pradhān sāhityik ghaṭnā*) like the rise of prose (*gadya*) in the modern period.[10] And one period led directly into another through a chain of causality that stemmed from political or cultural strengths and weaknesses. Under this thought system the heroism of the beginning period could not be sustained under 'Muslim rule,' which necessitated a turn inwards during the *bhakti* or 'early' (*pūrv*) stage of medieval literature.[11] Notably, it was during this *bhakti* period that Hindi is said to have reached a state of 'maturity' (*prauṛhtā*) before passing on the baton to *rīti* poets. The *rīti* or late (*uttar*) medieval phase, however, was constructed as a more scholarly and stilted style of writing that was too limiting and largely disappointing given the promise shown by earlier *bhakti* writers. One of Śukla's central findings on the subject of *rīti* literature was, 'People should have felt a strong sense of a lack (*abhāv*) but that never dawned on them.'[12] And in his account of the *rītigranth* (book of method), the *rīti* period's preeminent genre and a major vehicle of precolonial intellectual life in Hindi, Śukla repeatedly decried the poets' 'errors' (*bhram/bhrānt dhāraṇā*) and 'bungling' (*gaṛbaṛī*), their 'mistaken' (*pramādvaś*) and 'incoherent' (*asaṁgat*) ideas. He implied that during this era immediately preceding the modern period Hindi was running out of creative stimuli, to the point of risking stagnation:

9. The question of whether or not it makes sense to split medieval Hindi literature into two periods has subsequently been raised by other scholars, notably Gaṇpaticandra Gupta, who holds that the medieval period is best viewed as a single unit (spanning the years from 1350 to 1857) throughout which a range of literary trends like *bhakti*, *rīti*, and martial traditions coexisted. See Gaṇpaticandra Gupta, *Hindī sāhitya kā vaijñānik itihās*, Candigarh: Bhāratendu Bhavan,1965, pp. 4-7; 149-54. It is regrettable that this otherwise cogent system is marred by its reductionist treatment of 'Muslim rule' as religiously intolerant, prone to war, and overly luxury-loving.

10. Śukla, 'Foreword to first edition,' in *Itihās*, pp. 5-6.

11. Śukla, *Itihās*, p. 34.

12. Śukla, *Itihās*, p. 131.

> The tradition of writing *rītigranths* also proved an obstacle to the extensive development of literature. The poets ignored the diverse forms of nature, the various concerns of life and the many mysteries of the world. Literature became in a way bound, and limited in scope. Its field was limited. The literary stream (*vāgdhārā*) began to flow only in narrow rivulets... .[13]

And the contrast with Śukla's more favourable treatment of *bhakti* literature—its spiritualism, its purported advocacy of social uplift and Muslim-Hindu unity (just to name a few of its vaunted qualities), is striking.

It is no secret that Śukla wrote his *Itihās* in a hurry, and it was never intended to be viewed as the last word on Hindi literary history. The work was originally designed to be an introduction to the *Hindī śabdsāgar* (Ocean of Hindi words), the first scholarly Hindi lexicon of the modern period, and not the comprehensive literary historical milestone it has subsequently become. It is telling that in the foreword to the first edition Śukla explicitly stated that he had not conducted any significant new research into what he was newly terming the *rīti* authors, preferring to draw on earlier sources like the *Miśrabandhuvinod.*[14] His ideas were only meant to be 'preliminary indicators.'[15] It is therefore all the more surprising that so much of his model remains intact.

It is not that there was never again to be another literary history for Hindi. Dozens have been written since 1929, in both Hindi and in English. There have been numerous corrections and augmentations to the state of general knowledge about the Hindi past. New texts have been discovered, and Śukla's findings amended accordingly. Collected works (*granthāvalī*) and studies of key authors continue to be published in Hindi. There have also been fervent debates about Hindi's literary-historical categories and the periods they encompass, with some scholars even going so far as to propose new categories for organizing Hindi literature. But the proposed new names have done little to alter the core terms of engagement with respect to late precolonial Hindi literature. It is telling that the new historiographical construct that was accorded the most credence as a proposed replacement for *rītikāl* proved to be *śṛṅgārkāl* (period of eroticism). To advocate a *zeitgeist* of eros rather than mannerism does not advance the cause very far, for its

13. Śukla, *Itihās*, pp. 130-1.

14. Distinctly lacking in the *Miśra* brothers' work, however, is the dismissive tone that characterizes Śukla's analysis of rīti. The time constraints he faced in assembling his teaching notes into a book are mentioned in Śukla, 'Foreword to first edition,' in *Itihās*, p. 4.

15. '*Rītikāl yā aur kisī kāl ke kaviyoṁ ke sāhityik viśeṣtāoṁ ke saṃbandh meṁ maiṁne jo saṃkṣipt vicār prakaṭ kiye haiṁ, ve digdarśan mātr ke liye*' (The cursory opinions I have expressed with respect to the literary specificities of poets from the *rīti* period or any other period are merely preliminary indicators). Śukla, 'Foreword to first edition,' in *Itihās*, p. 6.

defining concept still participates in the very same cultural field of courtly decadence as *rīti*.[16]

The *rīti* period continues to be treated as a time of cultural embarrassment—even failure—long after Śukla wrote his *Itihās*.[17] In addition to being guilty of 'mannerism', the charge of 'decadence' always seems to hover over Brajbhasa poets from the *rīti* period, for according to the logic of literary history at its crudest, these poetic vices are the necessary concomitant to writing at a later moment. Often considered a standard symptom of this putative decadence-disorder is *rīti* poets' concern with literary convention and ornament (*alaṅkār*). But serious students of premodern Indian literature know that these were the essential building blocks for most poetry, even that of many *bhakti* authors, up to the modern period. After all, it is not without good reason that literary theory, one of the most sophisticated branches of learning in precolonial India, was known as the 'science of ornaments' (*alaṅkāra-śāstra*).

If principles of interpretive generosity concerning other styles of literature from other times, which may be animated by aesthetic criteria potentially very different from those of the present day, do not by themselves prompt the desire for a review of discourses about *rīti*, at the very least we should demand more historical precision of the model, for most of its defining imagery of a supposed decline from *bhakti* to *rīti*, from early to late, from maturity to decadence, etc., is based not on any careful assessment of the empirical data but on vague, unquestioned assumptions about Indian cultural history. Do we not need to be more intellectually wary of designations like 'early' or 'mature' (both associated with *bhakti* literature in

16. The argument for a *śṛiṅgārkāl* is found in Viśvanāth Prasād Miśra, *Hindī sāhitya kā atīt*, vol. 2, 2nd ed., Varanasi: Vāṇī Vitān Prakāśan, 1966, pp. 374-88. For a good overview of important elements in the debates on both the naming practices and periodization of Hindi literary history, see Gaṇpaticandra Gupta and Nagendra, 'Pūrvpīṭhikā,' in *Hindī sāhitya kā itihās*, ed. by Nagendra, 1973. I am struck by how even Gaṇpaticandra Gupta, whose *Hindī sāhitya kā vaijñānik itihās* (Scientific history of Hindi literature) is perhaps the most radical overhaul of Śukla's system, is still able to say that Śukla's ideas about rīti literature are 'in many respects still valid today.' Gupta and Nagendra, 'Pūrvpīṭhikā,' p. 14. A rare work that focuses on the successes rather than shortcomings of rīti literature is Kiśorīlāl, *Rītikālīn kaviyoṁ kī maulik den*, Allahabad: Sāhitya Bhavan, 1971.

17. The trend is found in scholarly writings in English no less than in Hindi. The most influential of the English-language Hindi literary histories designates the entire *rīti* period by the chapter heading 'a waning era,' in contrast to the section on the *bhakti* period, which is entitled 'the years of maturity.' See Ronald Stuart McGregor, *Hindi Literature from its Beginnings to the Nineteenth Century*, vol. 8, pt. 6 of *A History of Indian Literature*, ed. by Jan Gonda, Wiesbaden: Harrassowitz, 1984. Compare the recent characterization of *rīti* as a 'degeneration' from *bhakti* in Trivedi, *Progress*, 2003, p. 984.

Śukla's model) as descriptors for creative processes?[18] In the study of art, literature, and other artifacts of culture, the *early* is too easily romanticized as pure, simple, and free from artifice. Many ideas about earlier simplicity or 'classicism' versus later ornateness or 'decadence' seem to have been unthinkingly transplanted from the field of European art history and literature to the Indian cultural terrain. It is not at all clear that these remain useful terms for the cultural history even of their place of origin, let alone for that of India.[19] Literary-historical terms like 'early' and 'mature' also seem suspiciously more relevant as descriptors of processes in the natural world than critical tools for handling man-made literary production.[20] One thing is certain: such concepts do not leave much latitude for any poet that should be unfortunate enough to follow in their wake. For according to a biologic logic based on observing the life trajectory of flowers, or of aging people, what ineluctably happens after the 'mature' phase? Decline, decay, death. At least this seems to have been the fate of *rīti* literature in the eyes of most modern critics, who, in accepting that *rīti* literature is defined by its position as a 'late-medieval' (*uttar madhyakālīn*) cultural entity have usually—even relentlessly—constructed it as the tired, enervated, literary successor to *bhakti*.

Mapping the concepts of *rīti* and *bhakti* onto a linearly temporal structure permitted another teleological problem to enter the historiographical picture. *Rīti* literature was not just 'late medieval,' but its specific point of emplotment on a time line also served to forge an inextricable link with a perceived cultural weakness that had allowed the British to conquer India. A common trend in post-Śukla literary-historical discourse is to introduce rīti poetry with a lament about India's downfall under supposedly decadent, overly luxury-loving Mughal rulers.[21] This practice is not only tedious but also intellectually suspect insofar as the nature and extent of eighteenth-century Mughal decline—once thought to be a fatal rupture point in Indian society according to principles of colonial

18. 'Pūrv madhyakāl' is, as noted above, a synonym for the *bhakti* period. And the word *'prauṛhtā'* is used repeatedly to characterize it. See, for instance, Śukla, *Itihās*, pp. 35, 68, 129.

19. A good exposé of these unhelpful but widespread thought structures is Partha Mitter, '"Decadence in India": Reflections on a Much-Used Word in Studies of Indian Art and Society,' in *Sight & Insight: Essays on Art and Culture in Honour of E. H. Gombrich at 85,* ed. by John Onians, London: Phaidon Press, 1994. I thank Pika Ghosh for the reference.

20. A questioning of the merit of such 'organicist tropes' and a cogent articulation of the need to forge new models for South Asian literary history are offered by Shelden Pollock, 'Literary History, Region, and Nation in South Asia: Introductory Note,' *Social Scientist* 23.10-12 (1995), pp. 1-7. A recent embodiment of alternative literary-historical practice is Pollock, *Literary Cultures.*

21. Typical is Nagendra, *Rītibaddh kāvya*, vol. 6 of *Hindī sāhitya kā bṛhat itihās*, Varanasi: Nāgarī Pracāriṇī Sabhā, 1974, but there are innumerable others.

historiography—has recently been much-debated by historians.[22] And already damaging tropes about *rīti's* connections with Mughal decadence are often further exacerbated by unfavourable comparisons with twentieth-century literary trends such as a new emphasis on prose and more utilitarian poetic sensibilities. Viewed from a modern nationalist perspective *rīti* was historiographically poised to embody the 'backwardness' from which reformers like Mahāvīr Prasād Dvivedī were busy trying to rescue Indian culture. In sum, the modern periodization of Hindi literature as pioneered by Śukla and since his day reaffirmed with few changes by generations of critics constructs *rīti* as the era where medieval literature declined from maturity to near death, before its putative resurrection through the new genres and literary systems infused by the cultural currents of colonial and nationalist modernity.

What is *Rīti*, and When Did it Begin?

The point is not that literary processes do not take place in history. Literary sensibilities do change. New literary forms arise. Some genres die out, and others flourish. Patronage conditions shift. Some moments in time seem—whether to contemporaries or later observers or both—especially rich for literature. Other periods may not appear so outstanding. And some of this flux is susceptible to being measured. But we need to measure it with appropriate tools, not with cultural tropes about maturity and decadence, or political tropes centered in the stock imagery of decline and fall.

If we are accurately to mark *rīti's* origins and degrees of separation from *bhakti*, we should at least begin by defining more precisely what this *rīti* is, and see if it is possible to track a transition between *bhakti* and *rīti* with reference to particular authors and places. And once the originary *rīti* moment occurred, if such a thing can be said ever to have occurred, or at least if it can somehow be pinpointed in the context of known Braj textual history, we might be able to determine if an antecedent, and superior, devotional poetry really did give way to a later, inferior, worldly poetry. But we should remain open to other logics for theorizing literary trends, some of which may muddle rather than clarify the boundaries between authors or genres or across time periods. Literary cultures are one of the most significant manifestations of human creativity, and they are nothing if not

22. Recent overviews of critical debates in Mughal historiography are *The Mughal State 1526-1750*, ed. by Muzaffar Alam and Sanjay Subrahmanyam, New Delhi: Oxford University Press, 1998; *The Eighteenth Century in India*, ed. by Seema Alavi, New Delhi: Oxford University Press, 2002, and *The Eighteenth Century in Indian History*, ed. by P. J. Marshall, New Delhi: Oxford University Press, 2003.

complex. This is a complexity that standard literary history is often ill-equipped to handle.[23]

Indeed, while the basic temporal contours of Śukla's model of an earlier *bhakti* followed by a later *rīti* literature do not completely lack historical validity, there are enough exceptions to warrant a strong sense of hesitation about his approach. It is true that if one focuses on two major cultural developments—the Vaishnava efflorescence in the Braj region from the early sixteenth century, and the expansion of courtly patronage networks from the early seventeenth century—then a linear chain of causality whereby *bhakti* literature in Brajbhasha was eventually superseded by *rīti* styles seem plausible. However, a significant number of texts cannot be accommodated by this paradigm. For instance, how do we account for the poet Viṣṇudās, who composed two epics at the Tomar court in Gwalior between 1435 and 1442? These texts, which were apparently unknown to Śukla, lack the type of religiosity that defines *bhakti* literature, and we need to account for the fact that two major features of rīti, namely court patronage and a more secular spirit, characterized the literary production of a location very near the Brajmaṇḍal well before the explosion of Krishnaite literature.[24]

A strictly historical approach to rīti's defining genre, the *rītigranth,* complicates even more dramatically the idea of a transition from *bhakti* to *rīti* in the mid-seventeenth century. The practice of writing textbooks on poetics principles surely dictated his choice of name for the *rītikāl*, but, as Śukla himself acknowledged, in terms of brute chronology *rītigranths* were already being written more than a full century before his proposed beginning date of 1643 for the *rīti* period. Pertinent here is the figure of Kṛpārām, author of the first known Braj work on poetics, the *Hittaraṅginī* (River of love, 1541?), a reworking of Bhānudatta's Sanskrit *Rasamañjarī* (Bouquet of emotion, *c.* 1500).[25] Less equivocally dated is a subsequent Braj version of

23. A pertinent Europeanist's perspective on some of the problems with a historical approach to tracking literary style is that of John M. Steadman, *Redefining a Period Style*, Pittsburgh: Duquesne University Press, 1990, pp. 1-12.

24. The question of whether Viṣṇudās should be considered a specifically Brajbhasha poet has yet to be fully resolved. R. S. McGregor has termed the language of his oeuvre 'early Brajbhasha,' whereas H. N. Dvivedī, the other major scholar to have seriously studied this corpus, distinguishes it as Gwaliyari. See Ronald Stuart McGregor, 'A Narrative Poet's View of his Material: Viṣṇudās's Introduction to his Brajbhāṣā *Pāṇḍav-carit* (AD 1435),' in *The Banyan Tree*, ed. by Mariola Offredi, vol. 2, New Delhi: Manohar, 2000, pp. 335-42; Hariharnivās Dvivedī, *Mahābhārat (Pāṇḍav-carit)*, Gwalior: Vidyā Mandir Prakāśan, 1973, pp. 90ff.

25. Some dispute the chronogram that dates the *Hittaraṅginī* to 1541, and posit borrowings from later authors such as Bihārīlāl or even Raslīn. Neither R. S. McGregor nor Sudhākar Pāṇḍey sees reason to doubt the earlier dating. Significantly, Kṛpārām mentions predecessors (*Hittaraṅginī,* v. 1.4—although whether they wrote in Sanskrit or Braj is unspecified), so even this probable early work may be no absolute beginning point for vernacular poetics, just the earliest available. See McGregor, *Hindi Literature,* p. 124;

the *Rasamañjarī* by Nanddās (fl. 1570). With their highly structured, technical literary expositions these are *rīti* works in form, but they also evince a strong *bhakti* ethos, both in their opening dedications and in the illustrations (*udāharaṇ*) of definitions (*lakṣaṇ*) with Rādhā-Kṛṣṇa verses, raising questions about the extent to which devotional and scholarly orientations can be considered separate.

The inseparability of the concepts *bhakti* and *rīti* seems particularly pronounced in a third 'pre-*rīti*' *rītigranth*, Keśavdās's *Rasikpriyā* (1591). In fact, judging from several striking instances of word play in the *Rasikpriyā,* which merge the terminology of classical aesthetics with that of spiritual practice, it is as though Keśavdās set out to compose a work that would emphasize the synergy between the devotional and scholastic realms. In his opening address to his readers (called, *rasik* or savourers), the poet states that Kṛṣṇa should be worshiped as 'he who consists of the nine rasas' (*navrasmay*).[26] Thus, savouring is to be seen as *both* an aesthetic (*rīti*) and a religious (*bhakti*) activity. Further crossovers between these categories occur in the closing to chapter three on the subject of the quintessentially *rīti* topic *nāyikābheda,* where Keśavdās proclaims that the subject matter of his poetry is Rādhā, 'heroine of the world's hero' (*jaganāyaka kī nāyikā*). Similarly suggestive is the *bhakti-rīti* pun '*darśana rasa*' used in the next line to describe lovers' meetings, a phrase which aside from its literal, worldly sense also invokes a devotee's intimate experience of an icon in a temple.[27]

Further confounding the discreteness of the categories is the very title of the work, which may also have been intended as a double entendre. From a *rīti* perspective the compound *Rasikpriyā* yields the translation '*A Handbook for Poetry Connoisseurs.*' But the word *rasik* can also mean 'Kṛṣṇa' and *priyā* (with the feminine long-*ā* ending) would then mean 'beloved,' i.e. Rādhā. From this angle, the work presents itself as a Vaishnava meditation upon God and his lover. Following the traditional custodians of literary history we would have to ask whether Keśavdās was a *bhakti* or *rīti* poet. Although Śukla placed him in the *bhaktikāl,* the real answer is that he was both. The point, however, is precisely that we do not have to make some ultimate determination about whether the *Rasikpriyā* (or the *Hittaraṅginī,* or

---

Sudhākar Pāṇḍey, Introduction to *Kṛpārām granthāvalī*, Varanasi: Nāgarī Pracāriṇī Sabhā, 1969, pp. 31-40.

26. *Rasikpriyā* of Keśavdās, in *Keśavgranthāvalī*, ed. by Viśvanāth Prasād Miśra, vol. 1, Allahabad: Hindustani Academy, 1954, v. 1.2.

27. *Rasikpriyā,*, v. 3.74. The full *dohā* reads, '*jaganāyaka kī nāyikā, baranī Kesava-dāsa/tinake darsana-rasa kahaum̐, sunau prachanna prakāsa*' (Keśavdās has described the heroine of the world's hero. Now I will speak of the joys they experience in seeing one another—listen to the different types, both hidden and revealed).

Nanddās's *Rasmañjarī*) is a *rīti* or a *bhakti* work.[28] Attempts to separate out these elements contravene its spirit.

Aspects of Keśavdās's later writerly and patronage profile, however, do tip the scales in favour of a more pronounced *rīti* persona when compared with his recent predecessors Kṛpārām and Nanddās. In the case of Nanddās in particular, the *rīti* dimension constitutes only a relatively minor segment of his oeuvre, and his overall profile is that of a *bhakti* writer. But when it comes to Keśavdās, scholarly writings on poetics in the *rītigranth* genre make up a far more significant portion of his overall oeuvre (3 of 8 works[29]). His *rītigranths* are also far more complex than anything in the earlier Brajbhasha tradition, covering an extensive range of topics and showing a predilection for more elaborate meters like *kavitt* or *savaiyā* as opposed to the simple *dohā.* This tendency towards stylistic elaboration also needs to be seen as an important component of any definition of what constitutes rīti. In addition to writing *rītigranth* works Keśavdās also experimented with classical *mahākāvya* modes, and the proliferation of metrical forms coupled with deepening lexical and thematic complexity was certainly a new direction for Brajbhasha literature. Furthermore, aside from genre and stylistic proclivities Keśavdās, unlike Nanddās, composed his works not in religious communities but for kings, and court patronage for Braj poets became a dramatic new force in Hindi literary culture from that point on.[30]

The sense that Keśavdās worked and wrote in a courtly milieu is largely incidental to the *Rasikpriyā,* but it becomes quite pronounced from the time of his *Kavipriyā* (Handbook for poets, 1601), written a full decade later. Although Rādhā-Kṛṣṇa verses are still significant in number, the work has a much greater range of subject matter—some of it distinctly urbane and relatively secular. Keśavdās also frames the *Kavipriyā* within a context of courtly culture, with lengthy introductory chapters that detail his patron's family history, the story of the founding of Orcha, as well as contemporary circumstances at Orcha. An entire section of this *rītigranth* (chapter eight) is devoted to kingly topics. The interest in royal subject matter would reach its highest development in his late *kāvya* works like *Vīrsiṁhdevcarit* (1607) and

28. The same can be said for the case of Bihārīlāl, an argument developed by Rupert Snell in 'Bhakti versus Rīti? The Satsaī of Bihārīlāl,' *Journal of Vaishnava Studies* 3.1 (1994), pp. 153-70. Of course, there were significant precedents for this interpenetration of *bhakti* and *rīti* in sixteenth-century Gauṛīya Vaishnavism, where *bhakti* achieved prominence in the domain of aesthetic discourse as a fully-fledged rasa in texts such as Rūpa Goṣvāmin's *Bhakti-rasāmṛtasindhu.* An outline of the development of *bhaktirasa* and its place in Gauṛīya theology is Neal Delmonico, 'Sacred Rapture: The Bhakti-rasa Theory of Rupa Goswamin,' *Journal of Vaishnava Studies* 6.1 (1998), pp. 75-98.

29. The three *rītigranths* are *Rasikpriyā, Kavipriyā,* and *Chandamālā.*

30. Kṛpārām's precise literary milieu is uncertain. His reference to the Betwa river, which flows through Orcha, in one of his poems (*Hittaraṅginī,* v. 308) suggests a possible connection to that court. See McGregor, *Hindi Literature*, p. 124.

the *Jahāngīrjascandrikā* (1612), dedicated to an Orcha king and Mughal emperor, respectively.

If one must insist on a watershed moment for a historical transition between *bhakti* and *rīti* literature, then perhaps it should be marked by the composition of Keśavdās's *Kavipriyā,* in 1601, and not the year 1643. But under Śukla's system the most qualified poet for the title of first *rīti* poet was placed in the *bhakti* period![31] And yet the point here is not to quibble over forty years or so. What is at stake is not so much whether the *rīti* period started in 1601 or in 1643, but whether the dichotomous model works at all. The model makes it impossible to account for many premodern Hindi literary practices, given that *rīti* tendencies clearly predate even Keśavdās, and *bhakti* ones postdate him by centuries.

If the *bhakti-rīti* historical model is so tough to map onto known literary conditions, perhaps we should consider moving away from a paradigm structured by fixed dates and stiff categories—and dates and categories based on presuppositions that from a postcolonial perspective have become completely untenable anyway—to a more flexible system that better accounts for the interplay of diverse literary personalities and processes. There are numerous Brajbhasha poets who would fall under the rubric of *rīti* in terms of the era in which they lived, but whose oeuvre cannot be accurately assessed without factoring in *bhakti.* In some cases, a poet's *bhakti* or *rīti* orientation may be given pride of place for a particular community at a particular moment, as when the poems of Ānandghan (fl. *c.* 1740) were anthologized by two different interest groups in two different collections: one that emphasized the religious verses, and the other the erotic ones.[32] Or poets may move back and forth between literary modes over a lifetime, as in the case of Sūratī Miśra (fl. 1740), in whose vast oeuvre can be found both *bhakti*-centered and distinctly *rīti* compositions. Or how do we account for a *'rīti'* author like Nāgarīdās (fl. mid-17th century), who began life as a king, wrote on numerous courtly themes, but ultimately retired a bhakta in Vrindavan? [33] There are all kinds of reasons why terms like '*rīti*' and 'rīti' do have some relevance for the pre-modern literary world: as broad indicators of genre or style or patronage context. But their differentiation on chronological grounds has only a marginal validity at best. Indeed, the two tendencies were actually synchronic, interactive, and often present in one and the same author—or even the same work. Even a cursory glimpse at Braj textual history suggests that *bhakti* and *rīti* seem preferable as general terms

31. Śukla, *Itihās*, pp. 114-19. This choice was critiqued by subsequent scholars, who now mostly do consider Keśavdās the founder (*pravartak*) of *rīti* literature. See Gupta and Nagendra, 'Pūrvpīthikā,' p. 15.

32. See Bangha, 'Lover and Saint,' pp. 180ff.

33. Heidi Pauwels, 'Romancing Rādhā,' illustrates how the categories *bhakti* and *rīti* inhibit rather than enhance our understanding of Nāgarīdās.

for encapsulating the expressive potentialities of a poet rather than the inescapable fate of a writer destined to be born in a particular period.

Conclusion

Literary history is supposed to serve as an organizational tool that aids in understanding and theorizing a culture's significant creative processes and trends. In the case of the *bhakti-rīti* system for framing precolonial Hindi textual production the model does more to impede than to advance the understanding of a critical component of north Indian literary self-expression. At the time Śukla's *Itihās* was written, colonial-period historiographical structures were still dictating principles about the contours of the Indian past, and an excess of historical determinism underlies the book's conception. If one of your principal cultural reference points is living under colonial rule, which was an inescapable reality for the pioneering Hindi scholars of Śukla's generation, you needed a model that would account for the political, but also cultural, weakness of India (for the two are generally—no doubt too crudely—perceived to be correlated), which had putatively set the stage for the region's colonization from the eighteenth century. And that weakness was found in the intellectual and literary practices of *rīti* poets, perhaps precisely because Śukla expected it to be there.

The bifurcation of so-called medieval Hindi literature into an earlier, meritorious *bhakti* period and a later, substandard rīti period lingers on as a primary organizing principle more than seventy-five years after its original conception, and its continued survival is a discredit to the field. An important early stream of Brajbhasha writing (but, as evident from the figure of Viṣṇudās, by no means the earliest) is undeniably religious in orientation, which must have provided the inspiration for Śukla. But as Brajbhasha poets began to attract courtly patronage, embrace a greater range of themes, and experiment with stylistic elaboration, a trend already observable at a relatively early moment in the work of Keśavdās, *bhakti* motifs hardly ceased. *Rīti* and *bhakti* aesthetics can indeed overlap in the persona of a single poet or in the lines of a single poem. The terms *bhakti* and *rīti* also point to distinctions in the social worlds—roughly expressible in terms of the court and temple—where literature was produced, but patronage at the one did not preclude patronage at the other. As potentially overlapping socio-aesthetic categories, then, *rīti* and *bhakti* may retain some conceptual validity, but as discrete literary-historical terms they trap us in the logic of early and late, mature and decadent, simple and artificial, and it is a logic that should now be retired when it comes to the scholarly appraisal of the late precolonial Hindi literary past.

Padas of Gurū Nānak in Rajasthani Manuscripts

Winand M. Callewaert

'This is dynamite,' Hew McLeod wrote to me about twenty years ago and Sikh scholars in Delhi who had agreed to help me to identify the *pada*s in the *Ādi Granth* (*ĀG*) politely discontinued the collaboration when they saw the material. Five 'Bhakti conferences' passed till eventually I decided to bring the material to the Heidelberg conference and tell, not what I think, but what the manuscripts tell us. At this moment two basic questions are not satisfactorily answered: *When* did these *pada*s come to Rajasthan, and *how*? I attempt to give an answer and I am convinced and hopeful that Sikh scholars will be better equipped to speculate about this, looking at what the manuscripts tell us about the beginning of the seventeenth century in north-west India.

This, however, is certain: The manuscript material leads the student into the very fascinating world of the study of manuscripts and back to the times when we hear devotee-singers who travelled from one village to another in the neigbouring regions of Punjab and Rajasthan, possibly even before A.D. 1600.

Why, of the 974 compositions of Gurū Nānak and the 2218 compositions of Gurū Arjan in the *ĀG*, were 26 *pada*s and *c.* 200 *sākhī*s[1] with the *bhaṇitā* '*nānak*' circulated in the oral transmission in Rajasthan and scribed there in Dādūpanthī manuscripts dated A.D. 1614 till 1676? And why precisely these *pada*s and *sākhī*s? What are the changes that occurred in that transmission and is there a pattern in these changes? As the *ĀG* was compiled in A.D. 1604, is it possible that these *pada*s were circulating outside Punjab even before that date?

In the Rajasthani manuscripts all these *pada*s are listed as *'nānak ke pad.'*

---

1. I give here only an analysis of the *pada*s. The *sākhī*s may be the subject of another study (the films with a copy of these texts are now in the South Asia Institute, University of Heidelberg).

— Ten of these *padas* are in the *ĀG* attributed to *mahalā* 1 or Nānak.
— Thirteen *padas* with the *bhaṇitā 'nānak'* in the Rajasthani manuscripts have in the *ĀG* the *bhaṇitā 'nānak'* (as is customary), but are attributed to *mahalā* 5 or the fifth Gurū, Arjan, the compiler.
— Two *padas* are so far not found in the *ĀG.*

Over a period of twenty-five years (since 1973) I have copied manuscripts with, amongst other text genres, *Sarvāṅgī*s and *Pañc-vāṇī*s. Although the *Pañc-vāṇī*s and the *Sarvāṅgī*s were both compiled within the Dādūpanth in the early seventeenth century, they are clearly independent products of compilation. In fact even the different *Pañc-vāṇī*s were independent products of compilation, as has been amply illustrated in my earlier publications.[2] Does this mean that the *padas* with the *bhaṇitā 'nānak'* published here are not derived from one archetypal source, either a travelling singer or a written document? They may have entered Rajasthan along different paths and through different villages. Do they rely on different sources in Punjab? Keeping these questions in mind let us look at the variants, in the text and in the *rāgas*.

Manuscripts in Rajasthan

The following manuscripts were copied with, amongst other, compositions with the *bhaṇitā 'nānak.'* Manuscripts *B* (possibly compiled in 1620) and *C* (possibly compiled in 1627) give the *Sarvāṅgī*s compiled by Rajab and Gopāldās, respectively, but the manuscripts copied by me on film are of a later date. I classify these manuscripts according to their 'date of compilation' because only few variant readings are found in those manuscripts.[3] All the other manuscripts are of the *Pañc-vāṇī* type, which has been abundantly described in my earlier publications.[4]

---

2. See *Bhakti Literature: An Oral-Scribal Archetype*. In *Voice, Text, Hypertext*, ed. by Ramona Modiano, Leroy F. Searle and Peter Shillingsburg, Seattle and London: University of Washington Press, 2003, pp. 115-24.
3. See *The Sarvāṅgī of the Dādūpanthī Rajab* (Orientalia Lovaniensia Analecta 4), Leuven, 1978; 446 pp.; *The Sarvāṅgī of Gopāl Dās,* New Delhi: Manohar, 1993; 520 pp.
4. See especially *The Hindī Songs of Nāmdev*, with Mukund Lath (Orientalia Lovaniensia Analecta 29), Leuven: Departement Oriḷntalistiek, Katholieke Universiteit, 1989; 432 pp.; also published by Motilal Banarsidass, Delhi. *The Life and Works of Raidās,* with P. Friedlander, New Delhi: Manohar, 1992; 335pp.; see pp. 67ff. and p. 73: 'There are six observed instances where *pads* in the *ĀG* and in the Rajasthani manuscripts have different attributions. In five instances a *pad* "of Ravidās" in the *ĀG* is attributed to another Santa in Rajasthani manuscripts and *pad* 66 "of Nānak" in the *ĀG* is attributed to Raidās in the Rajasthani manuscripts.'

	Year
A	1614 *Pañc-vāṇī,* Sanjay Śarmā Saṅgrahālay, Jaipur, the oldest such manuscript discovered so far; 8 *padas*.
B	(1620)[5] The *Sarvāṅgī* compiled by Rajab; manuscript *r* in Callewaert and Lath, pp. 83-5; 2 *padas*.
C	(1627) The *Sarvāṅgī* compiled by Gopāldās; manuscript *g* in Callewaert and Lath, pp. 83-5; 20 *padas*.
D	1636 *Pañc-vāṇī,* Dādūmahāvidyālay, Jaipur, No. 12, fol. 309-12; manuscript *d* in Callewaert and Lath, pp. 83-5; 8 *padas*.
E	1658 *Pañc-vāṇī,* Vidyā Bhūṣaṇ Saṅgrah, Jaipur, No. 34, (sections 21-2 in the catalogue); manuscript *v* in Callewaert and Lath, pp. 83-85; 14 *padas*.
F	1675 *Pañc-vāṇī,* Guru Nanak Dev University Amritsar, No. 875, fol. 366b-72; manuscript *a* in Callewaert and Lath, pp. 83-5; 16 *padas*.
G[6]	1676 *Pañc-vāṇī,* Dādūmahāvidyālay, Jaipur, No. 2, fol. 162; manuscript *m* in Callewaert and Lath, pp. 83-5; 15 *padas*.

Abbreviations

ĀG	*Ādi Granth*
al. (*alii*)	the other manuscripts or versions
ĀG/E<>al. means:	in the *ĀG* and in manuscript *E*, there is a reading which is different in the other manuscripts (al.)
ĀG<>al.	the reading in the Rajasthani manuscripts is uniform but different from the reading in the *ĀG*

5. For the study of the *Sarvāṅgīs* (MSS *B* and *C*) of Rajab and Gopāldās (see above, n. 3) I consulted copies of the original of (possibly) A.D. 1620 and of 1627, respectively; therefore I give the dates in brackets.

6. This manuscript *G* was apparently also consulted by B. P. Śarmā: *Guru Nānak Vāṇī (Hindī),* Candigarh: Viśva Bhāratī Prakāśan, 1978.

E<>al.	Rajasthani manuscript E has a reading different from the reading found in the other Rajasthani manuscripts *and* in the *ĀG*
Nā	*mahalā* 1 or Gurū Nānak
Ar	*mahalā* 5 or Gurū Arjan

For the *Pañc-vāṇī* manuscripts (except *A*, dated 1614) I give also the reference letter in my edition of the Hindī-songs of Nāmdev:[7] in the analysis published there it is clearly seen that there was not one, but several *Pañc-vāṇī* compilers. Based on the analysis of the *padas* of Nāmdev, I classified these manuscripts in several groups: *d*, *v*, *a* (dated 1636, 1658, 1675) and *m* (dated 1676).

It is generally accepted that the Bhagat literature (e.g. Kabīr) started to be incorporated into the pre-*ĀG* singing (or writing?) repertoires in Punjab. Taking Kabīr as a test-example, we clearly see that the *structure* of the *padas* of Kabīr in the Rajasthani manuscripts is uniformly different from the structure of those *padas* in the *ĀG*. The refrain (called *ṭeka* in the Rajasthani manuscripts) was most probably sung after each stanza; in the manuscripts the *ṭeka* line is written at the beginning of the *pada*. In the *ĀG* that refrain is called *rahāu* and is usually or often given after the first stanza. Let us look at *pada* 416 in my edition of Kabīr,[8] and compare the structure in the Rajasthani versions (R) and the Punjabi versions (P).

Raj. Mss. Structure R	*ĀG* Structure P
0 *ṭeka*	0b *rahāu*
1	2
2	0a
--	(3 added in *ĀG*)
3	4

The *padas* of the Bhagats like Kabīr etc. are in the *ĀG* given in a different line-order when compared with the 'original' version found in the *Bījak* and the Rajasthani manuscripts. We may accept that 1) the earliest structure of the *padas*—as composed by Kabīr—is Structure R found in the Rajasthani versions and in the *Bījak*, 2) for reasons of their own the Punjabi (post?-)Nānak singers quoting and spreading Kabīr's *padas* in Punjab changed that structure into Structure P. Thus they adjusted the *pada*-structure of the Bhagat compositions to the structure commonly found in the

7. See note 4.

8. Callewaert, *The Millenium Kabīr Vāṇī*, New Delhi: Manohar, 2000, pp. 8ff.

ĀG for the Sikh compositions. The reasons for this kind of structure are explained by Sikh scholars.

As can be seen in the 26 compositions quoted below, the *rahāu* lines in the '*nānak padas*' are often given in different places (see e.g. *pada* 9). As my research was started taking the Rajasthani manuscripts as basic text, I give the lines in the order found in those manuscripts.

This, then, is the tricky question. When we examine the structure of the '*nānak padas*' found in the Rajasthani manuscripts, we note that without one exception, the P Structure of the compositions is changed into the R Structure. By whom and why? Exactly the reverse process that was applied to Kabīr's compositions entering Punjab. Did the travelling singers going south to Rajasthan change the structure? Or did the Dādūpanthī scribes separately compiling the *Sarvāṅgī*s and *Pañc-vāṇīs* (in the plural, i.e. not following one single archetype!)? If we accept that the '*nānak padas*' (of Gurū Nānak or Gurū Arjan) were originally composed and sung in the P Structure, *why* was that order changed in Rajasthan?

Why, by whom and at what time? The compositions of the first five gurus of the Sikh tradition and of the north-Indian Bhagats were brought together in one huge volume in 1604. That immense effort by Gurū Arjan was most probably based on already existing manuscript collections predating 1604. Did the compositions quoted below find a basis in the pre-1604 texts, or are they based on what Gurū Arjan compiled? If we accept that the *Pañc-vāṇī*s—the earliest manuscript used here is dated 1614—are not copies of one single archetype, but were produced independently by different *Pañc-vāṇī* compilers in the Dādūpanth, it is not unlikely that the first so-called '*nānak* compositions' entered Punjab before Gurū Arjan commissioned the compilation of the *ĀG*.

There is no doubt that the versions quoted below are *not* going back to one single archetype, in Rajasthan or Punjab. If one singer or singers' family would have brought this collection to Rajasthan during their evening singing sessions under a tree in Rajasthani villages, we might be able to construct a kind of stemma. There is no sensible stemma, not of the variant readings and not of the *rāga*s. Let me give only one illustration: *pada* 1 (see above for the abbreviations), in which there are as many examples of all Rajasthani manuscripts uniformly having a reading that is variant from the *ĀG* (marked below in grey) as there are lines where one or more Rajasthani manuscripts give the *ĀG* reading which is different from the remaining Rajasthani manuscripts.

A<>*ĀG* /al.
ĀG <>al.
ĀG <>al.
EF<>al.
D<>al.
ĀG <>al.
ĀG <>al.
ĀG /*D*<>al.
ĀG <>al.
F<>al.
ĀG <>al.
ĀG/*F* <>al.
A <>al.
ĀG/*C* <>al.
ĀG/*F* <>al.
E <>al.
F <>al.
ĀG <>al.
AC <>al.
ĀG /*F*<>al.

There is no consistency whatever in the variant readings. *ĀG* <>al. is a pattern one would expect, but how do we explain *ĀG*/*C* <>al. and *ĀG*/*F*<>al., or *EF*<>al. And *D*<>al.? This lack of consistency is seen throughout, suggesting a very nebulous interaction in the singing period. I presume that most variants were not introduced during the scribal transmission.

Like the compilers of the Dādūpanthī *Pañc-vāṇīs*, the Sikh singers and scribes hired by Gurū Arjan meticulously classified their material according to the *rāga.*[9] As I have no access to the earliest manuscripts of the *ĀG*, I have for the time being to accept that the *rāga* to which a particular composition was to be sung, is the *rāga* found in the current editions of the *ĀG.* Interestingly, that possibly standardized *rāga* for each composition of Gurū Nānak or Gurū Arjan found in the selection below, is not uniformly found in the repertoires of the Rajasthani manuscripts, as can be seen from the list below.

Most *padas* in the Rajasthani manuscripts are classified under a *rāga* that is different from the *rāga* in the *ĀG.* I have marked in grey the *padas* that have the same *rāga* in both the *ĀG* and the Rajasthani manuscripts. Of the *padas* assigned to *mahalā* 1 (Gurū Nānak), only two have the same *rāga*

9. See Callewaert (ed.), *Śrī Gurū Granth Sāhib*, with complete Index, 2 vols., Delhi: Motilal Banarsidass, 1996, pp. 15-24, 161-98.

in both regions: this may mean that in the case of the Nānak compositions, the singing and transmission tradition may be said to be most corrupted.

1: *ĀG mārū, A, C, D, F mārū <> E bhairū.*
2: *ĀG āsā <> A gauḍī <> B <> E āsāvarī <> C bilāval.*
3: *ĀG sirī <> C, F, G āsāvarī.*
4: *ĀG āsā <> A, D, E, F bilāval <> G āsāvarī.*
5: *ĀG dhanāsarī; B, C dhanāsarī.*
6: (*mahalā* 5, or Gurū Arjan) *ĀG dhanāsarī; G dhanāsarī.*
8: (*mahalā* 5, or Gurū Arjan) *ĀG āsā <> C, F janglī gauḍī.*
9: (*mahalā* 5, or Gurū Arjan) *ĀG jaitsarī <> E, F, G dhanāśrī.*
10: *ĀG tilaṅg <> F vasanta.*
11: *ĀG sirīrāg <> A jaṅgal; <>C bilāval <> D, E, F, G jaṅglī gauḍī.*
12: (*mahalā* 5, or Gurū Arjan) *ĀG ṭoḍī <> C dhanāśrī.*
13: (*mahalā* 5, or Gurū Arjan) *ĀG ṭoḍī <> C, E, F dhanāśrī.*
14: (*mahalā* 5, or Gurū Arjan) *ĀG bhairū; C bhairū.*
15: *ĀG sirī; A jaṅgal, C jaṅgalī, F jaṅglī gauḍī.*
16: *Pada* 16 is not found in the *ĀG; A jaṅgal, C jaṅgalī, F jaṅglī gauḍī.*
17: *Pada* 17 is not found in the *ĀG; A jaṅgal, C jaṅgalī, F jaṅglī gauḍī.*
18: *ĀG sirī <> A jaṅgal, C jaṅglī gauḍī.*
19: (*mahalā* 5, or Gurū Arjan) *ĀG bilāval; C bilāval.*
20: *ĀG āsā <> C jaṅglī gauḍī.*
22: (*mahalā* 5, or Gurū Arjan) *ĀG āsā; C āsāvarī.*
23: (*mahalā* 5, or Gurū Arjan) *ĀG bilāvalū; C bilāvarī.*
24: (*mahalā* 5, or Gurū Arjan) *ĀG āsā <> C rāmgirī.*
25: (*mahalā* 5, or Gurū Arjan) *ĀG āsā <> C jaṅglī gauḍī.*

Most *padas* in the Rajasthani manuscripts are classified under a *rāga* that is different from the *rāga* in the *ĀG*. I have marked those that have the same *rāga* in both the *ĀG* and the Rajasthani manuscripts. Of the *padas* assigned to *mahalā* 1 (Gurū Nānak), only two have the same *rāga* in both regions: this may mean that in the case of the Nānak compositions, the singing and transmission tradition may be said to be most corrupted.

	ĀG p.		A 1614	B (1620)	C (1627)	D 1636	E 1658	F 1675	G 1676
1	Nā 1035	अरबद नरबद धूंधूंकार	*		*	*	*	*	
2	Nā 360	मन मतिवाला रांम रस	*		*	*	*	*	*
3	Nā 14	हरि बिन जीव जलि		*	*		*	*	*
4	Nā 359-60	जुगतां जीव जुगे जुगि	*			*	*	*	*
5	Nā 13	कैसी आरती करां निरंजनां		*	*		*	*	*
6	Ar 679	गुर के बचन बसैं जीव नाले							*
7	Ar 978	जंन कौं भई तुंम्हारी धीर							*
8	Ar 384	चूका निहोरा सषी सहेली			*			*	
9	Ar 700	लोडीदां सजन मेरा वे					*	*	*
10	Nā 722	मैं कुरवांणीं जांउं मिहरवाना						*	
11	Nā 24	तु मति जांणैं गल्ही	*		*	*	*	*	*
12	Ar 711	हरि बिसरत सदा षुवारी रे			*		*	*	*
13	Ar 713	मांगूं दांन ठाकुर नांउं			*		*	*	*
14	Ar 1145	साध सेती करै बाद			*		*		
15	Nā 74-75	पहलै पहरै रैंणि दै बणजारिया	*	*	*	*	*	*	*
16 ?		मुझ कूं डर है रे उस	*		*	*	*	*	*
17 ?		हक मरणां गोवलि चरणां	*		*	*	*	*	*

ĀG	p.		A 1614	B (1620)	C (1627)	D 1636	E 1658	F 1675	G 1676
18	Nā 23	अब दिन थोरङे थके	*		*	*	*	*	*
19	Ar 824	धीरौं देषि तुम्हारे रंगा			*				
20	Nā 359	दयाल इहि बिधि कांमणि मोही			*				
21	Ar[10] 455	जा कूं षोजै असंष			*				
22	Ar 384	बाहरि सुत्र सकल सूं मौला			*				
23	Ar 808	सुनि मेरी मनसा मनहीं मांहि			*				
24	Ar 461	द्यौस रैंनि कमाइङा			*				
25	Ar 384	चूका निहोरा सषी सहेली			*			*	
26 ?	---	मन रे हरि भजि रांम संवेरे							*

10. Verses '21' are *chant* 1.3-4.6 on pp. 455-6 in the *ĀG*, attributed to *mahalā* 5, Gurū Arjan with the *bhaṇitā* '*nānak*' at the end of each *chant*.

— Ten of these *padas* (marked with न) are attributed to *mahalā* 1 or Nānak in the *ĀG*.
— Thirteen *padas* (all attributed to Nānak in the Rajasthani manuscripts) are in the *ĀG* attributed to *mahalā* 5 or the fifth Gurū, Arjan, the compiler. I have marked them with *Ar*.
— *Pada* 26 is in B.P. Śarmā, *Gurū nānak vāṇī*, p. 32, reprinted with some variants (adapting the reading to modern Hindī!) from the same manuscript of 1676 A.D. in the Dādū Mahāvidyālaya, Jaipur that I copied. In a note the author states that 'this *pada* is also found in the *Ravidās vāṇī*, with the name Raidās,' but so far I have not been able to locate the *pada*.

The Devnagari text of the *ĀG* is taken from Callewaert, *Śrī Gurū Granth Sāhib*, 1996, vol. I. The English translation is based on the 2004 Gurbani-CD (www.gurbanifiles.org).

Pada 1[11]

For endless aeons, there was only utter darkness.
There was no earth or sky; there was only the infinite Hukam.

न 15 1a अरबद नरबद धुंधूकारा ॥ धरणि न गगना हुकमु अपारा ॥
A 1 अरबद नरबद धुंधूकार ॥ धरंणि न गगन न अंगेस अपार ॥*A*<>*ĀG*/al.
C 1 अरबद नरबद धूंधूंकार ॥ धरणि न गगन न हुकम अपार ।
D 0 अरबद त्रबद धूंधूकार । धरणि गूगन न हुकम अपार ।
E 0 अरबद नरबद धुंधुंकार । धूंरणि न गगन न हुकम अपार ।
F 1 अर्वद नर्वद धूंधूंकार । धरणि न गगन न हुकंम पसार ।

There was no day or night, moon or sun; God sat in profound Samadhi. || 1 ||

न 15 1b ना दिनु रैनि न चंदु न सूरजु सुंन समाधि लगाइदा ॥ *ĀG* <>al.
A 1 ना तदि रैंणी चंदन सूर ॥ सुंनि समाधि लगांईदा ॥
C 1 ना तदि रैंणीं चंद न सूरिज । सुनि समाधि लगांईंदा ॥
D 0 ना तदि रैंणि न चंद न सूरज संन समाधि लगांईदा ॥
E 0 नां तदि रैंणीं चंद सूरिज । सुंनि संमाधि लगांईदा ॥
F 1 नां तदि रैंणीं चंद न सूर । शुंनि समाधि लगांइंदा ॥

---

11. The marking in grey on the following pages is intended to draw the attention to particular variants or clusters of variants. *ĀG*, pp. 1035-6, न15 *mārū*; *A, C, D, E, F mārū*; *E bhairū.*

There were no sources of creation or powers of speech, no air or water.
There was no creation or destruction, no coming or going.

न 15 2a खाणी न बाणी पउण न पाणी ॥ ओपति खपति न आवण जाणी ॥ *ĀG* <>al.

A 2 षांणी न बांणी पवन न पांणी ॥ उतपति षपति नहीं आंवण जांणीं ॥

C 2 षांनीं न बांनीं । पवन न पांनीं । उतपति षपति नहीं आंवन जांनीं ।

D 1 षांणी न बांणी पवन न पांणी । उतपति षपति नहीं आंवंण जांणीं ।

E 2 षांनीं न बांनीं पवन न पांनीं । उषति षपति नही आंवंण जांणीं । *EF*<>al.

F 2 षांनीं न वांनीं पवन न पांनीं । उपति षपति नहि आंवन जांनीं ।

There were no continents, nether regions, seven seas,
rivers or flowing water. ॥ 2 ॥

न 15 2b खंड पताल सपत नही सागर नदी न नीरु वहाइदा ॥

A 2 षंड पताल सप्तनहीं सागर ॥ नदी न नीर बहांईदा ॥

C 2 षड पताल सपत नहीं सागर । नदी न नीर बहांईदा ॥

D 1 षंड पताल सपत नहीं सागर । नदिषां न नीर बहांईदा ॥

E 2 षंड पताल सप्त नहीं सागर । नदीयां न नीर बहांइंदा ॥

F 2 षंड पताल सपत नहीं सागर । नदियं न नीर वहाईंदा ॥

There were no heavenly realms, earth or nether regions of the underworld.
There was no heaven or hell, no death or time.

न 15 3a ना तदि सुरगु मछु पइआला ॥ दोजकु भिसतु नही खै काला ॥

A 3 ना तदि श्रग न मंछ पयाला ॥ दोजक भिस्ति नहीं ष्यौ काला ॥

C 3 नां तदि श्रग न मंछ पयाला । दोजग भिस्त नहीं ष्यौ काला ।

D 2 ना तदि सरग नरक पताला । दोसग भिस्ति नहीं ष्यौ काला । *D*<>al.

E 3 नां तदि सुरगु न मंछ पयाला । दोजगि भिस्ति नहीं ष्यै काला ।

F 3 नां तदि सरग न मंछ पयालां । दोजग भिस्ति नहीं ष्यौ कालां ।

There was no hell or heaven, no birth or death, no coming or going. ॥ 3 ॥

न 15 3b नरकु सुरगु नही जंमणु मरणा ना को आइ न जाइदा ॥

A 3 नरग सरग नहीं जां मन मंरणां ॥ ना को आइ न जांईदा ॥

C 3 नरक सरग नहीं जांमण मरणां । नां को आइ न जाईदा ॥

D 2 नरक सरग नहीं जांमण मरणां । ना को आई न जाईदा ॥

E 3 नरग सरग नहीं जांमण मरंणां । नां कों आइ न जाइदा ॥

F 3 नरक न सरक नहि जांमण मरणां । नां को आइ न जाइ ॥

There was no Brahma, Vishnu or Shiva. No one was seen, but the one Lord.

न 15 4a ब्रहमा बिसनु महेसु न कोई ॥ अवरु न दीसै एको सोई ॥
A 4 ब्रह्मा बिश्न्र महेस न कोई ॥ और न दीसै ऐकै सोई ॥
C 4 ब्रह्मा बिश्न महेस न कोई । और न दीसै एकौ सोई ।
D 3 ब्रह्मां बिस्न सहेस न कोई । और न दीसै येकै सोई ।
E 4 ब्रह्म बिश्र महेस न कोई । और न दीसै एकौ सोई ।
F 4 व्रंह्मा विश्र महेस न कोई । और न दीसै ऐकै सोई ।

There was no female or male, no social class or caste of birth;
no one experienced pain or pleasure. || 4 ||

न 15 4b नारि पुरखु नही जाति न जनमा ना को दुखु सुखु पाइदा ॥ *ĀG* <>al.
A 4 नारी पुरिष नंही कुल जनमां ॥ नां सुष दुष को पांईदा ॥
C 4 नारी पुरिष नहीं कुल जनमां । नां सुष दुष को पाईंदा ॥
D 3 नारी पुरिष नहीं कुल जनमां । नां सुष दुष को पांईदा ॥
E 4 नारी पुरिस नहीं कुल जंनमा । नां सुष दुष को पाइंदा ॥
F 4 नारी पुरिस नहीं कुल जन्मं । नां शुष दुष को पांइंदा ॥

There were no people of celibacy or charity; no one lived in the forests.
There were no Siddhas or seekers, no one living in peace.

न 15 5a ना तदि जती सती बनवासी ॥ ना तदि सिध साधिक सुखवासी ॥ *ĀG* <>al.
A 5 नां तदि जती तपी सन्यासी ॥ नां तदि सिध साधिक बनवासी ॥
C 5 नां तदि जती तपी सिन्यासी । नां तदि सिध साधिक बनबासी ।
D 4 ना तदि जती सती स्यान्यासी । ना तदि सिध साधिक बंनबासी ।
E - - *E* <>al.
F 5 नां तदि जती तपी स्यंनासी । नां तदि सिध साधिक वनवासी ।

There were no Yogis, no wandering pilgrims, no religious robes;
no one called himself the master. || 5 ||

न 15 5b जोगी जंगम भेखु न कोई ना को नाथु कहाइदा ॥
A 5 जोगी जंगम सेषू कोई ॥ नो को नाथ कहांईदा ॥ 5 ॥
C 5 जोगी जंगम सेष न कोई । नां को नाथ कहांईदा ॥
D 4 जोगी जंगंम सेष न कोई । ना को न्यथ कहांईदा ॥
E - -. *E* <>al.
F 5 जोगी जंगम सेष न कोई । नां को नाथ कहांइंदा ॥

There was no chanting or meditation, no self-discipline, fasting or worship.
No one spoke or talked in duality.

न 15 6a जप तप संजम ना ब्रत पूजा ॥ ना को आखि वखाणै दूजा ॥
A 6 जप तप संजम ना व्रत पूजा ॥ ना को आषि बषाणै दूजा ॥
C 6 जप तप संजम नां ब्रत पूजा । नां को आषि बषांणैं दूजा ।
D 5 जप तप संजम ना ब्रत पूजा । ना को आषि बषणैं दूजा ।
E 5 जप तप संजम नां ब्रत पूजा । नां को आंषि बषांणैं दूजा ।
F 6 जप तप संजम नां व्रत पूजा । नां को अषि वषांणैं दूजा ।

He created Himself, and rejoiced; He evaluates(!) Himself. ॥ 6 ॥

न 15 6b आपे आपि उपाइ विगसै आपे कीमति पाइदा ॥
A 6 आपै आप उपाइ बिगासी ॥ आपै कीमति पाईंदा ॥
C 6 आपैं आप उपाइ बिगासी । आपैं कीमति पांईदा ॥
D 5 आपै आप उपाई बिगाती । आपै की+ता पांईदा ॥
E 5 आपै आप उपाइ बिगासे । आपै कीमति पाइंदा ॥
F 6 आपै आप उपाइ विणासै । आपै कीमति पाइंदा ॥

There was no purification, no self-restraint, no malas of basil seeds.
There were no Gopis, no Krishna, no cows or cowherds.

न 15 7a ना सुचि संजमु तुलसी माला ॥ गोपी कानु न गऊ गुोआला ॥
A 7 नां सुचि संजम तुलसी माला ॥ गोपी कान्ह न गउ गुवाला ॥
C 7 नां सचु संजम तुलछी माला । गोपी कांन्ह न गऊ गोवाला ।
D 6 ना सुचि संजम तुलसी माला । गो+ कांन्ह न गऊ गुवाला ।
E 6 ना सुचु संजम तुलछी माला । गोपी कांन्ह न गउ गोवाला ।
F 7 ना सत संजम तुलसी माला । नां गोपी कांन्ह नहीं गोवाला ।

There were no tantras, no mantras, no hypocrisy; no one played the flute. ॥ 7 ॥

न 15 7b तंतु मंतु पाखंडु न कोई ना को वंसु वजाइदा ॥
A 7 तंत मंत पांषंड न कोई ॥ नां को बस बजांईदा ॥
C 7 तंत मंत पाषंड न कोई । नां को बंस बजांईंदा ॥
D 6 तंत मंत पांषंड न कोई । ना को बस बजाईदा ॥
E 6 तंत मंतं पाषंड न कोई । नां को बंस बजाइदा ॥
F 7 तंत मंत पाषंड न कोई । नां को वंस वजांइंदा ॥

There was no karma, no Dharma, no buzzing fly of Maya.
Social class and birth were not seen with any eyes.

न 15 8a करम धरम नही माइआ माखी ॥ जाति जनमु नही दीसै आखी ॥
ĀG/D<>al.
A 8 क्रंम ध्रंम ना माया मांषी जाति न जन्म न दीसै आंषी ॥
C 8 कर्म धर्म न माया मांषी । जाति न जनम दीसै आंषी ।
D 7 करंम धरम नही माया माषी । जाति न जन्म न दीसै आंषी ।
E 7 करम न धरम न माया माषी । जाति न जंनम नहीं दीसै आषी ।
F 8 करम न धरम न माया मांषी । जाति न जन्म नहीं दस आंषी ।

There was no noose of attachment, no death inscribed upon the forehead;
no one meditated on anything. ‖ 8 ‖

न 15 8b ममता जालु कालु नही माथै ना को किसै धिआइदा ॥
A 8 ममिता जाल काल नहीं माथै ॥ नां को किसहीं ध्यांइदा ॥
C 8 ममिता जाल काल नहीं माथै । नां को किसहीं ध्याईंदा ॥
D 7 ममिता जाल काल नहीं मांथैं । ना को किसहीं ध्याईदा ॥
E 7 ममिता जाल काल नहीं माथै । नां को किसहीं ध्याइदा ॥
F 8 ममिता जाल काल नहि माथैं । नां को किसहीं धांइंदा ॥

There was no slander, no seed, no soul and no life.
There was no Gorakh and no Machindra.

न 15 9a निंदु बिंदु नही जीउ न जिंदो ॥ ना तदि गोरखु ना माछिंदो ॥ *ĀG* <>al.
A 9 नाद न ब्यंद नहीं जीव ज्यंदु इ गोर्ष नां माछांडु ॥
C 9 नाद न बिंद नहीं जीव जिंदू । इंदू गोरष नां मांछिदू ।
D 8 नाद न ब्यंद नहीं जीय ज्यंदू । ईं गोरष ना मांछ्यंदू ।
E 8 नाद न ब्यंद नहीं जिय जिदू । इडू गोरष ना मछिंडू ।
F 9 नां तदि व्यंद नहीं जीय ज्यंदू । इंदू गोरष ना माछिंडू । *F*<>al.

There was no spiritual wisdom or meditation,
no ancestry or creation, no reckoning of accounts. ‖ 9 ‖

न 15 9 ना तदि गिआनु धिआनु कुल ओपति ना को गणत गणाइदा ॥ *ĀG* <>al.
A 9b नां तदि ग्यांन ध्यांन ष्यौ काला ॥ नां गिणंति गिणंति गिणंईदा ॥
C 9 नां तदि ग्यांन ध्यांन ष्यौ काला । नां को गिणिति गिणांईंदा ॥
D 8 ना तदि ग्यांन ध्यांन ष्यो काला । ना को गिंणिति गिणांइंदा ॥
E 8 नां तदि ग्यांन ध्यांन ष्यौ काला । नां को गिणति गिणांइदा ॥
F 9 नां तदि ग्यांन ध्यांन ष्यौ काल । नां को गिणति गिणांइंदा ॥

There were social classes, no religious robes, no Brahmin or Kshatriya.
There were no demi-gods or temples, no cows or Gayatri prayer.

न 15 10a वरन भेख नही ब्रहमण खत्री ॥ देउ न देहुरा गऊ गाइत्री ॥

A 10 बरंण भेष नहीं ब्राह्मण षत्री ॥ देव न देहुरा गउ न गायत्री ॥

C 10 बरण भेष नहीं ब्राह्मण षत्री । देव न देहुरा गऊ न गावत्री ।

D 9 बरंण भेष नहीं ब्राह्मण षत्री । देव न देहुरा गउ न गावत्री ।

E 9 बरण भेष नहीं ब्राह्मण षत्री । देव न देहुरा गउ न गावत्री

F 10 वर्ण भेष नहि व्रांह्मण षत्री । देव न देहुरा गऊ न गावत्री ।

There were no burnt offerings, no cleansing rituals at shrines of pilgrimage;
no one worshipped in adoration. ॥ 10 ॥

न 15 10b हो म जग नही तीरथि नावणु ना को पूजा लाइदा ॥

A 10 होम जग्य नही तीरथ न्हांवण नां को पूजा लाईदा ॥

C 10 होम जग्य नहीं तीर्थ न्हांवण । नां को पूजा लाईंदा ॥

D 9 होम जज नहीं तीरथ न्हांणां । नां को पूजा लाईदा ॥

E 9 होम जगि नही तीरथ न्हांवण । नां को पूजा लाइदा ॥

F 10 होम न जग्य नहीं तीरथ न्हांवण । नां को पूजा लाइंदा ॥

There was no Mullah, no Qazi; there was no Shaykh, or pilgrims to Mecca.

न 15 11a ना को मुला ना को काजी ॥ ना को सेखु मसाइकु हाजी ॥

A 11 नां को मूलां नां को काजी ॥ नो को सेष मसाइक हाजी ॥

C 11 नां को मुलां नां को काजी । नां को सेष मसाइक हाजी ।

D 10 ना को मुलां ना को काजी । ना को सेष नसाइक हाजी ।

E 10 नां को मुलां नां को काजी । नां को सेष मसाइक हांजी

F 11 नां को मुलां नां को काजी । नां को सेष मसाइक हाजी ।

No king or subjects, no worldly egotism; no one spoke of himself. ॥ 11 ।

न 15 11b रईअति राउ न *हउमै* दुनीआ ना को कहणु कहाइदा ॥ *ĀG/F* <>al.

A 11 रइति राव न हुकमैं दुनियां ॥ नां को षांन कहांईदा ॥ *A* <>al.

C 11 रईत न राव न *हूंमैं* दुनियां । नां को षांन कहांईंदा ॥

D 10 रईत्य राव न होती दुनिया । नां को षांन कहांईंदा ।

E 10 रईत्य राव न होमैं दुनियां । नां को षांन कहांइदा ॥

F 11 रयत्य राव न होते दुनियां । नां को कहन कहांइंदा ॥ *ĀG/C* <>al.

There was no love or devotion, no Shiva or Shakti—no energy or matter.
There were no friends or companions, no semen or blood.

न 15 12a भाउ न भगती ना सिव सकती ॥ साजनु मीतु बिंदु नही रकती ॥
A 12 भाव न भगती नां सिव सक्ती ॥ सांजन मींत बिंद नहीं रक्ती ॥
C 12 भाव न भगती नां सिव सकती । साजन मींत ब्यंद नहीं रकती ।
D 11 भाव न भगति नहीं सिव सक्ती साजन मींत ब्यंद नहीं रक्ती ।
E 11 भाव न भगत नां सिव सकती । साजन मीत ब्यंद नहीं रक्ती ।
F 12 भाव न भक्ती नां सो सक्ती । साजन मींत व्यंद नही रक्ती ।

He Himself is the banker, and He Himself is the merchant.
Such is the Pleasure of the Will of the True Lord. ॥ 12 ॥

न 15 12b आपे साहु आपे वणजारा साचे एहो भाइदा ॥
A 12 आपैं साह आप बणिजारा ॥ साचे ईवैं भाईदा ॥
C 12 आपैं साह आपैं बणिजारा । साचै ईंवैं भांईंदा ॥
D 11 आपै साह आपै बंणिजारा । साचे ईवै भांईंदा ॥
E 11 आपैं साह आपैं बंणिजारा । साचे वैं भाइदा ॥
F 12 आपैं साह आपैं वनिजारा । साचे इमैं भाइंदा ॥

There were no Vedas, Korans or Bibles, no Smritis or Sastras.
There was no recitation of the Puranas, no sunrise or sunset.

न 15 13a बेद कतेब न सिंम्रिति सासत ॥ पाठ पुराण उदै नही आसत ॥*ĀG/F* <>al.
A 13 बेद कतेब न सुम्रिति पुरांणां ॥ उदै न असू नहीं आंवण जांणां ॥
C 13 बेद कतेब न सुमृत पुरांनां । उदै न अस्त नहीं आंव न जांनां ।
D 12 बेद कतेब न सुम्रित पुरांणां । उदै अस्त नहीं आवंण जांणां ।
E 12 बेद कतेब – सुम्रित पुरांनां । उदै नहीं अस्त न आवण जांणां ।
F 13 वेद कतेव न शुम्रिति पुरांनां । उदै न अस्त नहीं को जांनां ।

The unfathomable Lord Himself was the speaker and the preacher;
the unseen Lord Himself saw everything. ॥ 13 ॥

न 15 13b कहता बकता आपि अगोचरु आपे अलखु लखाइदा ॥ *ĀG* <>al.; *F* <>al.
A 13 कहता श्रुरत आप अगोचर ॥ आपै अलष लषांईदा ॥
C 13 कहता सुरता आप अगोचर । आपैं अलष लषाईदा ॥
D 12 कहता सुरता आप अगोचर । आपै अलष लषांईंदा ॥
E 12 कहता सकता आप आगोचर । आपैं अलष लषाइदा ॥ *E* <>al.
F 13 शुरता वक्ता आप अगोचर । आपै अलष लषांइंदा *F* <>al.

When He so willed, He created the world.

Without any supporting power, He sustained the universe.

न 15 14a जा तिसु भाणा ता जगतु उपाइआ ॥ बाझु कला आडाणु रहाइआ ॥

ĀG/F

<>al.

A जां तिस भाया जगत उपाया ॥ बाज कलां आंडांण रहाया ॥

C 14 जा तिस भाया जगत उपाया । बाझ कला आडांण रहाया ।

D 13 जा तिस भांयां जगत उपायां । बाझ कला आडंब रछाया ।

E 13 जा तिसु भाया जगत उपाया । बाज कला अडांण रहायां ।

F 14 जा तिशु भण ता जगत उपाया । वाज कलांयां अव निरहायां ।

He created Brahma, Vishnu and Shiva; He fostered attachment to Maya ॥ 14 ॥

न 15 14b ब्रहमा बिसनु महेसु उपाए माइआ मोहु वधाइदा ॥

A 14 व्रह्मा बिश्न्न महेस उपाया ॥ माया मोह बंधांईदा ॥

C 14 ब्रह्मा बिश्न महेस उपाया । माया मोह बंधांईंदा ॥

D 13 ब्रह्मा बिस्न महेस उपाया । माया मोह बधाईदा ॥

E 13 ब्रह्मां बिश्र महेस उपाया । माया मोह बधाइदा ॥

F 14 व्रंह्मा विश्न महेस उपाया । माया मोह वधांइंदा ॥

How rare is that person who listens to the Word of the Guru's Sabad.

He created the creation, and watches over it; His Hukam is over all.

न 15 15a विरले कउ गुरि सबदु सुणाइआ ॥ करि करि देखै हुकमु सबाइआ ॥

ĀG <>al.

A 15 बिरले कूं गुरि सबद सुणांयां ॥ करि करि चषें हुकम सवाया ॥

C 14 बिरले कूं गुर सबद सुणाया । करि करि चषे हुकम सवाया ।

D 14 बिरले कौं गुर सबद सुणांयां । करि करि चंषे हुकम सवाया ।

E 14 बिरले कूं गुरि सबद सुणाया । करि करि चिष हुंकम सवाया ।

F 15 विरले कूं गुरि सवद शुनाया । करि करि चिषे हुकंम सवाया ।

He formed the planets, solar systems and nether regions,

and brought what was hidden to manifestation. ॥ 15 ॥

न 15 15b खंड ब्रहमंड पाताल अरंभे गुपतहु परगटी आइदा ॥

A 15 षंड ब्रह्मंड पताल आरंभे ॥ गुपता प्रगट आईंदा ॥

C 15 षंड ब्रह्मंड पाताल आरंभे । गुपता प्रगट रहांईंदा ॥

D 14 षंड ब्रह्मडु पताल आरभे । गुपता प्रगट रहांइंदा ॥

E 14 षंड ब्रह्मड पाताल अरंभ । गुपता प्रगट रहांइदा ॥

F 15 षंड व्रह्मंड पताल आरंभें । गुप्ता प्रगट आइंदा ॥

No one knows His limits. This understanding comes from the perfect Gurū.

न 15 16a ता का अंतु न जाणै कोई ॥ पूरे गुर ते सोझी होई ॥

A 16 ता का अंनत पावै कोई ॥ पूरे गुर थै सोधी होई ॥ *AC* <>al.

C 16 ता का अंत न पावैं कोई । पूरे गुर थैं सोधी होई ।

D 16 ता का अंत न जांणैं कोई । पूरे गुर थैं सोधी होई ।

E 16 ता का अंत न जांनैं कोई । पूरे गुर तैं सोधी होई ।

F 16 ता का अंत न जांनैं कोई । विरले गुर तैं सोधी होई ।

O Nanak, those who are attuned to the truth are wonderstruck;
singing His glorious praises, they are filled with wonder. ॥ 16 ॥ 3 ॥ 15 ॥

न 15 16b नानक साचि रते बिसमादी बिसम भए गुण गाइदा ॥ *ĀG/F*<>al.

A 16 नांनिक दास रता विसमाधी ॥ बिसम भया गुण गांईदा ॥ 16 ॥ 1 ॥

C 16 नांनिक दास रता बिसमाधी । बिसम भया गुण गांईंदा ॥

D 15 नानिक दास रत बिसमाधी । बिसं भया गुण गायंदा ॥ dictation?

E 15 नानिका दास रता बिसमाधी । बिसम भयौ गुंण गांईदा ॥

F 16 नांनिक साचि रता विसमाधी । विसम भये गुर सांइंदा ॥

Pada 2[12]

O Baba, the mind is intoxicated with the Name, drinking in its nectar.
It remains absorbed in the Lord's love.

न 38 1c बाबा मनु मतवारो नाम रसु पीवै सहज रंग रचि रहिआ ॥

ĀG/DF<>al.; *ĀG*<>al.; *ĀG/G*<>al.

A 0 ---- मन मतिवाला रांम रस पीवै ॥ सहज रंग रंमि रहिया ॥

C 0 ---- मन मतिवाला रांम रस पीवै । सहज रंग रंमि रहिया ।

D 0 बाबा मन मतिवाला रांम रस पीवै । सहज रंग रंमि रहिया ।

E 0 ---- मंन मतिवाला रांम रस पीवै । सहज रंग रंमि रहिया ।

F 0 वावा मन मतिवाला रांम रस पीवै । सहज रंग रमि रहिया ।

G 0 ---- मन मतिवाला रांम रस पीवै । सहजि रंगि रचि रहिया ।

Night and day, remaining attached to the Love of the Lord,
the celestial music of the Sabad resounds. ॥ 1 ॥ Pause ॥

न 38 1d अहिनिसि बनी प्रेम लिव लागी सबदु अनाहद गहिआ ॥ रहाउ ॥

A अहनिसि बनी प्रेम ल्यौ लागी ॥ सबद अनाहद गहिया ॥ टेक ॥

C 0 अहनिसि बनी प्रेम ल्यौ लागी । सबद अनाहद गहिया ॥

D 0 अहनिसि बनी प्रेम ल्यौ लागी । सबद अनाहद गहिया ॥

12. *ĀG*, p. 360, न 38 *āsā*; *A gauḍī*; *B, E āsāvarī*; *C bilāval.*

E 0 अहनिसि बंनी प्रेम लिव लागी । सबद अंनाहद गहिया ॥

F 0 अहनिस वनीं प्रेम ल्यौ लागी । सवद अनाहद गहिया ॥

G 0 अनिसि बंनीं प्रेम ल्यौ लागी । सबद अनाहद गहिया ॥

Make spiritual wisdom your molasses, and meditation your scented flowers; let good deeds be the herbs.

न 38 1a गुड़ु करि गिआनु धिआनु करि धावै ॥ करि करणी कसु पाईअै ॥

A गुड़ करि ग्यांन ध्यांन करि ध्यावै करु करणी कस पाइये ॥

C 1 गुङ करि ग्यांन ध्यांन करि ध्यावै । करि करणीं कसु पाइये ।

D 1 गुङ करि ग्यांन ध्यांन करि पावै । करू करांणी कस पाईऐ ।*D* <>al.

E 1 गुङ करि ग्यांन ध्यांन करि धावै । करु करनीं कस पईए ।

F 1 गुङ करि ग्यांन ध्यांन करि ध्यावै । करु करणीं कसु पाइये ।

G 1 गुङ करि ग्यांन ध्यांन करि धावै । करु करणीं कस पाइये ।

Let devotional faith be the distilling fire, and your love the ceramic cup. Thus the sweet nectar of life is distilled. ॥ 1 ॥

न 38 1b भाठी भवनु प्रेम का पोचा इतु रसि अमिउ चुआईअै ॥

ĀG/E<>al.; *ĀG*<>al.

A भाठी भुवन प्रेम का पोता ॥ इत बिधि अंमी चुवाइये ॥

C 1 भाठी भाव प्रेम का पोता । इत बिधि अंमीं चुवाइये ॥

D 1 भाठी भवन प्रेम का पोता । ईत बिधि अंमी चुवाईऐ ॥

E 1 भाठी भुवन प्रेम का पोचा । इस बिधि अंमी चुवाइए ॥

G 1 भाठी भुवन प्रेम का पोता । इस बिधि अंमी चुवाईये ॥

F 1 भाठी भवन प्रेम का पोता । नांहीं इंन विधि अमीं चुवाइये ॥

One who trades in this Nectar, how can he ever love the wine of the world? ॥2॥

न 38 2b अंम्रित का वापारी होवै किआ मदि छूछै भाउ धरे ॥

2a/2b inverted: *ĀG/AC*<>al.

A 2b अंम्रित का ब्यापारी होवै ॥ तौ क्या मदि छोछै भाव धरै ॥

C 2b अंमृत का ब्यौपारी होवै । तौ क्या मद छोछै भाव धरै ॥

D 2 अंम्रित का ब्यौपारी होवै । क्यूं मदि छोछै भाव धरौ ॥

E 2 अंम्रित -- ब्यापारी होवै । सु क्या मदि छोछैं भाव धरै ॥

F 2 अंम्रित का व्यौपारी होवै । सो क्यौं मद छोछै भाव धरै ॥

G 2 अंम्रित का ब्यौपारी होवै । सु क्या मद छोछै भवि धरै ॥

The perfect Lord naturally gives the cup of truth,
to the one upon whom He casts His glance of grace.

न 38 2a पूरा साचु पिआला सहजे तिसहि पीआए जा कउ नदरि करे ॥ *ĀG* <>al.; *ĀG/E*<>al.
A 2a पूरा सचु पियाला साज्या ॥ जिनि पीया ते नजरि करै ॥
C 2a पूरा आप पियाला साचा । जिसै पिलावै तिसै नजरि करै ।
D 2 पूरा सचु पियाला साज्या । जिंनिं पीया ते कदरि करै । *DF*<>al.
E 2 पूरा सचु पियाला साचा । तिसै पियावै जिस नदरि करै ।
F 2 पूरा साचु पियाला साज्या । जिनि पीया ते कदरि करै ।
G 2 पूरा सचु पिया साजै । जिंनिं पीया तिसै नजरि धरै ।

The teachings of the Gurū, the ambrosial Bani —
drinking them in, one becomes acceptable and renowned.

न 38 3a गुर की साखी अंम्रित बाणी पीवत ही परवाणु भइआ ॥ *ĀG/CE*<>al.
A गुर की साषी अंम्रित चाषी ॥ पीवंदड़ा प्रमांण -- ॥
C 3 गुर की साषी अंमृत बांणी । पीवत हीं परिवांन भया ।
D 3 गुर की साषी अंम्रत चाषी । पीवतङा परवांणि भया ।
E 3 गुर की साषी अंम्रित बांनीं । पीवतही परवान भया ।
F 3 गुर की साषी अंम्रित चाषी । पीवतङा परवांणि भया ।
G 3 गुर की साषी अंम्रित बांणी । पीवतङा परंवांनिं भया ।

Unto the one who loves the Lord's court, and His Darshan,
of what use is liberation or paradise? ॥ 3 ॥

न 38 3b दर दरसन का प्रीतमु होवै मुकति बैकुठै करै किआ ॥
A दर दरसंण का व्यापारी होवै ॥ तौ मुकति बैकुंठै कहा करै ॥ *AC*<>al.
C 3 दर दरसन का सेवग होवै । तौ मुकति बैकुंठैं करै कहा ॥
D 3 दर दरसन का प्रीत्म होवै । मुकति बैकुठहि करै कहा ॥
E 3 दर दरसंन का प्रीतंम होवै । तौ मुकति बैकुठहि करै क्या ॥
F 3 दर दरसन का प्रीत्म होवै । मुक्ति वैकुंठहि करैं कहाया ॥
G 3 दर दरसन का प्रीतम होवै । सो मुकति बैकूंठहि करै कहा ॥

Imbued with the Lord's praises, one is forever a renunciate,
and one's life is not lost in the gamble.

न 38 4a सिफती रता सद बैरागी जूऐ जनमु न हारै ॥ *ĀG/C*<>al.
A सिफती रता सहजि बैरांगी ॥ जुवै जनम न हारी ॥
C 4 सिफिती रता सद बैरागी । जूवै जनम न हारै ।
D 4 सिपती रता सहज वैरागी । जूवै जंन्म न हारी ।
E 4 सिपति रता सहजि बैरागी । जूवै जंनम न हारे ।

F 4 सिपती रता सहजि वैरागी । जूवै जनम न हारी रे ।

G 4 सिपती रता सबद बैरागी । जवा जंन्म न हारी । *G*<>al.

Says Nanak, listen, O Bharthari Yogi: drink in
the intoxicating nectar of the Lord. ॥ 4 ॥ 4 ॥ 38 ॥

न 38 4b कहु नानक सूणि भरथरि जोगी खीवा अंम्रित धारै ॥

A कहु नांनिक श्रुणि भरथरी योगी ॥ पीवै अंम्रित धारी ॥ *AD*<>al.

C 4 कहै नांनिक सुणि भरथर जोगी । षींवां अंमृत धारै ॥

D 4 कहि नानिक सुंणि भरथर जोगी । पीवा अंम्रित धारी ॥

E 4 कहु नांनिक सुंणि भरथरि जोगी । षीवां अंम्रित धारे ॥

F 4 कहि नानिक शुंणि भरथर जोगी । षीवै अंम्रित धारी ॥

G 4 कहू नांनक सुंणि भरथर जोगी । षिंवां अंम्रित धारी ॥

Pada 3[13]

Without the Lord, my soul is scorched and burnt.

न 1 1d हरि बिनु जीउ जलि बलि जाउ ॥

B 0 हरि बिन जीव जलि बलि जाव ।

C 0 हरि बिन जीव जलि बलि जाव ।

E 0 हरि बिण जीव जलि बलि जाउ ।

F 0 हरि विन जीव जलि वलि जाव ।

G 0 हरि बिंनिं जीव जलि बलि जाव ।

I consulted my Gurū, and now I see there is no other place at all. ॥ 1 ॥ Pause ॥

न 1 1e मै आपणा गुरु पूछि देखिआ अवर नाही थाउ ॥ 1 ॥ रहाउ ॥ *ĀG* <>al.

B 0 – आपणां गुर पूछि देष्या । नहीं आंन उपाव ॥

C 0 – आपणां गुर पूछि देष्या । नहीं आंन उपाव ॥

E 0 – आपणां गुर पूछि देष्या । नही आन उपाव ॥

F 0 – आपणां गुर पूछि देष्या । नहीं आंन उपाव ॥

G 0 मैं आपनां गुर पूछि देष्या । नांहीं आंन उपाव ॥ *ĀG/G*<>al.

---

13. *ĀG*, p. 14, न 1 *sirī*; *C*, *F*, *G āsāvarī*.

If I had a palace made of pearls, inlaid with jewels,

न 1 1a मोती त मंदर ऊसरहि रतनी त होहि जड़ाउ ॥
B 1 मोती त मंदिर ऊसरै । रतन हूंहि जड़ाव ।
C 2 मोती त मंदिर ऊसरैं । रतने त होइ जड़ाव ।
E 3 मोती त मंदिर ऊसरैं । रतनने त हूंहि जड़ाव ।
F 4 मोती ति मंदिर ऊसरैं । रतने त हुंहि जड़ाव ।
G 2 मोती त मंदिर उसरैं । रतने त हूंहिं जड़ाव ।

If the floor of this palace was a mosaic of diamonds and rubies,
and if my bed was encased with rubies,

न 1 2a - - धरती त हीरे लाल जड़ती पलघि लाल जड़ाउ ॥
$\bar{A}G/C$<>al. $\bar{A}G/B$<>al.
B 2 लाल धरती लाल जड़ती । पलिंग लाल जड़ाव ।
C 1 - - धरती त हीरे लाल जड़ती । लाल पलिंग जड़ाव ।
E 1 लाल धरती लाल जड़ती । लाल पिंलग जड़ाव ।
F 1 लाल धरती लाल जड़ती । लाल पलिंग जड़ाव ।
G 1 लाल धरती लाल जरती । लाल पिंलग जड़ाव ।

and if heavenly beauties, their faces adorned with emeralds,
tried to entice me with sensual gestures of love—

न 1 2b मोहणी मुखि मणी सोहै करे रंगि पसाउ ॥
B 2 मोहनीं बहु संगि बनिता । बिषै संगि पसाव ॥ B<>al.
C 1 मोहनीं मुष मनीं सोहै । रंग करै पसाव ॥
E 1 मोहंनी मुष मनीं सोहै रंग करैं पसाव ।
F 1 मोहणीं मुष मणीं सोहै । रंग करैं पसाव ॥
G 1 मोहनी मुंष मनीं सोभैं । करैं रंग पसाव ॥

scented with musk, saffron and sandalwood, a sheer delight to behold—

न 1 1b कसतूरि कुंगू अगरि चंदनि लीपि आवै चाउ ॥
inversion/omissions $\bar{A}G$<>al.;
B - - B<>al.
C 2 अगर चंदन लेपनां । मति देषि आवै चाव ॥
C 3 हाथी तघोड़े पाइगा । नौबति नीसांण घाव । C/F *add*<>al.
E 3 अगर चंदन लेपना । मंति देषि आवै चाव ॥
F 4 अगर चंदन लेपनां । मति देषि आवै चाव ॥
F 2 हाथी तघोड़ै पाइगै । नौवति निसांण वजाव ।
G 2 अगर चंदन लेपनां । मति देषि आवै चाव ॥

seeing these, I might go astray and forget You,
and Your Name would not enter into my mind. ‖ 2 ‖

न 1 1c मतु देखि भूला वीसरै तेरा चिति न आवै नाउ ॥ 1 ॥
B 1 मति देषि भुलां बीसरां । तेरा चिति न आवे नांउ ॥
C 3 मति देषि भूलूं बीसरूं । तेरा चिति न आवै नांव ॥
E 1 मति देषि भूलूं बीसरुं । तेरा चिति न आवै नांव ॥
F 2 मति देषि भूलौं वीसरूं । तेरा चिति न आवै नांव ॥
G - -

If I were to become a Siddha, and work miracles, summon wealth and
न 1 3a सिधु होवा सिधि लाई रिधि आखा आउ ॥
B 3 सिध है साधि कहोऊं । रिधि आषौं आव ।
C 4 सिध होऊं स्यंध्य लांऊं । रिधि आषूं आव ।
E 2 सिध होऊं साधि लाऊं । रिधि आंषूं आव ।
F 3 सिध होऊं साधि ल्यांऊं । रिधि आषूं आव ।
G 3 सिध होउ साधि ल्यांउं । रिधि आंषौं आव ।

become invisible and visible at will, so that people would hold me in awe—
न 1 3b गुपतु परगटु होइ बैसा लोकु राखै भाउ ॥
seeing these, I might go astray and forget You,
and Your Name would not enter into my mind. ‖ 3 ‖
न 14 3c मतु देखि भूला वीसरै तेरा चिति न आवै नाउ ॥ *ĀG*<>al.

B 3 गुप्त प्रगट होइ बैठां । लोक रषन भाव ॥
C 4 गुपत प्रगट होइ बैठू । लोक राषैं भाव ॥
E 2 गुपत प्रगट होइ बैसूं । लोक राषैं भाव ॥
F 3 गुपत प्रगट होइ वैठूं । लोग राषैं भाव ॥
G 3 गुपत परगट होइ बैसौं । लोक राषै भाव ॥

If I were to become an emperor and raise a huge army,
and sit on a throne, issuing commands and collecting taxes—
न 1 4a सुलतानु होवा मेलि लसकर तखति राखा पाउ ॥ *ĀG/B*<>al.
B 4 सुलतांन होवां मेलि लसकर । तषति रषा पाव ।
C 5 पातिसाह होऊं मेलि लसकर । तषति राषू पाव ।
E 4 पातिसाह होऊं मेल्हि लसकर । तषति राषूं पावं ।
F 5 पातिसाह होऊं मेलि लसकर । तषति राषूं पाव ।
G 4 पातिसाह हौं मेल्हि ल्हसकर । तषति राषौं पाव ।

O Nanak, all of this could pass away like a puff of wind.

न 1 4b हुकमु हासलु करी बैठा नानका सभ वाउ ॥

seeing these, I might go astray and forget You,
and Your Name would not enter into my mind. ॥ 3 ॥

न 1 4c मतु देखि भूला वीसरै तेरा चिति न आवै नाउ ॥ ĀG<>al.

B 4 हुकम हासिल करी बैठा । नांनका सब बाव ॥

C 5 हुकम हासिल करूं बैठा । नानका सब बाव ॥

E 4 हुकम हासिल करूं बैठा । नानिका सब बाव ॥

F 5 हुकंम हासिल करूं ठा । नानिका सव वाव ॥

G 4 हूंकम हासिल करौं बैठौ । नांनिका सब बाव ॥

Pada 4[14]

O father, the soul which is united in union as a Yogi,
remains united in the supreme essence throughout the ages.

न 37 1c बाबा जुगता जीउ जुगह जुग जोगी परम तंत महि जोगं ॥ *ĀG* <>al.

A 0 -- जुगता जीव जुगैं जुगि जीवै ॥ परंम तत मै योगी ॥

D 0 -- जुगतर जीव जुगो जुगि जीवै । परंम तत मैं जोगी ।

E 0 -- जुगता जीव जुगैं जुग जीवै । परंम तत महि जोगी ।

F 0 -- जुगता जीव जुगे जुगि जीवै । परम तत मैं जोगी ।

G 0 -- जुगतां जीव जुगे जुगि जीवै । परंम तत महि जोगी ।

One who has obtained the ambrosial Name of the immaculate—
his body enjoys the pleasure of spiritual wisdom. ॥ 1 ॥ Pause ॥

न 37 1d अंम्रितु नामु निरंजन पाइआ गिआन काइआ रस भोगं ॥ रहाउ ॥

A 0 अंम्रित नांऊ निरंजन पाया ॥ ग्यांन काया रस भोगी ॥ टेक ॥

D 0 अंम्रित नांव निरंजन पाया । बिग्यान काया रस भोगी ॥ *D/F*<>al.

E 0 अंम्रित नांउं निरंजन पाया । ग्यांन काया रस भोगी ॥

F 0 अंम्रित नांवं निरंजन पाया । विग्यान काया रस भोगी ॥

G 0 अंम्रित नांव निरंजंन पाया । ग्यांन काया रस भोगी ॥

14. *ĀG*, pp. 359-60, न 37 *mahalā* 1, *āsā*; *A*, *D*, *E*, *F bilāval*; *G āsāvarī*.

Let the Word of the Guru's Sabad be the ear-rings in your mind,
and wear the patched coat of tolerance.

न	37 1a	गुर का सबदु मनै महि मुंद्रा खिंथा खिमा हढावउ ॥	
A	1	गुर का सबद मनहीं भां मुद्र ॥ षिंथा षिमा हंठांवा ॥	
D	1	गुर का सबद मनहीं मैं मुद्रा । ष्यंथ्या षिमा चटावा ।	*D* <>al.
E	1	गुर का सब्द मंनहि मैं मुद्रा । षिथा षिमां हंटांई ।	
F	1	गुर का सवद मंनहीं मैं मुद्रा । षंथा षिमां हंढाऊं ।	
G	1	गुर का सब्द मन महिं मुद्रा । थिथां षिमां हंढांवां ।	

Whatever the Lord does, look upon that as good;
thus you shall obtain the treasure of Sahaj Yoga. ॥ 1 ॥

न	37 1b	जो किछु करै भला करि मानउ सहज जोग निधि पावउ ॥	*ĀG*<>al.
A	1	जे कुछ करै भला करि मांनै ॥ सहजैं योग नि पावा ॥ 1 ॥	
D	1	जे कुछू रै भला करि मांनैं । सहजै जोग नि पावा ॥	
E	1	जो कछू कहै भला करि मांनैं । सहजै जोग निज पाई ॥	
F	1	जे कछु करे भला करि मांनैं । सहजैं जोर नि पांऊं ॥	
G	1	जे कछू करै भला करि मांनैं । सहजैं जोग निं पांवां ॥	

In the Lord's city, he sits in his yogic posture,
and he forsakes his desires and conflicts.

न	37 2a	सिव नगरी महि आसणि बैसउ कलप तिआगी बादं ॥	
A	2	सिव नंग्री मैं आसंण बैठा ॥ कलप तियागी बादा ॥	
D	2	सिव नग्रि मै आसंण माड्या । अवालप तियागी बादा ।	*D*<>al.
E	2	सिव नगरी मैं आसंन बेठा । कलप तियागी बादां ।	
F	2	सिव नग्री मैं आसणि वैठा । अकलप तियागी वादा ।	
G	2	सिव नंगरी मैं आसन बैठा । कलप तियांगी बांदी ।	

The sound of the horn ever rings out its beautiful melody,
and day and night, he is filled with the sound current of the Nād. ॥2॥

न	37 2b	सिंडी सबदु सदा धुनि सोहै अहिनिसि पूरै नादं ॥	*ĀG*/<>al.; *ĀG*/*FG*<>al.
A	2	सींगी श्रुति सदा संगि सोहै ॥ अह निसि पूरै नादा ॥	
D	2	सींगी सुरति सदा सुनि सोहै । अहिनिसि पूरै नादा ॥	
E	2	सींगी सुरति सदा सुणि सोहै । अहनिसि पूरां नादां ॥	
F	2	सींगी शुरति सदा धुंनि सोहै । अहिनिसि पूरै नादा ॥	
G	2	सींगी सुरति सदा धुंनि सोहै । अहनिंसि पूरै नादी ॥	

My cup is reflective meditation, and spiritual wisdom is my walking stick;
to dwell in the Lord's presence is the ashes I apply to my body.

न 37 3a पतु वीचारु गिआन मति डंडा वरतमान बिभूतं ॥
A 3 चत्र विचार ग्यांन मति डंडा ॥ बरतंनिमन बिभुता ॥
D 3 पत्र बिचार ग्यांन मत्य डंडा । बरतंणिमन बिभूता ।
E 3 पतु बिचारि ग्यांन मति डंडा । बरतंनमंन बिभूता ।
F 3 पत्रु विचार ग्यांन मति डंडा । वरतंणिंमंन विभूता ।
G 3 पत्रु बिचारि ग्यांन मति डंडी । बरतंणिंमन विभूता ।

The praise of the Lord is my occupation;
and to live as Gurmukh is my pure religion. ॥ 3 ॥

न 37 3b हरि कीरति रहरासि हमारी गुरमुखि पंथु अतीतं ॥ *ĀG*<>al.
A 3 हरि कीरति रहरासि हंमारी ॥ गंरमुंषि कथां आतीता ॥
D 3 हरि कीरति रहंणि हंमारा । गुरमुषि कथ्या अतीता ॥ *DF*<>al.
E 3 हरि कीरति रहरासि हंमारी । गुरमुषि कंथ अतीतं ॥
F 3 हरि कीरति रहंणि हमारी । गुरमुषि कथ्या असितेता ॥
G 3 हरि कीरति रहरासि हंमारी । गुरमुंषि कथा अतीता ॥

My arm-rest is to see the Lord's light in all,
although their forms and colors are so numerous.

न 37 4a सगली जोति हमारी संमिआ नाना वरन अनेकं ॥
A 4 सगली जोति तुम्हारी स्वांमी ॥ नांनां बरंण अनेका ॥
D 4 सगली जोति तुम्हारी स्वांमी । नांनां बरंण अनेका ।
E 4 सगली जोति तुम्हारी स्वंम्पां । नांनां बरंण अंनेकौं ।
F 4 सगली जोति तुम्हारी स्वांमीं । नांनां वरण अनेका ।
G 4 सगली जोति तुंम्हारी स्वांमीं । नांनां बरण अंनेकं ।

Says Nanak, listen, O Bharthari Yogi:
love only the supreme Lord God. ॥ 4 ॥ 3 ॥ 37 ॥

न 37 4b कहु नानक सुणि भरथरि जोगी पारब्रहम लिव एकं ॥
A 4 नांनिक कहै श्रुणौ भरथर योगी ॥ पारव्रह्म लिव ऐका ॥
D 4 कहु नानिक सुंणि भरथर जोगी । पारब्रह्म ल्योह ऐका ॥
E 4 कहु नानिक सुंणि भरथरि जोगी । पारब्रह्म लिव एकौं ॥
F 4 कहु नांनिक शुंनि भरथर जोगी । पारव्रंह्म ल्यौ ऐका ॥
G 4 कहू नांनक सुंणि भरथर जोगी । पारब्रह्म लिव ऐकं ॥

Pada 5[15]

What a beautiful Ārtī service this is!

O destroyer of fear, this is Your ceremony of light.

The unstruck Sabad is the vibration of the temple drums. ‖ 1 ‖ Pause ‖

न 31 1c कैसी आरती होइ भव खंडना तेरी आरती अनहता सबद वाजंत भेरी ॥ 1 ॥रहाउ॥

B 0 कैसैं आरती होइ अनाहदा सबद बाजंत भेरी । भौषंडणा? तेरी ॥*ĀG*<>al.; *B*<>al.

C 0 कैसी आरती करां निरंजनां तेरी । अनाहदा सबद बाजंत भेरी ॥

E 0 अैसी आरती करां निरंजनां तेरी । अंनाहद सबद बाजंत भेरी ॥

F 0 अैसी आरती करां – – – –

G 0 अैसी आरती करां निरंजनां तेरी । अनाहद सबद बाजंत भेरी ॥

Upon that cosmic plate of the sky, the sun and the moon are the lamps.

The stars and their orbs are the studded pearls.

न 3 1a गगन मै थालु रवि चंदु दीपक बने तारिका मंडल जनक मोती ॥

B 1 गगन महि थाल रवि चंद दीपक बनें । तारिका मंडला जनक मोती ।

C 1 गगन मह थाल रबि चंद दीपक बनें । तारिका मंडला जनक मोती ।

E 1 गगन महि थाल रवि चंद दीपक बंने । तारिका मंडल जंनक मोती ।

F 1 गगन मैं थाल रवि चंद दीपक वनें । तारिका मंडल जनक मोती ।

G 1 गगन मैं थाल रवि चंद दीपक बन्यौ । तारिका मंडल जनक मोती ।

The fragrance of sandalwood in the air is the incense, the wind is the fan.

All the plants of the world are the altar flowers, O Luminous Lord. ‖ 1 ‖

न 3 1b धूपु मलआनलो पवणु चवरो करे सगल बनराइ फूलंत जोती ॥*ĀG/B*<>al.

B 1 धूप मनआनलौ पवन चौरौ करै । सकल वनराइ फूलंत जोती ॥

C 1 ध्रब लिवंड नित पवन चवरु करै । सकल बनराइ फूलंत जोती ॥

E 1 ध्रूव लिवंड नित पवन चंवरू करैं । सकल बंनराइ फूलंति जोती ॥

F 1 धूव लिवंड नित पवन चवरू करै । सकल वनराइ फूलंत जोती ॥

G 1 धूब लवंड नित पवन चौरु करैं । सकल वनराइ फूलंत जोती ॥

You have thousands of eyes, and yet You have no eyes.

You have thousands of forms, and yet You do not have even one.

न 3 2a सहस तव नैन नन नैन हहि तोहि कउ सहस मूरति नना एक तुोही ॥

ĀG<>al.; *ĀG/EF*<>al.; *CFG*<>al.

B 2 असंष तोहि नैंन ननां नैंन हैं तोहि कौं । असंष सूरति ननां एक तूंही ।

C 2 असंष तोहि नैंन अरु नैंन नहीं तोहि कूं । असंष सूरती न एक तूंहीं ।

E 2 असंष तोहि नैंन अरु नैंन हि तोहि कूं । असंषि मूरते न एक तूहीं ।

15. *ĀG*, p. 13, न 3 *mahalā* 1, *dhan asarī*; *B*, *C dhanāsarī*.

F 2 असंषि तोहि नैंन अरु नैंन नहि तोहि कूं । असंषि मूरति नहीं ऐक तूंहीं ।
G 2 असंषि तोहि नैंन अरु नैंन नहिं तोहि कौं । असंष सूरती नहीं ऐक तूंही ।

You have thousands of lotus feet, and yet You do not have even one foot.
You have no nose, but you have thousands of noses.
This play of Yours entrances me. ‖ 2 ‖

न 3 2b सहस पद बिमल नन एक पद गंध बिनु सहस तव गंध इव चलत मोही ‖ 2 ‖
ĀG<>al.; *ĀG/B*<>al.
B 2 असंष पद बिमल ननां एक पद गंधु बिन । सकल गंध्रप यूं चरित मोही ‖
C 2 असंष पद बिमल एक पद गंध बिन । असंष गंध्र तेरे चरित मोही ‖
E 2 असंष पद बिबल एक पद गंध बिन । असंषि गंध्यू तेरे चरत मोही ‖
F 2 असंष पद विमल ऐक पद गंध विन । असंष गंधौ तेरे चरित्र मोही ‖
G 2 असंषि पद बिमल ऐक पद गंध बिंन । असंषि गंधू तरे चरित मोही ‖

Amongst all is the light—You are that light.
By this illumination, that light is radiant within all.

न 3 3a सभ महि जोति जोति है सोइ ‖ तिस दै चानणि सभ महि चानणु होइ ‖
B 3 सक्ल मैं जोति जोति न सोइ । जिस कै चांनणि सब मैं चांनणुं होइ ।*ĀG/B*<>al.
C 3 सर्ब मैं जोति है जोति मैं सोई । जास कै चांदिणैं चांदियां होई ।
E 3 श्रब मैं जोति है जोति मैं सोई । जास कै चांणिैं चांदिणां होई ।
F 3 श्रव मैं जोति है जोति मैं सोई । जास कै चांदिणैं चांदिणां होई ।
G 3 श्रब मैं जोति है जोति मैं सोई । जास कै चाहिनैं चांदनां होई ।

Through the Gurū's teachings, the light shines forth.
That which is pleasing to Him is the lamp-lit worship service. ‖ 3 ‖

न 3 3b गुर साखी जोति परगटु होइ ‖ जो तिसु भावै सु आरती होइ ‖*ĀG/B*<>al.
B 3 गुर साषी जोति प्रगट होइ । जां तु भांणीं तां आरती होइ ‖
C 3 गुर प्रसादि जोति प्रगट भई । जां तैं भांणीं तां आरती होई ‖
E 3 गुर प्रसादि जोति प्रगट भई । जा तैं भंणीं ता आरती होई ‖
F 3 गुर प्रसादि जोति प्रगट भई । जहां भांण तहां आरती होई ‖
G 3 गुर प्रसाद जोति प्रगट भई । जहां तैं भांणीं तहां आरती होई ‖

My mind is enticed by the honey-sweet lotus feet of the Lord.
Day and night, I thirst for them.

न 3 4a हरि चरण कवल मकरंद लोभित मनो अनदिनुो मोहि आही पिआसा ‖
B 4 हरि चरन कवल मकरंद लोभित मनो । अनदिन मोहि याही प्यासा ।
B 4 *होइ जातें तेरे नाइ बासा ‖*
C 4 हरि चरण मकरंद भजि लोभ करि तो मनां । अनदिनां मोहि या ईत आसा ।

E 4 हरि चरंन मकरंद भजि लोभ करि तो मंनां । अंनदिन मोहि या ईत आसा ।
F 4 हरि - मकरंद भजि लोभ करि तो मनां । नदिनां मोहि या ईत आसा ।
G 4 हरि चरण भजि लोभ करि तो मनां । अनदिंन सेवीये इत आसा । *ĀG*<>al.

Bestow the water of Your mercy upon Nanak, the thirsty song-bird,
so that he may come to dwell in Your Name. ॥ 4 ॥ 3 ॥

न 3 4b क्रिपा जलु देहि नानक सारिंग कउ होइ जाते तेरै नाइ वासा ॥ *ĀG/B*<>al.
B 4 कृपा जल देहु नानक सारंग कौं । होइ जाचौं तेरे नांइं वासा ॥
G 4 क्रिपा जंन नांनक करौ सारंग धर । होइ जाचौं तेरे नांइं वासा ॥
F 4 कृपा जन नांनिक करहु सारंग धर । होइ जाचौं तेरा नांइं वासा ॥
C 4 क्रिपा जन नांनिक करहु सारंग धर । होइ जाचूं तेसे नांइ बासा ॥
E 4 क्रिपा जंन नांनिक करहु सारंग धर । होइ जाचूं तेरे नांई बासा ॥

Pada 6[16]

The Gurū's Word abides with my soul.

अ 32 1c गुर का बचनु बसै जीउ नाले ॥
G 0 गुर के बचन बसैं जीव नाले ।

It does not sink in water; thieves cannot steal it, fire cannot burn it. ॥ 1 ॥
Pause ॥

अ 32 1d जलि नही डूबै तसकरु नही लेवै भाहि न साकै जाले ॥ रहाउ ॥
G 0 जलि नहीं डूबै तसकर नहीं लेवै । भाहि न सकैं जाले ॥

Remembering, remembering, remembering Him in meditation, I find peace;
with each and every breath, I dwell upon Him.

अ 32 1a सिमरउ सिमरि सिमरि सुख पावउ सासि सासि समाले ॥
G 1 सुंमिरौं सुमिरि सुष पाउं । सास सास संमाले ।

In this world, in the world beyond, He is with me, as my help and support;
wherever I go, He protects me. ॥ 1 ॥

अ 32 1b इह लोकि परलोकि संगि सहाई जत कत मोहि रखवाले ॥
G 1 इंहिं लोकि परलोकि संगि सषा है । जित तित मोहि रषवाले ॥

---

16. This *pada* is in the *Ādi-granth* attributed to *mahalā* 5, or Gurū Arjan (अ 32). As usual it has '*nānak*' as *bhaṇitā*. *ĀG*, p. 679, 32, *dhanāsarī*; *G dhanāsarī*.

It is like wealth to the poor, a cane for the blind, mother's milk for the infant.
अ 32 2a निरधन कउ धनु अंधुले कउ टिक मात दूधु जैसे बाले ॥
G 2 निधन कौ धंन अंधले की टेका । मात दूध जैसें बाले ।

In the ocean of the world, I have found the boat of the Lord;
the merciful Lord has bestowed His mercy upon Nanak. ॥ 2 ॥ 1 ॥ 32 ॥
अ 32 2b सागर महि बोहिथु पाइओ हरि नानक करी क्रिपा किरपाले ॥
G 2 सागर मैं जैसें बोहिथ पायौ - नांनक क्रिपा करी क्रिपाले ॥

Pada 7[17]

Whoever has You for support,
अ 3 1a जा कउ भई तुमारी धीर ॥
G 0 जंन कौं भई तुंम्हारी धीर ।

has the fear of death removed;
peace is found, and the disease of egotism is taken away. ॥ 1 ॥ Pause ॥
अ 3 1b जम की त्रास मिटी सुखु पाइआ निकसी हउमै पीर ॥ रहाउ ॥
G 0 जंम की त्रास मिटी सुष पाया । निकसी हौमैं पीर ॥

The fire within is quenched, and one is satisfied
through the ambrosial word of the Gurū, as the baby is satisfied by milk.
अ 3 1c तपति बुझानी अंम्रित बानी त्रिपते जिउ बारिक खीर ॥ *ĀG*<>*G*
G 1 अंम्रित बांनीं तपी बुझांनीं । जैसें बालिक त्रिपत्यौ षीर ।

The saints are my mother, father and friends.
The saints are my help and support, and my brothers. ॥ 1 ॥
अ 3 1d मात पिता साजन संत मेरे संत सहाई बीर ॥
G 1 मात पिता साजन संत मोरै । संत सहाई बीर ॥

The doors of doubt are thrown open, and I have met the Lord of the world;
God's diamond has pierced the diamond of my mind.
अ 3 2a खुले भ्रम भीति मिले गोपाला हीरै बेधे हीर ॥
G 2 षुलै भ्रंम भीति मिलै गोपाला । जैसें हीरै बेध्यौ हीर ।

---

17. This *pada* is in the *Ādi-granth* attributed to *mahalā* 5, or Gurū Arjan (अ3). As usual it has '*nānak*' as *bhaṇitā*. *ĀG*, p. 978, न 3 *naṅ nārāin*.

Nanak blossoms forth in ecstasy, singing the Lord's praises;
my Lord and Master is the ocean of virtue. ॥ 2 ॥ 2 ॥ 3 ॥

अ 3 2b बिसम भए नानक जसु गावत ठाकुर गुनी गहीर ॥

G 2 बसष भया नांनक गुंण गावत । ठाकुर गुंनी गहीर ॥

Pada 8[18]

My pride is gone, O friends and companions; my doubt is dispelled,
and the Gurū has united me with my Beloved. ॥ 1 ॥ Pause ॥

अ 53 1b चुका निहोरा सखी सहेरी ॥ भरमु गइआ गुरि पिर संगि मेरी ॥ रहाउ ॥

C 0 चूका निहोरा सषी सहेली । भरम गया तब पीव संग षेली ॥ *ĀG*<>al.

F 0 चूका हो निहोरा सषी सहेली । भरम गंमाया तव पीव संगि षेली ॥

I suffered in pain, when I thought He was far away;
but now, He is ever-present, and I receive His instructions. ॥ 1 ॥

अ 53 1a दूखु घनो जब होते दूरि ॥ अब मसलति मोहि मिली हदूरि ॥ *ĀG*<>al.

C 1 दुष घणां जब रहती दूरि । इब मोहि मजलिसि भई हजूरि ॥

F 1 दुष घणां जव रहती दूरि । अव मोहि मंजलसि भई हजूरि ॥

My beloved has drawn me near to Him, and seated me on his bed;
I have escaped the clutches of others. || 2 ||

अ 53 2 निकटि आनि प्रिअ सेज धरी ॥ काणि कढन ते छूटि परी ॥ *ĀG*<>al.

C 2 निकट सेज प्रभू आंणि धरी । काढ कढण थैं छूटि परी ॥

F 2 निकट सेज प्रभू आंणि धरी । काढण थैं अव छूटि परी ॥

In the mansion of my heart, shines the light of the Sabad.
My husband Lord is blissful and playful. ॥ 3 ॥

अ 53 3 मंदरि मेरै सबदि उजारा ॥ अनद बिनोदी खसमु हमारा ॥ *ĀG*<>al.

C 3 मंदिर हमारै सबद उजाला आंनंद बिनोदी प्रभू हमारा ॥

F 3 मंदिर हमारै सवद उजाला । अनंद विनोदी प्रभू हमारा ॥

---

18. This *pada* is in the *Ādi-granth* attributed to *mahalā* 5, or Gurū Arjan (अ 53). As usual it has '*nānak*' as *bhaṇitā*. *ĀG*, p. 384, न 53 *āsā*; *CF janglī gauḍī*.

According to the destiny on my forehead, my husband has come home to me.
Servant Nanak has obtained the eternal marriage. ॥ 4 ॥ 2 ॥ 53 ॥

अ 53 4 मसतकि भागु मै पिरु घरि आइआ ॥ थिरु सोहागु नानक जन पाइआ ॥
C 4 मस्तकि भाग जिसि पीव घरि आया । थिर सुहाग नांनिक जनि पाया ॥
F 4 मस्तकि भाग जिनि पीय घरि आया । थिर शुहाग नांनिक जनि पाया ॥

Pada 9[19]

I seek my Friend the Lord.

अ 4 1aaलोडीदड़ा साजनु मेरा ॥
E 0 लोडीदा सजंनं मेरा वे ।
F 0 लोड्यंदा सजन मेरा वे ।
G 0 लोडीदां सजन मेरा वे ।

Worship and adore Him in good times and in bad times;
do not ever forget Him.

अ 4 1b सुखि अराधनु दुखि अराधनु बिसरै न काहू बेरा ॥ *ĀG*<>al.
E 0 दुषि याराधंन सुषि याराधंन । बिसरै न काहू बेरावे ॥
F 0 दुषि आराधन दुषि आराधन । विसरै न काहू वेरा वे ॥
G 0 दुषि आराधंन सुषि आराधन । बिसरि न काहू वेरा वे ॥

In all the spaces and interspaces, everywhere, whatever we see is Yours.

अ 4 2a थानि थनंतरि सभनी जाई जो दीसै सो तेरा ॥
E 3 थांन थनतरि सबहीं थईयां । जो दीसै सो तेरा वे ॥
F 1 थांन थनंतरि सवनीं थाई । जे दीसै सो तेरा वे ॥
G 2 थांन थनंतर सबनीं थाई । जो दीसै सो तेरा वे ॥

Chanting the Name, the light of millions of suns shines forth,
and the darkness of doubt is dispelled. ॥ 1 ॥

अ 4 1c नामु जपत कोटि सूर उजारा बिनसै भरमु अंधेरा ॥
E 2 नांव जपत कोटि सूर उजियारा । बिनसे वा भरंम अंधेरा वे ॥
F 2 नांव जपत कोटि सूर उजाला । विनसे वा भरम अंधारा वे ॥
G 3 नांव जपत कोटि सूर उजियारा । बिंनसे वा भर्म अंधेरा वे ॥

---

19. This *pada* is in the *Ādi-granth* attributed to *mahalā* 5, or Gurū Arjan (अ 4). As usual it has '*nānak*' as *bhaṇitā*. *ĀG*, p. 700, न 4 *jaitsarī*; *E, F, G dhanāśrī*.

In each and every home, sing the sublime songs of rejoicing;
He abides in each and every heart. ॥ 1 ॥ Pause ॥

अ 4 1ab घरि घरि मंगल गावहु नीके घटि घटि तिकसहि बसेरा ॥ रहाउ ॥
E 1 घरि घरि मंगल गावैं नीका । घटि घटि तिसे बसेरा वे ॥
F 3 घरि घरि मंगल गावैं नीका । घटि घटि तिंहि वसेरा वे ॥
G 1 घरि घरि मंगल गावै नींका । घटि घटि तिसहि बसेरा वे ॥

One who finds the society of the saints, O Nanak,
is not consigned to reincarnation again. ॥ 2 ॥ 3 ॥ 4 ॥

अ 4 2b संतसंगि पावै जो नानक तिसु बहुरि न होई है फेरा ॥
E 4 जंन नानिक साधू सग पाया । बहुड़ि न भवजलि फेरा वे ॥
F 4 जन नांनिक साधू संगति पाया । वहुरि न भौजलि फेरा वे ॥
G 4 जन नांनक साधू संग पाया । बहुरि न भौजलि फेरा वे ॥

Pada 10[20]

I am a sacrifice, O dear merciful Lord; I am a sacrifice to You.
न 3 1c हंउ कुरबानै जाउ मिहरवाना हंउ कुरबानै जाउ ॥
F 0 मैं कुरवांणीं जांउं मिहरवाना मैं कुरवांणीं जांउं ।

I am a sacrifice to those who take to Your Name.
न 3 1d हंउ कुरबानै जाउ तिना कै लैनि जो तेरा नाउ ॥
F 0 मैं कुरवांणीं जांउं तिन्हां परि लेह ज तेरा नांउं ॥

Unto those who take to Your Name, I am forever a sacrifice. ॥ 1 ॥ Pause ॥
न 3 1-5 लैनि जो तेरा नाउ तिना कै हंउ सद कुरबानै जाउ ॥ रहाउ ॥

This body is conditioned by Maya, O beloved; this cloth is dyed in greed.
न 3 1a इहु तनु माइआ पाहिआ पिआरे लीतड़ा लबि रंगाए ॥
F 1 यहु मन माया फाहिया वारी दीतड़े सव रंगाइ ।

My husband Lord is not pleased by these clothes, O Beloved;
how can the soul-bride go to His bed? ॥ 1 ॥

न 3 1b मेरै कंत न भावै चोलड़ा पिआरे किउ धन सेजै जाए ॥
F 1 मेरे कंत न भावै चोलनां वारी । क्यौं धन सेझैं जाइ ॥

---

20. *ĀG*, pp. 721-2, न 3 *mahalā* 1, *tilaṅg*; *F vasanta*.

If the body becomes the dyer's vat, O beloved,
and the Name is placed within it as the dye,

न 3 2a काइआ रंङणि जे थीऐ पिआरे पाईऐ नाउ मजीठ ॥

F 2 काया रंगणि जे थिर होवै । पावै नांउं मजीठ ।

and if the dyer who dyes this cloth is the Lord Master —
O, such a color has never been seen before! ॥ 2 ॥

न 3 2b रंङण वाला जे रंङै साहिबु ऐसा रंगु न डीठ ॥

F 2 रंगनवाला ऐह्वा मेल्हैं । जेहा रंग न दीठ ॥

Those whose shawls are so dyed, O Beloved,
their husband Lord is always with them.

न 3 3a जिन के चोले रतडे पिआरे कंतु तिना कै पासि ॥

F 3 जिंहि गलि चोले रतङ वारी । कंत तिन्हां कै पासि ।

Bless me with the dust of those humble beings, O dear Lord.
Says Nanak, this is my prayer. ॥ 3 ॥

न 3 3b धूडि तिना की जे मिलै जी कहु नानक की अरदासि ॥

F ------

He Himself creates, He Himself imbues us. He bestows His glance.

न 3 4a आपे साजे आपे रंगे आपे नदरि करेइ ॥

O Nanak, if the bride becomes pleasing to her husband,
He Himself enjoys her. ॥ 4 ॥ 1 ॥ 3

न 3 4b नानक कामणि कंतै भावै आपे ही रावेइ ॥

F 3 षाक संतां की जो मिलै । वावै नांनिक की अरदासि ॥

Pada 11[21]

Do not think that your husband Lord can be obtained by mere words.

न 27 1c1 -- मतु जाण सहि गली पाइआ ॥

A 4 तूं मति जांणैं वे गाल्ही पाया ॥

C 0 तूं मति जांनैं वै गाल्ही पाया ।

D 0 तु मति जाणैं गाल्ही पाया ।

E 0 तूं मति जांनैं वै गल्हा पायां ।

F 0 तु मति जांणैं गल्ही पाया ।

G 0 तूं मति जांन वे गल्हां पाया ।

21. *ĀG*, p. 24, न 27 *mahalā* 1 *sirīrāg*; *A jaṅgal*; *C bilāval*; *D, E, F, G jaṅglī gauḍī*.

In the pride of wealth and the splendour of beauty,
You are wasting this life ॥ 1 ॥ Pause ॥

न 27 1c2 माल कै माणै रूप की सोभाइतु बिधी जनमु गवाइआ ॥ रहाउ ॥

A माला का मणियां रूप की छाया ॥ इत बिधि जनम गमाया ॥ *A*<>al.

C 0 माल कै मांणैं रूप की सोभा । इत बिधि जनम गवाया ॥

D 0 माला का मणियां रूप की सोभा । ईत बिधि जन्म गवाया ॥

E 0 माल का मता रुप की सोभा । ईहि बिधि जंनम गंवाया ॥

F 0 माला का मणियां रूप की सोभा । इत विधि जन्म गंवाया ॥

G 0 माला कै मांनैं रूप की सोभा । इत बिधि जनम गमाया ॥

Make good deeds the soil, and let the word be the seed;
irrigate it continually with the water of truth.

न 27 1a अमलु करि धरती बीजु सबदो करि सच की आब नित देहि पाणी ॥

C 1 अमल करि धरती बीज करि कलमां । सच की आब नित देहु पांणीं ।

D 1 अमल करि धरती बीज करि कलमा । स की आंब देह नित पांणीं ।

E 1 अंमल करि धरती बीज करि कलमां । सचु की आंब नित देहु पांनीं ।

A अमल करि धरतीं बीज करि कलमां ॥ सच की आंब नित देहु पांणी ॥

F 1 अमल करि धरती वीज करि कलमां । सत की आंव देह नित पांणीं ।

G 1 अंमल करि धरती बीज करि कलंमां । सचु की आब निंत देह पांनीं ।

Become such a farmer, and faith will sprout.
This brings knowledge of heaven and hell, you fool! ॥ 1 ॥

न 27 1b होइ किसाणु ईमानु जंमाइ लै भिसतु दोजकु मूड़े एव जाणी ॥

A होहु किसांण ईमान जमाइ ले ॥ भिस्ति दोजग मूढै ईवैं जांणीं ॥

C 1 होह किरसांण ईमांन जमाइ ले । भिस्त दोजग मूंढे इव जांणीं । *CF*<>al.

D 1 होह क्रिसाण ईमांन जमाई ले । भिस्ति दोजग मूढा. ईव जांणीं ॥

E 1 होह किरसांन ईमांन जमाइ ले । भिस्ति दोजगि मुंढे इवैं जांनीं ॥

F 1 होह किंरसांण ईमांन जमाइ ले । भिस्ति दोजग मूढा इवैं जांणीं ॥

G 1 होह किरसांन इंमांन जंमाइ लै । भिस्ति दोजिग मूंढैं इंवैं जांनीं ॥

The defect of the body which leads to sin is the mud puddle,
and this mind is the frog, which does not appreciate the lotus flower.

न 27 2 अैब तनि चिकड़ो इहु मनु मीडको कमल की सार नही मूलि पाई ॥ *ĀG*<>al.

A यहु तन कीचड़ यहु मन मींडक ॥ कवल की सार नहीं मूलि पाई ॥

C 2 यहु तन किचङ यहु मन मींडक । कवल की सार नहीं मूलि पाई ।

D 2 यहु तन कीचङा वहु मन मींड का कवल की सार नहीं मूलि पाई ।

E 2 यहु तंज कीचङ यहु मंन मीडक । कंवल की सार नहीं मूल पाई ।

F 2 यहु तन कीचङ यहु मन मींडक । कवल की सार नहीं मूल पाई ।

G 2 यहु तन कीचङ यहु मंन मींडक । कंवल की सार नही मूंल पाई ।

This speaking and listening is like the song of the wind,
for those whose minds are colored by the love of Maya.

न 27 3 आखणु सुनणा पउण की बाणी इहु मनु रता माइआ ॥ *ĀG/C*<>al.
C 3 आषणां सुणणां पवन की बांणीं । यहु मन रता माया ही ।
D ---
E ---
G ---

The grace of the Master is bestowed upon those who meditate on Him alone.

न 27 3 खसम की नदरि दिल पसिंदे जिनी करि एकु धिआइआ ॥ *ĀG/C*<>al.
C 3 षसम की नजरि दिल पंस न करि । जिनि इक मनि करि ध्याया ही ॥
A ---
D ---
E ---
G ---

The bumble bee is the teacher who continually teaches the lesson.
But how can one understand, unless one is made to understand? ॥ 2 ॥

न 27 2 भउरु उसतादु नित भाखिआ बोले किउ बूझै जा नह बुझाई ॥ 2 ॥
A 2 भवर उस्ताद नित भाषिया बोलै क्यं न बूझै बुझाई ॥
C 2 भवर उस्ताद नित्र भाषिया बोलै । क्यूं बूझै तिसै नां बुझाई ॥
D 2 भर उस्ताद नित भाष्या बोलै । क्यूं न बूझै बुझाई ॥
E 2 भवर उसताद नित भाषिया बोलैं । क्यूं न बूझै बुझाई ॥
F 2 भवर उस्ताद नित भ्यष्या वोलै । क्यौं न वूझै वूझाई ॥
G 2 भंवर उस्ताद नित भाषिया बोलैं । क्यौं न बूझै बुझाई ॥

You may observe the thirty fasts, and say the five prayers each day,
but 'Satan' can undo them.

न 27 4 तीह करि रखे पंज करि साथी नाउ सैतानु मतु कटि जाई ॥ *ĀG*<>al.
A 2 सत करि राषी पंजरि साषी ॥ नांम सैतांन मति काढि जाई ॥
C 4 तीह करि साषी । पवै सैतांन मति कटि जाई ।
D 3 तस कर राषी पंजर साषी । नामु सैतन काटि जाई ।
E 3 तीस कर राषौं पंज करि साषी । पावैं सेतांन मति लुटि जाई ।
F 3 तस कर राषी पंजर साषी । नांमु सैतन काटि जाई ।
G 3 तस कर राषी पंजर साषी । नव सैतांन मति काटि जाई

Says Nanak, you will have to walk on the path of death,
so why do you bother to collect wealth and property? ॥ 4 ॥ 27 ॥

न 27 4 नानकु आखै राहि पै चलणा मालु धनु कितकू संजि आव्ली ॥ 4 ॥ 27 ॥ *ĀG*<>al.
A 3 नानिक आषैं राह पैं चलनां ॥ माल धन किसकूं संचाई ॥ 3 ॥ 4 ॥
C 4 नांनिक आषै राह पै चलणां । माल धन कितकूं संचाई ॥
D 3 नानिक राषे राह पै चललां । माल धन किसकौं सचाई ॥
E 3 नांनिक अषै राह पैं चलनां । माल धंन किसकूं संचाई ॥
F 3 नांनिक आषै राह पै चलणां । माल धन किसकूं चाई ॥
G 3 नांनक अषै राह पैं चलनां । माल धंन किसकौं संचाई ॥

Pada 12[22]

Forgetting the Lord, one is ruined forever.
अ 2 1a हरि बिसरत सदा खुआरी ॥
C 0 हरि बिसरत सदा षुवारी रे ।
E 0 हरि बिसरत सदा ष्वारी रे ।
F 0 हरि विसरत सदा षारी रे ।
G 0 रे हरि बिसरत सदा षुवारी ।

How can anyone be deceived, who has Your support, O Lord? ॥ Pause ॥
अ 2 1b ता कउ धोखा कहा बिआपै जा कउ ओट तुहारी ॥ रहाउ ॥ *ĀG*<>al.
C 0 तिन कौं धोषा कहा बियापै । जे जन सरनि तुम्हारी रे ॥
E 0 तिन कूं धोषा कहा बियापै । जोई जंन सरंन तुम्हारी रे ॥
F 0 तिन कूं धोषा कहा वियापै । जे जन सरणि तुम्हारी रे ॥
G 0 तिन कौं धोषा कहा बियापै । जे जन सरनि तुंम्हारी ॥

One may rule over the nine regions of the earth,
but in the end, he shall have to depart, losing the game of life. ॥ 1 ॥
अ 2 1d नव खंडन को राजु कमावै अंति चलैगो हारी ॥ *ĀG*<>al.
C 1 नवां षंडां कौ माल उगाह्यौ । अंति चल्यौ सब हारी ।
E 1 नवां षंडां कौ माल उगाह्यौ । अंति चल्यौ सब हारी ।
F 1 नवां षंडां का माल उगाह्यौ । अंति चलैगौ हारी रे ॥
G 1 नवौं षंडा कौ माल उगाह्यौ । अंति चल्यौ सब हारी ।

Without meditating in remembrance on the Lord, life is like a burning fire,
even if one lives long, like a snake.
अ 2 1c बिनु सिमरन जो जीवनु बलना सरप जैसे अरजारी ॥

---

22. This *pada* is in the *Ādi-granth* attributed to *mahalā* 5, or Gurū Arjan (अ 2). As usual it has '*nānak*' as *bhaṇitā*. *ĀG*, pp. 711-72, अ 2 *ṭoḍī*; *C dhanāśrī*.

C 1 बिन सुमिरन कैसौ जीवनौ रे बलमां । श्रप जिसी अरजारी रे ॥
E 1 बिन सुंमिरंन कैसा जीवनां बलमां । श्रप जिसे अरजारी ॥
F 2 विन शुमिरन कैसा जीवनां वलमां । श्रप जिरो अरजारी ॥
G 1 बिण सुंमिरण कैसा जीवना रे बालम । श्रप जिसौ अरजारी ॥

He alone sings the glorious praises of the Lord, the treasure of virtue,
upon whom the Lord showers His grace.
अ 2 2a गुण निधान गुण तिन ही गाए जा कउ किरपा धारी ॥
C 2 गुण निधांन तेरे गुण गाये । जन परि कृपा धारी ।
E 2 गुंण निधान तेरे गुंण नहीं गाए । जंन कूं क्रिपा धारी । *EF*<>al.
F 3 गुन निधांन तेरे गुन नहि गावै । जन परि क्रिपा धारी रे ॥
G 2 गुंण निधांन तेरे गुंण जिनिं गाये । तिन परि क्रिपा धारी ।

He is at peace, and his birth is blessed; Nanak is a sacrifice to him. ‖ 2 ‖ 2 ‖
अ 2 2b सो सुखीआ धनु उसु जनमा नानक तिसु बलिहारी ॥
C 2 धंनि सोई सुषिया धनि तिस जनमां । जन नांनिक बलिहारी ॥
E 2 सो सुषिया धंनि जिस घरि जंनम्यां । नानिक ता बलिहारी ॥ *E*<>al.
F 4 सो शुषिया धंनि तिस जन्मां । जन नांनिक तिस वलिहारी रे ॥
G 2 सोई सुषिया धंनिं तस जनमां । जन नांनक तिस बलिहारी ॥

Pada 13[23]

I beg for the gift of Your Name, O my Lord and Master.
अ 6 1a मागउ दानु ठाकुर नाम ॥
C 0 मांगूं दांन ठाकुर नांउं ।
E 0 मांगूं दांन ठाकुर नांम ।
F 0 मांगूं दांन ठाकुर नांउं ।
G 0 मांगूं मैं दांन ठाकुर नांव ।

Nothing else shall go along with me in the end;
by Your grace, allow me to sing Your praises. ‖ 1 ‖ Pause ‖
अ 6 1b अवरु कछू मेरै संगि न चालै मिलै क्रिपा गुण गाम ॥ रहाउ ॥ *ĀG*<>al.
C 0 और कछू मेरे संगि नहीं चलणां- । करि किरपा गुन गांऊं ॥
E 0 और कछू मेरे संग नही चलनां । करु क्रिपा गुंन गांऊं ॥
F 0 अवर -- मेरे संगि नहि चलणां । करु क्रिपा गुन गांउं ॥

23. This *pada* is in the *Ādi-granth* attributed to *mahalā* 5, or Gurū Arjan (अ 6). As usual it has '*nānak*' as *bhaṇitā*. *ĀG*, p. 713, अ 6 *ṭoḍī*; *C, E, F dhanāśrī*.

G 0 और कछू मेरै संगि नहिं चलनां । करि क्रिपा गुंन गांव ॥

Power, wealth, various pleasures and enjoyments,
all are just like the shadow of a tree.

अ 6 1c राजु मालु अनेक भोग रस सगल तरवर की छाम ॥

C 1 राज माल अनेक भोग रस । सकल तरवर की छांह ।

E 1 राज माल अंनेक भोग रस । सकल तरवर की छांह ॥

F 1 राज माल अनेक भोग रस । सकल रवर की छांह ॥

G 1 राज पाट और अंनेक भोग रस । सकल तरवर की छांम । *G*<>al.

He runs around in many directions, but all of his pursuits are useless. ॥ 1 ॥

अ 6 1d धाइ धाइ बहु बिधि कउ धावै सगल निरारथ काम ॥ *ĀG*<>al.

C 3 ध्यावत कूं ध्यावै बहु बिधि करि । सकल निराफल कांम ॥

E 3 धांवत कूं धावैं बहु बिधि करि । सकल निरफल कांम ॥

F 3 धावत कूं धावै सव विधि करि । सकल निफल कांम ॥

G 3 धावत कूं धावै सव विधि करि । सकल निफल कांम ॥

Except for the Lord of the Universe, everything he desires appears transitory.

अ 6 2a बिनु गोविंद अवरु जे चाहउ दीसै सगल बात है खाम ॥ *ĀG*<>al.

C 2 बिन गोबिंद और कछू चाहै । सकल बात काची षांम ॥

E 2 बिन गोब्यंद अवर कछू चाहै । सकल बात काची षांम ॥

F 2 विन गोव्यंद और कछू चाहै । सकल वात काची षांम ॥

G 2 बिनां गोबिंद और कछू चाहै । सकल बात काची ष्यांम ।

Says Nanak, I beg for the dust of the feet of the saints,
so that my mind may find peace and tranquility. ॥ 2 ॥ 1 ॥ 6 ॥

अ 6 2b कहु नानक संत रेन मागउ मेरो मनु पावै बिस्राम ॥ *ĀG*<>al.

C 4 जंन नानिक साधू रेन मांगै । मेरां मंन पावै बिश्रांम ॥

G 2 जन नांनक साधू रेन मांगैं । मेरौ मन पावै बिश्रांम ॥

C 4 जन नांनक साधू रेणि मांगै । मेरा मन पावै बिश्रांम ॥

F 4 जन नांनिक साधू रैंनि मांगै । मेरा मन पावै विश्रांम ॥

Pada 14[24]

Those who argue and fight with the saints —
those slanderers find no happiness at all. ‖ 1 ‖ Pause ‖

अ 34 1c संतसंगि करहि जो बादु ॥ तिन निंदक नाही किछु सादु ॥ रहाउ ॥ *ĀG*<>al.
C 0 साध सेती करै बाद । तिस निंदक कछू नहीं स्वाद ॥
E 0 साध सेती करै बाद । तिस निदक कछू नही स्वाद ॥

the saints, the mortal wanders in reincarnation.
Slandering the saints, he is diseased.

अ 34 1a संत की निंदा जोनी भवना ॥ संत की निंदा रोगी करना ॥
C 1 साध की निंद्या जोनी भवनां । साध की निंद्या रोगी करनां ।
E 1 सांध की निद्या जोनी भवनां । साध की निद्या रोगी करंनां ।

Slandering the saints, he suffers in pain.
The slanderer is punished by the messenger of death. ‖ 1 ‖

अ 34 1b संत की निंदा दूख सहाम ॥ डानु दैत निंदक कउ जाम ॥
C 1 साध की निंद्या दुष सहमां डंड देगौ निंदक कूं जंमां ॥
E 1 साध की निद्या दुष सहंमां । डंड देगो निदकं कूं जंमां ॥

Slandering the devotees, the wall of the mortal's body is shattered.
Slandering the devotees, he suffers in hell.

अ 34 2a भगत की निंदा कंधु छेदावै ॥ भगत की निंदा नरकु भुंचावै ॥ *ĀG*<>al.
C 2 साध की निंद्या कंद छिदावै । संत की निंद्या नरक भुचावै ।
E 2 साध की निद्या कंध छिदावै । संत की निद्या त्रक भुचावै ।

Slandering the devotees, he rots in the womb.
Slandering the devotees, he loses his realm and power. ‖ 2 ‖

अ 34 2b भगत की निंदा गरभ महि गलै ॥ भगत की निंदा राज ते टलै ॥ *ĀG*<>al.
C 2 संत की निंद्या ग्रभ मांहिं गलै । संत की निंद्या राज थैं टलै ॥
E 2 संत की निद्या ग्रभ मांहि गलैं । संत की निद्या राज थैं टलै ॥

The slanderer finds no salvation. He eats only what he himself has planted.

अ 34 3a निंदक की गति कतहू नाहि ॥ आपि बीजि आपे ही खाहि ॥
C 3 निंदक कूं गति कितहूं नांहि । आपणां बीज्या आप हीं षांहि ।
E 3 निंदक कूं गति कितहूं नांहिं । आपणां बीज्या आप हीं षांहि ।

---

24. This *pada* is in the *Ādi-granth* attributed to *mahalā* 5, or Gurū Arjan (अ 34). As usual it has '*nānak*' as *bhaṇitā*. *ĀG*, p. 1145, अ34 *bhairū*; *C bhairū*.

He is worse than a thief, a lecher, or a gambler.
The slanderer places an unbearable burden upon his head. ‖ 3 ‖

अ 34 3b चोर जार जूआर ते बुरा ॥ अणहोदा भारु निंदकि सिरि धरा ॥
C 3 चोर जार जुवारी थैं बुरा । अणहूंदा भार निंदक सिरि धरा ॥
E 3 चोर जार जुवारी थैं बुरा । अंणहूंदा भार निदक सिर धरा ॥

The devotees of the supreme Lord God are beyond hate and vengeance.
Whoever worships their feet is emancipated.

अ 34 4a पारब्रहम के भगत निरवैर ॥ सो निसतरै जो पूजै पैर ॥ *ĀG*<>al.
C 4 पारब्रह्म की भगति त्रिबैर । सो निस्तरै जिनि पूजै पैर ।
E 4 पारब्रह्म की भगति निरबैर । से निस्तरै जै पूजै पैर ।

The primal Lord God has deluded and confused the slanderer.
O Nanak, the record of one's past actions cannot be erased. ‖ 4 ‖ 21 ‖ 34 ‖

अ 34 4b आदि पुरखि निंदकु भोलाइआ ॥ नानक किरतु न जाइ मिटाइआ ॥
C 4 आदि पुरिषि निंदक भुलाया । नांनिक क्रित न मिटै न मिटाया ॥
E 4 आदि पुरिषि निदक भुलाया । नानिक क्रित न मिटै न मिटाया ॥

Pada 15[25]

In the first watch of the night, O my merchant friend,
you were cast into the womb, by the Lord's command.

न 1 1a पहिलै पहरै रैणि कै वणजारिआ मित्रा हुकमि पइआ गरभासि ॥ *ĀG*<>al.
A 0 पहिलै पहिरै रैणि दै बणिजारिया ॥ तेरा हुकम पया ग्रभवास रे ॥
C 1 पहलै पहरै रैंणि दै बणजारिया । तेरा हुकम पया गर्भवास वे ।
D 0 पहलै पहरैं रयाणि दै बणिजारिया । हुकम पया ग्रभवास वे ।
E 1 पहलै पहरै रैंणिं दै बंणिजारिया । हुकमु पया ग्रभवास वे ।
F 1 पहलै पहरै रैंणि कै वणिजारिया । - - -
G 1 पहलै पहरै रैंणि दै बंणिजारिया । हुकम पया ग्रभ वास वे ।

25. *ĀG*, pp. 74-75, न 1 *mahalā* 1 *sirī*; (see also *ĀG* p. 75, न 2) *A jangal*, *C jangalī*, *F janglī gauḍī*. A similar four-part *pada* by Dādū is found in Callewaert and Op de Beeck: 1991, p. 205 (Monika Thiel-Horstmann [ed.], *Dādū: Lieder*, Stuttgart: Franz Steiner Verlag, 1991, (1.32), pp. 80-1, and by Raidās in Callewaert, *Devotional Hindi Literature*, Delhi: Manohar, 2000 and Friedlander, *The Life and Works Of Raidās*, Delhi: Manohar, 1992, pp. 123-4.

Upside-down, within the womb, you performed penance,
O my merchant friend, and you prayed to your Lord and Master.

न 1 1b उरध तपु अंतरि करे वणजारिआ मित्रा खसम सेती अरदासि ॥ *ĀG*<>al.
A 1 उर्ध तपु अंदरि कीया बणिजारिया ॥ षसंम सेती अरदासिवे ॥
C 1 उरध तपु अंदरि करै बणजारिया षसम सेती अरदास वे ।
D 0 उरध तप अंदरि करै बंणिजारिया । षसम सेती अरदासि वे ।
E 1 उरध तपु अंदरि करैं -- षसंम सेती अरदास वे ।
F 1 --- -- षसम सेती अरदास वे ।
G 1 उर्ध तप अंदरि करै -- षसम सेती अरदासि वे ।

You uttered prayers to your Lord and Master, while upside-down,
and you meditated on Him with deep love and affection.

न 1 1c खसम सेती अरदासि वखाणै उरध धिआनि लिव लागा ॥
A 1 षसंम सेती अरदासिं बणांवै ॥ उर्ध ध्यांन ल्यौ लागा ॥
C 1 षसम सेती अरदासि बणावै । उरध ध्यांन ल्यौ लागा वे ।
D 1 षसम सेती अरदासि बषांणै चे । उरध ध्यांन ल्यौ लागा ।
E 1 षसंम सेती अरदासि बणांवै । उरध ध्यांन ल्यौ लागा वे ।
F 1 षसम सेती अरदास वषांणैं । उरध ध्यांन ल्यौ लागा वे ।
G 1 षसम सेती अरदासि बषांणैं । उर्ध ध्यांन ल्यौ लागा ।

You came into this dark age of Kaliyuga naked,
and you shall depart again naked.

न 1 1d ना मरजादु आइआ कलि भीतरि बाहुङि जासी नागा ॥ *ĀG*<>al.
A 1 नां म्रजाद भया कलि अंदरि ॥ बाहुड़ि जासी नागा वे ॥
C 1 नां मरजाद भया कलि अंदरि । बहुङि जासी नागा वे ।
D 1 ना मरजाद भया कलि अंदरि । बहुङि जासौ नागा ।
E 1 नां मरजाद भया कलि अंदरि । बाहुङि जासी नागा वे ।
F 1 नां मरजाद भया कलि अंदरि । वाहुङि जासी नागा वे ।
G 1 नां व म्रजाद भया कलि अंदरि । बहूङि जासी नागा ।

As God's pen has written on your forehead, so it shall be with your soul.

न 1 1e जैसी कलम वुडी है मसतकि तैसी जीअडे पासि ॥ *ĀG*<>al.
A 1 जेही कलम लिषी इत मस्तकि ॥ तेही जियड़ै पासि वे ॥
C 1 जेही कलम लिषी इत मसतकि । तेही जीवडे पास वे ।
D 1 जेही कलम लिषी ईत मस्तकि । तेही जीयडे पास वे ।
E 1 जेही कलंम लिषी इत मसतकि तेही जियडे पास वे ।

F 1 जेही कलम लिषी इत मस्तकि । तेही जियडै पास वे ।
G 1 जेई कलम लिषी इत मस्तकि । तेई जीयरे पासि वे ।

Says Nanak, in the first watch of the night,
by the Hukam you enter into the womb. ॥ 1 ॥

न 1 1f कहु नानक प्राणी पहिलै पहरै हुकमि पइआ गरभासि ॥
A 1 कहु नांनिक प्रांणी पहिलै पहिरै ॥ हुकम पया ग्रभंवास वे ॥
C 1 कहु नांनक प्रांणीं पहलै पहरै । हुकम पया गर्भवास वे ॥
D 1 कहु नानिक प्रांणी पहलै पहरै । हुकम पया ग्रभवास वे ॥
E 1 कहु नानिक प्रांणीं पहलै पहरै । हुकमु पया ग्रभवास वे ॥
F 1 कहु नांनिक प्रांणीं पहिलै पहिरै । हुकंम पया ग्रभवास वे ॥
G 1 कहु नांनिक प्रांणीं पहलै पहरै । हुकम पया ग्रभवास वे ॥

In the second watch of the night,
O my merchant friend, you have forgotten to meditate.

न 1 2a दूजै पहरै रैणि कै वणजारिआ मित्रा विसरि गइआ धिआनु ॥ *ĀG*<>al.
A 2 दूजै पहिरै रैणि दै बणिजारिया ॥ तूं बिसरि गया सब ध्यांन वें ॥
C 2 दूजै पहरै रैंनि दै बणजारिया । तूं बिसरि गया सब ध्यांन वे ।
D 2 दूजै पहरै रेंईणि दै बंणिजारिया । तू बिसरि गया सब ध्यांन वै ।
E 2 दूजै पहरै रैंणिं दै बंणिजारिया । – – – –
F 2 दूजै पहिरै रैंणि कै वणिजारिया । विसरि गया सव ध्यांन वे ।
G 2 दूजै पहरै रैंणि दै बणिजारियां । तूं बिसरि गया सब ध्यांन वे ।

From hand to hand, you are passed around,
O my merchant friend, like Krishna in the house of Yashoda.

न 1 2b हथो हथि नचाईऐ वणजारिआ मित्रा जिउ जसुदा घरि कानु ॥ *ĀG*<>al.
A 2 हाथूं हाथ षिलाया बांणीजारिया ॥ ज्यूं जसवै घरि कांन्ह वे ॥
C 2 हाथूं हाथ षिलाइया बजारिया । ज्यूं जसवै घरि कांन्ह वे ।
D 2 हाथूं हाथि षिलाईया बणिजारिया । ज्यूं जसवै घरि कांन्ह वे ।
E -- ज्यूं जसुवै घरि कांन्ह वे ।
F 2 हाथूं हाथि षिलाइया वणिजारिया । ज्यौं जसव घरि कांन्ह वे ॥
G 2 हाथौं हाथि षिलाइया बंणिजारिया । ज्यौं जसघा घरि कांन्हं वे ।

From hand to hand, you are passed around,
and your mother says, 'This is my son.'

न 1 2c हथो हथि नचाईऐ प्राणी मात कहै सुतु मेरा ॥
ĀG<>al.
A 2 हाथूं हाथ षिलाया प्रांणीं ॥ मात कहैं सुत मेरा ॥

C 2 हाथू हाथ षिलाया प्रांणीं । मात कहै सुत मेरा वे ।
D 2 हाथूं हाथि षिलायां प्रांणीं । मात कहै सुत मेरा वे ।
E 2 हाथूं हाथ षिलाया प्रांणीं मात कहै सुत मेरा ।
F 2 हाथूं हाथि षिलाइया प्रांणीं । मात कहै शुत मेरा वे ।
G 2 हाथौं हाथ षिलाइये प्रांणीं । मात कहै सुत मेरा ।

O, my thoughtless and foolish mind, think:
In the end, nothing shall be yours.

न 1 2d चेति अचेत मूड मन मेरे अंति नही कछु तेरा ॥
ĀG<>al.
A 2 चेति अचेत मूढें दिल अंदरि ॥ अंति नहीं कछु तेरा ॥
C 2 चेति अचेत मूंढे दिल अंदरि । अंति नहीं कुछ तेरा वे ।
D 2 चेत अचेत मूढ दिल अंदरि । अंति नहीं कुछ तेरा वे ।
E 2 चेति अचेत मूंट दिल अंदरि । अंति नहीं कुछ तेरा वे ।
F 2 चेत अचेत मूढ दिल अंदरि । अंति नहीं कछु तेरा वे ।
G 2 चेति अचेत मूंढ दिल अंदरि । कोई नहीं कछू तेरा ।

You do not know the One who created the creation.
Gather spiritual wisdom within your mind.

न 1 2e जिनि रचि रचिआ तिसहि न जाणै मन भीतरि धरि गिआनु ॥ *ĀG*<>al.
A 2 जिनि रच रच्या तिसहि न चेतै ॥ मन अंदरि करि ग्यांन वे ॥
C 2 जिनि रच रच्या तिसहि न चेतै । मन अंदरि करि ग्यांन वे ।
D 2 जिंनिं च रच्य जिसहि न चेतै । मन अंदरि करि ग्यांन वे ।
E 2 जिनि रच रच्या तिसहि न चेतै । मंन अंदरि करि ग्यांन वे ।
F 2 जिनि रच रंच्याति सहि न चेतै । मन अंदरि करि ग्यांन वे ।
G 2 जिंनिं रच रचिया तिसहि न चेतै । मन अंदरि करि ग्यांन वे ।

Says Nanak, in the second watch of the night, you forgot to meditate. ॥ 2 ॥
न 1 2f कहु नानक प्राणी दूजै पहरै विसरि गइआ धिआनु ॥
A 2 कहि नांनिक प्रांणी दूजै पहिरै ॥ बिसरि गया सब ध्यांनु वे सुचे ॥ 2 ॥
C 2 कहु नांनक प्रांनीं दूजे पहरै । बिसरि गया सब ध्यांन वे ॥
D 2 कहु नानिक प्रांणीं दूजै पहरै । बिसरि गया सब ध्यांन वे ॥
E 2 कहु नांनिक प्रांणीं दूजै पहरै । बिसरि गया सब ध्यांन वे ॥
F 2 कहु नांनिक प्रांणीं दूजै पहिरै । विसरि गया सव ध्यांन वे ॥
G 2 कहु नांनिक प्रांणीं दूजे पहरै । विसरि गया सब ध्यांन वे ॥

In the third watch of the night, O my merchant friend,
your consciousness is focused on wealth and youth.

न 1 3a तीजै पहरै रैणि कै वणजारिआ मित्रा धन जोबन सिउ चितु ॥ *ĀG*<>al.

A 3 तीजै पहिरै रैणि दै बणिजारिया ॥ तौरा धनु जोबन स्यूं चितु वे ॥

C 3 तीजे पहरै रैंणि दै बणजारिया । तेरा धन जोबन सूं चित वे ।

D 3 तीजे पहरै रैंणि दै बंणिजारिया । तेरा धन जोबन स्यूं चित वे ।

E 3 तीजे पहरै रैंणि दै बंणजारिया । तेरा धंन जोबंन सौं चिंतु वे ।

F 3 तीजे पहरै रैंणि दै वणिजारिया । तेरा धन जोवन स्यौं चित वे ।

G 3 तीजे पहरै रैंणिं दै बंणिंजारिया । तेरा धन जोबन सौं चित वे ।

You have not remembered the Name of the Lord,
O my merchant friend, although it would release you from bondage.

न 1 3b हरि का नामु न चेतही वणजारिआ मित्रा बधा छुटहि जितु ॥ *ĀG*<>al.

A 3 हरि का नांउं न चेतहीं बणिजारिंया ॥ बंध्या छूटै जिंतु वे ॥

C 3 हरि का नांव न चेतहीं बणजारिया । बंध्यां छूटै जितु वे ।

D 3 हरि का नांवा न चेतहीं बंजिारिया । बंध्या छूटौ जित वे ।

E 3 हरि का नांव न चेतहीं बणजारिया । बंध्या चूटै जितु वे ।

F 3 हरि का नांउं न चेतही वणिजारिया । वंध्या छूटै जित वे ।

G 3 हरि का नांव न .चेतही बंणिंजारिया । बंध्या छूटै जिन वे ।

You do not remember the Name of the Lord, you become confused by Maya.

न 1 3c हरि का नामु न चेतै प्राणी बिकलु भइआ संगि माइआ ॥

A 3 हरि का नांउ न चेतै प्रांणी ॥ बिकल भंया संगि माया ॥

C 3 हरि का क चैतै प्रांणीं । बिकल भया संगि माया वे ।

D 3 हरि का नाव न चेतै प्रांणीं । विकल भया संगी माया ।

E 3 हरि का नांव न चेतै प्रांणीं । बिकल भया संगि माया वे ।

F 3 हरि का नांउं न चेतै प्रांणीं । विकल भया संगि माया ।

G 3 हरि का नांव न चेतही प्रांणीं । विकल भया संगि माया वे ।

Revelling in your riches and intoxicated with youth,
you waste your life uselessly.

न 1 3d धन सिउ रता जोबनि मता अहिला जनमु गवाइआ ॥

A 3 धनं स्यूं रता जोबन मता ॥ अहला जनम गमाया ॥

C 3 धन सूंर ता जोबन मता । अहला जनम गवाया वे ।

D 3 धंन सूं रता जोबन मतां । अहला जनम गमाया वे ।

E 3 धंन सौं रत जोबंन मता । अहला जंनम गंवाया वे ।

F 3 धन स्यौं रता जोवन मता । अहला जन्म गंमाया वे ।
G 3 धंन सौ रता जोबन मंता । अहला जनम गंमाया ।

You have not traded in righteousness and Dharma;
you have not made good deeds your friends.

न 1 3e धरम सेती वापारु न कीतो करमु न कीतो मितु ॥ *ĀG*<>al.
A 3 धरंम सेतीं ब्यापर न किता ॥ रांम न किता मिंत वे ॥
C 3 धर्म सेती ब्यौपार न कीता । रांम न कीता म्यंतु वे ।
D 3 ध्रम सेती ब्यौहार न कीता । रांम न कीता मींत वे । *DF*<>al.
E 3 धंरम सेती ब्यौपार न कीनां । रांम न कीता मीतु वे ॥
F 3 ध्रंम सेती व्यौहार न कीया । रांम न कीता म्यंत वे ।
G 3 ध्रम सेती ब्यापार न कीता । रांम न कीया म्यंत वे ।

Says Nanak, in the third watch of the night,
your mind is attached to wealth and youth. ‖ 3 ‖

न 1 3f कहु नानक तीजै पहरै प्राणी धन जोबन सिउ चितु ॥
A 3 कहु नांनिक प्रांणी तीजै पहिरै ॥ तेरा धन जोबन स्यूं चित वे ॥ 3 ॥
C 3 कहु नांन प्रांणीं तीजै पहरै । तेरा धन जोबन सूं चितु वे ॥
D 3 कहु नानिक प्रांणीं तीजै पहरै । तेरा धंन जोबन स्यूं चित वे ॥
E --
F 3 कहु नांनिक प्रांणीं तीजै पहरै । तेरा धन जोवन स्यौं चित वे ॥
G 3 कहु नांनक तीजै पहरै । धंन जोबंन सौं चित वे ॥

In the fourth watch of the night, O my merchant friend,
the grim reaper comes to the field.

न 1 4a चउथै पहरै रैणि कै वणजारिआ मित्रा लावी आइआ खेतु ॥ *ĀG/F*<>al.
A 4 चौथै पहिरै रैणि दै बणिजारिया ॥ तेरा जाई आया षेंतु वे ॥
C 4 चौथै पहरै रैंणि दै बणजारिया । तेरा लाई आया षेतु वे ।
D 4 चौथे पहरे रैंणि दै बंणिजारिया । तेरा लावी आया षेत वे ।
E 4 चौथै पहरै रैंणि दै बणिजारिया । तेरा लाई आया षेतु वे ।
F 4 चौथैं पहरै रैंणि कै वणिजारिया । तेरा लांवनि आया षेतु वे ।
G 4 चौथै पहरै रैंणिं दै बंणिजारिया । तेरा लांवीं आया षेत वे ।

When the messenger of death seizes and dispatches you, O merchant friend,
no one knows the mystery of where you have gone.

न 1 4b जा जमि पकड़ि चलाइआ वणजारिआ मित्रा किसै न मिलिआ भेतु ॥
A 4 जो जमि पकड़ि चलाईया बणिंजारिया ॥ किसहिं न दीयां भेतु वे ॥
C 4 जां जंमि पकड़ि चलाइया बणजारिया । किसहीं न दीया भेतु वे ।

D 4 जा जंमि पकरि चलाईया बणिजारिया । किसहि न मिल++ तु + ।
E 4 जा जंमि पकङि चलाइया बंणजारिया । तां किसही न मिलिया भेतु वे ।
F 4 जां जंमि पकङि चलाइया वणिजारिया । जां किसहि न मिलिया भतु वे ।
G 4 ज्यूं जंमिं कपङि चलाइया बंणिंजारिया कहु किसै मिलावै हेत वे ।

So think of the Lord! No one knows this secret,
of when the messenger of death will seize you and take you away.
न 1 4c भेतु चेतु हरि किसै न मिलिओ जा जमि पकङि चलाइआ ॥ *ĀG*<>al.
A 4 भेतु हेतु करि किसहि न दीयां ॥ जां जंमि पंकड़ि चलाया ॥
C 4 भेत सेत करि किसहीं न मिलिया । जा जंमि पकङि चलाया वे ।
D - -
E 4 भेतु सेतु करि किसहि न मिलिया । जा जंमि पकङि चलाया वे ।
F 4 भेतु सेतु करि किसहि न मिलिया । जा जंमि पकङि चलाया वे ।
G 4 हेत भेत कहू किसै मिलावै । जब जंम पकङि चलाइया ।

All your weeping and wailing then is false.
In an instant, you become a stranger.
न 1 4d झूठा रुदनु होआ दोआलै खिन महि भइआ पराइआ ॥
A 4 झूठा रुदन भया है द्वारै ॥ छिन मैं भया पराया ॥
C 4 झूठा रूदन भया है द्वालै । छिन मैं भया पराया वे ।
D - -
E 4 झूठा रुदन भया है द्वालै । छिंन मैं भया पराया वे ।
F 4 झूठा रुदन भया है द्वालै । छिन मैं भया पराया वे ।
G 4 झूठा रूदन भया है द्वारै । छिन मैं भया पराईया ।

You obtain exactly what you have longed for.
न 1 4e साई वसतु परापति होई जिसु सिउ लाइआ हेतु ॥
A 4 सोई बस्त परापति हुई जा स्यूं लाया हेतु वे ॥
C 4 सोई बस्त परापति हुई । जा सूं लाया हेतु वे ।
D - -
E 4 सोई बस्त परपति हुई । जा सूं लाया हेतु वे ।
F 4 सोई वस्त परापति हूई । जा स्यौं लाया हेतु वे ।
G 4 सोई बस्त प्रापति हूई । तिस सौं लाया हेत वे ।

Says Nanak, in the fourth watch of the night, O mortal,
the grim reaper has harvested your field. || 4 || 1 ||

न 1 4f कहु नानक प्राणी चउथै पहरै लावी लुणिआ खेतु ॥
A 4 कहु नांनिक प्रांणी चौथै पहिरै ॥ तेरा लाई आया षेत वे ॥
C 4 कहु नांनक प्रांणीं चौथै पहरै । तेरा लाई आया षेतु वे ॥
D --
E 4 कहु नानिक प्रांणी चौथै पहरै । तेरा लाइ आया षेतु वे ॥
F 4 कहु नांनिक प्रांणीं चौथै पहरै । तेरा लांवंनि आया षेतु वे ॥
G 4 कहु नानिंक चौथै पहरै । लांवीं आया षेत वे ॥

Pada 16[26]

A 0 मुझ कौं डर है रे उस दिन का ॥ काल कराल फिरै फंदक ज्यूं ॥
C 0 मुझ कूं डर है रे उस दिन का । काल कराल फिरै फंधक ज्यूं ।
D 0 मुझ कौं डर है रे उस दिन का । काल कराल फिरै फंदक ज्यूं ।
E 0 मुझ कूं डर है वै उस दिंन का । काल कराल फिरै फंधक ज्यूं ।
F 0 मुझ कूं डर है रे उस दिन का । काल कराल फिरै फंदक ज्यौं ।
G 0 मुझ कौं डर है रे उस दिंन का । काल कराल फिरै फंदक ज्यौं ।
A 0 म्रिग पड़ै जैसै बन का ॥ टेक ॥
C 0 म्रिग पडै जैसैं बन का ॥
D 0 म्रिथ पडै जैसै बंन का ॥
E 0 म्रिघ परै जैसैं बंन का ॥
F 0 म्रिग पडै जैसैं वन का ॥
G 0 म्रिघ परै जैसैं बन का ॥
A 1 काची माटी काचे भांडा ॥ फूटत लागै ठण का ॥
C 1 काची माटी काचा भांडा । फूटत लागै ठन का ॥
D 1 काची मांटी काचा भांडा । फूटत लागै ठंण का ॥
E 1 काची माटी काचा भांड । फूटत लागै ठंण का ॥
F 1 काची माटी काची काया । फूटत लागै ठंन का ॥
G 1 काची मांटी काचा भांडा । फूटत लागै ठण का ॥
A 1 जम के आये बंधि चलाये ॥ सारा नांहीं किनका ॥
C 2 जंम के आंवैं बंधि भलांवैं । सारा नांहीं तिन का ॥
D 2 जंम के आरे बंधि चलाऐ । सारा नांहीं तिनका ॥
E 2 जंम के आए बंधि चलाए । सारा नांही तिनि का ॥
F 2 जम के आये वंधि चलाये । सारा नांहीं तिन का ॥

26. *Pada* 16 is not found in the *ĀG*; *A jaṅgal*, *C jaṅgalī*, *F jaṅglī gauḍī*.

G 2 जंम के आये बंधि चलाये । सारा नांही तिनका ॥

A 3 नांनिक कहै अब लेंषा पूरा ॥ ज्यूं मांला का मणिका ॥

C 3 नांनक कहै यहु लेषा पूगा । ज्यूं माला का मणिका ॥

D 3 नानिक कहै यहु लेषा पूगा । ज्यूं माला का मणीका ॥

E 3 नांनिक कहै यहु लेषा पूरा । ज्यूं माला का मंणिका ॥

F 3 नांनिक कहै यहु लेषा पूगा । ज्यूं माला का मनिका ॥

G 3 नांनक कहै यहु लेषा पूरा । ज्यौं माला का मंनिंका ॥

Pada 17[27]

A 0 हंक मरणां गोवलि चरणां ॥ भजि पवौ रांम दी सरणां ॥

C 0 हक मरणां गोवलि चरणां । तुम्ह करि ल्यौं रांम सुमिरणां ॥

D 0 – मरंणा गोवलि चरंणां । भजि पवो रांम दी सरणां ॥

E 0 हक मरंणां गोवलि चरंनां । तुम्ह करि ल्यौ रांम सुमिरनां ॥

F 0 हकि मरणां गोवलि चरणां । दिन दस करि ल्यौ रांम शुमिरणां ॥

G 0 हकि मरणां गोवलि चरणां । भजि पवो रांम दी सरणां ।

G तुंम करि ल्यौं रांम सुंमिंरणां ॥

A 0 कोई चौसई पहिरौ पैंसंई पहिरौ ॥ पहिरौ मुलमुल षासा ॥

C 1 कोई चौरी पहरौ पंचई पहरौ । पहरौ मलमल षासा वे ।

D 1 चौसी पदारौ पंसी पहरौ । पहरौ मलमल षासा ।

E 1 कोई चौसी पहरौ पचसी पहरौ । पहिरौ मलमल षासा ।

F 1 चौसी पहरौ पंचसी पहरौ । पहरौ मुलमुल षासा ।

G 1 कोई चौसी पहरौ पचसी पहरौ । पहरौ मुलमुल षासा ।

A 1 बींदी दे चौ तारा पहिरौ भी मरंणै दीआसा ॥

C 1 बींदी दे चौ तारा पहरौ । भी मरणैं दी आसा वे ॥

D 1 बींदी दे चौ तारैं पहरौं । + + दी आसा ॥

E 1 बींदी तै चौ तारा पहरौ भी मरणैं दी आसा ॥

F 1 वींदी दे चौ तारा पहरौ । भी मरणं दी आसा ॥

G 1 बीदी दे चौ तारा पहरौ । भी मरणैं दी आसा ॥

A 2 कोई बीस भीषटौ तीस भीषटौ ॥ षाटौ कोड़ि पचासा ॥

C 2 कोई बीस भीषटौ तीस भीषटौ । षटौ कोडि पचासा वै ।

D 2 कोई बीस भी जीवो तीस भी जीवो । जीवो बरस पचासा वे ।

E 2 कोई बीस भिषटौ तीस भिषटौ । षटौ लष पचासा ।

F 2 वीस भी जीवो तीस भी जीवो । जीवो वरस पचासा ।

27. *Pada* 17 is not found in the *ĀG*; *A jaṅgal*, *C jaṅgalī*, *F jaṅglī gauḍī.*

G 2 कोई बीस भी जीवौ तीस भ जीवौ । जीवो बरस पचासा ।

A ---
C 3 अंतकालि बरसां सौ जीवौ । भी मरणैं दी आसा वे ॥
D 2 अंतकालि बीसा सौ जीवे । भी मरणें दी आसा वे ॥
E 2 अंति कालि सौ बरसा जीवो । भी मरंणैं दी आसा ॥
F 2 अंतिकालि वरसा सौ जीवो । भी मरणं दी आसा ॥
G 2 अंति कालि बीसा सौ जीवो । भी मरणैं दी आसा ॥

A ---
C 3 कोई बीस ली जीवौ तीस भी जीवौ । जीवौ बरस पचासा वे ।
D 3 कोई बीस भी षाटौ । तीस भी षाटौ । षाटौ कोङि पचासा वे ।
E 3 कोई बीस भि जीवो तीस भि जीवो । जीवो बरस पचासा ।
F 3 कोई वीस भी जोङो तीस भी जोङौ । जोङौ कोङि पचासा ।
G 3 कोई बीस भी षटौ तीस भी षटौ । षटौ लष पचासा ।

A 2 अरब षरब बहुतेरा षटौ ॥ भी मरणैं दी आासा ॥
C 2 अर्बष र्ब बहुतेरे षटौ । भी मरणैं दी आसा वे ॥
D 3 अरबष रब बहुतेरा षाटौ । भी मरंणैं दी आसा वे ॥
E 3 अरब षरब बहुतेरे षटौ । भी मरणैं दी आसा ॥
F 3 अरवष रव वहुतेरे जोङौ । भी मरणं दी आसा ॥
G 3 अरबष रब बहुतेरे षटौ । भी मरणैं दी आसा ॥

A 3 किस दी धीया किस दा पूता ॥ किस दा यहु घर वासा ॥
C 4 किसी - धिया किस दा पूता । किस दा य घर वासा वे ।
D 4 किस दी धीया किस दा पूता । किस दा यहु घर वासा वे ।
E 4 किस दा धियां किस दा पूता । किस दा यहु घर वासा ।
F 4 किस दा धीया किस दा पूता । किस दा यहु घर वासा ।
G 4 किस दा धीया किस दा पूता । किस का यहु घर वासा ।

A 3 नांनिक कहै थिर रहणां नांहीं ॥ जगलि हैगा बासा ॥ 3 ॥
C 4 नांनक कहै थ्रि रहणां नांहीं । जंगलि हैगा बासा वे ॥
D 4 नांनिक कहै थीर रंहणां नांहीं । जंगलि है बासा वे ॥
E 4 नानिक कहै थिर रहणां नांहीं । जगलि हैगा बासा ॥
F 4 नांनिक कहै थिर रहणां नांहीं । जंगलि है गावासा ॥
G 4 नांनक कहै थिर रहनां नांहीं । जंगलि हैगा बासा ॥

Pada 18[28]

Be happy, dear beloved, as long as your youth is fresh and delightful.

न 24 1b रंगु माणि लै पिआरिआ जा जोबनु नउ हुला ॥

But your days are few—you have grown weary,

and now your body has grown old. ॥ 1 ॥ Pause ॥

दिन थोड़ड़े थके भइआ भइआ पुराणा चोला ॥ 1 ॥ रहाउ ॥

line न 24,1b-a/b is internally inverted; also *ĀG/CF*<>al.

A 0 अब दिन थोरड़े थक वे ॥ इब रंगु माणि लै ॥ कि हरि रस जांणि लै ॥
C 0 अब दिन थोरड़े थके । इब रंग मांणि लै । कि हरि रस जांणि लै ।
D 4 – दिन थोरड़े थके वै । – रंग माणि लै हरि ज़स जांणि ले ।
E 0 – दिन थोरड़े थके वे । – रंग मांणि लै हरि जस जांणि लै ।
F 0 – दिन थोरड़े थके वे । इव रंग मांणि लै । हरि रस जांणि लै ।
G 0 – दिन थोरड़े थके । – रंग मांणिं लै हरि जस जांणिं लै ।
न 24 see above न24; 1b
A 0 मेरी ज्यंदूडी ये भया बें पुरांणां मैंडा चोला चौणा वे ॥ टेक ॥
C 0 मेरी जिंदुड़ि ये । भया वै पुरांणां मैंडा चोलणां वे ॥
D 4 मैं जीज्यंदुड़ी वे । भयां – पुरांणां मैंजा चोला चोलणा वै ॥
E 0 मेरी जिहूड़ी ए भया वे पुरांणां मैंडा – चोलनां वे ॥
F 0 मैंडी ज्यंदड़ी वे । भया – पुरांणां मैंडा चोला चोलणां वे ॥
G 0 मेरी जिंदुड़ी ये भया वे पुरांणां – चोल चोलणां वे ॥

Wealth, the beauty of youth and flowers are guests for only a few days.

न 24 1aa धनु जोबनु अरु फुलड़ा नाठीअड़े दिन चारि ॥ *ĀG*<>al.
A 1 धन जोबन नव हुलणें (?) पांहुनड़े दिन चारि वे ॥
C 1 धंन जोबन नव हुलणें । पांहुंनड़े दिन चारि वे ।
D 5 धंन जोबंन ना हूलगो । पांहुणड़े दिन चारे वै ।
E 1 धंन जोबन नव हुलणें । पांहुंनड़े दिन चारि वे ।
F 1 धन जोवन न हुलणां । पांहुणड़ा दिन चारि वे ।
G 1 धंन जोबन नां हूलनां । पाहूनड़ा दिन च्यारि वे ।

Like the leaves of the water-lily, they wither and fade and finally die. ॥ 1 ॥

न 24 1ab पबणि केरे पत जिउ – – – ढलि ढुलि जुंमणहार ॥ *ĀG*<>al.
A 1 पड़वंणां केजे पतु ज्यूं ॥ मैडी अंमावंणी ॥ भुरि भुरि भये चलणहार वे ॥
C 1 पड़वणि केरे पात ज्यूं । मैंडी अमांवणीं । भुरि भुरि थइ चलनहार वे ॥

28. *ĀG*, p. 23, न 24 *mahalā* 1 *sirī*; *A jaṅgal*, *C jaṅglī gauḍī*.

D 5 पङवणि केरे पतं ज्यूं मैंडी अंमांवांणी । भरी भुरि थऐ चलणहार वै ॥
E 1 प्रवणि केरे पात ज्यूं मेरी अंमावङी । भरि भुरि थए चलणहार वे ॥
F 1 पङवणि केरे पत ज्यौं । मैंडी अंमांवांणीं । भरि भुरि भये चलणहार वे ॥
G 1 पङवनिं केरे पात ज्यौं । मैंडी जिंदूङीये भुरि भुरि थयें चलणहार वे ॥ *G*<>al.
ĀG - -
A 2 जे जाणौं तिल हुलणां ॥ सामरि गाद भरां उवे
C 2 जे जांणां तिल दुलणां । सांवरि गोद भरेऊं वे ।
D 6 जे जांणौं तिल हुलहणां । सांवंणि गोद भरे हुवे ।
E 2 जे जांणूं तिल डुलणां । सांवरि गोद भरे उंवे ।
F 2 जे जांणूं तिल डुलणां । सांवरि गोद भरींऊं वे ।
G 3 जे जांणौ तिल झुलणां । सांवरि गोद भरेव वे । *G*<>al.
ĀG - -
A 2 जे जांणौं जगु छडणां मेरी अमांवणीं ।इत तनि थोड़ा थोड़ां मांण करेउ वे ॥
C 2 जे जांणां जग छडणां । मैंडी अमांवणीं । इस तनि थोडा थोङा मांन करेऊं वे ॥
D 6 जे जांणूं जगु छडणां । मैडी अंमांवणी । ईत तनि थोङा थोङा माण करेहु वै ॥
E 2 जे जांणां जग छडणां । मेरी अंमावङी । इस तंनि थोङा थोङा मांन करेंउं वे ॥
F 2 जो जांणूं जग छडणां मैंडी अंमांवांणीं । इ तनि थोङा थोङा मांन करींउं वे ॥
G 3 जे जांणूं जग छडणां । मैंडी अंमांवंणी । - - थोङा थोङा मांन करेव वे ॥

Haven't you heard the call from beyond, O beautiful soul-bride?
न 24 3a की न सुणेही गोरीए आपण कंनी सोइ ॥ *ĀG*<>al.
A 3 निहुड़ीये इक सीष सुणि ॥ सास केरी सोई वे ॥
D 7 नहुङिये ऐक सीष सुणि । सासू केरी सोई वै ।
C 3 निहुङिए इक सिष सुणि । सासू केरी सोइ वे ।
E 3 नाहुलियै इक सीष सुंणि । सासु केरी सोइ वे ।
F 3 नहुङी ऐक सीष शुंणि । सासू हंदी सोइ वे ।
G 4 नहूङी ऐकै सीष सुंणि । साहू हंदी सोइ वे ।

You must go to your in-laws; you cannot stay with your parents forever. ॥ 3 ॥
न 24 3b लगी आवहि साहुरै - - - - - - - नित न पेईआ होइ ॥ *ĀG*<>al.
A 3 मैं भी वंजा साहुरै मैडी असावणी नित निपेयो (?) पेया होइ वे ॥
C 3 मैं भी वंजां -हुरै मैंडी अमांवंणीं नित निपेइया निपेइया होइ वै ॥
D 7 मैं भी वंजा साहरै मैडी अंमांवांणीं नित नपेई षाई होइ वै ।
E 3 मैं भी बज्या साहुरै मैंडी अंमावङी निति नांऊं निपेया पीया होइ वे ॥
F 3 मैं भी वंजां साहुरै मैंडी अंमांवांणीं नित न पीया (?) पीया होइ वे ॥
G 4 मैं भी बंज्यां साहूरै - । - - - निंत न पीया पीया होइ वे ॥

My playful friends have gone to sleep in the graveyard.

न 24 2a सजण मेरे रंगुले जाइ सुते जीराणि ॥ *ĀG*<>al.
A 4 साजन मैंडा रंगला ॥ जाइलं थैसी लैंण वे ॥
C 4 सजन मैंडा रंगुला जाइल थैसी लैंण वे ।
D 8 सजण मैंडा रंगुले जाई । लंथे सीलाण वे ।
E 4 साजंण मैंडा रंगुला । जाइल थैं सीय लैणि वे ।
F 4 साजन मैंडा रंगुला । जाइल थेसी लैंण वे ।
G 2 साजन मैंडा रंगुला । जाइ उलथ से लैंण वे ।

In my double-mindedness, I shall have to go. I cry in a feeble voice. ॥ 2 ॥

न 24 2b हं भी वंञा डुमणी – – – – रोवा झीणी बाणि ॥ 2 ॥ *ĀG*<>al.
A 4 मैं भी आवंण दूमणी ॥ मैंडी असोवणी ॥ कुकी सगली रैंणिं वै ॥
C 4 मैं भी आंमण दूंमणीं मैंडी अमांवणीं । कूकी सगली रैंणि वे ॥
D 8 मैं भी आंमण दूमणीं । मैंडी अंमांवांणी । कूकी सगलो रैणि वै ॥
E 4 मैं भी अमंण दुमंणी । मैडी अंमांवणीं कुकी सारी रैंणिं वे ॥
F 4 मैं भी आंमण दूंमाणीं । मैंडी अंमांवाणीं । कूकी सीहली रैंणि वे ॥
G 2 मैं भी आंमण दूंमणीं । मैंडी अंमांवणींक कूकी सगली रैंणिं वे ॥

O Nanak, know that she who sleeps in her parents' home
is plundered in broad daylight.

न 24 4a नानक सुती पेईअै जाणु विरती संनि ॥ *ĀG*<>al.
A नांनिक सुती पेइया ॥ देषि बरंती सधि वे ॥
C 5 नांनक सुती पेइये । देषि बरती संधि वे
D 9 नानिक सूती पेईयां । देषि बरती संधि वे ।
E 5 नांनिक सुती पैइयैं । देषि बरीति संधि वे ।
F 5 नांनिक सूती पेइयां । आय वरती संधि वे ।
G 5 नांनिंक सूती पेइयां । देषि बरंदी संधि वे ।

She has lost her bouquet of merits; gathering one of demerits,
she departs. ॥ 4 ॥ 24॥

न 24 4b गुणा गवाई गंठङी अवगण चली बंनि ॥ *ĀG*<>al.
A गुंणहि गवांई गांठड़ी मैंडी अमावणी ॥
C 5 गुणहि गंवाई गंठङी । नैंङी अमांवणीं
D 9 गुणंहं गवांई गंटङी । मैंडी अंमांवांणीं ।
E 5 गुंणहं गंमाई गंठङी । मैंडी अंमावणीं ।
F 5 गुणह गंवांईं गंठङी । मैंडी अंमांवांणीं ।

G 5 गुंनह गंमांई गंठडी मैडी जिंदुडीये ।

ĀG - -

A 5 औगुंण चलीं पलै बंधि वे ॥

C 5 औगुण चली पलै बंधि वे ॥

D 9 औगुण चली पलै बांनि वे ॥

E 5 अवगुंण चली चली पहलै बंधि वे ॥

F 5 चली औगुण पलै वंधि वे ॥

G 5 औगुंण चली पलै बंधि वे ॥

Pada 19[29]

I am reassured, gazing upon Your wondrous play.

अ 101 1a धीरउ देखि तुम्हारे रंगा ॥

C 0 धीरौं देषि तुम्हारे रंगा ।

You are my Lord and Master, the Inner-knower, the searcher of hearts;
You dwell with the holy saints. ॥ 1 ॥ Pause ॥

अ 101 1b तुही सुआमी अंतरजामी तूही वसहि साध कै संगा ॥ रहाउ ॥

C 0 तुम्ह हौ स्वांमीं अंतरजांमीं । तुमहि बसौ साधू कै संगा ॥

In an instant, our Lord and Master establishes and exalts.
From a lowly worm, He creates a king. ॥ 1 ॥

अ 101 1c खिन महि थापि निवाजे ठाकुर नीच कीट ते करहि राजंगा ॥ *ĀG*<>al.

C 1 छिन मैं थापि करै मेरौ ठाकुर । कीरति नीच करहि राजंगा ॥

May I never forget You from my heart;
slave Nanak prays for this blessing. ॥ 2 ॥ 15 ॥ 101 ॥

अ 101 2 कबहू न बिसरै हीए मोरे ते नानक दास इही दानु मंगा ॥

C 2 निमष न बिसरौ मेरे जीयरे तैं । नांनिक दास इहै दांन मांगा ॥

---

29. This *pada* is in the *Ādi-granth* attributed to *mahalā* 5, or Gurū Arjan (अ 101). As usual it has '*nānak*' as *bhaṇitā*. *ĀG*, p. 824, न 101 *bilāval*; *C bilāval*.

Pada 20[30]

O my Love, I am fascinated by Your many glories;
Your glorious virtues are not found in any other. ॥ 1 ॥ Pause ॥

न 35 1c लाल बहु गुणि कामणि मोही ॥ तेरे गुण होहि न अवरी ॥ रहाउ ॥
C 0 दयाल इहि बिधि कांमणि मोही । तेरे ए गुण लहां न तोही ॥

If the pearl of the mind is strung like a jewel on the thread of the breath,

न 35 1a मनु मोती जे गहणा होवै पउणु होवै सूत धारी ॥ *ĀG<>C*
C 1 नांव मोती जे होवै गहणां । पवन होइ सुरति धारी ।

and the soul-bride adorns her body with compassion,
then the Beloved Lord will enjoy His lovely bride. ॥ 1 ॥

न 35 1b खिमा सीगारु कामणि तनि पहिरै रावै लाल पिआरी ॥ *ĀG<>C*
C 1 काया षिमां सिंगार करह री । तौ तूं लाल पियारी ॥

If the bride wears the garland of the Lord's name, har har, around her neck,
and if she uses the toothbrush of the Lord;

न 35 2a हरि हरि हारु कंठि ले पहिरै दामोदरु दंतु लेई ॥
C 2 हरि हरि हार कठि ले पहरा दामोदर दत देई ।

if she fashions and wears the bracelet of the creator Lord around her wrist,
then she shall hold her consciousness steady. ॥ 2 ॥

न 35 2b कर करि करता कंगन पहिरै इन बिधि चितु धरेई ॥
C 2 कर करते के कांगण पहरां । इहि बिधि चित धरेई ॥

She should make the Lord, the slayer of demons, her ring,
and take the transcendent Lord as her silken clothes.

न 35 3a मधुसूदनु कर मुंदरी पहिरै परमेसरु पटु लेई ॥ *ĀG<>C*
C 3 मिहरवांन मुदियां करि पहरां । परमेसुर पट लेई ।

The soul-bride should weave patience into the braids of her hair,
and apply the lotion of the Lord, the great lover. ॥ 3 ॥

न 35 3b धीरजु धङी बंधावै कामणि स्रीरंगु सुरमा देई ॥
C 3 धीरज धङी बंधावै कांमणि । श्रीरंग सुरमां देई ॥

---

30. *ĀG*, p. 359, न 35 *mahalā* 1, *āsā*; *C jaṅglī gauḍī.*

If she lights the lamp in the mansion of her mind,
and makes her body the bed of the Lord,
न 35 4a मन मंदरि जे दीपकु जाले काइआ सेज करेई ॥
C 4 इहि मंदिर ले दीपक जालै । काया सेज करेई ।

then, when the king of spiritual wisdom comes to her bed,
He shall take her, and enjoy her. ‖ 4 ‖ 1 ‖ 35 ‖
न 35 4b गिआन राउ जब सेजै आवै त नानक भोगु करेई ॥ *ĀG<>C*
C 4 ग्यांन ध्यांन दोऊ सेजर मांडै । जन नांनिक भोग करेई ॥

Pada 21[31]

CHANT: Countless silent sages and innumerable ascetics seek Him;
अ 5 1-3 जा कउ खोजहि असंख मुनी अनेक तपे ॥
C 0 जा कूं षोजै असंष । मुनीं अनेक तपे ।

millions of Brahmas meditate and adore Him;
he spiritual teachers meditate and chant His Name.
अ 5 1-4 ब्रहमे कोटि अराधहि गिआनी जाप जपे ॥
C 1 ब्रह्मे कोटि अराधैं । ग्यांनी जाप जपैं ।

Through chanting, deep meditation, austere self-discipline, religious rituals,
sincere worship, endless purifications and humble salutations,
अ 5 1-5 जप ताप संजम किरिआ पूजा अनिक सोधन बंदना ॥
C 1 जप तप संजम करी पूजा अनेक सोधन बंदनां ।

wandering all over the earth and bathing at sacred shrines of pilgrimage,
people seek to meet the Pure Lord.
अ 5 1-6 करि गवनु बसुधा तीरथह मजनु मिलन कउ निरंजना ॥
C 1 करि गवन बसुधा तीरथ मैंजन । मिलन कूं निरंजनां ।

Mortals, forests, blades of grass, animals and birds all meditate on You.
अ 5 1-7 मानुख बनु तिनु पसू पंखी सगल तुझहि अराधते ॥
C 1 मांनूष बन तिन पसू पंषी । सकल तुझै अराधते ।

The merciful beloved Lord, the Lord of the universe is found;
Nanak, joining the company of the holy, salvation is attained. ‖ 1 ‖
अ 5 1-8 दइआल लाल गोबिंद नानक मिलु साधसंगति होइ गते ॥

---

31. These verses (*chant* 1.3- 4.6, *ĀG*, pp. 454-5) are in the *Ādi-granth* attributed to *mahalā* 5, or Gurū Arjan (v 5). They are preceded by 2 *saloku*s (1.1-2). As usual they have '*nānak*' as *bhaṇitā*.

C 1 मिलि दयाल लाल गोबिंद नांनिक । साधसंगति है गते ॥

Millions of incarnations of Vishnu
and Shiva, with matted hair yearn for You,

अ 5 2–1 कोटि बिसन अवतार संकर जटाधार ॥

C 2 कोटि बिश्न अवतार । संकर जटाधार ।

O merciful Lord, their minds and bodies are filled with infinite longing.

अ 5 2–2 चाहहि तुझहि दइआर मनि तनि रुच अपार ॥

C 2 वै चांहैं तुझ दयाल । मनि तनि रुचै अपार ।

The Lord Master, the Lord of the universe, is infinite and unapproachable;
God is the all-pervading lord of all.

अ 5 2–3 अपार अगम गोबिंद ठाकुर सगल पूरक प्रभ धनी ॥

C 2 अपार अगिनत अथाह ठाकुर । सकल पूण प्रभु धणीं ।

The angels, the Siddhas, the beings of spiritual perfection, the heavenly heralds and celestial singers meditate on You.
The Yakhshas and Kinnars chant Your glorious praises.

अ 5 2–4 सुर सिध गण गंधरब धिआवहि जख किंनर गुण भनी ॥

C 2 सुर सिध गंणां गंध्रप ध्यांवैं । जिषि किंनर गुन भणीं ।

Millions of Indras and countless gods and super-human beings
meditate on the Lord Master and celebrate His praises.

अ 5 2–5 कोटि इं अनेक देवा जपत सुआमी जै जै कार ॥

C 2 कोटि इं अंनेक देवा जपैं स्वांमीं जै जै करैं ।

The merciful Lord is the Master of the masterless, O Nanak;
joining the company of the holy, one is saved. ‖ 2 ‖

अ 5 2–6 अनाथ नाथ दइआल नानक साधसंगति मिलि उधार ॥

C 2 अनाथ नाथ दयाल नांनिक । साधसंगति मिलि उधरैं ॥

Millions of gods and goddesses of wealth serve Him in so many ways.

अ 5 3–1 कोटि देवी जा कउ सेवहि लखिमी अनिक भाति ॥

C 3 कोटि देवी जा कूं सेवैं लिषिमीं अनेक भांति ।

The invisible and visible beings worship Him in adoration,
along with wind and water, day and night.

अ 5 3–2 गुपत प्रगट जा कउ अराधहि पउण पाणी दिनसु राति ॥

C 3 गुपत प्रगट जा कूं अराधैं । पवन पांणीं दिवस राति ।

the stars, the moon and the sun meditate on Him;
the earth and the sky sing to Him.

अ 5 3-3 नखिअत्र ससीअर सूर धिआवहि बसुध गगना गावए ॥
C 3 नषियत ससिहर सूर ध्यांवैं । बसुधा गगन गांवहीं ।

All the sources of creation, all languages meditate on Him, forever and ever.

अ 5 3-4 सगल खाणी सगल बाणी सदा सदा धिआवए ॥
C 3 चारि षांणीं चांरि बांणीं । सदा सदा हरि ध्यांवहीं ।

The Smritis, Puranas, four Vedas and six Shastras meditate on Him.

अ 5 3-5 सम्रिति पुराण चतुर बेदह खटु सासत्र जा कउ जपाति ॥
C 3 सुम्रित पुरांण चत्रु बेदा । षट सास्त्र जा कूं जपैं ।

He is the purifier of sinners, the lover of His saints;
O Nanak, He is met in the society of the saints. ॥ 3 ॥

अ 5 3-6 पतित पावन भगति वछल नानक मिलीऔ संगि साति ॥
C 3 पतित पांवन भगति बछल । नांनिक मिलि अघ कपैं ॥

As much as God has revealed to us, that we can speak with our tongues.

अ 5 4-1 जेती प्रभू जनाई रसना तेत भनी ॥
C 4 जीती प्रभु जणाई । रसनां तेत भणीं ।

Those unknown ones who serve You cannot be counted.

अ 5 4-2 अनजानत जो सेवै तेती नह जाइ गनी ॥
C 4 अणजांणत ज सेवैं । तेत न जाइ गिणीं ।

Imperishable, incalculable, and unfathomable is the Lord and Master;
He is everywhere, inside and out.

अ 5 4-3 अविगत अगनत अथाह ठाकुर सगल मंझे बाहरा ॥
C 4 अबिगत अगिणत अथाह ठाकुर । सकल मंझे बाहरा ।

We are all beggars, He is the one and only giver;
He is not far away, but is with us, ever-present.

अ5 4-4 सरब जाचिक एकु दाता नह दूरि संगी जाहरा ॥
C 4 सर्ब जाचिक एक दाता । नहीं दूरि संगी जाहरा ।

He is in the power of His devotees; those whose souls are united with Him
— how can their praises be sung?

अ 5 4-5 वसि भगत थीआ मिले जीआ ता की उपमा कित गनी ॥
C 4 बसि भगति थीया मिले जीया । तिन की उपमां केत गिणीं

May Nanak receive this gift and honor,
of placing his head on the feet of the holy saints. ॥ 4 ॥ 2 ॥ 5 ॥
अ 5 4-6 इहु दानु मानु नानकु पाए सीसु साधह धरि चरनी ॥
C 4 यहुं दांन मांन नांनिक पावै । स साधां धरै चरणीं ॥

Pada 22[32]

My mind is attached to the true Name.
My dealings with other people are only superficial. ॥1॥
अ 54 1a साचि नामि मेरा मनु लागा ॥ लोगन सिउ मेरा ठाठा बागा ॥

Outwardly, I am on good terms with all;
but I remain detached, like the lotus upon the water. ॥ 1 ॥ Pause ॥
अ 54 1b बाहरि सूतु सगल सिउ मउला ॥ अलिपतु रहउ जैसे जल महि कउला ॥ रहाउ ॥
C 0 बाहरि सुत्र सकल सूं मौला । अलिपत रहै जैसैं जल मैं कवला ॥

By word of mouth, I talk with everyone; I keep God clasped to my heart. ॥ 2 ॥
अ 54 2 मुख की बात सगल सिउ करता ॥ जीअ संगि प्रभु अपुना धरता ॥
C 1 मुष की बात सब इन सूं करता । जीव प्रांण अपनैं प्रभु धरता ॥

I may appear utterly terrible, but my mind is the dust of all men's feet.
अ 54 3 दीसि आवत है बहुतु भीहाला ॥ सगल चरन की इहु मनु राला ॥
C 2 ऊभा दीसै आवत बीहाला । यहु मन सकल चरन की राला ॥

Servant Nanak has found the Perfect Gurū.
Inwardly and outwardly, He has shown me the one Lord. ॥ 4 ॥ 3 ॥ 54 ॥
अ 54 4 नानक जनि गुरु पूरा पाइआ ॥ अंतरि बाहरि एकु दिखाइआ ॥
C 3 जन नानक थिर सतगुर पाया । बाहरि भीतरि एक धियाया ॥

Pada 23[33]

Listen to me, people: behold, and consider this within your mind.
अ 31 1c सुनि मेरी मनसा मनै माहि सति देखु बीचारि ॥
C 0 सुनि मेरी मनसा मनहीं मांहि । सति देषि बिचार ।

---

32. This *pada* is in the *Ādi-granth* attributed to *mahalā* 5, or Gurū Arjan (अ 54). As usual it has '*nānak*' as *bhaṇitā*. *ĀG*, p. 384, v 54 *āsā*; *C āsāvarī*.
33. This *pada* is in the *Ādi-granth* attributed to *mahalā* 5, or Gurū Arjan (अ 31). As usual it has '*nānak*' as *bhaṇitā*. *ĀG*, p. 808, न 31 *bilāvalū*; *C bilāvarī*.

The siddhas, the seekers, house-holders and yogis
have forsaken their homes and left. ‖ 1 ‖ Pause ‖

अ 31 1d सिध साधिक गिरही जोगी तजि गए घर बार ॥ रहाउ ॥

C 0 सिध साधिक जोगा ग्रिही । तजि गये घर बार ॥

This perishable realm and world has been made like a house of sand.

अ 31 1a म्रित मंडल जगु साजिआ जिउ बालू घर बार ॥

C 1 म्रित मंडल जग साजियौ । बालू घर बार ।

In no time at all, it is destroyed, like the paper drenched with water. ‖ 1 ‖

अ 31 1b बिनसत बार न लागई जिउ कागद बूंदार ॥

C 1 बिणसत बार न लागई । कागद बूंदार ॥

Where are your brothers and friends? Open your eyes and see!

अ 31 3a कहा सु भाई मीत है देखु नैन पसारि ॥

C 2 कहां स भाई मींत हौ । देषि नैंन पसारि ।

Some have gone, and some will go; everyone must take his turn. ‖ 3 ‖

अ 31 3b इकि चाले इकि चालसहि सभि अपनी वार ॥

C 2 एक चले हो खल सनीं । सब अपनीं बार ॥

This world is like a dream in the night.

अ 31 2a जैसा सुपना रैनि का तैसा संसार ॥

C 3 जैसा सुपिनां रैंनि का । तैसा संसार ।

Those who serve the true Gurū, remain ever-stable at the door of the Lord.

अ 31 4a जिन पूरा सतिगुरु सेविआ से असथिरु हरि दुआरि ॥

C 4 पूरा प्रभू जिनि सेविया । से अस्थिर हरि द्वारि ।

Servant Nanak is the Lord's slave;
preserve his honor, O Lord, destroyer of ego. ‖ 4 ‖ 1 ‖ 31 ‖

अ 31 4b जनु नानकु हरि का दासु है राखु पैज मुरारि ॥

C 4 नानक हरि कौ दास है । पैज राषि मुरारि ॥

Pada 24[34]

Those actions you perform, day and night, are recorded upon your forehead.

अ 13 1aa दिनु राति कमाइअड़ो सो आइओ माथै ॥

C 0 द्यौस रैंनि कमाइड़ा । सु आया माथैं ।

And the One, from whom you hide these actions —
He sees them, and is always with you.

अ 13 1abजिसु पासि लुकाइदड़ो सो वेखी साथै ॥

C 0 तिस पासि लुकांइदड़ा । सु देषै साथैं

The Creator Lord is with you; He sees you, so why commit sins?

अ 13 1b संगि देखै करणहारा काइ पापु कमाईऐ ॥

C 0 संगि देषै करणहारा । कांइ पाप कमाइये ।

Perform good deeds and chant the Name; you shall never have to go to hell.

अ 13 1c सुक्रितु कीजै नामु लीजै नरकि मूलि न जाईऐ ॥

C 5 सुक्रित कीजै नांव लीजै । नरकि मूलि न जाइये ।

Twenty-four hours a day, dwell upon the Lord's Name in meditation;
it alone shall go along with you.

अ 13 1d आठ पहर हरि नामु सिमरहु चलै तेरै साथे ॥

C 5 आठा पहर हरि नांव सुमिरौ । चुलै तुम्हारै साथै ।

So vibrate continually in the company of the holy, O Nanak,
and the sins you committed shall be erased. ॥ 1 ॥

अ 13 1e भजु साधसंगति सदा नानक मिटहि दोख कमाते ॥

C 5 भजि साधसंगति सदा नांनका । मिटै पाप कमाते ॥

Practicing deceit, you fill your belly, you ignorant fool!

अ 13 2a वलवंच करि उदरु भरहि मूरख गावारा ॥

C 6 बलवंच करि उदर भरि रे । मूरिष गंवारा ।

The Lord, the great giver, continues to give you everything.

अ13 2b सभु किछु दे रहिआ हरि देवणहारा ॥

C 6 सब कुछ देइ रह्या प्रभू देवणहारा ।

---

34. This *pada* is in the *Ādi-granth* attributed to *mahalā* 5, or Gurū Arjan (अ 13). As usual it has '*nānak*' as *bhaṇitā*. *ĀG*, p. 461, न 13, *āsā*; *C rāmgirī*.

The great giver is always merciful.
Why should we forget the Lord master from our minds?
अ 13 2c दातारु सदा दइआलु सुआमी काइ मनहु विसारीऔ ॥
C 6 देवणहारु दातारु सदा दयाल स्वांमीं । कांइ मनहुं बिसारिये

Join the company of the holy and vibrate fearlessly;
all your relations shall be saved.
अ 13 2d मिलु साधसंगे भजु निसंगे कुल समूहा तारीए ॥
C 6 भजि साधसंगे जपि निसंगे । कुल सबूवा तारिये ।

The siddhas, the seekers, the demi-gods, the silent sages and the devotees,
all take the Name as their support.
अ 13 2e सिध साधिक देव मुनि जन भगत नामु अधारा ॥
C 6 सिध साधिक देव मुनि जन भगति नांव अधारा ।

Prays Nanak, vibrate continually upon God, the one creator Lord. ॥ 2 ॥
अ 13 2f बिनवंति नानक सदा भजीऔ प्रभु एकु करणैहारा ॥
C 6 बिनवंत नांनिक सदा जपिये । एक करणहारा ॥

Do not practice deception—God is the assayer of all.
अ 13 3a खोटु न कीचई प्रभु परखणहारा ॥
C 7 षोट न कीजै प्रभू परषनहारा ।

Those who practice falsehood and deceit are reincarnated in the world.
अ 13 3b कूड़ु कपटु कमावदड़े जनमहि संसारा ॥
C 7 कूड़ कपटु कमांवंदाड़े मरि जनमें संसारा

Those who meditate on the one Lord, cross over the world-ocean.
अ 13 3c संसारु सागरु तिन्ही तरिआ जिन्ही एकु धिआइआ ॥
C 7 संसार सागर तिनहि तिरिया । जिन्हि एकु ध्याया ।

Renouncing sexual desire, anger, flattery, slander, they enter the refuge of God.
अ 13 3d तजि कामु क्रोधु अनिंद निंदा प्रभु सरणाई आइआ ॥
C 7 तजि कांम क्रोध अन्यंद न्यंदा । तजि प्रभू सरनैं आया ।

The lofty, inaccessible and infinite Lord and Master
is pervading the water, the land and the sky.
अ 13 3e जलि थलि महीअलि रविआ सुआमी ऊच अगम अपारा ॥
C 7 जलि थलि महियलि रम्यां स्वांमीं । ऊंचा अगम अपारा ।

Prays Nanak, He is the support of His servants;
His lotus feet are their only sustenance. ॥ 3

अ 13 3f बिनवंति नानक टेक जन की चरण कमल अधारा ॥

C 7 बिनवंत नांनक टेक जन की । चरन कवल अधारा ॥

Behold-the world is a mirage; nothing here is permanent.

अ 13 4a पेखु हरिचंदउरङी असथिरु किछु नाही ॥

C 8 पेषि हरिचंदौरङियां । प्रांणीं असाथिर किछु नांहीं ।

The pleasures of Maya which are here, shall not go with you.

अ 13 4b माइआ रंग जेते से संगि न जाही ॥

C 8 माया के रंग रूप । तेरे संगि न जांहीं ।

The Lord, your companion, is always with you; remember Him day and night.

अ 13 4c हरि संगि साथी सदा तेरै दिनसु रैणि समालीऐ ॥

C 8 संग साथी सदा तेरै । द्यौस रैंणि संमालिये ।

Without the one Lord, there is no other; burn away the love of duality.

अ 13 4d हरि एक बिनु कछु अवरु नाही भाउ दुतीआ जालीऐ ॥

C 8 उस एक बिन को नाहि दूजा । भाव दुतिया जालिए ।

Know that the one God is your friend, youth, wealth and everything.

अ 13 4e मीतु जोबनु मालु सरबसु प्रभु एकु करि मन माही ॥

C 8 मींतु जोबन मालु सरबस । एकु करु मन मांहीं ।

Prays Nanak, by great good fortune, we find the Lord,
and merge in peace and celestial poise. ॥ 4 ॥ 4 ॥ 13 ॥

अ 13 4f बिनवंति नानकु वडभागि पाईऐ सूखि सहजि समाहि ॥

C 8 बिनवंत नांनक बडभागि पाइए । सहज सुष संमांहीं ॥

Pada 25[35]

My pride is gone, O friends and companions; my doubt is dispelled,
and the Gurū has united me with my beloved. ॥ 1 ॥ Pause ॥

अ 53 1b चुका निहोरा सखी सहेरी ॥ भरमु गइआ गुरि पिर संगि मेरी ॥ रहाउ ॥

C 10 चूका निहोरा सषी सहेली । भरम गया तब पीव संग षेली ॥

F 0 चूका हो निहोरा सषी सहेली । भरम गंमाया तव पीव संगि षेली ॥

---

35. This *pada* is in the *Ādi-granth* attributed to *mahalā* 5, or Gurū Arjan (अ 53). As usual it has '*nānak*' as *bhaṇitā*. *ĀG*, p. 384, *āsā*; *C jaṅglī gauḍī*.

I suffered in pain, when I thought He was far away;
but now, He is ever-present, and I receive His instructions. || 1 ||

अ 53 1a दूखु घनो जब होते दूरि ॥ अब मसलति मोहि मिली हदूरि ॥
C 1 दुष घणां जब रहती दूरि । इब मोहि मजलिसि भई हजूरि ॥
F 1 दुष घणां जव रहती दूरि । अव मोहि मंजलसि भई हजूरि ॥

My Beloved has drawn me near to Him, and seated me on His bed;
I have escaped the clutches of others. || 2 ||

अ 53 2 निकटि आनि प्रिअ सेज धरी ॥ काणि कढन ते छूटि परी ॥
C 2 निकट सेज प्रभू आंणि धरी । काढ कढण थैं छूटि परी ॥
F 2 निकट सेज प्रभू आंणि धरी । काढण थैं अव छूटि परी ॥

In the mansion of my heart, shines the light of the Sabad.
My husband Lord is blissful and playful. || 3 ||

अ 53 3 मंदरि मेरै सबदि उजारा ॥ अनद बिनोदी खसमु हमारा ॥
C 3 मंदिर हमारै सबद उजाला आंनंद बिनोदी प्रभू हमारा ॥
F 3 मंदिर हमारै सवद उजाला । अनंद विनोदी प्रभू हमारा ॥

According to the destiny written on my forehead, my husband has come home to me. Servant Nanak has obtained the eternal marriage. || 4 || 2 || 53 ||

अ 53 4 मसतकि भागु मै पिरु घरि आइआ ॥ थिरु सोहागु नानक जन पाइआ ॥
C 4 मस्तकि भाग जिसि पीव घरि आया । थिर सुहाग नांनिक जनि पाया ॥
F 4 मस्तकि भाग जिनि पीय घरि आया । थिर शुहाग नांनिक जनि पाया ॥

Pada 26[36]

G ॥ नांनक जी का पद ॥ राग सोरठ ॥
G 0 मन रे हरि भजि रांम संवेरे ।
G 0 जैसा करै तैसा ही पावै । प्रभु मेरा हाथौं हाथ न बे रे ॥
G 1 बहुते जगि करे रघुराजा । मन मैं भई बडाई ।
G 1 करि अहंकार तपे रथ जोये । जोनि सरप की पाई ॥
G 2 मन अभिमांन कीयौ थौ रांवणिं । कूंभकरण देषि भाई ।
G 2 दसरथि नंदनिं मारि बिडार्‍यौ । लंक बभीषाणिं पाई ॥
G 3 दुबे प्रीति गई जादवनिंमौ । मन मैं कपट रचाया ।

36. *Pada* 26 is in Śarmā, *Gurū Nānak vāṇī*, Candigarh: Viśva Bharatī Prakaśan, 1978, p. 32, reprinted with some variants (adapting the reading to modern Hindī!) from the same manuscript No. 2 of A.D. 1676 in the Dādū Mahāvidyālaya, Jaipur that I copied. In a note the author states that 'this *pada* is also found in the *Ravidās vāṇī*, with the name "Raidās" ', but so far I have not been able to locate the *pada*.

G 3 करि निंद्या साधू हरि जंन की । अपनां बंस गंमाया ॥
G 4 यहु संसारु कजल की कोठी । यहु जगु बिष का कूवा ।
G 4 कहि नांनक माया जगु षाया । ज्यौं नलनीं भ्रंमिं सूवा ॥

The 'Other' in the World of the Faithful

Vasudha Dalmia

In the debates around communalism and secularism, which became acute from the late 1980s on, it was Ashis Nandy who brought the term 'faith' into circulation again. Nandy suggested that the monoliths constructed in the modern age, particularly those which had positioned themselves as mutually hostile communal blocs in South Asia, could best be understood if religion were viewed in two ways: the one as a way of life and the other as ideology. This has proved to be a controversial suggestion, which has been variously contested. Almost as if in anticipation of this debate, Nandy himself not only admitted that both terms did, indeed, seem inadequate, he specified in what sense he was using them:

> By faith I mean religion as a way of life, a tradition which is definitionally non-monolithic and operationally plural. I say 'definitionally' because unless a religion is geographically and culturally confined to a small area, it has as a way of life, in effect, to turn into a confederation of a number of ways of life which are linked by a common faith that has some theological space for the heterogeneity which everyday life introduces. Witness the differentiation between Iranian and Indonesian Islams, two cultures which can be said to be divided by the same faith. The two forms of Islam are interlocking, not isomorphic, in relation to each other.
>
> By ideology I mean religion as a sub-national, national or cross-national identifier of populations contesting for or protecting non-religious, usually political or socio-economic interests. Such religion-as-ideologies usually get identified with one or more texts which, rather than the ways of life of the believers, then become the final identifiers of the pure forms of the religions. The texts help anchor the ideologies in something seemingly concrete and delimited, and in effect provide a set of manageable operational definitions.[1]

---

1. Ashis Nandy, 'The Politics of Secularism and the Recovery of Religious Tolerance,' in *Mirrors of Violence: Communities, Riots and Survivors in South Asia*, ed. by Veena Das, New Delhi: Oxford University Press, 1990, p. 70.

The idealized folk-ways, which make for religion-as-faith, rooted as they still are in the pre-modern, allow theological leeway for the heterogeneity of every-day life. It follows that religion-as-ideology, which Nandy identifies with one or more texts, is a modern phenomenon. If we could return to the pre-modern form, he seems to be suggesting, we could recover the pluralistic and the tolerant. The problems here are manifold; they arise partly because Nandy in proposing the first category (religion-as-faith) is operating on the principle of unity-in-diversity, evolved and propagated by the very nationalist ideologues who, according to him, contributed to the construction of the second idiom (religion-as-ideology). It seems to be a circular argument, not substantiated by historical or sociological data, one of the traps for the unwary who seek to by-pass the communal-secular divide by positing new categories, which may or may not square with historical data or indeed with contemporary experience.

Historically, faith has not precluded intolerance; in periods of intense proselytization, precisely when faith at its most intense is being evoked, there can be and has been violent rivalry. And in times of political change, past as much as present, matters of faith have often been politicized, though not quite on the scale made possible by modern media.[2] Thus tolerance and intolerance, diffuse religiosity and ideologically driven religiosity, could and did coexist in past periods. Yet to insist that there have been no major shifts in these patterns during the colonial period and thereafter, would make for another kind of myopia. Clearly, we need to be more attentive to the self-definitions and demarcations of religious communities in the pre-modern period, and note particularly how they proclaimed their difference to each other and the level of tolerance they accorded or denied each other. Perhaps we can make small beginnings by viewing the modes through which those pre-modern traditions which sought to define and demarcate themselves clearly, themselves defined difference. Eventually, we may be able to pool enough information to arrive at clearer notions of intra-regional linkages and hostilities and to evolve a vocabulary which does justice to these. We may then be able to map the larger sub-continental picture.

The so-called bhakti movements and the religious communities or *sampradāya*s, which swept through North India from the late fifteenth century onwards were surely 'faith' based. However, the rivalries within a given cluster of religious groups were often bitter, precisely because the message they preached was not so dissimilar and the audiences they addressed comprised of similar social groups. Did faith make for more tolerance, particularly when a given community sought to distinguish itself from competing groups? What resources could it muster to outpace the

2. See Vasudha Dalmia, 'Mosques, Temples and Fields of Disputation in a Late Eighteenth Century Chronicle,' *Studies in History* 20.1 (January-June 2004), pp. 59-72.

others? As Richard Burghart pointed out many years ago, when speaking of the Rāmānandī movement which began to gain momentum and acquire a large following from the sixteenth century onwards:

> In order to maintain themselves over time, the ascetics of the various Hindu sects required access to three important resources: devotees and disciples, pilgrimage routes and pilgrimage centers, and political patronage. The availability of these resources was limited. Although some ascetic sects were founded in the outlying regions of the sub-continent, nearly all of them, like the Ramanadi sect, eventually spread over the Ganges basin where, given the number of sects operating on that territory, the competition for these resources was very intense. In the competition for devotees and disciples, Ramanand's sect gained a significant advantage over the rival sects. The servant castes, untouchables, women, and former Hindus who had converted by choice or by threat of force to Islam comprised more than three fourths of the population of the Ganges basin and constituted an immense hitherto unexploited source of devotees and disciples for an ascetic sect.[3]

The web of ascetic and indeed non-ascetic orders, offering old and new paths of salvation, competed at the same locations, to attract the same kinds of people. Future recruits were obviously most easily to be found on pilgrimage routes and at pilgrim centres. It was at these sites that both kinds of groups were to be met—those who were still seeking and those who thought they had already found the answers. Both could respond to the power of a message and the mode of its conveyance.

However, at pilgrimage centres, there was also the additional problem of relating to, or indeed sharing power, with the all-powerful temple-deity, or in some credible way contesting it. We shall see that this is an issue, which the text discussed below addresses directly. And finally there was the question of political patronage, though it was of greatest importance in a later phase, when consolidation was the order of the day. In the earlier, expansive preaching phase, the devotees themselves were the major consideration. Here it was surely the message itself, that which distinguished a given *sampradāya* from all the others, which counted most. Thus, even if the conversion 'took place along a continuum,' between 'sought fixities and practised fluidities' and the boundaries between *sampradāyas* did indeed seem porous, it was precisely the effort to preserve difference and prevent overlapping that propelled the move towards 'icy clarities.'[4] Transgressions could only be fiercely and remorselessly punished.

3. Richard Burghart, 'The Founding of the Ramandi Sect,' *Ethnohistory* 25, pp. 121-39, p. 126.

4. Thus Sangari's on the process we encounter repeatedly in the texts at hand: 'Evidently, till the seventeenth century, conversion, conventionally defined as a sudden shift from one

In viewing the terms in which the Puṣṭimārg, or the way of fulfillment, one of the two major devotional communities centred around Kṛṣṇa-worship, came to define itself in relationship to other groups which today comprise Hinduism at large, I hope to trace its modes of demarcation, not in order to insist on their continued validity today, but to make it possible to map out more precisely the shifts when they did occur.

Definitions and Demarcations of New Movements: the Puṣṭimārg

The Puṣṭimārg was established in 1492 by Vallabha (1478-1530), to be further expanded and consolidated by his son Viṭṭhalnāth (1516-86), whose period of activity coincided with the expansion and consolidation of the Mughal empire. If we go by the later hagiographical compendia, it was the very groups of which Burghart speaks, the servant castes and women, who were the prime addresses of the Puṣṭimārg in its initial phase.

The Vallabha *sampradāya* has attracted much research: in his *The Bhakti Sect of Vallabhācārya* (1976) Richard Barz has offered the most extensive account of its theological basis in English.[5] The art, music and ritual which the *sampradāya* developed to such fine arts have inspired a steady spate of monographs.[6] But we possess relatively little knowledge of the life worlds of the people who were drawn to it, though Richard J. Cohen offered some sociological information in the article, 'Sectarian Vaishnavism: the Vallabha Sampradaya.'[7] Who were the first devotees, what information do we have on their lives? How were they drawn into Vallabha's fold? I

---

belief system to another, took place along a continuum ... Conversion was also tied to illumination—the sudden eruption of a new faith through miracles, sight of a holy person, teaching of preceptors, leading to an 'awakening' or immediate transformation. Finally, conversion was often interleaved in individual trajectories of eclectic experimentation, moving from faith to faith though the pathways of intellectual curiosity, spiritual quest, theological attraction, personal friendship and dialogue.' Kumkum Sangari, 'Tracing Akbar: Hagiographies, Popular Narrative Traditions and the Subject of Conversion,' in *Mapping Histories: Essays Presented to Ravinder Kumar*, ed. by Neera Chandhoke, New Delhi: Tulika, 2000, p. 93.

5. Faridabad: Thomson Press (India) Ltd.

6. To name a few: Anne-Marie Gaston, *Krishna's Musicians: Music-Making in the Temples of Nathdvara Rajasthan*, New Delhi: Manohar, 1997, on the music of Nathdwara; Norbert Peabody, *Hindu Kingship and Polity in Precolonial India*, Cambridge: Cambridge University Press, 2003, on ritual and political power, and Tryna Lyons, *The Artists of Nathdwara: The Practice of Painting in Rajasthan*, Bloomington: Indiana University Press, in association with Mapin Publishing, Ahmedabad, 2004, on the artists of Nathdwara as they negotiated the transition into the modern.

7. In *Identity and Division in Cults and Sects in South Asia*, ed. by Peter Gaeffke and David A. Utz. Proceedings of South Asia Seminar, 1980-1981, Philadelphia: Department of South Asia Regional Studies, University of Pennsylvania, 1984, pp. 69-72.

have turned repeatedly to the hagiographical compendia of the *sampradāya* in the effort to glean information on the religious and emotional lives of people represented as the ordinary followers, who often left all their worldly possessions to follow their teacher.[8] My interest has remain focused on the *Caurāsī vaiṣṇavan kī vārtā*, or the account of the eighty-four Vaiṣṇavas who are considered the first followers of the *sampradāya*, initiated by Vallabha himself, who is referred to as *Ācāryajī* or preceptor. There exists also a second important compendium, comprising the tales of the two hundred and fifty-two followers credited to Viṭṭhalnāth. To draw information on the lives of the first community as celebrated in a hagiographical compendium is a risky enterprise. The lives have already been moulded to form a pattern, to become exemplary. Yet the self-representation does offer some indication of the people being addressed, since it was to move them that the tales were cast into a particular form to be then told and retold to the generations that followed.

According to Hariharnāth Ṭaṇḍan, who has to date offered the most comprehensive study of the two compendia,[9] the collections first comprised just the kernel of the tales circulating orally in the *sampradāya* which were then written down by Kṛṣṇa Bhatt, one of the elect. Gokulnāth, in the third generation of the Vallabha clan, is credited with officially acknowledging the presence and importance of these tales. They were later ordered in compendia of eighty-four and two hundred and fifty-two tales each, and yet later, in the fourth generation, and by this time Brajbhāṣā had almost entirely replaced Sanskrit as the liturgical language of the community, Gokulnāth's nephew and pupil Harirāyjī further reworked them by folding them into a commentarial frame which located these tales firmly within the theology of the *sampradāya*. The commentary often tempered the radical content of the tales and softened the rough edges, offering much further biographical information on the life circumstances of the devotees. Harirāyjī is supposed to have been completed this commentarial work around A.D. 1696, towards the end of his life.[10]

---

8. See Vasudha Dalmia, 'Forging Community: The Guru in a Seventeenth Century Vaishnava Hagiography,' in *Charisma and Canon: Essays on the Religious History of the Indian Subcontinent*, ed. by Vasudha Dalmia, Angelika Malinar and Martin Christof, Delhi: Oxford University Press, 2001, and id., 'Women, Duty and Sanctified Space in a Vaiṣṇava Hagiography of the Seventeenth Century,' in *Constructions hagiographiques en Inde: entre mythe et histoire*, ed. by Françoise Mallison, Paris: École Pratique des Hautes Études, IVième Section – Sciences historiques et philologiques – Serie II: Hautes Études Orientales, 2001.

9. Hariharnāth Ṭaṇḍan, *Vārtā-sāhitya (Ek bṛhat adhyayan)*, Aligarh: Bhārat Prakāśan Mandir, [1960].

10. Cf. Barz, *The Bhakti* Sect, p. 102. I have based my study on the edition by Dvārikādās Parīkh, *Caurāsī vaiṣṇavan kī vārtā (tīn janma kī līlā bhāvanā vālī)*, Mathura: Śrī Bajraṅg Pustakālay, V.S. 2027 (A.D. 1970). Parīkh has put the original *vārtā* or tale in bold print, so

The main *vārtā* or *prasaṅga*s relate, if taken by themselves, in a somewhat unmediated way—for they are often raw tales of emotion and release—the experience of the ecstasy, preceded by one kind of trial or another, which follows the encounter with Ācāryajī and the life of intimacy with the Ṭhākurjī, or the lord, which he mediates. In considering the ideology as embedded in the tales and the commentary thereon, we have to bear in mind that the *vārtā*s are not the site for detailed theological debates; they are, much more, rough and ready models of lives in the devotional mode. The biographical details of the devotee's life, before he or she was received by Ācārayajī, are invariably contained in the *Bhāv-prakāś* or commentary section, rather than the original *vārtā*. It is here that we are told the *jāti* name of the devotee and informed of the family circumstances and the exact nature of the suffering which first moved the devotee to seek spiritual guidance. It is impossible to know whether these are fictional accounts, added later for effect, or whether, in fact, they are based on 'real' facts and figures, certainly Ṭaṇḍan treats them thus.

The suffering of which the tales speak is of two kinds, either loss or deprivation of one kind or another, which leaves the devotee with almost no resource to fall back upon, or, the suffering which ensues when the devotee is early in life overcome by the kind of *vairāgya* or intense detachment which leaves him unfit to lead a normal house-holding life. He can then wander from one kind of mendicant to another, one false teacher to another, till he alights upon Ācāryajī or one of his followers, who then enlightens the devotee also in regard to the falseness of the previous teaching. Clearly there is much scope here for description of other routes to salvation and those who preach them, even if it is only to dismantle their claim.

How are other religious groups and figures of religious authority, then, described? *Anya* or other, is the most important term used in this regard. *Anyāśraya* means to seek refuge of another, *anyamārgīya* is a person who follows another path. Some of the *anya* will be found to be so outside the pale, that they will be roundly condemned and rejected. At other points, it will be more important to establish equations rather than indulge in outright rejection. This will be the case with the great Vaiṣṇava temple deities at the most powerful pilgrimage centres, as we will see below. The treatment of other temples and gods and goddesses will be more condescending. And in one interesting case, the deity considered alien will just be replaced.

As for mainstream Brahminical religious authority, we will find that Smārta ritual will be held up to ridicule and thus disempowered. This will

---

that the commentary, which frames the tale and often intersperses it, become visible as such. Parīkh maintains that his intentions are literary; his claim being that the Brajbhāṣā prose in which these tales are told is the earliest written prose in Brajbhāṣā to document living speech.

also be the treatment reserved for other religious leaders of the time, particularly the Vaiṣṇava leaders. And finally, the punishment for seeking refuge with leaders of other faiths, 'folk' or otherwise, will be violent, in some cases leading to death.

Distancing from Smārta Rites and Rituals: *Varṇāśramadharma*, *Saṃskāras* and *Vartās*

There is no violent detachment from Smārta Brahminical prescriptives, but a myriad tales suggest that the Puṣṭimārg regards itself as a sharp departure from the dictates of *varṇāśramadharma*, from *karmakāṇḍa* or ritual, particularly the life-cycle rituals and fasting and from Śaṅkara's *māyāvād*.[11] These are regarded as polarities and are often subject to extreme polemics.

To begin with the vexed question of *varṇa* and the question, whether in fact, the faith was open to the lower castes and the status accorded to those from the lower castes who were accepted in the fold. It is not as if the matter is explicitly thematized and a definitive stand taken with regard to it. Once again, it is likely that there were many changes after the first period, particularly after the *sampradāya* was firmly established and there was enough princely patronage to ensure its high status, public visibility and obvious stability. It is clear, however, that in this first period, Brahmans did not automatically have the higher status, particularly if they were *anyamārgīya*. A closer look at a *vārtā* centrally placed in the compendium would lead us to conclude that though at the end of the tale, the *varṇa* hierarchy is not finally destabilized, it is at least much qualified ideologically, reflecting presumably the lived reality of that early period which forms the mainstay of the tales.

The central protagonist of the *vārtā* is one Viṣṇudās Chīpā[12] from a village near Agra. The *vārtā* consists of three episodes or *prasaṅgas*, two of which have to do with matters of *varṇa* hierarchy. In the first episode, Ācāryajī happens to be passing through the bazaar in Agra, when his eyes

---

11. See Dalmia, 'Forging Community,' p. 138 for a brief discussion of the conflictual relationship with *māyāvād*.

12. 'Not only are the Chīpās distinctly low-caste, they are, additionally a mixture of Hindus and Muslims, since many groups amongst them were early converted to Islam. The Chīpās form a distinct caste who employ themselves in printing and stamping chintz or other cotton cloths, and are said to have originally come from Pindarpore in the Deccan. They are Hindus as well as Musalmans ... Some of them also work as tailors... They [the Musalman Chīpās] follow the same calling as the Hindu Chīpās, and also comprise several tribes of converted Rajputs who are said long ago, to have adopted the profession of dyers. They form a distinct caste from that of the Rangrez, and do not marry the latter. They are Sunnis.' (Munshi Hardyal [*sic!*] Singh, *The Castes of Marwar*, 2nd ed., Jodhpur: Book Treasure, 1995 [1st ed. 1984], p. 170.)

fall upon bales of beautifully printed calico cloth. He instructs his follower Kṛṣṇadās to purchase these. The seller is a young man, Viṣṇudās, who sells his father's wares in Agra. Viṣṇudās asks fourfold the usual price of the cloth and to his surprise receives it. But he is alarmed, once he realizes the identity of the buyer, that he is a close disciple of the powerful Ācārya. It seems better not to have to do with such folks; who knows what kind of renunciatory activity could ensue, once their money found entry into the cloth printers' workshop? His effort to undo the transaction are unsuccessful. He finally asks to see Ācāryajī and when he does so, he is moved by some deep inner compulsion to throw himself at his feet and ask to be accepted into the fold. Ācāryajī poses his usual question: 'You live in the Chīpan, the cloth printers' quarter; will you be able to practise the ways of the Puṣṭimārg?' Viṣṇudās assures him that he will either persuade his family to adopt them also, or separate himself entirely from them. Ācāryajī communicates the contents of his teaching to Viṣṇudās in a remarkably short space of time but he asks him not to follow him to Arel, but to wait rather in the Braj area till Śrī Gusāiṁjī comes to settle in Gokul. This is where the *vārtā* text proper sets in. Viṣṇudās has become aged, he is immensely learned, but he has remained unassuming and he waits at Śrī Gusāiṁjī's door. He soon observes that Śrī Gusāiṁjī gets a string of Brahman visitors who engage him in debate. They are invariably defeated, but it means strain for Śrī Gusāiṁjī. So, Viṣṇudās decides to deal with their arguments and send them off (*prati uttar kari bidā kari deuṁ*). Eventually Śrī Gusāiṁjī notices that he has been thus relieved and puts a stop to it, pronouncing that though Viṣṇudās has knowledge of the *śāstras*, thanks to Śrī Ācāryajī, the Brahmans who come to his door cannot be allowed to go away empty-handed; he will therefore engage with them himself. Thus Gusāiṁjī seems to be restoring the older balance of power.

But there are contradictions in the attitude of Gusāiṁjī himself, for the crowning incident in the matter of caste hierarchy takes place when Śrī Gusāiṁjī has to fulfill a wish expressed by his own father-in-law, a Bhaṭṭ from Mathura. The Bhaṭṭ regularly asks to be allowed to feed the Vaiṣṇavas of the area and Śrī Gusāiṁjī as regularly asks him to stay out of these matters. Once when Śrī Gusāiṁjī is himself to dine at his father-in-law's place, he asks Viṣṇudās to accompany him. He trusts Viṣṇudās above all other Vaiṣṇavas, when it comes to reacting appropriately in a tricky situation. After Śrī Gusāiṁjī has eaten at his father-in-laws house, he leaves his left-overs, considered very auspicious (*mahāprasād*) for Viṣṇudās to partake of and himself departs. The Bhaṭṭ tries to serve him fresh food, but Viṣṇudās declines. He refuses, in fact, to let the Bhaṭṭ touch his food, it would become impure. The Bhaṭṭ is angered and follows Śrī Gusāiṁjī to Gokul to expressly ask him, how it was that he, a Brahman, could pollute a Śūdra's food? The answer is clear. It is spelt out at great length in the *Bhāv-*

prakāś that follows: Do not take from the hands of one that follows another path (*anya margīya ke hāth ko sarvathā na leno*, p. 285), even if he is a high standing Brahman and a close relative at that. Viṣṇudās is placed higher in the hierarchy than the Brahman father-in-law because he is a Vaiṣṇava.

The matter is further explicated in the *Bhāv-prakāś* passages which introduce the *vārtā* of Bhagvāndās, Sārasvat Brahman from Hājīpur. Bhagvāndās asks: 'Maharāj, a Śūdra fetches your water and scours your vessels for you. I am a Brahman, why don't you let me carry out these tasks?' Śrī Ācāryajī replies: 'In our faith (*mat*) those who do not know God are more down and out than Śūdras. And those who do know God are the highest Brahmans. This is how much difference there is (p. 290).'

Brahminical authority is also undermined in connection with the performance of life cycle rituals, or the chief *saṃskāras*, which are so formative a feature of *dvija* or twice-born identity and make for a sense of community.[13] However, in the Puṣṭimārg which is constituting itself as an autonomous community, there will be little tolerance for any kind of Smārta *saṃskāra*s. Evidence of this is found scattered through the compendium. I have selected two tales, which focus upon two life cycle rituals: *caula* or *muṇḍana*, that is, the tonsure of the head performed in early childhood,[14] and the death rites. Not only is the Brahminical performance of these rites negated but also the merit of performing them at particularly auspicious pilgrimage sites.[15] Thus, *muṇḍana*, or the *saṃskāra* of shaving the head in Prayag, which is supposed to bring particular fruit, is explicitly highlighted as a fruitless exercise. As the *Bhāv-prakāś* which precedes his *vārtā* tells us, Gopāldās of Banswara is born of a father who had pledged that if this child

---

13. Cf. Kane: 'The saṃskāras had been treated from very ancient times as necessary for unfolding the latent capacities of man for development and as being outward symbols or signs of the inner change which would fit human beings for corporate life and they also tended to confer a certain status on those who underwent them.' (Pandurang Vaman Kane, *History of Dharma-śāstra (Ancient and Mediaeval Religious and Civil Law)*, vol. 2.1, 2nd ed., Poona: Bhandarkar Oriental Research Institute, p. 192).

14. Cf. Kane: 'First as to the purpose of the saṃskāras. Manu (II. 27-28) says in the case of dvijātis, the taints (or sins) due to seed and the uterus (i.e. derived from parents) are wiped off by the *homas* (burnt oblations) performed during pregnancy and by jātakarma (ceremonies on birth), caula (tonsure) and the tying of the girdle of muñja grass. This (human body) is rendered fit for the attainment of *brahma* by the study of the Veda, by the vrata called traividya, by worship (of gods, sages and manes), by generations of sons, by the performance of the five daily sacrifices and by (solemn Vedic) sacrifices.' (Ibid., p. 191) As Kane further clarifies, there is great divergence of opinion about the number of obligatory *saṃskāras*. However, all the *smṛtis* mention *caula* or *cūḍākarma* (Ibid., p. 197).

15. As Bharadwaj has shown, life cycle rituals performed at sacred places have particular significance and there has evolved a functional specialization of sacred places, thus Gaya for *śrāddha* rituals, but also Kurukshetra and Pehoa 'specialize in the performance of death rites for a person whose death occurred accidentally or in bed.' (Surinder Mohan Bhardwaj, *Hindu Places of Pilgrimage in India [A Study in Cultural Geography]*, Berkeley, Los Angeles: University of California Press, 1973, p. 150).

survived, his head would be shorn in Prayag. But he is a Khatrī, much occupied with his trade; he does not find the time and the leisure to fulfill this pledge. When Gopāldās is ten or eleven years old, his father hires a carriage and sends him with a *gumāśtā*, an agent, to Prayag, so that this *saṃskāra* is performed and his marriage can take place. But the child Gopāldās refuses to do so, when he gets there. He says: 'Do you want to send me straight to hell by doing this?' His father has made a fool of himself by making this pledge. And he deliberately goes five *kroṣas* outside this area to have his head shaven. And soon after this, he accosts Ācāryajī on the banks of the river and asks to be accepted by him (pp. 164-5).

Death rites at particularly auspicious sites are treated with similar disdain. When Prabhudās Bhāṭ, Khatrī from Singhnand, reaches old age and becomes decrepit and so weak that he has no idea of where he finds himself, his relatives take him to Pṛthodaka *tīrtha* or modern Pehoa to die. When Prabhudās becomes aware of where his relatives have brought him, he protests vigorously. He demands to be taken back to Singhnand, so that he can take leave of this life in the presence of his *svarūpa*. His relatives refuse to heed this plea. But Prabhudās becomes well enough to be taken back to Singhnand. It is there, safe at the feet of his *svarūpa*, that he takes leave of his body. Then all the Vaiṣṇavas there collect to praise him. He had held death at bay for so long in order *not* to die in a *tīrtha* (pp. 140-1).

There is general discouragement of ascetic practice, of making the body suffer excessively, and in this connection the *vārtā*s propagate a teaching which is against fasting at large. In a culture where fasting is rampant, fasts are not explicitly forbidden. However, they are severely restricted,[16] only certain very specific fasts are to be observed.[17] This is brought out very clearly in a *vārtā* which seems to be included in the compendium precisely to illustrate this. The two devotees who are its focus remain unnamed, they are known simply as the husband and wife from Singhnand. From early in their lives they deny themselves pleasure. As they see it, the delights of the world are good enough for dogs and donkeys; they have taken human birth in order to learn how to discipline and control the senses. And so they ignore the pleas of their parents to enjoy life while they are young and find instead a hundred ways to afflict their body with suffering in order to practise asceticism. One day as they are standing

---

16. Cf. Kane: 'There is an immense literature on vratas. There is no topic of Dharmaśāstra except probably that of the tīrthyatra and of śrāddha on which the Purāṇas wax so eloquent as on vrata. Some of the Purāṇas contain thousands of verses on vrata.' (Kane, *History of Dharmaśāstra*, vol. 5.1 [1974], p. 57).

17. This is hardly surprising in a *sampradāya* in which the yearly ritual calendar would lay so much importance on food, and go on to develop one of the finest temple cuisines in North India. See Paul M. Toomey, *Food from the Mouth of Krishna: Feasts and Festivities in a North Indian Pilgrimage Centre*, Delhi: Hindustan Publishing Corporation, 1994.

shivering in the river in the cold of the evening, Śrī Ācāryajī arrives at the bank of the river to perform his evening ablutions. He asks: 'Who are these two, who stand in the cold water, looking extremely weak (*mahā durbal*)?' He is told that they afflict the body with great hardship in the hope that it will dry up altogether. Ācāryajī asks that they be brought to him so that he find some resolution to this self-negating life style. And he explains to them that this is not the way to gain the lord, particularly in this life, as they desire. They take shelter with him; he gives them a *svarūpa* and a mantra and he hands them over to the Vaiṣṇavas of Singhnand, proclaiming that these two, man and wife, are mine. Look to their needs. And he explains to the two that only five fasts are to be observed, the four *jayantī*s and *ekādaśī*, since they are connected to Viṣṇu. All other fasts are no longer to be observed. Once their time in Singhnand is over, the husband and wife move on to another place. This is where the *vārtā* takes over and relates the incident where Ṭhākurjī is so pleased with their humble, self-denying ways, that he begins to speak with them, though once again, this is the kind of good fortune, which they have no means at their disposal to receive without feeling inadequate (pp. 323-7). The *vārtā* leaves the auditor in little doubt as to the advisability of such extreme behaviour; Ācāryajī tempers it, so that it becomes bearable to themselves and the community.

As Padmarāval tells Ācāryajī, when he seeks refuge with him, he has little idea of right and wrong. He belongs to the Brahmans of Ujjain, who are *karma-jaḍa smārtas*, that is, Smārtas who are duped by the belief that performing certain *saṃskāra*s and sacrifices can bear sufficient fruit. They pain him with their ways, which are ostensibly ineffective. Why else would he have sought refuge with Ācāryajī, if not to seek guidance out of the maze that they create (p. 172)?

Pilgrimage Sites and Temple Deities

How does this new propagation of a faith which claims ancient roots relate to the existing centres of authority, particularly the kind of authority radiated by old and powerful sites of power and the deities ensconced in the most sacred temples there? Not surprisingly, it is the Vaiṣṇava centres, which play the most prominent role. But, as in the tale of Rānā Vyās, not one of the four Vaiṣṇava *dhām*s, or places of pilgrimage, can alone provide the succour the devotee seeks. In fact, the tale offers incisive critique of the practices prevalent in these centres. Rānā Vyās arrives first in Badrinath, receives *darśan*, but he receives no happiness; it is too cold here, he thinks. And the way here is such that one could well lose one's life. Thereafter, he goes to the Jagannāth temple in Puri. Here he does receive some succour, but he falls ill soon after and it takes him a whole month to recover. So, he takes the southerly direction in order to obtain *darśan* of Śrī Raṅganāthjī. But, he reflects, how is it possible to obtain a view of the entire image? If I look at the feet, I don't see the visage of the deity, and if I look at his visage, then I lose sight of his feet. He is too large. Let me try Dvarka. When he manages to obtain *darśan* of Raṇchoṛjī, he is asked to touch the feet of the image. But then the *paṇḍā* in charge says, you have to give so and so much money, only then will it become possible for you to do so. Then Rānā Vyās thinks, the *brahmacārī*s who allow the touching of feet for money, will take away that money afterwards, so it is not appropriate to stay here. And he takes leave of Dvarka. The stage is now set for his encounter with the true path (pp. 195-6).

But Ācāryajī does make some concessions for those who have deep faith in the temple deities of these powerful pilgrimage sites. In fact, he often takes the form of the images in the most famous shrines, to provide the devotees with gratification in the mode they deserve. In the *vārtā* of Gopāldās, we are told how Gopāldās persuades three others who believe in Raṇchoṛjī of Dvarka to take refuge with Ācāryajī. As he says to Padmarāval, Sāñcorā Brahman, Raṇchoṛjī has manifested himself lately and in this manifestation he speaks and holds dialogue. The reference is to Śrī Ācāryajī, who resides in Arel near Prayag. Padmarāval then persuades Māvjī Paṭel (who is obviously powerful and wealthy) and his own wife Vīrjo to go to Arel with him. Ācāryajī anticipates their coming and sends a boat across the river to fetch them, and then appears to them repeatedly in the form of Raṇchoṛjī. The *Bhāv-prakāś* points out that the three will receive their due in Dvarka *līlā*, a *līlā* obviously inferior, in some unspecified way, from the Gokula *līlā* (p. 171).

Ācāryajī also identifies at times with Jagannāthjī, the deity residing in Puri, as the two brothers, Narhari Jośī and Jagannāth Jośī, who seek out Ācāryajī in Puri, find out. They are sent to the temple by Ācāryajī himself, who thus dispels all doubts about where true power truly lies, for the two brothers find when they get to the temple, that Ācāryajī is standing next to the icon of Jagannāth. When they rush back to him to confirm whether he is still at his own place, they find him seated there as well. And thus they recognize the true god (p. 188). There are many other such tales, whereby Ācāryajī either merges into Raṇchoṛjī or Jagannāthjī or supersedes them. Many a time, it is the deity who advises the given devotee to seek out Ācāryajī: Śrī Jagannāthrāyjī, says to Narhardās Gauḍīya Brahman from Bengal: 'Go you in the morning to Śrī Ācāryajī and become his servant... Śrī Vallabhācārya is famous. Anyone you ask can tell you. Thus understand Śrī Ācāryajī as my *svarūpa*, as my own true form (p. 71).'

However, there is little tolerance for a powerful shrine nearer home, the famous temple of Keśavdev or Keśavrāi in the heart of Braj country. Keśavrāi had long been the presiding deity of Mathura. Worship at the temple went back at least to the early medieval period; it was built and destroyed several times, the last of the magnificent structures which stood at the site had been razed to the ground by Aurangzeb in 1669.[18] Though it is nowhere explicitly clarified in the *vārtā*s, the Vaiṣṇavas who visit shrines such as Keśavrāi's, follow ways which are deeply antithetical to the way of Puṣṭi. They are sometimes described as Maryādāmārgīya Vaiṣṇavas. The fate of such errant devotees is sombre, as related in the *vārtā* of Govinddās Bhallā Kṣatrī. The introductory *Bhāv-prakāś* clarifies that Govinddās, who was conscious of being very wealthy, had given up his wife, making a financial settlement for her at Ācāryajī's bidding, since she was not a *daivī jīva*. He had then been accepted into the fold and had followed Ācāryajī to Mahavana. However, he was arrogant and unbending and his service displeased Śrī Nāthjī. In fact, it is here, rather abruptly, that the main *vārtā* sets in: Śrī Nāthjī communicates to Ācāryajī that he is most displeased. To cut the meanderings which then follow short and to come to the point which concerns us here, Ācāryajī tells him unceremoniously *'sevā choḍ dehu,'* 'leave off performing *sevā'* (p. 101). Govinddās goes to Mathura, but since he has become accustomed to *sevā*, he now performs it for Śrī Keśorāy. But this of course is *viparīt* or contrary behaviour. He is duly punished in the episode which then follows. The triviality of the occurrence which brings about heavy retribution is somehow characteristic of the often almost banal level of action related in the *vārtā*. Govinddās procures a very fine bedstead for Śrī Keśorāy. The Muslim Hākim of Mathura, who is a friend of his, desires a similar bedstead. Govinddās has it made, but someone says to the Hākim, your bed is not as fine as the one made for Keśorāy. This angers the Hākim who comes and seats himself on Keśorāy's bedstead. Govinddās beats him and is in his turn killed by the Hākim's servants. The Vaiṣṇavas perform the crematory rites for him. All is not lost, however. In answer to the Vaiṣṇava's query as to how such a fate could befall a Vaiṣṇava, Ācāryajī explains that he would come to no harm in the beyond (*paraloka*). He had been a buffalo belonging to Nāndrāy and Śrī Ṭhākurjī would often sit astride him. Once he swiped him with his tail and was punished for this offence. Thus the fate of Maryādāmārgī Vaiṣṇavas. However, lest there be any doubt on this score, the tale is concluded with the clear injunction: Do not leave the service of the Ṭhākurjī of Puṣṭimārg and perform it instead for Śrī Ṭhākurjī for Maryādāmārg (p. 103).

However, these equations need not be belaboured as far as Śiva is concerned. He gives way easily to this new path. When a devotee inquires, whether there is any difference between Śrī Ṭhākurjī and Mahādevjī, which of the two is greater, the answers are simple, as we see in the *vārtā* of

---

18. For a dispassionate documentation of the successive temples of Keśavdev, see Alan W. Entwistle, *Braj: Centre of Krishna Pilgrimage*, Groningen: Egbert Forsten, 1987.

Kavirāj Bhāṭ, Sanoḍiyā Brahman, resident of Mathura. The *vārtā* text dispels all doubts on this score:

> Thus one day when he [Kavirāj Bhāṭ] was reciting his own *kavitta* on Bhūteśvar Mahādev on Viśrānt Ghāṭ, Śrī Ācāryajī arrived in Mahavana from Mathura. As he was performing his evening ritual on Viśrānt Ghāṭ, Kavirāj Bhāṭ saw Śrī Ācāryajī. And realizing that he appeared to be a very learned, he asked him something. He threw himself headlong on the ground in obeisance and put a question to him: 'Mahārāj, is the goddess greater, or Mahādev?' Then Śrī Ācāryajī said, according to the *śāstras*: 'Ṭhākurjī is the greatest.' Then Kavirāj Bhāṭ asked: 'Mahārāj, what difference is there between Śrī Ṭhākurjī and Mahādevjī? Both are called *Īśvar*.' Śrī Ācāryajī said: 'It is said in the *Bhāgavata Purāṇa* that when Bhagavān assumed the form of Mohinī, he was able to cast a spell on Mahādeva. And if Mahādeva assumed some other form, he was never able to cast a spell on Śrī Ṭhākurjī. Therefore, Mahādeva is subservient to Bhagvān and Bhagvān is not subservient to Mahādeva; that is the distinction (p. 335).'

Once he hears this, Kavirāj Bhāṭ's mind is purified and cleansed. And he and his two brothers duly receive initiation from Śrī Ācāryajī. Whereas the goddess is not even mentioned again, Śiva is subordinated in time-honoured way by being assigned the role of a devotee. Thus Viśveśvar Mahārāj or the powerful Viśvanāth of Kashi subordinates himself voluntarily to Ṭhākurjī, there is not even the hint of a tussle. There are several small incidents in the *vārtā* of Seṭh Govinddās, an ardent devotee of Śrī Ācāryajī and Śrī Ṭhākurjī, which provide evidence of and thus confirm this subordinate relationship. Viśveśvar Mahārāj almost pleads with the Seṭh to award him some attention. He says: 'You never come to visit me, you maintain not even village ties with me. You could come by sometimes, so that I also partake of *mahāprasād*.' And so the Seṭh deigns to go there, much to the surprise of the people who come there regularly, though not as a devotee, for he does not fall flat in obeisance. In fact, he regularly carries the *mahāprasād* to Viśveśvar Mahārāj, who thus acquires the stature of a devotee of Ṭhākurjī and begins to feel so responsible for the welfare of the Seṭh that he even posts the fierce Kāl Bhairav at the Seṭh's mansion, so that he can protect the many Vaiṣṇavas who go in and out of his house at odd hours (pp. 62-3).

Village deities are seldom considered worthy foes.[19] However, Vallabha's followers are not averse to replacing even these, as we see in the

19. Cf. Komal Kothari on 'folk' gods: 'For a moment keep in mind that Krishna, Shiva, or for that matter, Buddha and Mahavir, are not folk gods. When devotees turn to them for personal salvation, they have to embark on a rigorous process of different disciplines-tapasya, sadhana, yoga, or whatever. But so far as folk gods and goddesses are concerned, they can be approached more directly with the faith that they will be able to intervene in the

following tale, which is contained in the *Bhāv-prakāś* or commentary section leading up to the *vārtā* of the three friends, Bābā Benu, Sārasvat Brahman; Kṛṣṇadās, Ghagharī Kṣatrī, and Yādavendradās, Baniyā. The ruse adopted is simple. Though worshipped as a Devī, since such was the preference of one the three friends, the mistake consisted in not being able to recognize the true form, which was from the beginning that of a *svarūpa* of Ṭhākurjī. It will take Ācāryajī to recognize this and to effect the transformation back to the true form. The village will once again receive the image of a goddess, a Devī, and a Brahman priest will be appointed to perform the due ritual. But the lives of the three friends will be saved; they will henceforth become devotees of Ṭhākurjī. The first two were born in good *jātis*, the third but was born as a Yādava and served Bābā Benu, who at the time was a worshipper of the goddesss, and considered her superior to all. The *Bhāv-prakāś* proceeds then to relate the following tale:

> So one day, Śrī Kalyāṇrāy Ṭhākurjī appeared in a dream to Bābā Benu and said, I am Kalyāṇīdevī and I am in the pond of such and such village. Take me out and perform my worship. In the morning Bābā Benu told Kṛṣṇadās of this and the two friends descended into the pond. There was chest deep water in that pond and after he had searched all over, Kalyāṇrāyjī came into his hands. And with the money he had, he built the little house above the pond into a temple and believing her to be a Devī, installed her in the temple. She was called Kalyāṇīdevī. The village folk, knowing her to be a Devī, made many offerings to her and so Bābā Benu, Kṛṣṇadās and Jādavdās earned their livelihood. As five years passed thus, Śrī Ācāryajī came there on his way from Kashi to Arel and thus it came to pass that he came to this village and set himself up under a mango tree near the temple of Kalyāṇrāyjī. At this time Bābā Benu and Kṛṣṇadās had gone to a nearby village. Then Kalyāṇrāyjī called out to Ācāryajī from his temple, saying, come inside. Then Ācāryajī entered the temple and saw that he was wearing a *lehaṁgā* and *lugrā* (skirt and upper garment). Then Śrī Ācāryajī asked: 'Why are you sitting here like a Devī?' Śrī Ṭhākurjī said: 'What should I do, no one knows of Ṭhākurjī here in this village. And Bābā Benu, Kṛṣṇadās and Yādavdās are *daivī jīvas*. It is for their benefit that I made myself into a Devī and sit here and have my worship performed by Bābā Benu. And why? Because Bābā Benu is a worshipper of Devī. So now make me into a *svarūpa* of Ṭhākurjī. And stay here for four watches, and leave only after you have accepted Bābā Benu, Kṛṣṇadās and Yādavdās [into your fold].' Then Śrī Ācāryajī took off the *lehaṁgā* and hung it up on a hook, and he tore up the upper garment to make a dhoti and a turban. And then he betook himself to the mango tree. In the meantime, Bābā Benu, Kṛṣṇadās and Yādavdās came back. When they entered the temple of

---

most ordinary problems of everyday life. Once I understood this principle, it became easier for me to decide who is folk god and who isn't.' (Rustom Bharucha, *Rajasthan: An Oral History: Conversations with Komal Kothari*, Delhi: Penguin, 2003, p. 119).

> Kalyāṇrāyjī, they saw that he was securely ensconced there, wearing turban and dhoti. Then Bābā Benu said: 'Who came here and took off my Devī's garments?' Kalyāṇrāyjī said: 'Don't touch me, I am Kalyāṇrāyjī Ṭhākur.' Then Bābā Benu said: 'No one worships the Ṭhākur here in this village. And what offence have I given that you forbid me to touch you?' Then Kalyāṇrāyjī said: 'Śrī Ācāryajī is seated under the mango tree. Go become his servant. And if the people of the village don't worship Ṭhākurjī, what do I have to do with them? Seven hundred rupees are buried under your house, take those out and perform my *sevā* and worship' (pp. 239-41).

This part of the story ends with another Devī being installed in the village temple and a Brahman being entrusted with the performance of due worship. Bābā Benu and Kṛṣṇadās are in their turn taught how to take care of their *svarūpa*, with Yādavdās in attendance. Later they give the *svarūpa* to Kṛṣṇadās's two brothers and themselves depart in the direction of Brajbhūmi, where they will enter into *līlā*. This will then form the main *vārtā* tale, which depicts the passing away into *līlā* of the three friends.

In the welter of deities and sites of religious authority and power, a hierarchy of approval and disapproval, of downgrading and negation, is thus established. Some allowance is made for the authority radiated by the deities ensconced at the most powerful Vaiṣṇava sites, by means of merger, or uneasy coexistence, though there is little tolerance for the service of Keśorāy in Mathura, who is a more immediate rival. Clearly, only one manifestation of Kṛṣṇa is finally acceptable. Non-Vaiṣṇava deities, the old rival Śiva, as Viśveśvar Mahārāj of Kashi, is given short shrift, whereas goddesses, particularly as folk deities, are entirely sidelined and replaced.

Contemporaneous Vaiṣṇava Figures of Authority

If it is one thing for Vallabha and his followers to compete with temples and temple icons, it is quite another to compete with Vaiṣṇava religious leaders whose teachings so closely resemble Vallabha's own as to be virtually indistinguishable at the popular level. It is for these charismatic figures that the *vārtā*s reserve a special kind of violence and ire, which ranges from ridicule to outright abuse. The connection to these teachings cannot be denied, but there is ostensible need to establish distance and the firm claim to be the only true path to Kṛṣṇa.

In the *vārtā* of Gadādhardās Kapil Sārasvat Brahman (pp. 83-95), there is a lengthy introductory *Bhāv-prakāś* section which clarifies the standing of the Puṣṭimārg amongst other Vaiṣṇava *sampradāya*s. Gadādhardās goes to Prayag to the banks of the meeting rivers for Makara-*snāna*, where Ācāryajī has also alighted. Gadādhardās has an uncle there who is a Śaiva and who is eager to go to Ācāryajī to seek resolution to a query. The two go to Ācāryajī and the uncle asks: 'If there is only one Ṭhākurjī, Mahārāj, why do the different Vaiṣṇava *sampradāya*s worship different ones?[20] Some worship Kṛṣṇa, some Rāma, some Nṛsiṃh, some Nārāyaṇa etc, who then is definitively the Ṭhākur, the lord of them all?' Then Ācāryajī said: 'Just as a Cakravartī Rājā or Supreme King reigns over the whole earth and other Rājās rule over the different regions and different villages and are addressed as Rājā but remain subservient to the Cakravartī, in just such a way, the Pūrṇapuruṣottam, the perfect and supreme being, Śrī Kṛṣṇa, reigns above all. And all the incarnations are only parts thereof (*aṃśakalā*) and subservient to Śrī Kṛṣṇa, though you can address them all as Ṭhākur.' Gadādhardās's uncle remained silent. But Gadādhardās was a *daivī jīva* and the resolve took firm root within him that he needed to seek refuge with Ācāryajī if he was to attain Śrī Kṛṣṇa. The main *vārtā* is then concerned with the loyalty, devotion and steadfastness of Gadādhardās.

The relationship of Vallabha and his followers to the Gauḍīya *sampradāya* was particularly frought. As Barz[21] and Vaudeville[22] have discussed at some length, the Gauḍīyas were firmly established in Vrindavan, and had gained control of the very shrine of Govardhan from which the Vallabhites derived their legitimation and authority. The Gauḍīyas were to be ousted by violent means and some outright trickery from the temple of Śrī Nāthjī at Govardhan. The *Caurāsī vaiṣṇavan kī vārtā* gives a detailed account of the string of episodes narrating these deeds in the life of the Kṛṣṇadās, who came to be included in the prestigious group of *aṣṭachāp*, the eight seals or poets, whose poetic works were considered the crowning glory of the liturgical corpus of the *sampradāya*. In the words of Vaudeville:

> The aggrieved Bengalis went to complain to their own gurus, the Gosvāmīs Rūp and Sanātan, then at Mathurā, where a violent quarrel broke out between their party and Kṛṣṇadās Adhikārī escorted by a troup of armed Brajvāsīs. The Vallabhite party had more influence at the Moghul court so that the quarrel was finally settled by the emperor Akbar in their favour: they remained in possession of Śrī Govardhannāthjī, whereas the Bengalis accepted the Śrī Madanmohanjī *svarūpa* as compensation.[23]

Thus the Vallabhites had a stake in undermining the authority of Rūpa and Sanātana in particular as well as the Gauḍīyas at large. A particularly vivid

---

20. It is perhaps no coincidence that it is a Śaiva who puts this question about the many forms and incarnations about Viṣṇu, since this is a long standing topos in the Śaiva-Vaiṣṇava encounters. I am grateful to Catherine Clémentin-Ojha for drawing my attention to this.
21. Barz, *The Bhakti Sect*, pp. 270ff.
22. Charlotte Vaudeville, 'The Govardhan Myth in Northern India,' *Indo-Iranian Journal* 22 (1980), pp. 1-45.
23. Vaudeville, 'The Govardhan Myth in Northern India,' p. 45.

tale, woven into the *vārtā* of Prabhudās Jaloṭā of Singhnand, proceeds then to discredit not only the person of Caitanya but also of his followers Rūpa and Sanātana:

> Once Śrī Ācārayajī Mahāprabhu arrived in Mathura. He was performing his *sandhyāvandanā*, evening prayers, in his *baiṭhak*, seat/residence, in Viśrānt Ghāṭ. Besides him were standing four Vaiṣṇavas. At this point in time and at this place, Kṛṣṇa Caitanya's followers Rūpa-Sanātana, came to obtain the *darśan* of Śrī Ācāryajī and prostrated themselves before him. Thereafter Rūpa-Sanātana asked Śrī Ācāryajī: 'Mahārāj, who are these Vaiṣṇavas?' Ācāryajī said: 'These are my followers.' Then Rūpa-Sanātana asked: 'Your *mārg*, path, is that of *puṣṭi* or grace, why then do they appear so weak?' Then Ācāryajī said: 'I had fended them off, saying, don't get involved in this path (*yah mārag meṃ mati paro*) but they did not listen to me. Hence they partake of the fruits of it.' In this deep way did Ācāryajī speak but Rūpa-Sanātana understood nothing. Thereafter, taking their leave, Rūpa-Sanātana went to obtain *darśan* of Śrī Jagannāth Rāy [presumably they have now come to Puri]. There Kṛṣṇa Caitanya asked: 'Where do you come from?' Rūpa-Sanātana said: 'We have come from the *darśan* of Braj.' Kṛṣṇa Caitanya then asked: 'Did you obtain *darśan* of Śrī Vallabhācārya?' Rūpa-Sanātana said that they had received his *darśan* on Viśrānt Ghāṭ in Mathura. Kṛṣṇa Caitanya asked: 'Did you do *vārtā* tales?' Rūpa-Sanātana said: 'We asked, your way is that of *puṣṭi*, why are your Vaiṣṇavas so weak? And he said, I kept them off, saying, don't get involved in this path, but they did not listen to me. Hence they partake of the fruits of it.' As soon as they heard this, he was overcome by the *bhāv* of Śrī Ācāryajī and he fell into a faint for a whole *muhūrta*. This was said thrice and thrice did he fall into a faint. When he asked for a fourth time, Rūpa-Sanātana said: 'We can repeat this no more.' So Kṛṣṇa-Caitanya understood this partially (p. 134).

Rūpa and Sanātana apparently grasp enough and absorb enough of the words of Vallabha and the power that inheres in them to convey them to Caitanya, who in his turn is endowed with enough divine grace to be deeply affected by their power, though without comprehending the words fully. The *vārtā* is here invoking the popularly known image of Caitanya as particularly prone to fainting in fits of ecstasy and excess emotion. However, in doing so, the *vārtā* is focusing on one aspect alone of a personality of whom indeed very little is known but whom Dimock describes thus:

> It is clear that he was an ascetic and withdrawn individual, having at the same time an extraordinary personal magnetism. He was almost certainly, especially in the later stages of his life, mad, whether this be interpreted as

> the divine madness of the holy fool, the random madness of the irresponsible child, or, as A.C. Sen prefers, epilepsy.[24]

But Dimock also gives us some information concerning Caitanya's visits to the Braj area and presumably his reputation there. Apparently, his first attempts to go to Vrindavan were abortive, since so large a retinue of followers planned to accompany him there that it became impractical to do so. When he did set out to go there, it was

> ... in relative secret, and accompanied only by a *brāhmaṇa* and that *brāhmaṇa's* servant. While he was in Vṛndavana he was in constant ecstasy, and this so frightened his companions that they escorted him away from the place before, in his frenzy, an accident occurred.[25]

Before going on to cite the *Bhāv-prakāś* comment on these passages, it is perhaps also important to turn to the popular reputation that Rūpa and Sanātana enjoyed, which Dimock thus summarizes:

> Rūpa and Sanātana, and their nephew Jīva, were brilliant men, learned in the *śāstras* and every conceivable category of learning from esthetics to grammar.[26]

Once again, the *vārtā*s present a one-dimensional image, playing upon the more dominant traits alone, as in Caitanya's case or completely reversing them, as with the Gosvāmīs, Rūpa and Sanātana. Thus the explications that the *Bhāv-prakāś* undertakes covers as much as it uncovers, when it sets out to explain Kṛṣṇa Caitanya's behaviour:

> He understood something of the *svarūpa* (true being, divine being) of Śrī Ācāryajī. Therefore he understood only partially. If he had understood all of it, he would have take leave of his body. And that Śrī Ācāryajī said, don't get involved in this path, and they did not understand, so they partook of the fruits of it, this is as in the *Pañcādhyāyī* when the devotees from Braj are told by Śrī Ṭhākurjī: 'Go home,' but the devotees from Braj do not agree to this. Only then do they obtain the fruits of Rāsalīlā.
>
> This was said in the way of *maryādā*. The way of the Veda is as follows, if someone comes in order to become a follower, a 'no' has to be said once. This is in order to test the firmness of the follower. Later, when this follower forms the

24. Edward C. Dimock in *Caitanya Caritāmṛta of Kṛṣṇadās Kavirāja: A Translation and Commentary* by Edward C. Dimock, Jr. With an Introduction by Edward C. Dimock, Jr. and Tony K. Stewart, ed. by Tony K. Stewart (Harvard Oriental Series 56), Cambridge, Mass.: Department of Sanskrit and Indian Studies, Harvard University, 1999, p. 23.
25. Ibid., p. 21.
26. Ibid., p. 24.

resolve of obtaining full love, only then does he obtain the remaining fruits of it. Hence one has to say to say 'no' to a Vaiṣṇava (p. 135).

The message seems to be that Kṛṣṇa Caitanya, deeply affected as he is, yet does not possess enough divine grace to fully absorb the teaching of Vallabha, and the learning that Rūpa and Sanātana possess yet debars them from grasping the true meaning of Vallabha's words, which a Maryādāmārgī could in any case never fully comprehend.

There are further insidious suggestions regarding the true character of Caitanya's teaching in later passages, which apparently provides cover for, at worst *mleccha*, at best, syncretic practices. The *vārtā* part of the tale of Sundardās and Mādhodās, wherein these suggestions are made, is comparatively long. Though the commentarial introductory portion is also long, the *Bhāv-prakāś* on the whole confines itself to brief comment in the portions *interspersing* the *vārtā*, leaving it to tell its own tale, so to speak. In the introductory portion, however, we are told that Sundardās and Mādhodās are friends. Both are Brahmans, the one a Sārasvat Brahman, the other born into a Gaṅgāputra family. But Mādhodās's father had placed his faith in a *pīr*, and to disguise it, had pretended to be affiliated to Kṛṣṇa Caitanya. He had no son, so he had pledged himself to the *pīr* and had named the son born to him Mādhodās, so that people would give credence to his allegiance to Kṛṣṇa Caitanya. Mādhodās's father would place his food offerings before Ṭhākurjī but he would call upon the *pīr* to partake of it. As against this duplicitous behaviour, which Mādhodās had inherited from his father, Sundardās Gaṅgāputra was truly devoted to holy men and would serve all who came into the village faithfully. Once when Śrī Ācāryajī came by the village on his way to Jagannāthpurī, Sundardās offered his services to him and after some hesitation, Śrī Ācāryajī, recognizing him to be a *daivī jīva*, accepted him into this fold. However, and this is where the *vārtā* sets in, Sundardās also wanted Mādhodās to give up *anyāśraya* (p. 383) so he asked him to become Śrī Ācāryajī's follower. But Mādhodās protested, saying that Kṛṣṇa Caitanya was his all. Mādhodās further disclosed that he had found that when Śrī Ācāryajī offered food to Ṭhākurjī, it remained whole. And he pointed out to Sundardās that this was strange. When he, Sundardās offered food to his image, it disappeared almost entirely. Through a series of encounters and conversations, it becomes clear that this is so, because the *pīr* comes in the guise of a *bhūt* or spirit and gobbles up the food. Śrī Ācāryajī is able to exorcise the *bhūt* by setting him afire, when he traps him in the act and when Mādhodās refuses to believe that this is what happens, he is physically beaten in the night by followers of Ācāryajī who force him into submission. Śrī Ācāryajī desires to rescue him because Sundardās and Mādhodās are true friends and the latter, through no fault of his own, for he has been misguided by his father, inherited habits which he can unlearn. And a further miracle is performed when Śrī Ācāryajī feeds the whole village *mahāprasād* from that modest portion which is usually reserved for Mādhodās and his family. All that is needed, as he tells the incredulous Mādhodās, is firm belief (p. 386). *Anyāśraya* in this tale then is an intermingling of belief in the *pīr* with only ostensible belief in Kṛṣṇa Caitanya, leaving us with the intriguing question whether this is a reference and refutation of the syncretic practices of Bauls and *pīr*s in Bengal which are so closely allied to Sahajiyā Vaiṣṇava devotional practices.

Apart from Kṛṣṇa Caitanya, it is Mīrābāī, the other vastly popular and beloved devotional figure in the Kṛṣṇa bhakti movements of the period, though with no affiliation to any sectarian tradition, for whom derision and rejection are reserved. The encounters with Mīrābāī are both violent and abusive. The first mention, derogatory in the extreme, is in the *vārtā* of Govind Dube, who once goes to the house of Mīrābāī and spends some days there, conversing about godly matters. When Śrī Gusāīṁjī hears of this, he sends her a Sanskrit *śloka*, the meaning of which the *vārtā* paraphrases thus:

> If you ride once on an elephant, you leave off riding on a donkey, not even if you have to give up your life. So also, having tasted of the pollen of his lotus feet, do not take taste the rasa of another, even if you have to bear suffering for the rest of your life.

Govind Dube then cannot be persuaded by Mīrābāī to stay at her side even for a moment. He goes straight to Gusāīṁjī, who repeats the injunction so often heard in such context: Do not speak of your *mārga* to *anyamārgīya*, those who follow other paths (p. 215).

The second mention of Mīrābāī takes place in the *vārtā* of Rāmdās, Mevāṛā Brahman. He sings Śrī Ācāryajī's *kīrtan* in front of Mīrābāī's Ṭhākurjī. Then Mīrābāī says to him: 'Sing some *viṣnupada*s of Śrī Ṭhākurjī.' It is then that Rāmdās realizes that he is transgressing. He abuses her: 'Dārī, Rāṁṛ! Do these *pada*s belong to your lord?' And after this, he resolves to never again set eyes on her again (p. 269). The *Bhāv-prakāś* concludes the tale with the absolute prohibition it reserves for such acts: do not go to an *anyamārgīya*, follower of alien path, and if you go, do not speak of your path. Do not sing the *kīrtans* of your path, if you do so, you will suffer much pain. The listener of the tale shares Rāmdās's thought processes: I should not stay in this village, if I do so, I may have to set eyes on her face again. I am a Brahmin, Mīrābāī's *purohita*, house-priest, on top of that. And the lure of money is such a bad thing in this world. It is greed which makes one lose one's dharma. So I should take my departure from this village, along with my family, so that I never have to drink water here again.

Faith in the lord is a mediated act, however direct the access preached. And the mediators are less than generous about sharing space with like-minded teachers of faith.

Alien Religious Authority Figures

There are, however, multiple sources of authority in every day life which take care of domestic problems and often provide immediate local relief, but even these are not spared the wrath of Ācāryajī, who watches over his followers jealously and expressly forbids taking recourse to the remedies they suggest, explicitly designating it as *anyāśraya*.

The Ḍākotiā[27] is an important figure in village life. Connected to the cult of Śani, he performs astrological functions for lower castes. He becomes the cause of much family distress in the *vārtā* of Dāmodardās Harsānī, whose wife came from a rich family (pp. 4-13). In spite of her high birth, she was very devoted to Ācāryajī and performed all *sevā* related work herself. Ācāryajī once asked Dāmodardās whether he had any wish that he could fulfill. Dāmodardās said, he had none, whereupon Ācāryajī bade him ask his wife. She answered willingly, the only wish that remained for them was to have a son. This wish was granted. However, while she was pregnant, a Ḍākotiā came to the village and all the Smārta women of the village flocked to him to ask him questions. They also asked Dāmodardās' wife whether she would go with them. She did not go with him, but she allowed a young girl to put a question to him about the gender of her child. With this, she gave in to a weakness, the implication being that she did not simply trust in Ācāryajī's power to grant her the son she had asked for. The Ḍākotiā did indeed confirm that she would bear a son, but the mischief was done. When Ācāryajī next came by and Dāmodardās went to pay his respect, Ācāryajī forbade him to touch him. Dāmodardās was innocent and could not understand this reaction. Ācāryajī's pronouncement was grim: 'You have sought refuge of another (*anyāśraya bhayau hai*).' Once the matter was cleared, that Dāmodardās had not himself sought this advice and

27. Komal Kothari has thus explicated the function of the Dakotias, who perform different functions in different regions of Western India: 'One other community with dual functions is the Dakot, who also perform brahmanical ritual functions for low-caste communities in villages all over Rajasthan, while being identified as astrologers (*jyotishis*) for upper-caste families in Gujarat and Maharashtra. Recognized in their respective villages as the chief priests of Shani Maharaj, a potentially vindictive deity who has to be constantly appeased, the Dakots are identified as the horoscope makers of low-caste people. They themselves are involved in the rituals of low-caste groups and eat meat, drink liquor, and are generally treated as low-caste people themselves.' (Bharucha, *Rajasthan*, p. 211.) – Singh, *The Castes of* Marwar, p. 84, has a more straightforward classification: 'The Dakot Brahmans belong to the Punch-Gour group, and bear a proportion of 2.45 per cent to the total Brahman population in Marwar, and in the North-West Provinces are known by the name of Bhadries, or Bhaddalis, so called from following the tenets of Bhaddal, though Sir H.M. Elliot describes them as branch of the Dakot.'

the wife only tangentially, Ācāryajī relented, but only marginally. The couple would have a son, but he would soon become a *mleccha*. Whereupon, the wife pledged that she would not see the face of her son and that she would send him away to her mother the moment he was born, so that he could be brought up there. And this is what happens; a wet-nurse brings him up. Husband and wife lead a life of devotion and depart from life in due course without seeing the son, who does indeed become a *turk*.

Another 'folk' figure, the Nāgā Bairāgī, is similarly vilified. In fact, all connection to the Nāgā Bairāgīs, the ascetic militant groups attached to the Rāmānandī *sampradāya* and thus nominally Vaiṣṇava, is considered sheer loss of time, no further condemnation is needed: they are rogues and child snatchers. The *Bhāv-prakāś* which leads to the rather emotion-drenched main *vārtā* illustrating the consequences of associating with Nāgā Bairāgīs, tells us how Gopaldās Jaṭādhārī Gauṛ Brahman from Prayag comes to be attached to this group of people and spend his youth with them. As a six-year-old, Gopāldās had gone for the annual Makar-*saṃkrānti* ritual bath in the river. He began to cry when he lost sight of his father in the crowd. Then a Nāgā Bairāgī offered to take him to his father. And when the boy consented, he took him to his camp, where he took possession of his things. Later, he took the boy along with him to the south. And so Gopāldās came to live in his *jamāt*, till the Bairāgī passed away. He had reached the age of thirty, and he wanted to visit places of pilgrimage, so he accompanied a group of fifty to hundred Nāgās to Dvarka and from there he went to Mathura. There in the evening he accosted Śrī Ācāryajī performing *sandhyā* on Viśrānt Ghāṭ. And he stood still watching him. Then Kṛṣṇadās Meghan who had accompanied Ācāryajī asked Gopāldās why he remained standing there and did not join the Nāgā Bairāgīs. And Gopāldās answered: 'I lost sight of my group (*saṅg*) many births ago. If Ācāryajī will have mercy on me, I will attain the company of devotees and of the lord himself.' Tellingly, he does not refer to his father; it is the religious affiliation which is uppermost in his mind. And it is as if Ācāryajī has known this all along. For he calls out: 'Gopāldās, have you come?' And Gopāldās throws himself on the floor in obeisance and replies: 'Mahārāj, take mercy on me, I have come. I have strayed a lot. I have committed many evil deeds in evil company on many paths. I was swept away by the utterly depraved. With your grace I shall cross the ocean of this *saṃsāra*.' He is duly initiated; he serves faithfully and dies faithfully (p. 365).

Conclusion

It is then important to distinguish between the kind of faith based 'high' religion to which the Puṣṭimārg ultimately aspires and the 'folk' religion which prevails in everyday life, particularly in the village. The scripture in the case of the Puṣṭimārg is the *Bhāgavata Purāṇa* and the canon that the *sampradāya* itself is creating, much of it in Brajbhāṣā and some of it orally transmitted. It is a distinction that the teachers of the Puṣṭimārg themselves establish, though they are clearly seeking to attract the servant classes and women, as we have seen. The lines of demarcation however, are drawn in all directions, laterally and horizontally. The Brahminical Smārta traditions are undermined, if not explicitly demolished and the 'folk' traditions lower down the ladder are violently rejected. Horizontally, the various Vaiṣṇava orders are devalued and discredited, alternately mocked and abused. However, the modalities adopted to establish difference diverge from those used by modern day communalism. The self is not defined as 'not-other,' that is, as against the other, who is demonized for historical wrongs but rather, for all the violence involved, the claims which makes one set of beliefs superior to another are indeed presented as a matter of faith, as offering the ONLY path of salvation and are therefore primarily theological and eschatological. This state of affairs is, however, at all times open to change, once political power becomes aligned to it.

To idealize the world of faith then, is as problematic as demonizing communalism, particularly since we know that the lines separating them are thin and that communalism is itself a construct. To understand the nature of the construct and how faith plays itself out in rural and urban locations, where its many vulnerabilities lie today and where it intersects with the political public sphere, we need not only more historical data regarding past configurations, but also more contemporary study of alliances and hostilities between former foes and allies.

Textual Studies of the *Ādi Granth*: Current Issues

Balwant Singh Dhillon

The quadri-centennial of the compilation and installation of Sikh scriptures, the *Gurū Granth*, in Harimandir at Amritsar, was celebrated in 2004. As expected it has provided fresh impetus to studies on the Sikh scriptural tradition. A close look at the works on Sikh scriptures produced during the last three to four years reveals that a good number of scholarly works have come out and many more were produced to mark the solemn occasion. It is worth noting that in addition to the old textual issues of Sikh scriptures, a few new ones that have come to the fore which have got scholarly attention in these works. Besides attempting to identify the contentious issues of the Sikh scriptural tradition this study tries to trace the main lines of the debate in the works produced during the period under study.

The Sikh scriptures comprise the hymns of Gurū Nānak and his five successors, the medieval Hindu Bhagats, Muslim Sufi poets and other religious persons associated with the Sikh Gurūs. All these writings are collectively known as *Gurbāṇī*. In its literal sense it means 'speech,' 'words' or 'utterances' of the Gurus which have come down to them in a state of spiritual experience of God. Therefore *Gurbāṇī* is not merely a product of speculation but the very word of God. The history of the Sikh scriptural tradition dates back to the times of Gurū Nānak, the founder of Sikh religion. In fact, his experience of the numinous forms the core of the Sikh scriptures. To express his spiritual experience, Gurū Nānak has devolved a curious blend of music and poetry which has an enchanting effect on the listeners. We are informed that during his missionary tours to various lands, Gurū Nānak carried with him a book which is believed was nothing else but a collection of his hymns, including the writings of medieval Bhagats that he had collected over the years.[1] Lastly when he settled at Kartarpur (now in Pakistan on the right bank of river Ravi) he directed Bhāi Lehnā, his spiritual

1. Gurdās Bhallā, *Vārān Bhāī Gurdās*, ed. by Giānī Hazārā Singh, Amritsar: Khālsā Samācar, 1962, *vār* I.32.

heir, to compile his hymns into a codex which he bestowed on him on his succession to guruship.[2]

The next stage in the development of Sikh scriptural tradition relates to Gurū Amar Dās, the third Sikh Gurū. He not only added his own hymns to the Sikh scriptures but applying the thesis of *kacī* (ungenuine) versus *sacī* (genuine) *bāṇī* produced a fresh codex.[3] In the Sikh history we come across many references to Sikh Gurūs and their Sikhs engaged in copying the sacred writings and passing these on to their successors.[4] Sources at our disposal indicate that in order to eliminate spurious writings as well as to provide the Sikhs with their own scriptures, in 1604 Gurū Arjan took up the gigantic task to compile the Sikh scriptures in a canonized form in a volume which is popularly known as the *Ādi Granth*.[5] According to the Sikh tradition the final canonization of Sikh scriptures occurred at Damdama (Talwandi Sabo, Bathinda) in 1706 when Gurū Gobind Singh for the first time incorporated the hymns of Gurū Teg Bahādur into the Sikh scriptures. The tradition holds that it was the Damdama volume which was invested with guruship by Gurū Gobind Singh upon his death in 1708. Thus, from the first revelation of Gurū Nānak to the final canonization, there is a time gap of more than two centuries. Before and after the final canonization in 1706, Sikhs of various hues have produced a number of documents primarily to preserve and transmit the *bāṇī* in their own manner. In order to reconstruct the history of Sikh scriptural tradition as well as to clarify the scriptural evolution and to fix the sure and certain text our critics have grappled with various textual issues which is the subject matter of this study.

The process of transmission of any text reveals the ways in which it has been received at different stages of its history. A close look at the history of Sikh scriptural tradition confirms that for its preservation and transmission various modes and traditions had come to exist in the pre- and post-*Ādi Granth* periods. Besides the scribal activities, recitation and singing were quite popular among the early Sikhs. The schismatic trends within the Sikh Panth also led to various ways of transmission of the *Gurbāṇī*. In certain recent studies the impression has been created that the transmission of *Gurbāṇī* took place in a linear manner. Consequently, three main sources of the early Sikh scriptural tradition have been identified to conclude that they have descended one after another.[6] But, by contrast, there are scholars who

---

2. Harjī, *Janamsākhī Gurū Nānak Dev jī*, ed. by Kirpāl Singh, Amritsar: Khālsā College, 1969, pp. 249-50; *Purātan janamsākhī*, ed. by Bhāī Vīr Singh, Amritsar: Khālsā Samācar, 1962, p. 114.

3. *Gurū Granth Sāhib*, p. 920; see also Balwant Singh Dhillon, *Early Sikh Scriptural Tradition: Myth and Reality*, Amritsar: Singh Brothers, 1999, p. 41.

4. *Gurū Granth Sāhib*, pp. 322, 544; Gurdās Bhallā, *o.c., vār* VI.12, XXIV.6, XXVIII.5.

5. Balwant Singh Dhillon, *o.c.*, pp. 46-60.

6. The three main sources are (i) *Gurū Har Sahāi Pothī*, (ii) *Goindvāl Pothīs* and (iii) MS #1245, Guru Nanak Dev University, Amritsar. For the use of these sources for textual

do not subscribe to the above approach.[7] They feel that the state of transmission of the Sikh scriptural tradition, especially its peculiar ways, means and traditions have not yet come into the focus of textual studies. For example early attempts to compile *Gurbāṇī* independent of the Sikh Gurūs, musical or oral repertoires, small prayer books *(guṭkās)* of personal use, early commentaries on the text, textual traditions preserved in the *Janamsākhī* literature and works outside the Sikh tradition especially in Rajasthan have not yet been fully explored for textual studies on the Sikh scriptures. To decide about the text families, cross-fertilization between various recensions and nature of variant readings, all these aspects of the *Gurbāṇī* transmission have remained out of focus.

The role played by the scribes in the transmission of scriptures was quite significant. The Sikh scriptural sources reveal that copying of sacred writings had developed into a pastime for pious Sikhs. Besides the main stream Sikhism, rivals of the Sikh Gurūs had also engaged scribes whose primary interest lay in projecting their peculiar beliefs and practices.[8] Then there were professional scribes also whose livelihood depended on the copying of the *Ādi Granth* text. They responded to the requirement of individuals and groups to produce a selection of particular hymns or a particular recension.[9] Thus not all the manuscripts which presently we find in different public and private collections are necessarily the product of mainstream scribes. Scribal habits associated with sectarian groups and coming from different centres of learning have not yet been fully identified by the critics. Similarly their criteria to select the text or their preference for a particular recension over the other recensions has to date eluded proper understanding.

For reconstructing the history of the Sikh scriptural tradition one is expected to go through a maze of sources especially those that pre-date 1604, the year of the *Ādi Granth*'s codification. The Sikh tradition informs us that Gurū Arjan while compiling the *Ādi Granth* had some other sources at his disposal besides the volume inherited from Gurū Rām Dās. Unfortunately none of the early sources nor the original writings of the early Sikh Gurus have survived. Some scholars, in their pursuit to reconstruct the history of Sikh scriptural tradition, have identified three main sources of

studies on the Sikh scripture, see Pashaura Singh, *The Guru Granth Sahib: Canon, Meaning and Authority*, New Delhi: Oxford University Press, 2000; Gurinder Singh Mann, *The Making of Sikh Scripture*, New Delhi: Oxford University Press, 2001.

7. Sahib Singh, *Ādi Bīr Bāre,* Amritsar: Singh Brothers, 1970, pp. 82-4; Pritam Singh (ed.), *Ahīāpur vālī pothī*, vol. I, Amritsar: Guru Nanak Dev University, 1998, pp. 66-239; Balwant Singh Dhillon, *Early Sikh Scriptural Tradition*, pp. 89-241.

8. Balwant Singh Dhillon, 'Traditions of Gurbani Transmission and Rival Traditions.' *The Journal of Religious Studies* 31 (Spring-Autumn 2000). Patiala: Punjabi University, pp. 138-52.

9. Balwant Singh Dhillon, *Early Sikh Scriptural Tradition*, pp. 274-5.

early Sikh scriptural tradition—the Gurū Har Sahāi Pothī, extant Goindvāl Pothīs, and MS #1245 of Guru Nanak Dev University, Amritsar. It has been concluded that these sources had originated one after another to culminate in the *Ādi Granth* in 1604.[10] Though these sources have been extensively used to reconstruct the three phases of the evolution of the Sikh sacred text, they have not yet been subjected to rigorous examination to probe their antecedents. Moreover family accounts or traditions have been taken at their face value to decide about the scriptures' very origin and purpose. Instead of an 'accurate description' sometimes a 'misleading account' has been provided.[11] Interestingly sometimes a scholar uses a source to illuminate the process of evolution of scriptures, but he has excluded the same while discussing the formation of the canon.[12] The variety of textual variants present in these sources proves that none of them is a direct copy, or a direct descendant, of another.[13] These sources represent three different text families which are the product of different groups who were interested in preserving a particular version of the scriptures.

What is of particular significance of a manuscript source is not that it has been displayed at a particular religious place or has been in possession of a family descending from the Sikh Gurūs. Inspite of all these merits, the antiquity, authority and authenticity of a source has to be established. For this rigorous inquiries are called for, such as: When was it recorded? Who was the scribe? Is it an original version or a copy of it? What was the use or purpose of it? Did the scribe record it for personal use, for an institution, for a group or for a patron? Each source or even its smallest parts have to be examined in an analytical manner.

It is widely believed that the compilations of *Gurbāṇī* that were current during the pre-*Ādi Granth* period had no canonical authority. Usually Gurū Arjan is credited for producing the first canonical text of the Sikh tradition. Analysis of *Gurbāṇī* indicates that during the guruship of Gurū Amar Dās three basic principles to fix the Sikh canon had come to be applied. Firstly, the writings of Gurū Nānak and hymns coming down from his legitimately appointed line of successors form an integral part of Sikh scriptural tradition. Secondly, the compositions of pseudo-gurus composed

10. Pashaura Singh, *The Guru Granth Sahib*, pp. 28-49; Gurinder Singh Mann, *The Making of Sikh Scripture*, pp. 32-62.

11. Jeevan Deol, 'Text and Lineage in Early Sikh History: Issues in the Study of the *Adi Granth*,' *Bulletin of the School of Oriental and African Studies* 64.1 (February 2001), pp. 34-58; Balwant Singh Dhillon, 'Early Sikh Scriptural Sources: The Question of Authenticity,' *The Journal of Religious Studies* 34 (Spring-Autumn 2003), pp. 117-127.

12. See for example Gurinder Singh Mann, 'Canon Formation in the Sikh Tradition,' in *Sikh Religion, Cultural and Ethnicity*, ed. by Christopher Shackle, Gurharpal Singh and Arvindpal Singh Mandair, Richmond, Surrey: Curzon Press, 2001, pp. 10-24 where he excludes MS #1245 from the discussion on the issue of canon formation.

13. Balwant Singh Dhillon, *Early Sikh Scriptural Tradition*, pp. 220-8.

in the veins of 'Nānak' are not acceptable. Finally, the unprincipled, false or forged writings that violate the basic tenets of Sikh faith are of no religious merit for the Sikhs.[14]

The internal evidence of Sikh scriptures points to a canonization process which is marked by three pivotal stages. The first stage occurred during the pontificate of Gurū Amar Dās when the 'ungenuine' writings of a pseudo-gurū which were likely to effect the originality of Sikh scriptures were not allowed to enter into the Sikh scriptural tradition. We observe that Gurū Amar Dās after applying the criterion of the *sacī* (true, genuine) versus *kacī bāṇī* (ungenuine, unripe) had prepared the codex afresh. During the second stage Gurū Rām Dās very zealously guarded the originality of Sikh scriptural tradition and did not allow the *kacī bāṇī* composed in the vein of 'Nānak' to interpolate the Sikh sacred writings. The third stage was related to the internal crisis created by the Mīṇās when the Sikh scriptural writings had come under serious threat of interpolation.[15] It resulted in the culmination of Sikh scriptures, the *Ādi Granth* by which Gurū Arjan rejected once for all the unauthentic writings which had come to be attributed to the Sikh Gurūs and Bhagats as well. Hence the canonization of the Sikh scriptural tradition should not be viewed as a late development related to Gurū Arjan Dev only, but it was an ongoing process, coextensive with the pontificate of his predecessors as well.

The issue of intertextuality in the *Ādi Granth* is an area which has not found adequate attention of scholars working on the Sikh text. A careful reading of the *Ādi Granth* indicates that certain of its compositions appear under the name of two authors. According to a recent study, it is a very complex phenomenon which for the sake of clarity can be reduced to following the three categories:[16]

I. *In certain cases the same composition that occurs at different places in the* Ādi Granth *has been attributed to two Gurūs, to a Gurū and a Bhagat, and to two Bhagats.*
II. *Some compositions of the* Ādi Granth *have been attributed differently in the non-Sikh sources.*
III. *In some cases the mark of authorship in the heading of a composition does not correspond to its* chapp *(poetic signature) line.*

How does a composition appear differently under the different authors of the *Ādi Granth* and other manuscripts of the Sikh scripture? How

14. Balwant Singh Dhillon, 'Early Sikh Scriptural Tradition: The Process of Canonization,' *Journal of Sikh Studies* 24.4 (2000), Amritsar: Guru Nanak Dev University, pp. 127-49.
15. Ibid., pp. 143-4.
16. Jeevan Deol, 'Sūrdās: Poet and Text in the Sikh Tradition,' *Bulletin of the School of Oriental and African Studies* 63.2 (June 2000), pp. 166-93.

come the dual authorship is attributed to a composition? Why does the mark of authorship in the heading of a composition come to be at variance with its poetic signature? How and when did a composition come to be attributed simultaneously to two authors? Though a few compositions of dual authorship in the *Ādi Granth* are available in non-Sikh sources, some of them do not appear in any other collection.[17] In this situation to resolve the issue of authorship of such compositions one has to go through all the Sikh and non-Sikh repertoires. Traditionally the compositions which carry dual authorship of a Gurū and a Bhagat have been taken as commentaries of a Gurū on the Bhagat verses. Similarly, where the mark of authorship in the heading and poetic signatures are at variance, all these compositions have been assumed to have been completed by Gurū Arjan on behalf of a Bhagat. Gurū Arjan purposely assumes the authority and voice of the Bhagats. It has been done to formalize the fluid identity of oral tradition, the source of the compositions in question. In that way the *Ādi Granth* text extends the identification of the Guru with a Bhagat through the phenomenon of intertextuality.[18] But some of the headings over such hymns in the *Ādi Granth* may indicate a source which was exclusively available to Gurū Arjan.[19] In fact the issue of intertextuality is a complex one which demands thorough investigation. Unless going through all the Sikh and non-Sikh sources, it cannot be resolved satisfactorily.

According to the Sikh sources, one of the basic concerns of Gurū Arjan in canonizing the Sikh scripture in 1604 was to protect it from interpolation as his rivals were circulating spurious hymns in the name of 'Nānak.' Except for accusing the Mīṇās for corrupting the Sikh text no worthwhile study on the extra-canonical compositions found in their literature has been carried forward.[20] Until recently the presence or absence of a few non-canonical writings in the *Ādi Granth* manuscripts has been at the center of the textual debate. Consequently, large corpora of extra-canonical compositions attributed to the Sikh Gurūs and Bhagats have not come under the focus of scholars working on the Sikh canon.

A close look at the contents of the Gurū Har Sahāi Pothī reveals that at least seven extra canonical compositions attributed to Kabīr (3), Nāmdev (2), Ravidās (1) and Madan Mohan Sūrdās (1) were present in it. A sizeable number of non-canonical compositions—Gurū Nānak (2), Gurū Rām Dās (1) Gulām Sadāsevak (14), Śaraf (1), Kabīr (a), Nāmdev (6), Trilocan (2), Benī

---

17. Ibid., p. 191.
18. Ibid., p. 193.
19. Balwant Singh Dhillon, 'Early Sikh Scriptural Tradition: The Process of Canonization,' p. 143.
20. Recently, Simarjit Singh has completed his Ph.D. thesis on 'The *Kachī-bāṇī* Composed by the Mīṇās under the Chhāp of "Nānak",' in the Faculty of Humanities and Religious Studies, Guru Nanak Dev University, Amritsar.

(1)—form part of the two extant Goindvāl Pothīs. Similarly MS #1245 is a rich repository of extra-canonical writings (total 48) that have been attributed to the Sikh Gurūs.[21] On examining the Mīṇā commentaries on the works of Gurū Nānak, we observe that their text is full of extra-canonical verses and stanzas. Recently a scholar has drawn our attention to some extra-canonical compositions attributed to Seventh and Ninth Sikh Gurūs, that are available in some seventeenth-century manuscripts of the *Ādi Granth*.[22] The *Janam-sākhī* literature also carries a number of apocryphal writings attributed to Gurū Nānak. Either the scholars are not aware of all these writings of extra-canonical nature or they shun discussion of them. As a result, significant textual issues emanating from these compositions have been ignored. What is the source of these writings? Are they really the compositions of the authors to whom they have been attributed? If yes, why have they not found a place in the Sikh canon? If no, who were the authors of these writings? How have they found their way into these sources? How and in what manner do these writings differ socially and theologically from the Sikh canon? These are some of the core issues to which scholars should respond. These issues need to be addressed dispassionately while applying the state-of-the-art techniques and methods of textual studies as well rigorous principles of manuscriptology.

21. For the text of extra-canonical writings in these sources, see Balwant Singh Dhillon, *Early Sikh Scriptural Tradition*, pp. 85-6, 173-82, 243-58.

22. Jeevan Deol, 'Non-Canonical Compositions Attributed to the Seventh and Ninth Gurus,' *Journal of the American Oriental Society* 121.2 (April-June 2001), pp. 193-203.

form part of the two extant Goindvāl Pothīs. Similarly MS #1245 is a rich repository of extra-canonical writings (total 48) that have been attributed to the Sikh Gurus.[11] On examining the Mīnā commentaries on the works of Guru Nānak, we observe that their text is full of extra-canonical verses and stanzas. Recently a scholar has drawn our attention to some extra-canonical compositions attributed to Seventh and Ninth Sikh Gurus, that are available in some seventeenth-century manuscripts of the *Ādi Granth*.[12] The *Janam-sākhī* literature also carries a number of apocryphal writings attributed to Guru Nānak. Either the scholars are not aware of all these writings of extra-canonical nature or they shun discussion of them. As a result, significant textual issues emanating from these compositions have been ignored. What is the source of these writings? Are they really the compositions of the authors to whom they have been attributed? If yes, why have they not found a place in the Sikh canon? If not, who were the authors of these writings? How have they found their way into these sources? How and in what manner do these writings differ socially and theologically from the Sikh tradition? These are some of the core issues to which scholars should respond. These issues need to be addressed dispassionately while applying the state-of-the-art techniques and methods of textual studies as well as rigorous principles of manuscriptology.

11. For the list of extra-canonical writings in these sources see Balwant Singh Dhillon, [illegible] *Sources* [illegible], pp. [illegible], 43-38.
12. Jeevan Deol, 'Non-Canonical Compositions Attributed to the Seventh and Ninth Gurus', *Journal of the Royal Asiatic Society* 12:2 (April-June [illegible]), pp. [illegible]-207.

Music in the Ashram, Then and Now: Introduction to the DVD

Daniel Gold

Although musical performance is not central to all Indian devotional traditions, it tends to play some part in most of them. But the part it plays, like much in contemporary India, is liable to change—particularly in guru-oriented traditions, which can undergo continuing modifications as a guru matures and substantial transformations as a new guru assumes authority. Over the last thirty-five years, I have been struck by changes in the roles music plays in a small ashram on the outskirts of Gwalior, Madhya Pradesh, which underwent a change in leadership in the early 1980s. I first became acquainted with the ashram—named Adhyatma Niketan—in 1968, when I was living in Gwalior as a Peace Corps volunteer and over the years have visited the place when catching up with acquaintances in the city. When I went in 2003 with the idea of making a video about the ashram, I was struck by the cumulative changes that had occurred there since the late 1960s. Many of these changes, moreover, seemed to reverberate in the types of music performed at the ashram and their roles in religious life.

Adhyatma Niketan was founded by Thakur Man Singh Kushwah—known to his devotees as Malik Sahib.[1] Sectarian circumstance had led Malik Sahib to follow a spiritual trajectory that is unusual in Hindu traditions, where an exclusivist guru-devotion is usually the norm: he recognized two main lineages and managed to integrate them for his disciples. His first guru was from a little-known offshoot of the Radhasoami line, which looks to precedent in the North Indian sant tradition and offers a devotional yoga featuring the steady cultivation of ecstatic states. The Radhasoamis started in Agra in the 19th century with Shiv Dayal Singh, called Soamiji. Several groups of Radhasoamis remain in Agra, while important sublineages stemming from Beas, Punjab, have started large establishments throughout North India. Malik Sahib's guru, known as

1. For more on the ashram in its contexts see my *The Lord as Guru: Hindi Sants in North Indian Tradition* (New York: Oxford University Press, 1987), pp. 166-69; and Mark Juergensmeyer, *Radhasoami Reality: The Logic of a Modern Faith* (Princeton, N.J.: Princeton University Press, 1991), pp 155, 167, 178n. A biography of Malik Sahib has been published in Hindi: Pītāmbar Miśra, *Divya caritāmrit* (New Delhi: Sudarshan Chopra, 1973).

Huzoor Data Dayala, was a disciple of Soamiji's younger brother, Pratap Singh. Data Dayala had grown up in Gwalior, which is not too far away from Agra, and started an ashram there.

When Huzoor Data Dayala died in 1940, Malik Sahib understood himself to be the guru's qualified successor. Although Malik Sahib's legitimacy was not acknowledged by important leaders at the late guru's ashram—which has remained under the care of a managing committee—it was recognized by a few members. Able to attract new devotees of his own, Malik Sahib eventually developed a modest following. In 1958, he came in touch with a guru named Yogendra Vijnani, who offered a yoga through a *śaktipāt* initiation.[2] That initiation produced a felt transference of power understood to offer a quicker path than that of the Radhasoamis, if one less sweet and subtle. Yogendra Vijnani recognized Malik Sahib's earlier attainment, and over an intense few days during the Holi festival, initiated him and gave him spiritual authority. Malik Sahib now had experienced two different yogic paths and could give his devotees access to them. This convergence of lineages would be unlikely to happen with a guru functioning in an established Hindu-style sectarian line; it is, moreover, what Adhyatma Niketan's devotees boast of as their independent ashram's specialty. In practice, for the majority of devotees, the *śaktipāt* initiation is experienced first, and the subtler Radhasoami states may become more prominent later.

Despite the growing number of devotees attracted by the *śaktipāt* initiation, Malik Sahib maintained a custom found at establishments, like the Radhasoamis', that look to a North Indian sant: the regular chanting of devotional hymns by gurus from both their own lineage and the broader sant tradition. The chanting was performed simply in a limited number of local melodies, usually by one of several ordinary devotees who had a predilection for it. A few of the regular chanters had good voices and could carry a tune nicely, but this was not the case with all of them: the music often seemed like an afterthought. There was also occasional singing of well-known Hindu devotional refrains, particularly when large groups gathered during seasonal events. In these, even disciples for whom Radhasoami states remained distant could participate with enthusiasm, and they became more frequent as devotees became increasingly drawn by the *śaktipāt* initiation. During Malik Sahib's lifetime, however, this general devotional singing tended to be organized spontaneously and was not a regular part of formal programs.

Today, the simple chanting of sant songs still goes on, but at the beginning of the twenty-first century, the singing of a wide range of devotional songs has become much more common and more crucial for religious life. The songs are performed by practiced, sometimes professional,

2. Yogendra Vijnani's major Hindi work is still in print: *Mahāyoga vijñāna* (Rishikesh: Vijñāna Bhavan, 4 Pushkar Mandir Marg, 1997 [1938]).

musicians—some conversant with different regional folk traditions, others proficient in classical styles, or, increasingly, in popular Indian film-song arrangements. This semi-professional style of performance features prominently in the public programs held by Malik Sahib's son Kripal, who has succeeded him as guru. The differences in styles of musical performance then and now reflect differences in the regional diversity and sociological composition of the devotees attracted to each guru and the ways in which they gain access to their gurus' spiritual power. These differences, in turn, derive from the gurus' different sociocultural eras and spiritual personalities.

The family of the gurus hails from the fading local gentry. They are Rajputs with a history of military service to the Scindia maharajas of Gwalior. Although Malik Sahib had inherited some land in Bhind and Morena districts, it wasn't enough to keep him. Working as a civil servant in Gwalior State and its successors in independent India, he had been occupied with his spiritual practices and never rose very high in the bureaucratic ranks. During Malik Sahib's day, many of the devotees were small town people with whom he had formed bonds during his various postings in the region. There were also many village Rajputs from Bhind and Morena districts, rough areas in the Chambal basin that in the 1960s was still rife with dacoits. Travelers in the area regularly protected themselves with firearms, and I remember occasionally being taken aback at seeing villagers visiting the ashram carrying rifles. Alongside these devotees from the Gwalior hinterlands, there were a number from Gwalior City, a sizable contingent from Jodhpur, and other individuals and small groups from various North Indian places who had found their way to the guru. Still, most of the disciples were from not too far away and when they gathered during seasonal festivals, the ashram retained a parochial, regional air.

When Malik Sahib died in 1983, spiritual authority passed to his middle son, Kripal. I was a little surprised when I heard about this some years after the event. I knew Kripal in the early days as a good boy, but not as the disciplined practitioner that his father was. Although he spent much of his time managing ashram affairs during his father's final years, he hadn't struck me as someone likely to be his father's *spiritual* heir. But he underwent a visible transformation at Malik Sahib's death, they say, and has obviously grown into the role of guru, having attracted a large number of new devotees of his own as Sant Kripal. One of the first major events in Sant Kripal's life as a guru was a tour to Himachal Pradesh, where he had been invited by a small group of Himachali disciples previously initiated by Malik Sahib. The enthusiastic response to Sant Kripal then by many who had never known his father seemed to bolster his confidence and to help establish him in his new role. Sant Kripal met similar responses on traveling to other places where his father had a few devotees, including Banda district, U.P., and several areas of Rajasthan. He now makes regular tours to all these regions.

Extended touring was not something that Malik Sahib had done. By the time he had many disciples outside his home region he was already on in years and didn't like to do a lot of traveling. Sant Kripal, by contrast, was in his early 30s when he succeeded his father, with plenty of energy and no other occupation. He had the means and motivation to extend his spiritual influence broadly. These days, the annual festivals—when disciples converge on the ashram—are no longer largely regional events, but are crowded with devotees from many areas of North India.

It was not only Sant Kripal's relatively youthful energy, however, that helped him attract more devotees than his father, but also his personal style. Malik Sahib had been a serious practitioner and active spiritual thinker in somewhat difficult personal and sectarian circumstances. Understandably, he developed a complicated personality. In discourses that sometimes seemed to escape him in energetic outflows, he would interpret Hindu scriptures in light of the internal experiences from his two lineages. But as his spiritual dynamism interacted with his worldly life, he sometimes appeared sharp and intense. Thus, although Malik Sahib had a graciousness about him that was recognized by many, he could also seem personally forbidding. Through most of the 1970s, I think, his devotees would probably be numbered in the hundreds. Sant Kripal's devotees, by contrast, can easily be numbered in the thousands. This is due in part to his very good social skills, which were honed during the final years of his father's life as he regularly dealt with devotees—smoothing over conflicts that inevitably arose during the crush of the seasonal festivals. Fate seems to have opened up a spiritual path fairly easily for Sant Kripal, who doesn't appear to have had to struggle very hard with either his practice or his life. He smiles a lot.

Sant Kripal, moreover, also has a different mode of initiating disciples than his father, one that is more fluid and easily accessible. Generally, Malik Sahib gave a *śaktipāt* initiation that he called *dīkṣā* to small groups at specific times of the year during the seasonal festivals. Twice a day over a three-day period he meditated with them in his special initiation room until they (ideally) got a sense of being linked to the guru's power. In public programs, he was liable to give complex spiritual commentaries on simply chanted verses. With Sant Kripal, by contrast, a sense of becoming linked to the guru's power is likely to happen during a public program itself, as people become extraordinarily moved during musical sessions conducted by trained performers. Listening to the music, people often get taken up in ecstasies and can look possessed. When this happens to new devotees, they are said to 'join' *(joṛnā)* the guru's force. Specific initiation is not seen as crucial and is not normally given in the way it was in Malik Sahib's day. Partly in its place, musical performance has taken on a vital new dimension.

The music at Sant Kripal's programs reflects both the diversity of the devotees and their predominantly middle-class tastes. For both father and son, devotees have been primarily upper-caste Hindu, although people of all castes can and do come—these days including ethnic Tibetans from Kulu and beyond who also revere the Dalai Lama. There are also several old Muslim devotees and, especially from the mid-1990s, a few foreigners. Following norms common to both sant traditions and more cosmopolitan urban circles, all the devotees, irrespective of caste, eat together when at the ashram. But the following that Sant Kripal has attracted is in fact more urban and cosmopolitan than that of his father, and runs in social circles that are broader and somewhat higher. In Gwalior itself, he is widely known as a spiritual personage and is frequently invited to local civic functions as a chief guest. In a higher proportion than those of his father, his devotees seem to be from the upper middle classes, whose diverse musical tastes he shares. He listens with apparent equanimity to devotional music sung in *filmī* arrangements as well as to those sung in classical ragas and folk-song styles.

Old devotees at the ashram, while recognizing the changes that have taken place there, are generally happy that they still have a living guru and a vital tradition. But not all are happy with all the different musical traditions that have developed. The 16-minute DVD *Music in the Ashram,* provided in PAL format with this volume, presents samples of the different current musical styles at Adhyatma Niketan and gives commentaries by the singers. These are intercut with excerpts from an interview by Sant Kripal. The DVD, which is subtitled, is also available in NTSC (as well as PAL) format from

The South Asia Program
170 Uris Hall
Cornell University
Ithaca, NY 14853
USA
http://www.einaudi.cornell.edu/SouthAsia

The Verbal Icon—How Literal?

John Stratton Hawley

Let me begin with a story. It comes from the *Caurāsī vaiṣṇavan kī vārtā* ('Accounts of Eighty-four Vaiṣṇavas'), the major hagiogaphical collection created in the Vallabh Sampradāy as early as 1640,[1] and it concerns the great Brajbhāṣā poet Sūrdās, whom the sect considers to be one of its leading lights.

The *vārtā* tells us that Sūr was already renowned in Braj before Vallabha (*c.* 1479-1531) travelled there from his home in Adail, near the *saṅgam* where the Jumna and Ganges meet at Allahabad. But when Sūr met Vallabha and became his disciple, it was a whole new ballgame. Sūr began to flower, and he did so in two temples where Vallabha held sway. That's where Vallabha took Sūr for inspiration after adopting him as the first of eight poets (*aṣṭachāp*) who were to serve as the liturgical backbone of his fledgling community.

The more important of these two sites was the great temple of Kṛṣṇa the Mountain Lifter atop that very Mount Govardhan. Bengalis, immigrants to Braj, had apparently transformed this temple in the preceding century, but as early as the 1530s it would come wholly under Vallabhite control.[2] The *vārtā* tells how Vallabha made Sūr a key player in his program of liturgical renovation.[3] The other locale that served as Sūr's inspiration, according to the *vārtā*, was Gokul, a spot associated with Kṛṣṇa's early childhood. When Sūr first visited it with Vallabha, it was just a hallowed place on the riverbank, but in the 1570s, as we learn from other sources, Vallabha's second son Viṭṭhalnāth established a network of family temples there.[4]

1. For a brief index of difficulties surrounding this date, see J. S. Hawley, *Sūr Dās: Poet, Singer, Saint*, Seattle: University of Washington Press, and Delhi: Oxford University Press, 1984), p. 7; Alan W. Entwistle, *Braj, Centre of Krishna Pilgrimage*, Groningen: Egbert Forsten, 1987, p. 165.

2. Entwistle, *Braj*, pp. 153-4.

3. It uses the word *samarāyā*: *Caurāsī vaiṣṇavan kī vārtā*, 'Sūrdās kī vārtā,' ch. 1, Mathura: Śrī Govardhan Granthamālā Kāryālay, 1970, p. 409.

4. Entwistle, *Braj*, pp. 160-1.

As the *vārtā* pictures it, Vallabha devoted his own main efforts to worshipping in the temple of Govardhannāth (i.e., Śrī Nāthjī) and Sūr performed his musical role there to his guru's great satisfaction. But once the community was well established and others could share his musical burden, Sūr liked to slip off to Gokul to worship before the tiny deity who reigned there, Sri Navanītapriyajī, Kṛṣṇa the child who loves fresh butter. There he encountered Vallabha's grandsons, the playful offspring of Viṭṭhalnāth. One of these boys, Gokulnāth, is remembered as the person who would later become the author of the *vārtā*.

In the *vārtā* Gokulnāth explains that Sūr had a great talent for recording exactly the way Sri Navanītapriyajī appeared in any given *darśan*. But how could this happen day after day?, the boys wanted to know. After all, Sūr was blind. They decided they would put him to the test. They conjured up a *darśan* so outlandish, so utterly beyond the canon, that it would test definitively whether Sūr was actually responding to the appearance of Sri Navanītapriyajī, or cheating by composing poems that were appropriate in a general way. It was the month of Asāḍh, deep in the hot season, and what they determined to do was dress the icon in nothing at all—no garments, that is, just pearls. Pearls on his forehead, pearls around his arms, pearls at his waist, ankles, and neck; then they affixed a *tilak*, a nosering, and earrings, and that was it.[5]

Needless to say, Sūr passed the test with flying colors. Already as they worked behind closed doors, he felt something remarkable was about to be divulged, and when the *darśan* began and the icon appeared, Sūr sang a poem with the following refrain: *dekhe rī hari naṅgamanaṅgā*: 'Hey, I've seen Hari naked, all naked!' The body of the poem goes on to marvel at how the deity's limbs blaze all over with pearls and nothing else, as he shrieks for joy, smearing butter over his mouth, laughing amid the girls of Braj.[6] Thus we have a playful but utterly convincing vindication of the notion that for religious poetry, at least, the visual icon is the prototype of its verbal counterpart.[7] Even if the poet is blind, this is how it works, and even if the visual display is so extreme that it seems to transgress the limits of divine propriety.

The theological point is clear. A poem of true inspiration takes its pattern from a *mūrti*, a deity in iconic form, by a process so pure that the physical faculty of vision is of only secondary importance. Real poets see what they

5. 'Sūrdās kī vārtā,' ch. 6, p. 421.

6. Ibid., p. 422.

7. We owe the phrase 'verbal icon' to W. K. Wimsatt and Monroe C. Beardsley, *The Verbal Icon: Studies in the Meaning of Poetry*, Lexington, Ky.: University Press of Kentucky, 1964. Kenneth Bryant is responsible for having brought it into the critical literature on the *Sūrsāgar*: *Poems to the Child-God*, Berkeley: University of California Press, 1978, pp. 72-112.

say—and do so by virtue of their initiation at the hands of a genuine guru. Hence it is entirely to be expected that, within the Vallabh Sampradāy at least, their poetry will align itself naturally with the seasons and times at which the community witnesses the Lord's self-manifestations: eight times a day, with a change of mood and vestment each time; in the annual calendar of festivals; and in an independent sequence at the time of Holī. Such is the shape of Vallabhite worship, and the poems of Sūrdās feature prominently in almost all its aspects. True, the community honors as ancient a collection of Sūr's poetry (the *Sūrsāgar*, 'Sūr's Ocean') that is not organized in this way at all—in the main, it follows the life of Kṛṣṇa—but a scholar such as Dharmanarayan Ojha finds no difficulty working out the points of connection. That is the mission of his hefty book *Sūr-sāhitya meṁ puṣṭimārgīya sevā bhāvanā* (The Vallabhite Spirit of Worship in the Literature of Sūr).[8] It attempts to remove any doubt about Sūr's having been a liturgical poet, and in doing so aligns him with the iconic base and cultic form that make the Vallabhite community what it is.

It sounds great. But alas, there are difficulties—difficulties too numerous to explore fully here. For one thing, if we turn to the oldest manuscripts of the *Sūrsāgar*, it turns out that Sūr's theology answers poorly to Vallabha's: the key concepts are missing, the language is distant. Moreover, unlike certain others belonging to the inner circle of Vallabhite poets (*aṣṭachāp*), Sūr doesn't ever refer to Vallabha. Most devastating of all for our present concern, there is not a single poem among those that can reasonably be shown to have been in circulation in the sixteenth century, in which we can see the peculiar features of either Śrī Govardhannāthjī or Śrī Navanītapriyajī. Yes, there are poems on the Mountain Lifter and the Butter Thief, but these are surprisingly rare—fewer than twenty in a corpus of more than 400—and none of them takes us directly to the distinguishing characteristics of the *mūrtis* in question. The diamond now embedded in Srināthjī's chin may not go back to Sūr's time,[9] so one can excuse its absence in Sūr's poetry, but if Sūr was taking his cues from this specific image of the Mountain Lifter, how could he not refer to its one truly distinctive feature: the lotus stalk held in its right hand?[10] Nor is there mention of the places that house these icons, as we might expect from the Tamil analogue—no Elephant Hill at Kanci, no shrine of Alavay, no Lord of Vittuvakkottu.[11] Yes,

8. Allahabad, Śodh Sāhitya Prakāśan, 1973.

9. Entwistle, *Braj*, p. 161.

10. For numerous depictions in painting, see Amit Ambalal, *Krishna as Shrinathji*, Ahmedabad: Mapin, 1987.

11. Steven Paul Hopkins, *Singing the Body of God*, New York: Oxford University Press, 2002, pp. 93, 99-100, passim; Indira V. Peterson, *Poems to Śiva*, Princeton: Princeton University Press, 1989, pp. 274-6; Vasudha Narayanan, *The Way and the Goal*, Washington: Institute for

we have plenty of the mystery of epiphany, as Kenneth Bryant has so clearly shown,[12] but it is the epiphany of a universal Lord in the form of a village child—not the Lord who adopts a particular place as his own, making 'our place,' the place where this temple stands, a *divya deśa*.[13] The stark virtuosity of the Tamil verb *nil* ('to stand [here]'), which Ramanujan has so beautifully explained,[14] is simply not present.

But what about the poem we just discussed, the one about nakedness? It is quite absent from every *Sūrsāgar* dating to the sixteenth or seventeenth century, and you won't even find it in the large 'vulgate' edition of the *Sūrsāgar* published by the Nāgarīpracāriṇī Sabhā of Benares in the middle years of this century.[15] The place-oriented sectarian claims for Sūr are a meaningful tradition with roots in the seventeenth century, but they are evidently not the same tradition of transmission that gave us the ever-expanding *Sūrsāgar* we know by that name today.

When we go back to the poems of Sūr that can be shown to have been in circulation by the end of his own century, the sixteenth, we also seem to leave behind any dependable relation between *Sūrsāgar* compositions and any specific moment of performance.[16] If Ojha's project were really to be fulfilled, we would expect that poems attributed to Sūrdās would be clearly and reliably associated with a particular festival or time of day. But again there are problems. It's not just that we lack Vallabhite liturgical anthologies ('hymnbooks,' *sevā praṇālīs*) going back anywhere near that far. It's that what we would expect to find there—a stable association between a given poem and the *rāga* in which it would have been performed—is absent in the manuscripts

---

Vaishnava Studies and Cambridge: Center for the Study of World Religions, Harvard University, 1987, p. 64.

12. *Poems to the Child-God*, pp. 24-35, 79-84.

13. Or in Tamil, *ukantaruḷiṇanilaṅkaḷ*. See Katharine Young, 'Beloved Places (*Ukantaruḷiṇanilaṅkaḷ*): The Correlation of Topography and Theology in the Śrīvaiṣṇava Tradition of South India,' Ph.D. dissertation, McGill University, 1978.

14. A. K. Ramanujan, *Hymns for the Drowning*, Princeton: Princeton University Press, pp. 122-6; cf. Hopkins on Vedāntadeśika, *Singing the Body of God*, p. 103.

15. Jagannāth Dās 'Ratnākar,' Nandadulāre Vājpeyī, et al., *Sūrsāgar*, Varanasi: Kāśī Nāgarīpracāriṇī Sabhā, 1972 and 1976 (originally 1948).

16. On the difficulties of historical musicology relating to *dhrupad* and Brajbhasha poetry, see Richard Widdess, 'Dhrupad as a Musical Tradition,' *Journal of Vaiṣṇava Studies* 3:1 (1994), pp. 65-70; Françoise 'Nalini' Delvoye, 'The Verbal Content of Dhrupad Songs from the Earliest Collections,' *Dhrupad Annual* 5 (1990), pp. 93-109; other essays by Delvoye listed F. N. Delvoye, 'Dhrupad Songs Attributed to Tansen,' in Alan Entwistle and Françoise Mallison, eds., *Studies in South Asian Devotional Literature*, New Delhi: Manohar, and Paris: École Française d'Extrême-Orient, 1994), pp. 426-7; and Hawley, Introduction, chapter 2, 'Performance, past and present,' in J. S. Hawley and K. E. Bryant, *Sūr's Ocean*, vol. 1 [forthcoming].

we do have, some of which are very old indeed. There a *rāga* is indeed specified for each poem, but the problem is that a given poem is often linked to several *rāgas*—one in one group of manuscripts, another in another. Even when the same poem is duplicated within a given manuscript, it is apt to be assigned a different *rāga* the second time around.[17] Hence it is not altogether surprising that the traditions of major Vallabhite temples vary as to when particular poems should be performed, even today when there is a common printed hymnbook to work from.[18] Either the original performance context for a given poem (if we may speak of such a thing) has been lost to the memory of at least some within the Sampradāy, or a musician had more latitude than we tend to think in choosing the *rāga* with which a certain poem belonged—and by the same token, its cultic context, its liturgical hour or season.

This is discouraging, perhaps, but let's not fold our tents and walk away. There are plenty of poems in the sixteenth-century *Sūrsāgar* that really do translate an image into words—an image of exactly the sort one might see in a temple. In his book on Sūrdās, Kenneth Bryant has dealt beautifully with one of these, the triply bent image of Kṛṣṇa as a flute-player (*tribhaṅgī veṇugopāl*), showing how it is the poet's purpose to bring that image to life before allowing it to return to bronze or stone.[19] I have tried to perform similar exegeses for poems that take, in fact, our friend *navanītapriya* Kṛṣṇa as their inspiration.[20]

---

17. An example is the well known poem *cakaī rī cali caran sarovar* (Hawley, *Sūr's Ocean* §420, Nāgarīpracāriṇī Sabhā 337), which is assigned to *rāg dhanāśrī* when it first appears in manuscript J1 (folio 4, #10) and to *rāg bilāval* when it recurs (folio 44, #16). J1 was apparently compiled from three separate pre-existing collections of poetry, in two of which this poem occurs. See G. N. Bahura and K. E. Bryant, (ed.) *Pad Sūrdās jī kā/The Padas of Surdas*, Jaipur: Maharaja Sawai Man Singh II Museum, 1982, pp. 7, 88.

18. For example, see Udaysankar Sastri, 'Sūrsāgar kī sāmagrī kā saṃkalan aur uskā sampādan,' *Bhāratīya Sāhitya* 17:1-2 (1972), p. 92, in relation to poems that cluster around the theme of stealing butter. *Kīrtankārs* in both the temple of Mathurādhīś in Kota and the *dvitīya pīṭh* in Nathdwara reported ways in which their singing of these poems varied—and in somewhat different ways—from what what is now specified in the printed *sevā praṇālī*. At Kota, for example, *mākhan corī* poems are sung from *kṛṣṇajanmāṣṭamī* to the new moon (*bhādrapad kṛṣṇa* 11-15), whereas the printed text specifies that they should be confined to *bhādrapad kṛṣṇa* 14-15. (Interviews, November 7, 1975; November 22, 1975; August 26, 1976.)

19. Nāgarīpracāriṇī Sabhā 1273, *Poems to the Child-God*, pp. 95-8. Bryant worked with the Nāgarīpracāriṇī Sabhā version of this poem, which is altered in several details by his critical edition, and these encourage certain changes in translation and interpretation (see Hawley and Bryant, *Sūr's Ocean* §46). But the overriding thrust of Bryant's exegesis remains intact.

20. I mean *navanītapriya kṛṣṇa* in the general sense, not the Vallabhite *mūrti* per se. See, e.g., Nāgarīpracāriṇī Sabhā 790, in *Krishna, the Butter Thief*, Princeton: Princeton University Press, 1983, pp. 109-12, but with an error regarding *kīḍā* on p. 111.

And one could present many, many more examples. But in no case does the form of Kṛṣṇa as seen in a particular temple emerge. Rather, these poems take as their basis such general iconographic canons as might be represented in a *śilpaśāstrī*'s book of archetypes—the sort of thing we find summarized in Gopinatha Rao's *Elements of Hindu Iconography* or Banerjea's *The Development of Hindu Iconography*.[21] This doesn't mean that a poet like Sūrdās 'enjoys' the Deity head to foot (*āpādacūḍānubhava*) any less than a poet such as Vedāntadeśika, as Steven Hopkins shows in his book *Singing the Body of God*.[22] But it does seem that Sūr's debt to a specific cultic environment is not so marked, no matter what the Vallabhite chroniclers of the seventeenth century and later may have wanted us to believe.

Ah, but perhaps you've been studying the list of poems that will comprise the critical edition and translation of the *Sūrsāgar* that Ken Bryant, Vidyut Aklujkar, and I—with help from many others—have been working on for so many years. Perhaps, on paging through it, you worked your way to the very last poem and found there a title line that promises to falsify all that I have said. The refrain reads *jai ho jai mādhau bainī*, and you are certain this must be a *stotra* addressed to Viṣṇu as we see him in the temple of Veṇī Mādhav at Allahabad, that is, Prayag. Here he is Mādhav of the Triveni, the triple confluence (*triveṇī saṅgam*) where the Ganges meets the Jumna and the invisible Sarasvati. Not only that, you think, this little known poem may provide surprise confirmation that Sūr really did venerate Vallabha, for here we have Sūr praising the local deity of the place from which Vallabha came when he travelled to Braj. After all, Veṇī Mādhav is just across the Jumna from Adail.

These are good instincts, for the Veṇī Mādhav temple has a substantial history. Located in Daraganj just north of the road and railway bridges that now connect Allahabad with cities farther east, and on the last bit of high ground before one descends to the *saṅgam* itself, it is mentioned in the *Caitanya caritāmṛta* as the very place where Caitanya met Vallabha.[23] Its antiquity—at least dating to Sūr's time—is confirmed by the fact that a replica was constructed across the river in Adail in the eighteenth century, billing itself, of course, the original (*ādi*) Veṇī Mādhav temple. The 'original' in its title is a dead give-away that it is, in fact, not. Here we may suspect another example of Vallabhite

21. T. A. Gopinatha Rao, *The Elements of Hindu Iconography*, Delhi: Motilal Banarsidass, 1985 (originally 1914); Jitendra Nath Banerjea, *The Development of Hindu Iconography*, New Delhi: Munshiram Manoharlal, 1974 (originally 1956).

22. *Singing the Body of God*, p. 162 and throughout chapter 5 (pp. 135-65).

23. Edward C. Dimock, Jr., and Tony K. Stewart, eds., *The Caitanya Caritāmṛta of Kṛṣṇadāsa Kavirāja*, Cambridge: Harvard University Press, 1999, *Madhya Līlā* 19.56-84, pp. 615-16.

Vallabhite attempts to reshape history after the fact, but I hasten to add that Mohan ji Sharma, the *adhikārī* who presently looks after the historic place (*baiṭhak)* where Vallabha established his residence in Adail, tells the story of the meeting between Vallabha and Caitanya in the correct way: it happened not in the Veṇī Mādhav temple in Adail but on the Allahabad side of the confluence.[24] Similarly there is a temple of Veṇī Mādhav on Prayag Ghat in Mathura, whose purpose is to bring Prayag to Mathura, making its benefits accessible to pilgrims traveling to Braj. As with Adail, it seems unlikely to me that this temple would have been in existence in Sūrdās's time, and Alan Entwistle apparently shared that view. He thought it might originally have been a Rāmānandī temple, although it has now passed into Śrī Vaiṣṇava hands. Whatever the precise date of its founding, it too bears witness to the original in Allahabad, confirming its prestige and suggesting its antiquity.[25]

So much for the temple, but what about the Veṇī Mādhav image itself? Veṇī Mādhav is a black, standing, four-armed icon of Viṣṇu, and his consort is similar. Satyanand Giri, the person currently in charge, reports that Veṇī Mādhav's accoutrements, invisible to me because of his garments, include a disc in the (proper) back right hand, a conch in the back left, and a club and lotus in the front right and left. This does not exactly match the presumed copy in Adail, which arrays three of these differently and dispenses with the fourth, giving the front right hand over to the gesture of generosity (*varada mudrā)* instead. This mismatch need not detain us, however, since the main point is clear. Veṇī Mādhav is clearly understood on both sides of the river as a four-armed Viṣṇu accompanied by a four-armed Lakṣmī, and there is every indication that he would have been so understood in Sūr's time, even if there is no precise way of attesting to the age of the image now installed in the temple in Allahabad.

Thereby hangs the tale. For if Sūr did compose his Veṇī Mādhav poem on a visit to the *saṅgam* temple, he nonetheless found no reason to greet the deity in his iconic form. He did not copy the image into words. This is what we hear instead:

---

24. Personal communication, October 13, 2003.

25. See Entwistle, *Braj*, p. 314; Prabhudayāl Mītal, *Braj dharm-sampradāyoṃ kā itihās*, Delhi: National Publishing House, 1968, p. 571.

Jai ho jai mādhau bainī[26]

1 Hail to Madhav's Braid, the confluence of rivers
2 That he mercifully manifested in the world
to give a way for those who'd lost the way.
3 It is as if Trivikram, the Triple-Victory Lord,
knowing this Kali age to be a harsh, crooked king
4 Whose body is adorned with armies of evil,
unsheathed his sword against him, in anger:
5 With Mount Meru for a hilt, glistening with great waters,
and purchased at enormous cost—
6 That Triple Confluence! How the waves of its body glint,
and the blade of its current is so very sharp
7 That the merest sight of it conquers Yama's soldiers—
Greeks, Kapalikas, Jains.
8 They take its one name as their boat and flee,
leaving their hells for a fine peaceful realm.
9 Heavenly damsels observe that water war
with lovely faces and lotus eyes,
10 Raise a great uproar among themselves, says Sūr,
and with their hands bear garlands for the
river of Narayan.

It's a wonderful poem, and it is full of the celebration of a particular place, the *triveṇī saṅgam*, yet there is nothing besides the name itself to root that place in the temple of Veṇī Mādhav or its cultus. Rather, Sūr constructs a vast and vastly different icon in which the triune Ganges—'that Triple Confluence' (*trisaṅgam*), braided from the Ganges, the Jumna, and the Sarasvati—becomes a great sword to Trivikram, 'the Triple Victory Lord.' So the triple nature of the *saṅgam* as sword actually seems to cause us to bypass Veṇī Mādhav, turning him into another form of Viṣṇu, Trivikram. Wielding the hilt of this massive weapon—the Himalayas ('Mount Meru,' *meru*, v. 5)—and using it to slash straight through the north Indian plains, he defeats the crookedness (*kuṭil*, v. 3) of the Kali age by drawing it back into a unity, as the metaphor of the braid suggests. In the process, Trivikram too is transfigured, for he comprehends not the three levels of the cosmos, as classically he should, but the three sorts of heretics who symbolize the confused dispersion of the Kali age. These are the divisions of Death's enemy army: Greeks (barbarians), Kapālikas (scull-begging Śaivas), and the heterodox Jains (v. 7).

26. The poem corresponds to Nāgarīpracāriṇī Sabhā 455, but is translated on the basis of the critically edited form worked out by Kenneth Bryant: Hawley and Bryant, *Sūr's Ocean* §433.

In making the Ganges into Viṣṇu's scimitar, the poet takes advantage of the fact that *dhār* (v. 6, translated in v. 7) can mean both 'blade' and 'current,' so I include both meanings in the translation. He also puns on *nāv* (v. 8), which can mean either 'name' or 'boat,' and must here mean both. The desperate enemies seize on that as their lifeboat—the name of Veṇī Mādhav, that is, who is at once the confluence and Viṣṇu himself. Foreigners, apostates, and heretics, they have oriented themselves to other 'names,' but in truth there is only one name: the name of Viṣṇu. When these lost souls flee (*bhaje*, v. 8) to that 'one name' as their refuge, their lifeboat, at the same time they 'sing' (*bhaje*) of Veṇī Mādhav. For *bhaje* too is a pun.

The 'heavenly damsels' (*dibi sundari*) who appear in the penultimate verse to celebrate all this provide the poet a way of pointing even more unambiguously to the One about whose name he has been speaking. For when, in a gesture that has for millennia fallen to such beauties, they present their garlands to the Ganges, they do so in the name of Nārāyaṇ (*narainī*, v. 10). Nārāyaṇī is one of the names of the Ganges, which it earned by originating in the heavens at the toe of Viṣṇu. This name, with which Sūr concludes his poem, is thus appropriate to the heavenly damsels with whom the poet associates it. As to their 'uproar' (*kulāhal*, v. 10) this may be the sound that is made when the Ganges and the Jumna coalesce. But it is also the sounds we hear here—in this very composition. The first eight verses can be interpreted as the damsels' uproar—and, of course, it is also the poet's. And as we move on to the refrain, as in performance we must, this becomes our uproar as well, for we in the audience freely join in singing as the refrain comes around: *jai ho jai mādhav bainī*, 'Hail to Mādhav's Braid!'

How self-referential! As the poet feeds the diction of the poem back into its refrain for a last time, causing the full composition to rest in its title, he seems to affirm that in his 'naming' he's been letting us discover how the Ganges' real name is Viṣṇu. She is Nārāyaṇī. And Nārāyaṇ (as we recall, moving on to the refrain) is Veṇī Mādhav, who braids her together from the three tributary strands that make her what she is.

Sūr may well have sat in the temple at the *saṅgam* when he composed this hymn, and he may well have addressed it to the deity installed there. I like to believe he did. But the verbal offering he makes is far from being a copy of anything he sees. If this poem is a verbal icon, it is not an 'icon of an icon,' the sort of thing Steven Hopkins sometimes sees in the place-specific *stotras* of Vedāntadeśika. Instead it is its own icon, a fully transsubstantiated form; and for this reason, as Hopkins elsewhere reports of Deśika's language, it is as divine as any image.[27] By situating itself as divine speech, by identifying its own uproar with the uproar of the 'heavenly damsels' (*dibi sundari*), this poem begs us to recognize it as being no less holy than the stone image that may have served as its occasion. A verbal icon, indeed.

27. Hopkins, *Singing the Body of God*, p. 165 (on the *Tiruvāymoḷi* in relation to *arcāvatara*) and p. 169 (on Deśika's poetic speech as divinely given, and therefore intrinsically appealing to the Deity); on the *phalaśruti*, see 'The Poet's Telescope,' pp. 339-41.

Dādūpanthī Anthologies of the Eighteenth and Nineteenth Centuries

Monika Horstmann

The sect of Dādū (d. 1603), the Dādūpanth, started forming during its founder's lifetime in Rajasthan and has its headquarter *c.* 70 km to the west of Jaipur, in Naraina. The life of Dādūpanthī male and female ascetics, at least for particular branches of them, is to this day governed by three types of activities: wandering (*rāmat*), conducting communal worship, and preaching. The lay followers, in their turn, organize for them and the local communities impressive feasts. This reciprocity has existed from the formative period of the sect. In this way the link between both groups is strengthened. Before print culture made its definitive impact, writing as a fourth activity ranged prominently among ascetics and this, in fact, established the fame of the Dādūpanth. They scribed manuscripts for themselves or others, or they committed them to professional scribes. The manuscripts were meant for their own use or for veneration as sacred objects in shrines. Especially the months of the rainy season, when ascetics more often than not stayed at the houses of laymen, lent themselves to writing.

Numerous aspects of the wealth of the Dādūpanthī manuscript tradition have been explored, most importantly by Svāmī Maṅgaldās and by Winand M. Callewaert. Whereas Sv. Maṅgaldās, in the earlier part of the twentieth century, established an overview of the sectarian authors and literature, Callewaert, starting in the early 1970s, filmed a host of texts and mainly aimed at the constitution of critical texts of Sant and related literature. Impressive and seminal to our understanding of the Dādūpanthī tradition and its mixing with traditions with which it shares the geographical and religious ground also is the catalogue that Harinārāyaṇ Purohit Vidyābhūṣaṇ prepared of his own collection, which was given to the Jaipur branch of the Rajasthan Oriental Research Institute, which also published the catalogue.[1] Sv. Maṅgaldās prepared a handlist of the precious loose leaf manuscripts and of select big bound anthologies kept in the main temple of the Dādūpanth at Naraina. In 2003, I started preparing a handlist of that

1. Gopālnārāyaṇ Bahurā and Lakṣmīnārāyaṇ Gosvāmī Dīkṣit (ed.), *Vidyābhūṣaṇ-granth-saṃgrah-sūcī*, Jodhpur: Rājasthān Prācya Vidyā Pratiṣṭhān, 1961.

collection and listed about a quarter to a third of the *c.* 150 anthologies that are now accessible and usable.[2] In the meanwhile, in February 2004, Brajendra Kumar Singhal from Jaipur, in collaboration with Gurumukhramji Ramsnehi, completed a catalogue of 637 MSS in the Naraina collection. This catalogue has to date remained unpublished.

My focus is on this collection of anthologies and the communal life that gave rise to them. I am consequently speaking of bound manuscripts that were scribed by monks for their own usage or commissioned by them to scribes. These hand-written books are called *guṭkās*. The owners and scribes, the date of completion of the manuscripts or of particular texts of these are given more often than not, and so are the lineage and place of residence or impermanent sojourn of their owners or scribes. Some of these books are tiny, but many have four to five hundred folios with scores of texts by various authors. The folios of the books were often numbered in the fashion of loose leaf manuscript folios before scribing and binding. This means that when bound, the second half of the book bore no page numbers which makes the cataloguing of those parts a little complicated, especially if the anthology contains a multitude of texts. Anthologies sometimes kept growing over several decades which is also the reason why they may bear more than one colophon. Physically, they are often divided into an inner block of folios and an outer one, which was actually meant not to be inscribed but to protect the manuscript pages from wear and tear. This outer block tended to be converted into a scrap-book and may contain anything, from short devotional texts to charms and recipes. A great part of these books was written in the eighteenth and nineteenth centuries. According to their most common function, these volumes, aesthetically so delightful with their often exquisite bindings, usually have a format convenient enough to serve travelling ascetics as vademecums. They were passed on from teacher to disciple or among the spiritual kin of a lineage. They represented sacred objects so that, also in case they were passed on to someone outside the lineage, they were supposed not to be sold, but given away for a ceremonial offering (*nichāvar*). In a contract affixed on the last page of one of these anthologies, it was stipulated in the presence of four witnesses that its new owner would never sell it.[3]

The writing of manuscripts in the Dādūpanth started with Dādū himself who appointed his disciple Mohandās Daftarī as his amanuensis. He wrote them down as and when he heard them uttered by his master. He did not put them together, however, at random, but gave the collection structure by alotting his master's sayings to appropriate chapters, accordings to topics

2. I acknowledge with gratitude the generous support extended to me in this by the abbot-in-chief of the Dādūpanth, Sv. Gopāldās, and I also thank Shri Sharad Chandra Ojha for his cooperation while listing the manuscripts.

3. NarG 65, V.S. 1832, agreement of V.S. 1876.

for the *sākhīs* (distichs) and according to *rāgas* for the *pads* (devotional songs). At least three authorities recorded Mohandās's activities, namely, Jangopāl, Dādū's disciple and hagiographer who finished his account of Dādū after his master's death; Dādū's disciple Ṭīlā, and Rāghavdās, who wrote in 1660. Jangopāl says,

> *siṣa mohana daphtarī bāṃcau hari guna liṣe re gura sūm sāṃcau/*
>
> I will name the disciple Mohan Daftarī, he writes down the praise of Hari, trustworthy through the guru.[4]

Jangopāl seems to say that what Mohandās writes is authenticated by the living testimony of Guru Dādū. Mohandās was a record-keeper (*daftarī*), and records needed to be authenticated by an authorized official. This fact is mentioned allegorically, as it seems. The process of preparing Dādū' *Vāṇī* is also mentioned by Ṭīlā in a devotional song in praise of Mohandās's devotion,[5]

> *bābā mohana āyo ho,*
> *ājñākārī sādha tho, thāṃ vegi bulāyo ho//ṭek//*
> *pada liṣato sāṣī liṣī, aru artha vicāryo ho/*
> *tumahī soṃ sanamuṣa rahyo, aura sabai nivāryo ho//1//*
> *hāṃjī hāṃjī hī kiyo, nāhīṃ kade na bhāṣyo ho/*
> *manasā vācā karmaṇā, mana tuma soṃ rāṣyo ho//2//*
>
> Bābā Mohan came,
> He was an obedient sadhu, you called him [that he come] speedily. (Refrain)
> He scribed the devotional songs, he scribed the distichs, and he thought about their meaning,
> His face was turned toward you, from everything else he abstained. (1)
> 'Yes, yes,' he said, but never anything [else],
> In thought, speech and deeds he kept his mind with you. (2)

---

4. Jangopāl, *The Hindī biography of Dādū Dayāl* (Dādū janma līlā), Delhi: Motilal Banarsidass, 1988, Chapter 13.25cd, translated by Callewaert as

> Mohan Dās Daftarī
> writes about the greatness of Hari
> who is above the guru.

This translation gives the line a meaning that runs against the belief of the Sants who would never call the guru inferior to Hari. I take *bāṃcau* as a 1st person singular, 'I will read, recite', unnasalized to rhyme with *sāṃcau*, 'true'.

5. Svāmī Maṅgaldās (ed.), *Sant-sāhitya-suman-mālā*, Jaipur: Śrī Svāmī Lakṣmīrām Ṭrasṭ, [V.S. 2022], pp. 4-5, 129 (no. 48).

Rāghavdās says about Mohandās's activities,[6]

> *dādūjī kī vāṇī ko khajānacī khabaradāra,*
> *vigati se likhata su mohana daphatarī/*
> *lekhanī ru dvāta saṃga kīnhī nāhī ājñā bhaṃga,*
> *śabada ucāra bhayo liyo likha tihiṃ gharī//*
> *jaise sūta sūtradhāra maṃdira uṭhāve dvāra,*
> *taise pada sākhī prakha jahāṃ kī tahāṃ dharī/*
> *raghavā dedīpyamāna ukati bhalo vicāra,*
> *saphala janama bhayo sevā guru kī karī//*

> Mohan Daftarī was the watchful treasurer of Dādūjī's *Vāṇī*,
> he wrote it down according to the context of the occasion,
> He carried with him pen and ink, he never failed to follow the order [to write],
> the moment a verse was uttered, he wrote it down.
> Like the puppeteer who sits in the house and pulls the [right] strings at the door,
> He examined the devotional songs and distichs and put them in their appropriate place.
> The bright [Mohan]–says Rāghav–thought thoroughly about the utterances,
> his life was fulfilled because he served the guru.

The earliest Dādūpanthī manuscript traced so far belongs to the Shree Sanjay Sharma Museum and Research Institute, Jaipur. Winand M. Callewaert reports its date as C.E. 1614 without giving its actual colophon.[7] That manuscript represents the *pañcvāṇī* type which is characteristic of the Dādūpanth in containing the works of Dādū, Kabīr, Nāmdev, Raidās and Haradās/Haridās. Unfortunately, Callewaert does not mention if the manuscript contains only the *pañcvāṇī* or also additional material. In any case, the manuscript gives evidence of the early emergence of a canon of scriptures created in the sect. Its underlying concept is that Dādū saw himself as member of the spiritual pedigree represented by those four Sants prior to him. Dādū saw himself indeed in a line with Kabīr, Nāmdev and Raidās, whereas he does not refer explicitly to Haradās/Haridās.[8] Jangopāl saw in him another Kabīr, whose vision he received in a state of profound

---

6. Rāghavdās, *Bhaktamāl, Svāmī Caturdās kṛt padya ṭīkā tathā (Sv. Nārāyaṇdās's)* Bhaktcaritra prakāśikā *gadya ṭīkā sahit,* ed. by Svāmī Nārāyaṇdās, Jaipur: Śrī Dādūdayāl Mahāsabhā, V.S. 2026, pp. 692-3, *manhar* 504. Mohandās Daftarī is not treated in a separate entry in the version of the *Bhaktamāl (Caturdās kṛt ṭīkā sahit)*, ed. by A. C. Nāhṭā, Jodhpur: Rajasthan Oriental Research Institute.
7. Winand M. Callewaert in collaboration with Swapna Sharma and Dieter Taillieu (ed.), *The Millennium Kabīr Vāṇī: A Collection of Pad-s*, New Delhi: Manohar, 2000, p. 21.
8. For references, see Winand M. Callewaert and Bart Op de Beeck (ed.), *Devotional Hindī Literature/Nirguṇ bhakti sāgar*, 2 vols., New Delhi: Manohar, 1991.

contemplation.[9] Right in the beginning of his hagiography he positions Dādū in the genealogy of the Sants which is justified, indeed, and authenticated by his master's life.[10] The *pañcvāṇī* type of manuscripts therefore clearly expresses the Panth's identity as it has been expressed from its formative period. There is no way to know if the material compiled by Mohandās Daftarī comprised texts besides Dādū's own sayings. Given the charismatic presence of Dādū and the size of the corpus of his sayings, it seems likely that Mohandās concentrated just on these. The unusual uniformity of the tradition of the *Dādūvāṇī*, notwithstanding a few *sākhīs* and *pads* more or less shifted to different places in different manuscripts, suggests that Mohandās's version of the *Dādūvāṇī* came to be considered canonical. Competition with the Sikh tradition which produced the first version of the *Ādi Granth* to be displayed as a sacred object in summer 1604 may have spurred the almost immediate acceptance of Mohandās's version as the standard. The scribing of only the sayings of Dādū with no other material added remained an ongoing practice in the Panth. There is one description of the *Dādūvāṇī* being installed as a sacred object in the temple of Naraina after Dādū's death. Dādū died on the eighth day of the dark half of the month of Jeṭh in the Vikrama year 1660, which corresponds to 23 April 1603. The description forms part of Mādhavdās's *Sant-guṇ-sāgar*, a text whose present form is fraught with problems. Mādhavdās was a disciple of Dādū who begun his composition in the village of Gūlar in V.S. 1650 and completed it on the third bright day of the month of Āṣāṛh of V.S. 1601, which corresponds to 20 June 1604. On the first anniversary of Dādū's death, the *Sant-guṇ-sāgar* was recited for the first time.[11] However, the text underlying the edition was certainly reworked so that we have before us a pastiche that represents also an answer to the needs of subsequent generations. With this reservation, I am here quoting the relevant passage,[12]

dohā
āṣāḍha śukla aṣṭamī, guruvāṇī tharapāya/
mandira meṁ jaya bola kari, bhoga prasāda lagāya//1//
indava chanda
mandira meṁguruvāṇi virājata, dāsa gupāla ju chāpa pujārī/
gādi khaṛāū su pustaka vastrahi, ṭopi ju kesaru sauṃja saṁvārī/
sauṃja banāya dharī takhatā pari, ūpara āṁcala dharahiṁ bhārī/
prātaka dhūpa niśā kari dīpaka, yoṁ kari pūjana sāṁjha saṁvārī//2//
bāṁcata santakathā guru grantha ju, dāsa gopāla ucāra karāī/
saṃta samāja sabai maṃḍalī mila, svamiju saṃta sabhā madha āī/

9. *Dādū janma līlā*, Chapter 2.3-4.
10. *Dādū janma līlā*, Chapter 1.3.
11. Mādhavdās, *Sant-guṇ-sāgar*, ed. and comm. by Pt. Bakśīrām Śāstrī, Bhairāṇā: Mahant Rāmvallabh Dās Svāmī, V.S. 2056, Chapter 25.26-7.
12. *Sant-guṇ-sāgar*, Chapter 25.1-6.

hota kathā nita doya muhūrata, saṃta kathā kari śabdahu gāī/
dhyāna dhareṁ aru bhojana pāvata, saṃta ju āsana jāya rahāī//3//
pāchali yāma su saṃta ru sādhu ju, nhāvata dhovana śauca karāī/
prāta su sāṁjha kareṁ mili gāvata, ḍholaka jhāṁjhu maṃjīra bajāī/
ārati sāṁjha kareṁ mili gāvata, baiṭhata hī pada maṃgala gāī/
āsana pe phira jāya virājata, yoṁ niśi vāsara saṃta rahāī//4//
pālaki chāpa dharī guru mandira, savya banāya subhāṁti sajāī/
jo apano gurupaṃtha upāsaka, pāsa rakhe guruvāṇī pujāī/
dāsa garība daī saba ko sudha, saṃta sudhānahiṁ vāṇi dharāī/
deśa diśā nija sādhuna ko paṭhi, mādhava vāṇiju kīrati gāī//5//
dādu guru nija āyasu pāvata, rajjaba mohana śrī jagannāthā/
sākhi hu śodha anukrama rākhata, tāla ru rāga garībahiṁ sāthā/
aṃga saiṁtīsa sākhi likhī saba, rāga satāisa śabdahiṁ gāthā/
yoṁ kari saṃta likhī guru vāṇiju, sthāna ru sthāna bhaī vikhyātā//6//

On the eighth day of the bright half of Āṣāṛh (24 June 1604), the *Guruvāṇī* was installed,
Hail was shouted in the temple, and food-*prasād* was served. (1)
The *Guruvāṇī* was residing in the temple, and Gopāl Dās received the designation of *pujārī*.
The *gādī,* the sandals, the book wrapt in cloth, and the saffron-coloured cap were arranged as items of veneration.
These items were placed on a throne, and above this a heavy curtain was suspended.
Early in the morning, by incense; at night, by a lamp; this is how the twilight worship was arranged. (2)
Gopāl Dās made a saintly homily, he recited from the *Gurugranth,*
All the local congregations of the holy society gathered in Svāmīju's hall of congregation.
For two *muhūrts*[13] there was always a homily, then the Sants sang devotional songs.
After meditation they were fed, upon which they retired to their places. (3)
At the last watch of the night, the Sants and Sadhus were made to purify themselves and bathe.
In the morning, they sang together at the twilight worship and played drums and cymbals.
The twilight *āratī* they performed together and sang, and in a sitting posture sang auspicious songs.
Then they retired again to their places. This is how the Sants were made to pass day and night. (4)
The Guru's temple received the name 'Palanquin', it was nicely arranged and decorated.
Those who were lay followers of the Guru's Path kept a *Guruvāṇī* which they worshipped.

---

13. A *muhūrt* lasts forty-eight minutes.

> Garīb Dās admonished and reminded every Sant that he should keep a scripture.
> Everywhere he sent his sadhus. Mādhav, the glory of the *Vāṇī* was sung. (5)
> Authorized by Guru Dādū himself, Rajjab, Mohan and Śrī Jagannāth
> revised the *sākhīs* and put them in order, for the *tālas* and *rāgas* [this was done] together with Garīb.
> All the *sākhīs* were written down in thirty-seven chapters, and the devotional songs in twenty-seven *rāgas*.
> In this way the Sant scribed the *Guruvāṇī* and it became famous everywhere. (6)

Garīb was Dādū's elder son and became his successor, Raj(j)ab[14] his Paṭhān disciple and a famous author, and Jagannāth, a Kāyasth by caste, was himself a poet and compiler of poetry.[15] As I said, the text may reflect that the Dādūpanth vied with the Sikhs for being first in installing their scripture as a sacred object, for the *Ādi Granth* as completed under Guru Arjan was installed in the Harimandir of Rāmdāspur (to be named subsequently Amritsar) on the first bright day of the month of Bhādoṁ of V.S. 1661/16 August 1604, that is, according to Mādhavdās, a little more than two months later than *Dādūvāṇī*.[16] If the report is authentic, the redaction of Dādū's sayings was made by the aforementioned four disciples and Dādū's son, respectively, one would think on the basis of the material gathered systematically by Mohandās. That Garīb should have been consulted for the *pads* has the obvious reason that he was an acclaimed musician besides being the chief authority of the Panth. These bits of information suggest that the first redaction of the scripture consisted exclusively of Dādū's sayings with the *pañcvāṇī* coming into use side by side with it.

The generation of Dādū's disciples also developed the tradition reflected in the later anthologies such as those under review. Already in that early period, we encounter anthologies either of the whole or parts of the *Dādūvāṇī* or the whole or parts of the *pañcvāṇī* plus additional material from the regionally and religiously related traditions. This is illustrated by MS 12 in the library of the Dādū Mahāvidyālay, Jaipur, dated C.E. 1636. Besides the *pañcvāṇī* it contains 'Gorakhanātha and other poets.'[17] Another case in point is MS 2 in the same library, forty years younger (C.E. 1676). Callewaert lists its contents,[18]

---

14. The MSS normally have the spelling 'Rajab', whereas modern editions replace this sometimes by the standard spelling 'Rajjab'.
15. Rāghavdās, *Bhaktamāl*, ed. A. C. Nāhṭā, p. 197, *chapai* 417.
16. Madanjit Kaur, *The Golden Temple Past and Present*, Amritsar: Guru Nanak Dev University, 1983, p. 16.
17. Winand M. Callewaert, 'Search for manuscripts of the Dādū-panthī literature in Rājasthān.' *Orientalia Lovanensia Periodica* 4 (1973), pp. 155-67, p. 166. Callewaert does not give the colophon and the Vikrama date of the manuscript.
18. Ibid., pp. 166-7. The colophon and the Vikrama date of the MS are not given.

DM 2, p. 1-64 Dādū - *Vāṇī* (1676), 70-78 Garīb - Vāṇī, 129-152 Nāmadev, Raidās and Haradās, 153-329 about 25 poets of different sects, 329-332 Jagannāth – *Mohamard rājā kī kathā*, 332-338 Nārāyaṇadās – *Citraket*, 342-346 Khemadās, 347 Harisiṃha – *Citāvanī* (347 *Dhūndhalī*... by Cain?), 348 Cain – *Karaṇīsār*, 348-351 Bājīd, 351-353 Nārāyaṇadās, 354-362 different minor poets, 362-390 Anantadās, 390-407 Janagopāl, 408 Haridās *nirañjanī*, 408-411 Bakhanā, 411-413 Jagajīvan – *Dṛṣṭānt sākhī*, 415 Jaimal, 416 Ṭīlājī, 424 Rajab, 430-460 Lāladās – *Itihās sār bhāṣā*, 460-499 Catradās – *Bhāgavat ekādaś bhāṣā*, 499-521 Dāmodarajī – *Mārkaṇḍey purāṇ*, 521-536 Jagannath – *Guṇagañjanāmā*, 536-547 Sundaradās – *Gyānasamudra*, 547-569 Nārāyaṇadās – *Bhāgavat aṣṭam skandha bhāṣā*.

An especially impressive anthology is MS 34 of the Vidyābhūṣaṇ Collection of the Rajasthan Oriental Research Institute, Jaipur, which bears two dates, namely, V.S. 1710 and V.S. 1715.[19] It contains 256 works by different authors. Whereas the aforementioned items are loose-leaf manuscripts, this last-mentioned one is a *guṭkā* of 581 folios. It ranges within a type of manuscripts in which the text material is arranged in a relatively loose sequence, albeit with a preference for presenting Dādū's work or that of one's own lineage ancestor towards the beginning and forming clusters according to the religious provenance of texts. This can be distinguished from a second type in which the material is arranged by topics. Of this, the model is the *Dādūvāṇī* itself which is characterized by thematic arrangement of the *sākhīs* and the musical one of the *pads*. Within the thematical groups and *rāgas*, respectively, the second type of *guṭkās* groups the material by literary genre and authors. Exemplars of this type are the huge compilations made by Gopāldās and Rajab, both of them very close to the lifetime of Dādū. Gopāldās finished his compilation in V.S. 1684/C.E. 1628 and Rajab at about the same time. [20] The anthologies share a number of features beyond those already mentioned:

1. They represent the contact of the Dādūpanth with other religious traditions of Rajasthan. In the first place the yogic tradition deserves to be mentioned, because it has been integral to the Dādūpanthī tradition which re-interprets it in its own Sant fashion. Pervasive, though less voluminous is the presence of western Indian traditions, such as that of the Panjab and Gujarat (Narasiṃha Mahetā), with a conspicuously minimal representation of the Mīrā tradition. The Jain tradition figures sparsely, too, whereas the Nirañjanī tradition is represented fairly well. The Dādūpanthī tradition has always been

19. Bahura and Dīkṣit, *Vidyābhūṣaṇ-granth-saṃgrah-sūcī*, pp. 38-53.

20. For Gopāldās, see the edition by Winand M. Callewaert, *The* Sarvāṃgī *of Gopāldās: A 17th Century Anthology of Bhakti Literature*, New Delhi: Manohar, 1993, and Callewaert's *The* Sarvāṅgī *of the Dādūpanthī Rajab*, Leuven: Katholieke Universiteit, Distributors: D. K. Publishers, New Delhi, 1978.

permeable to the wider Vaiṣṇava tradition and the non-sectarian narrative tradition. Prominently figure, in the period under review, the *Bhagavadgītā*, the *Bhāgavata ekādaśa skandha, Viṣṇusahasranāma* and Vaiṣṇava *stotras*. A good number of texts exhibit an interest in reflecting the six philosophical systems. All this shows not a sectarian offstandishness from the wider religious debates, but a lively participation in them. The Muslim tradition is prominently represented, mainly by its Panjabi intermediaries. This is due to the presence of Dādūpanthīs in the Panjab as well as of Sikhs south of the Panjab.[21] The most voluminous work of this origin to be found in Dādūpanthī anthologies is the translation of the abridged Persian version of Al-Ghazālī's *Iḥyā'*, the *Kīmiyā al-sa'ādat* by Aḍḍan, entitled *Pārasbhāg* in its translation.[22] The underlying Persian version enjoyed wide popularity, also in a later period when it was translated into Urdu and printed in1862.[23]

2. In the period under review, the Muslim disciples of Dādū, mainly of the line of Rajab, occupied pride of place in the Dādūpanthī manuscript tradition. They were no less present than in the beginning. Sv. Maṅgaldās published a number of editions of prominent Dādūpanthī authors. Wondering what may have been the principles of selection of the authors and their works, one discovers that he tacitly and most appropriately went by the criterion of the prominence given to them in the anthologies. These authors faithfully represent the trans-Hindu-Muslim stance of the sect.[24] Considering the Brahmanical reform imposed upon the sect in the beginning of the eighteenth century and the ban on Muslim teachers from it, their presence reveals the resilience in spirit and intellect and the catholicity of the group.
3. From the earliest phase of writing by Dādū's disciples, there has existed a productive interest in exegesis and homiletic practice. This

---

21. Prominent authors are, for example, Saman, Farīd, or Qāẓī Qādan. The Sikh influence on the Dādūpanth can hardly be overrated, but it remains to be studied systematically.
22. At least one MS containing the text forms part of Naraina's *guṭkā* collection. It was scribed in V.S. 1861 in the line of Banvārīdās, the man to whom the expansion of the Dādūpanth to Hisar and further on to wider parts of Panjab and Haryana and the creation of its Utarādhā branch is owed. I may point to two more MSS, one undated in a private collection, the other MS 4 of the Vidyābhūṣāṇ Collection.
23. Ulrike Stark, *An Empire of Books: The Naval Kishore Press and the Diffusion of the Printed Word in Colonial India 1858-1895* [forthcoming].
24. This may also have been the reason why Sv. Maṅgaldās devoted himself to the edition of these authors. He believed that the Sant tradition had a lesson to teach to the emerging nation, as he hoped a nation that would not be divided by distinctions of caste and creed. On the life and mission of that great Nirañjanī devotee, reformer and educational activist, see Surjandās Svāmī, *Tyāgmūrti Svāmī Śrī Maṅgaldās smṛti-granth*, Jaipur: Svāmī Śrī Maṅgaldās Smṛtigranth Prakāśansamiti, V.S. 2043.

is overwhelmingly demonstrated by the anthologies. I hinted at this earlier, when I mentioned the well-known fact that Dādū's own work is, for its distichs, arranged by topics. The modern practice to introduce a sermon or a performance of songs by, and to intersperse it with, thematically appropriate distichs is a mere continuation of the usage also reflected by the redactional principles of manuscripts. As far as the anthologies quote from Dādū's distichs, there seems to lie preference on the first four chapters, the others being quoted perhaps less frequently. A trace of this preference is found in modern editions where in the passages from the distichs of Dādū recommended for contemplation, the first few are clearly emphasised.[25] By the period under review, some of Sundardās's works must have attained liturgical status. These were certainly his 'Octaves' (*aṣṭaka*s), which form part of the daily liturgy. Probably also the chapter of his *Savaiyās* entitled 'Citāvanī' (Warning) as well as texts of the 'Warning' genre by other authors were popular. Like Sundardās's, these were often composed in *savaiyā* or related metres which are popular and effectfully usable in communal worship. The *savaiyā* metre was popular at the time, and also Dādūpathī authors excelled in it.

4. The anthologies abound in narrative hagiographical texts, among which Jangopāl's are probably the most frequently occurring.
5. Much space in the anthologies is occupied by the genre of examples. Most prominent is perhaps the composition by Jagjīvandās which we find from the early stage of the Dādūpanthī manuscript tradition.[26] There is a plethora of texts called 'miscellaneous (*phuṭkar*),' usually arranged systematically by topics so that pertinent ones could be found quickly. The genre finds its modern continuation in the six-volume collection of examples by Sv. Nārāyaṇdās 'Puṣkar.'[27] The genre of examples is supplemented by texts listing conceptual categories, such as cosmological, mythological, philosophical or theological ones. In this category, a sub-category would be that of lists of synonyms for key-terms of bhakti. The oldest within the Dādūpanth seems to be Garībdās's *Anabhayaprabodha*.[28] Whereas it

---

25. See Balrām Svāmī, *Śrī Dādū Dayālu nityapāṭhratnāvalī*, Jaipur: Śrī Dādū Satsāhitya Maṇḍal, V.S. 2027. Also Kanīrām Svāmī, *Svāmī Śrī Dādū Dayālu svādhyāy-saṃgrah*, Baṛāgāṃv (Dt. Jhuṃjhunūṃ): Śyāmsundar Omprakāś Bhānīrām, V.S. 2030.

26. Winand M. Callewaert, 'Search for manuscripts of the Dādū-panthī literature in Rājasthān,' p. 159. See also the passage quoted from this source on p. 172 of this contribution.

27. Svāmī Nārāyaṇdās 'Puṣkar,' *Śrīdṛṣṭānt-sudhā-sindhu*, 6 vols. Puṣkar: Author, n.d.-V.S. 2019.

28. Garībdās, *Garībdās jī kī vāṇī*, ed. by Svāmī Maṅgaldās. Jaipur: Śrī Svāmī Lakṣmīrām Trasṭ, V.S. 2004; Winand M. Callewaert, 'The *Anabhay-prabodha* of the Dādū-panthī

is true that it represents a kind of glossary, as Sv. Maṅgaldās, its first editor, appropriately classified it, it is more than a mere glossary of synonyms. Garībdās's copyists classify the text expressly as an exegetical and spiritual exercise, for they call it *adhyātam bodh*, 'spiritual understanding' as well as *adhyātam anabhay prabodh*, 'understanding of the spiritual experience.'[29]

6. The anthologies unite numerous exegetical texts. In these, the works of several Sant authors were supplemented by exegetical paraphrases, called *adhyātmik arth*. These have, therefore, a systematic connection with the word exegesis of the type produced by Garībdās. I may mention the example of an anthology, scribed in the middle of the eighteenth century and rich in that exegetical genre (NarG 39, V.S. 1801). Amongst its many texts are no less than five exegetical commentaries, namely, on Dādū's *Kāyābelī*, Kabīr's distichs and songs, Gorakhnāth's *Ulṭī bāṇī*, and Bakhanā's songs.[30]

The existence of innumerable Dādūpanthī anthologies with their particular inventory of textual genres can be understood conclusively if we only review the religious practice of the Panth as it can be reconstructed from Jangopāl's *Dādū janma līlā*. Also instructive is the perhaps too neat description given by Mādhavdās and quoted above.[31] The peripatetic life of Dādū and his following was the indispensable instrument for building up and maintaining local communities of the emerging sect. It provided for the 'domestication' of the Panth, to call it by a term used by Ivan Strenski, [32] that is, for the creation of a territorial structure binding ascetics and laity and making this dependent on the reciprocity of service, the exchange of spiritual well-being provided by the ascetics for material well-being provided by the lay followers. Jangopāl's work records over long passages a kind of itinerary of his master and his disciples who travelled from place to place, and it thereby displays the enormous importance that was attributed to this activity, an importance that it has retained for the present-day *virakts*, the monastic branch that emulates Dādū's itinerant life. With his following the master moved from village to village, from local community of followers to another local community. The arrival of the Dādūpanthī following of ascetics and lay supporters was celebrated by the village communities by religious functions

---

Garībdās,' *Orientalia Lovanensia Periodica* 5 (1974), pp. 163-85; (continued as:) 'Key for understanding mystical literature', *Orientalia Lovanensia Periodica* 8 (1977), pp. 309-30.

29. Callewaert, 'The *Anabhay-prabodha...*,' p. 163, fn. 1.

30. Bakhanā was a disciple of Dādū himself. His works were edited by Sv. Maṅgaldās as *Baṣanājī kī vāṇī*, Jaipur: Śrī Svāmī Lakṣmīrām Ṭrasṭ, 1937.

31. See pp. 169-71.

32. Ivan Strenski, 'On Generalized Exchange and the Domestication of the Sangha,' *Man* (NS), 18 (1983), pp. 463-77.

and communal feasts which were called *mahochau*. An example of this is given by Jangopāl in a chapter densely packed with the enumeration of such incidents.[33]

> 7. Rajab decided to organize a great festival
> and invited Svāmījī.
> He tried different ways to convince Svāmījī to come,
> saying that the Indweller would shower His grace on them.
> 8. He urged him repeatedly,
> till Svāmījī gave the order for the journey and
> got on his way after a week.
> He blessed the Sants he met on the way.
> 9. The first stop was Alhanyāvās
> and everybody worshipped the Indweller:
> Bohith, Khem Dās, Ṭīkā,
> Khetā, Tohā and Gobinda, all outstanding persons.
> 10. In Kārū lived an ascetic called Ghaḍasī,
> a man with the temper of a real ascetic.
> His family held a great festival,
> spending all they possessed.
> 11. Then they arrived in Kevalpur, where
> all Sants gathered when they heard his name.
> A great festival of devotion, with religious celebrations,
> was organized for four days, to the great joy of Rajab.
> 12. Rāghav, Gobinda, and Narāin were Rajab's disciples,
> experienced in devotion,
> Ṭhākur Dās invited him to Nilyā,
> making all the arrangements for his stay.
> 13. Govinda Dās also came there
> and seeing Dādū his hope was fulfilled.
> A great festival of devotion was held
> and Svāmījī gave joy to all.

The religious gatherings comprised preaching, singing, spiritual discussions, and also religious instruction, as is described a number of times.

> *āṃbanerī svāṃmī āye rājā parajā kai mani bhāye/*
> *nisadīna bhīra hoi darabārā kathā kīratana gyāṃna bicārā/*

> When Svāmījī came to Āmer,
> the King and the people were overjoyed.
> Day and night the crowds flocked to his house,
> to hear devotional songs and narratives.[34]

---

33. Jangopāl, *Dādū janma līlā*, 1988, Chapter 13.7-13; in the following the translation is Callewaert's unless otherwise stated.

34. Jangopāl, *Dādū janma līlā*, Chapter 4.1.

For the present purpose, the last line should be rendered more precisely as '[there took place] homilies (*kathā*), praise (*kīratana*) and reflection on wisdom (*gyāṃna bicārā*).' In Chapter 12, v. 24a, we read,

> *bahuta bhāṃti bhojana karavāyau kathā kīratanu ati suṣa pāyau/*

> He arranged for plenty of food and
> in the instruction and singing he found happiness.

Here, *kathā*, 'homily', is rendered by 'instruction' and *kīratanu*, 'praise,' by 'singing.' Similarly, Chapter 15, v. 13, reads,

> *mile narāiṃnadāsa ru svāṃmī mānūṃ pragaṭe aṃtarajāṃmī/*
> *kathā kīratana goṣṭi kīnīṃ thore hīṃ maiṃ saba lași līnīṃ/*

> When Narāin Dās met Svāmījī,
> it was as if the Indweller had appeared.
> Holy instructions, singing and discussions were organized,
> even a small participation fulfilled all purposes.[35]

Here again *kathā* and *kīratana* occur together, supplemented by *goṣṭi*, 'discussion'. To this may be added the term *[gura] upadesau*, 'instruction by the guru', which is also part of the discursive exercises.[36] Whereas *goṣṭ[h]i* and *upadesau* are more private than public and require two or more interlocutors, *kathā* and *kīrtan* are executed by a preacher before an audience and by a congregation, respectively. The *kathā* calls for rhetorical structure and the *kīrtan* for music. We know virtually no details about preaching in the Dādūpanth during its formative period and, for that matter, in the pre-contemporary period. The only information that we have concerns the timings and the length of the homilies. It occurs in a passage of the *Sant-guṇ-sāgar* which was quoted above.[37] The text says that the homilies held in front of the shrine containing Dādū's scripture took about one hour and a half. Today a *kathā* lasts around an hour and is executed at a relatively high speed, at least faster than ordinary speech, and makes use of the kind of material that one finds also in the *guṭkās*. To hold a sermon requires a thorough command of the literary tradition and that the orator can rely on homiletic tools or has preferably stored a good part of the relevant material

35. The last line of the translation would read more correctly, '... in a little while all purposes were fulfilled.'

36. For example, Jangopāl, *Dādū janma līlā*, Chapter 15.4.

37. See p. 170.

in his memory.[38] Also in the initial period of the Panth, preaching required a well-assorted arsenal of examples and stories to relate successfully to the audience. Hagiography especially praises Rajab's talent for fleshing out his sermons with examples.[39] Garībdās is reported to have been a powerful orator, spirited singer and accomplished musician, and with a stock comparison, though a telling one, the hagiographer Rāghavdās compares the three men to Vyāsa, Prahlāda and Nārada, respectively.[40]

From the earliest period, the celebration of the *āratī* has been at the heart of communal worship, and this was also an occasion for the visibly emotional, ecstatic ways of worshipping, such as dancing.[41] While Dādū was present in the flesh, he himself formed the object of the *āratī*.[42] Already during Dādū's lifetime, congregational places (*dvārau*) started springing up.[43] Dādū is, for example, reported to have stayed for three months at the *dvārau* somewhere in the region around Rodū, then again at Īḍvā, where a sizable structure of communal life had already emerged, for there was a sadhu who conducted the kitchen, and an extended sojourn of his at the *dvārau* at Punyānā is also reported.[44] The local communities must be assumed to have held *āratīs* in those congregational places also in the absence of Dādū. Dādū's own *āratī* compositions form part of the liturgy, additional *āratīs* by other authors may be added to them, and *āratī* collections are a particular genre frequently occurring in the *guṭkās.*

The earliest recorded religious practice in the Dādūpanth clearly required the kind of texts that form the contents matter of the manuscripts. Irrespective of certain variants, the types of manuscripts that came into use in the formative period of the Dādūpanth remained productive throughout its history. The anthologies of the eighteenth and nineteenth centuries hand down and update the material, but typologically they do not differ in principle from earlier exemplars. I argue that the Dādūpanth was a writing community from the beginning, no matter how impressive an oral tradition was at work side by side with the written. The scripture and the exegetical and homiletically relevant material was hardly committed to writing from memory, but from written material. Consequently, I do not share Winand M.

---

38. For contemporary Dādūpanthī preaching, see Monika Thiel-Horstmann, 'Dādūpanthī Sermons,' in Richard K. Barz and Monika Thiel-Horstmann (ed.), *Living Texts from India*, Wiesbaden: Otto Harrassowitz, 1989, pp. 144-83; Monika Thiel-Horstmann, 'An Oral Theology: Dādūpanthī Homilies,' in Ronald S. McGregor (ed.), *Devotional Literature in South Asia: Current Research, 1985-1988*, Cambridge: Cambridge University Press, 1992, pp. 36-47.

39. Rāghavdās, *Bhaktamāl*, ed. Agarcand Nāhṭā, p. 187, *chapai* 378; 189, *indav* 387.

40. Ibid., p. 184, *manhar* 366.

41. *Dādū janma* līlā, Chapters 14.4, 18, 26, and 15.6.

42. Ibid., Chapters 14.5, 14.18, 14.26, and 15.6.

43. Ibid., Chapters 13.21, 13.24.

44. Ibid., Chapters 13.4-5, 13.19-24, and 14.5, respectively.

Callewaert's 'disbelieving belief' that the huge compilations of the *Sarvāṅgīs* by a Rajab or a Gopāldās were produced from memory. He is of the opinion that these authors prepared their texts on the basis of the repertoires of singers.[45] Why, if already Dādū himself arranged for his sayings to be written down, should later authors have reverted to scribing on the basis of oral repertoires? It is rather likely that various and numerous individual repertoires were written down by redactors and used for the compilation of huge collections, whereas it is rather unlikely that they committed to writing their aural impression of individual repertoires. This is not to say that the oral, the aural and the written did not influence each other, though not in ways readily warranting the audacious hypothesis put forth by Callewaert. To test the hypotheses about the modes of textual transmission, the various works preserved in, and the variants of tradition reflected by, the anthologies under review commend themselves to further examination.

45. *The* Sarvāṅgī *of Gopāldās*, p. 6.

The Signs of Death According to the *Jñāndev Gāthā*

Catharina Kiehnle

Jñāndev, one of the most famous poet saints of Maharashtra, lived most probably at the end of the thirteenth century. He is mainly known for his *Bhagavadgītā* commentary called *Jñāneśvarī,* and his independent philosophical work *Anubhavāmṛt* which propagates a sort of Śaiva monism. He is also credited with about 1200 songs, *abhaṅgas*. The collection is called *Jñāndev gāthā*. The best known songs of the *Gāthā* are a collection of 27 *abhaṅga*s dedicated to god in the form of Hari or Viṣṇu, the *Haripāṭh*. It is considered the basic text of the Vārkarī Panth, as the Bhāgavata movement is called in Maharashtra. Apart from devotional songs on God and *guru*, the pilgrimage to Paṇḍharpūr and on various philosophical topics, the *Gāthā* also contains compositions on yoga, which I have dealt with elsewhere.[1] Moreover, one finds a very peculiar song on a subject otherwise not mentioned in devotional song collections, namely on the physical signs of approaching death.

In spite of being peculiar, the song seems to have been quite popular. Not only has it been included in all the printed *Gāthās* since 1877, it also occurs in the manuscripts collected by me in 1984 in Dhuḷe, Poona and Bombay. The quest resulted in 1654 Jñāndev songs. Since some of them are found more than once, a total of 784 of individual songs remains. In the 'hit list' of those songs the *abhaṅga* in question is high up, occuring 14 times. That is, at one time it must have been almost as popular as the *abhaṅga*s of Haripāṭh which occur 12 to 22 times in the manuscripts.

The text is published in the extant *Gāthās* with only a few and unspectacular variations which mostly concern orthography. It was, therefore, quite easy to prepare the following 'edition' with the printed material. 'A' refers to the oldest edition by R. S. Goṃdhḷekar of 1891, which is a reprint of 1867, 'F' to the edition by P. N. Jośī of 1969. B, C, C1, D, E, E1 stand for the editions published during the 100 years between 1891 and 1969.[2]

---

1. Catharina Kiehnle, 1. *Songs on Yoga*. 2. *Conservative Vaiṣṇava*, Jñandev Studies I-III, 2 vols., Stuttgart: Franz Steiner, 1997.

2. A: *Śrī Jñāndevācā Gāthā*, ed. by R. Ś. Goṃdhḷekar, Puṇe, A.D. 1891; A1: *Śrī Jñāneśvar Mahārājāṃcī Gāthā*, ed. by T. N. Pāṅgaḷ, Puṇe, 1927; B: *Śrī Jñāneśvarmahārājācyā*

A 604 (separation of words, numbering, and indication of *caraṇ*s by me)

kānīṃ ghāluniyāṃ boṭeṃ ' nāda je pāhāve //
na disatāṃ jāṇāveṃ ' naū divasa // 1 //
bhoṃvayā pāhātāṃ ' na dise jāṇā //
āyuṣyācī gaṇanā ' sāta divasa // 2 (dhru) //
ḍoḷāṃ ghāloniyāṃ boṭa ' cakra jeṃ pāhāveṃ //
na disatāṃ jāṇāveṃ ' pāṃca divasa // 3 //
nāsāgrāceṃ agra ' na dise nayanīṃ //
tarī teṃcī dinīṃ ' hmaṇā rāmakṛṣṇa // 4 //
jñānadeva hmaṇe ' heṃ sādhūceṃ lakṣaṇa //
aṃtakāḷīṃ āpaṇa ' pahā vegīṃ // 5 //

Variants

1a: B, E, E1, F *ghālūniyāṃ*; 2a: E, E1, F *pāhatāṃ*; 2b: A *pahāveṃ*; 3a: E, E1, F *ghāloniyāṃ*; 4a: E, E1, F *nāsāgrīceṃ*; 4c: A, E, E1, F *tecī*; 4c: F *dinī*; 4d: A, C, C1, E, E1, F *mhaṇā*; 5a: A1 *mhaṇeṃ*; C1, E, E1, F *mhaṇe*; 5b: D *sādhūṃceṃ*; 5d: D, E, E1, F *vegīṃ pāhā*.

Translation

After putting one's fingers into one's ears, and after not seing/perceiving the sounds one should see/perceive, one should know: nine days (1). When one looks [at] the brows and does not see [them], know: life's counting [is] seven days (2). After putting one's fingers into one's eyes and after not seeing the circles one should see, one should know: five days (3). [When] the tip of the nose is not visible with/in the eyes, then that very day say: Rāmakṛṣṇa (4). Jñānadeva says, that is the sign of (for) the wise one. At the time of the end, see quickly [by] yourself (5).

Of the 14 MSS 12 are from the Samartha Vāgdevatā Mandir, Dhuḷe (S), one from Rājvāḍe Saṃśodhan Maṇḍal, Dhuḷe (R), and one from Bhāratīya Itihās Saṃśodhan Mandal in Puṇe (Bh): S 132, 169, 217, 550, 604, 697, 1159, 1254, 1449, 1510, 1733, 2085, R 200, and Bh 482.3. Most of them are *bāḍ*s (S 169, 550, 604, 697, 1159, 1254, 1449, 1733, 2085) and *vahī*s (S 132, 1510, R 200, Bh 482.3). The latter look like copy-books, the former are more narrow, with the lines written parallel to the stitched middle fold of the long folios. S 217 is a professionally written *pothī*, that is,

---

Abhaṅgāṃcī Gāthā, ed. by G. N. Dātār, Muṃbaī, 1906; C: *Jñāndevācī Gāthā*, ed. by V. N. Jog, Puṇe, 1907; C1: *Śrīsakalasaṃtagāthā*, ed. by K. A. Jośī, Puṇe, 1967. D: *Śrījñāndevmahārāj yāṃcyā Abhaṅgāṃcī Gāthā*, ed. by T. H. Avṭe, Puṇe, 1923; E: *Śrījñāneśvarmahārāj yāṃcī Sārtha Gāthā*, ed. by V. N. Sākhre, Āḷaṃdī, 1934; E1: *Śrī Jñāneśvar Mahārāj viracit Amṛtānubhav, Cāṅgdevpāsaṣṭhī, Haripāṭh, Abhaṅgagāthā*; ed. by J. Paṃḍit; Āḷaṃdī, 1977; F: *Sārtha Śrī Jñāndev Abhaṅga Gāthā*; ed. by P. N. Jośī, Puṇe, 1969. For the description of the editions see Catharina Kiehnle, *Songs on Yoga*, pp. 21-4.

it consists of separate pages that are folded in the middle, like many Sanskrit scriptures. All MSS are written on paper, which is more or less thick and rough. S 550, 1449, and 1733 contain great collections of Jñāndev *abhaṅga*s and are well-written, perhaps also by professionals, just als S 1254. The other MSS, too, are quite readable, although the scribe of S 169 was not able to keep his syllables in a straight line. S 132 is mouse-eaten. Not much can be said about the age of the MSS, most of which come from Rāmdāsī *maṭha*s and institutions all over Maharashtra and Tanjore. Some of them may date back to the seventeenth century like the *maṭha*s themselves. Bh 482 looks the most ancient but is written in various scripts so that some parts of the contents may be younger than others. The edges of some of the MSS are worn off due to usage. S 550, 1254, 1449 and 1733, however, look quite fresh. None of the MSS under discussion here is dated—a common feature of many *abhaṅga* MSS.

Whereas the versions of the editions do not differ much, those of MSS do so, even quite considerably in some places. Since the *abhaṅga*s were transmitted partly orally and partly in writing, and because the texts have gone through many hands, ears and throats, it is of course impossible to arrive at something like an 'Urfassung' or a stemma. It is similarly impossible to produce a contamination-free version of the text. Considering that private singers and public *kīrtankār*s met and meet on all sorts of occasions, like home gatherings, temple performances or during the pilgrimage to Paṇḍharpūr, the exchange of 'readings' is not astonishing.

Still, the variants are not completely arbitrary but can be grouped into several types, and even reveal stages of transmission. The most important variant from the latter point of view concerns the number of stanzas in the editions. There are of course variations in the MSS because it is easy to forget a passage in the midst of very similar-sounding sentences—or to add one, as in S 217 after stanza 4. Most MSS, however, contain six stanzas as against five of the editions. A closer look reveals that most probably a scribe or editor jumped from stanza 4b to 5c, dropping the four *caraṇ*s in between. In the following, the forgotten *caraṇ*s, taken from S 550, are printed in bold:

nāsikācem̟ agra ' na dīse nayani /
taici traya dini ' urale jāṇā // 4 //
jīvhece te agra ' na dise nayani /
tarī temcī dinīm̟ ' rāmakṛṣṇa // 5 /

4. [When] the tip of the nose is not visible with/in the eyes, just then know, three days are left.
5. [When] the tip of the tongue is not visible with/in the eyes, then that very day: Rāmakṛṣṇa.

Or, in the version of 1449:

nāsikācem̥ agra ' pāhatām̥ na dise /
tari tem̥ āyuṣya ' doni divasa // 4 //
jīvhem̥ce paim̥ agra ' na disatām̥ nayanā /
teci divasīm̥ jāṇā ' rāmarāma // 5 //

4. [When] one looks [and] the tip of the nose is visible, then that life: two days.
5. [When] the tip of the tongue is not visible with the eyes, know on that day: Rāmarāma.

The fact that all the printed editions agree in the lacuna, and that they are the only ones that read against all MSS *naū* instead of *nava* in 1d, supports the suspicion that they are based on very few and very similar MSS. It also shows that the editors, if at all they had a look at the MSS again, mostly copied R. S. Goṃdhḷekar's *Gāthā* edition. Unfortunately the *Gāthā* MSS Goṃdhḷekar used have vanished, at least I could not find a single one of them. S 1733, which has the greatest similarity to the editions, does not seem to have been taken into account by the *Gāthā* publishers. While working on *yoga* songs of the *Gāthā*, I used the manuscript and noted considerable differences in comparison to the printed editions. Thus one cannot say when exactly the *caraṇ*s disappeared—during MSS writing or while printing.

Some variants in the MSS may be interpreted as indications of two main 'versions.' The tables in the appendix (where A of the editions has been included as the representative of the MSS on which the editions are based) have been arranged accordingly. The most important variant is found in 2b where A 604, S 217, 697, 1159, 1510, 1733, Bh 482 read *jāṇā*, and R 200 *jāṇāvā,* instead of *nayanā,* which occurs in the remaining MSS. Within the *jāṇā(vā)* group, A 604, S 697, 1510, 1733, and Bh 482 read *nāsāgrāce[m̥]* in 4a, as against *nāsikāce[m̥]* of the rest of all the MSS - which means that *nāsikāce[m̥]* belongs to a stage prior to the split of the *jāṇā* and the *nayanā* versions. *Kālī* in 5c is restricted to MSS of the *jāṇā* group that read *nāsikāce[m̥]* (S 1159, R 200). Within the *nayanā* group, one finds *pāhatā* (S 604, 1254, 1449, 2085) in 4b, and within this latter group *pāhatā dise nā* (S 604, 2085) in 5b, instead of *na dise/disatā nayanā*. *Ḍolayācyā bhovayā* instead of *bhovayā pāhatā* of S 1159, R 200, and S 132 in 2a within both the *nayanā* and the *jāṇā* versions, underlines Maas's verdict that 'gegen Kontamination ist kein Kraut gewachsen.'[3]

The most problematic stanza as far as contamination is concerned, is no. 4. Both within the *nayanā* and the *jāṇā* versions occur MSS that read *urale jāṇā* in 4cd (S 217, 550, 604, 1733, 2085, Bh 482.3), but also some that do not (A 604, S 169, 1159, 1254, 1449, 1510). The only explanation

3. Paul Maas, Textkritik, 2nd ed., Leipzig, 1950, p.31.

I can think of is that this division is quite young: an arrangement of the songs according to *urale* and non-*urale* occurrence does not yield any further common patterns. Due to special circumstances (perhaps the pilgrimage to Paṇḍharpūr) the two possibilities may have become known to singers and scribes of the *nayanā* as well as the *jāṇā* version.

As to the metre, the song is a *moṭhā*, 'great,' *abhaṅga*, based on the *ovī* metre. The number of syllables in a stanza should be, according to the 14th century poet saint Nāmdev, 6+6+6+4.[4] As I have shown elsewhere, one syllable more or less seems to have been permissible.[5] In the present song, only the versions of S 550 and 1449 are metrically correct in this sense. S 604, 1254 and 1510 are the most faulty versions. Most of the readings that are wrong from the point of view of syllable number can be identified as mistakes or emphatical additions. E.g. in 1a and 3a, the extended absolutive *ghālunīyā* of several versions is the cause of 8 syllables. Perhaps it was used because it gives more emphasis to the opening of a song or sentence than the simple absolutive *ghāluni*. In 5c, the explanatory *tari* is superfluous in the versions which also read *mhaṇā*. In S 1510.2a *pāhātā* was perhaps simply forgotten by the scribe. In S 132, R 200, the faulty metre shows the unsuccessful endeavor to accomodate readings both of the *urale* and the non-*urale* version. Similarly, in S 604.4b *pāhatā* was taken over from versions that do not read *nayanā* in 4b, which produces 9 syllables. In S 697.4c *tari* was perhaps forgotten by a scribe. This is suggested by the fact that all the *urale* versions, and most of the others, read *tari*. Therefore, also in S 1254.4c, *tari* is acceptable, and *-ve* of *jāṇāve* an unnecessary addition.

The rhyming pattern of the song is abbc (imperfect *ovī*)—except in the extra stanza after 4 in S 217, which is aaab (perfect *ovī*). The faulty rhymes are indicated by bold type in the last column of the tables. There are not too many deficient rhymes because the rhyme is such a basic structure that mistakes do not creep in easily, and if so, there is often a reason. E.g., in R 200.2bc the *-vā* of *jānāvā* (instead of simple *jānā*) was taken over from the *pāhāvā*s and *pāhāve*s of the previous and the following stanza. *Pāhāṇe* (instead of *pāhāve*) in S 604.3b may be a writing mistake.

As to the rest of the variants, there are some that occur in one manuscript only. Such readings may even cover one or more *caraṇ*s but are of no consequence for the general transmission. Examples are several passages of S 1510 which is in several places a product of creative writing. Quite frequent are, apart from writing mistakes, changes of word order, orthography and pronounciation like Koṅkanastha *anusvār*s, e.g. in loc. plural or neuter singular endings (as in the editions, in MSS S 1254, 1449, and occasionally in S 697), or variations of single syllables (as in *jo, je* and

4. Nāmdev, *Śrīnāmdev Gathā*, Mumbāī, 1970, song no. 1382.
5. Catharina Kiehnle, *Songs on Yoga*, vol. 1, pp. 46-51.

te, na dise and *na disatā*, or *ghālunī* and *ghālunīyā*). Such variants may change the meaning of a sentence, but since they easily occur during performance or manuscript copying, they may also be re-changed just as easily. That is also the case with changes in the order of the stanzas. Since the knowledge about the number of days one may live seems to be reserved to the *sant*s and unaccessible to the profane eye of the indologist, the order adopted here follows the majority of MSS.

The indologist, however, can contribute some suggestions as to where these notions about the approaching death may come from or where similar ideas occur. They are found for example in ayurvedic texts in the chapters about the *ariṣṭalakṣaṇa*s, 'signs of the hurt' or 'signs of calamity.' The term *ariṣṭa* is strange in this context, because it actually means since Vedic times 'unhurt, secure, safe' etc. (from *riṣ*, 'to be hurt or injured'), and in fact, some authors also call the signs *riṣṭalakṣaṇa*s.[6] Both terms are used for the indications that tell the physician when a patient is doomed to death and should therefore be avoided by the intelligent doctor from a distance (*dūrāt tam parivarjayet* and similar sentences as e.g. in *Carakasaṃhitā*, 'Indriyasthāna' 6.6, 7, 13, 15, 16, 17, 19 etc. are frequent in that context). Vāgbhaṭa (*Aṣṭāṅgasaṃgraha* 10.30) opines that such a man is in the company of messengers of death and *piśāca*s who destroy the potency of drugs. Caraka warns that treating incurable persons leads to loss of riches and reputation (*Carakasaṃhitā* 1.10.8). Suśruta states that *asādhyān naivopakramet*, 'he should not treat uncurable [diseases]' (*Suśrutasaṃhitā* 10.6).

There are two main types of *ariṣṭalakṣaṇa*s: *puruṣasaṃśrayaḥ*, 'located in a person,' and *puruṣānāṣrayaḥ*, 'not located in a person.'[7] To the latter belong the condition of the patient's shadow and of the messenger he sends to the doctor, moreover omens, incidents happening in the house of the patient, astrological indications, etc. Among the signs in the body of a patient are those which have been present since his birth like lines of his hands and feet (as can be determined by the *sāmudrikaśāstra*), then those that occur in the course of a disease, and those that appear invariably prior to death. The signs of the *abhaṅga* belong here. Generally, the perception on the part of the patient changes (*Carakasaṃhitā*, 'Indriyasthāna' 4.4-6). For example, he sees space as solid and earth as space-like, or he perceives

6. K. R. Srikantha Murthy, *Doctrines of Pathology in Āyurveda*, Varanasi, 1998, p. 126; Gerrit Jan Meulenbeld (ed., tr.), *The Mādhavanidāna and Its Chief Commentary: The Chapters 1-10*, Leiden, 1974, p. 442. For the doubtful *alpha privativum* in a positive sense see Jacob Wackernagel and Albert Debrunner I, *Altindische Grammatik*, 3 vols., Göttingen, 1957-75, vol. II.1, Nachträge p. 25; Walter Wüst, *Vergleichendes und etymologisches Wörterbuch des Alt-Indoarischen (Altindischen)*, 3 pts., Heidelberg, 1935, pp. 207f; Louis Renou, *BSOS* 10 (1939), No. 10, pp. 8f.

7. For this and the follwing see Srikantha Murthy, *Doctrines*, pp. 126-8, 164-89.

*preta*s and *rākṣasa*s, or whatever normally is not seen, and does not perceive what is normally perceived:

Carakasaṃhitā, 'Indriyasthāna' 4.19,20

aśabdasya ca yaḥ śrotā ' śabdān yaś ca na budhyate /
dvāv apy etau yathā pretau ' tathā jñeyau vijānatā //
saṃvṛtyāṅgulibhiḥ karṇau ' jvālaśabdaṃ ya āturaḥ /
na śṛṇoti gatāsuṃ taṃ ' buddhimān parivarjayet //

Someone who is a hearer of a non-sound and someone who does not perceive a sound [that exists]: both of them should be recognised as [people] whose life is gone by one who is able to distinguish. An intelligent [doctor] should abandon a diseased one as dead who, after closing with the fingers both ears does not hear the sound of fire.

Aṣṭāṅgasaṃgraha 10.6

niṣpīḍya karṇau śṛṇuyān na yo dhukadhukāsvanam [sa naśyati]
Who when pressing the ears does not hear the sound *dhukadhuka* [perishes].

This, in fact, is the only sign of the *abhaṅga* which I found mentioned in the medical texts. The others are in accordance with ayurvedic ideas, although their classification is not as clear as in the previous case. Not seeing the circles in one's eyes may be covered by a statement in

Carakasaṃhitā, 'Indriyasthāna' 4.17,18

vyākṛtāni vivarṇāni visaṃkhyopagatāni ca /
vinimittāni paśyanti rūpāṇy āyuḥksaye narāḥ //
yaś ca paśyaty adṛśyān vai dṛśyān yaś ca na paśyati /
tāv ubhau paśyataḥ kṣipraṃ yamakṣayam asaṃśayaḥ //

When life is declining people see without reason figures that are deformed, discoloured, with different number (of parts compared to reality?). Who sees [things] not to be seen, and who does not see [things] to be seen: without doubt both see soon the decay due to Yama.

The reason for not perceiving nose, tongue, or brows may among other things be due to failing eyesight:

Carakasaṃhitā, 'Indriyasthāna' 8.4

jaṭībhūtāni paksmāṇi dṛṣṭiś cāpi nigṛhyate /
yasya jantor na taṃ dhīro bheṣajenopapādayet //

Whose eyelashes have become matted, and whose vision is obstructed, him the wise one should not have treated with medicine…

Or, the organs themselves or their location may have changed:

Carakasaṃhitā, 'Indriyasthāna' 7.29:

vyāvṛttamūrdhajihvās yo bhruvau yasya ca vicyute /
kaṇṭakaiś cācitā jihvā yathā pretas tathaiva ca //

Whose head and tongue are turned back, whose brows are dislocated/have fallen down, [whose] tongue is covered with thorns [is] like dead/a ghost...

Aṣṭāṅgasaṃgraha 9.9

jihvā vā jihmā stabdhā suptāvaliptā gurvī śyāvā śūnā śuṣkā visarpiṇī kaṇṭakāciteva vā

...or the tongue is crooked/curved, stiff, asleep, coated, heavy, dark brown, swollen, dry, moving to and fro, or as if covered by thorns.

Carakasaṃhitā, 'Indriyasthāna' 8.14

stabdhā niścetanā gurvī kaṇṭakopacitā bhṛśam /
śyāvā śuṣkā 'thavā śūnā pretajihvā visa[r]piṇī //

...stiff, without sensation, heavy, intensively covered with thorns, dark brown, dry or swollen, [is] the tongue of a *preta*, moving to and fro.

The non-visibility of parts of the body may as well belong to changes perceived outside the person, which include changes of the shadow or the image in a mirror or water:

Aṣṭāṅgasaṃgraha 9.8

yasyātapādarśādiṣv akasmāt praticchāyā chinnā bhinnā hīnādhikākulā naṣṭā jihmāvākśirā viśirā dviśirā vistṛtā'nyathā vā vikṛtā vā dṛśyate... sa gatāyuḥ //

Whose image in the sun or in a mirror etc. looks without reason unexpectedly cut, split, deficient, with surplus, confused, disappeared/damaged, crooked, head downwards, headless, two-headed, expanded or otherwise changed... he [is one] whose life is gone.

It will be clear by now, that even though not all the signs mentioned in the song are present in ayurvedic texts, the idea of phenomena contrary to the normal as indications of approaching death was basic knowledge among medical doctors. It was also basic knowledge among the yogis, it seems. *Ariṣṭa*s are dealt with in the *Yogasūtra*s as they are today, in the chapter about the *vibhūtis/siddhi*s:[8]

---

8. The whole *sūtra* is treated in all the commentaries. Yet, it has also been noted by Michel Angot (Patañjali, *Yoga, La Parole sur le silence: Le* Yoga-Sūtra *de Patañjali,* Bhāṣya

Yogasūtra 3.22

sopakramaṃ nirupakramaṃ ca karma tatsaṃyamād aparāntajñānam ariṣṭebhyo vā //

Karma is advancing and non-advancing. By *saṃyama* (a particular method of meditation) on it [arises] knowledge of the end, or through the *ariṣṭa*s.

Bhāṣya

...ariṣṭebhyo veti / trividham ariṣṭam ādhyātmikam ādhibhautikam ādhidaivikaṃ ca / tatrādhyātmikaṃ ghoṣaṃ svadehe pihitakarṇo na śṛṇoti jyotir vā netre 'vaṣṭabdhe na paśyati / tathādhibhautikaṃ yamapuruṣān paśyati, pitṝn atītān akasmāt paśyati / tathādhidaivikaṃ svargam akasmāt siddhān vā paśyati / viparītaṃ vā sarvam ity / anena vā jānāty aparāntam upasthitam iti //

or through the *ariṣṭa*s: *ariṣṭa* is threefold: pertaining to the self, pertaining to [other] beings, pertaining to the gods. Among them pertaining to the self [means that] he does not hear the sound in his body, when he covers the ears, [or that] he does not see the light in the eye when he presses. In the like manner, pertaining to [other] beings [means that] he sees the servants of Yama, dead ancestors, [or] without reason/unexpectedly *siddha*s. Similarly, pertaining to the gods [means that] he sees without reason/unexpectedly heaven or *siddha*s, or everything as contrary [to what one normally sees]—or through that he knows [that] the end is near.

Tattvavaiśāradī

...ariṣṭebhyo vā / arivat trāsayantīty ariṣṭāni trividhāni maraṇacihnāni / viparītaṃ vā sarvaṃ māhendrajālādivyatirekeṇa grāmanagarādi svargam abhimanyate, manuṣyalokam eva devalokam iti //

Or through the *ariṣṭa*s: [*ariṣṭa*s means] they terrify like an enemy. The signs of death are threefold. Or contrary: he considers everything, except for magical tricks, villages, towns etc., as heaven, [and] even the world of men as the abode of gods.

Yogavārttika

ariṣṭajñānasyāpīdaṃ phalam iti sūtre prasaṅgād evoktam, saṃyamasiddhīnām eva prakṛtatvāt / ariṣṭāni maraṇacihnāni ca yoginā samādhyavadhānārtham avadhāraṇīyāni / tāni vyācaṣṭe - trividham iti / pihitakarṇaḥ svadehāntarghoṣam vahnijvālanaśabdavacchabdaviśeṣam na

---

de Vedavyāsa et le Yoga-Vārttika *de Vijñānabhikṣu*, ed. and tr. by Michel Angot, Paris, 2002, pp. 412-13, note 1080), that *ariṣṭebhyo vā* might be a pre-*bhāṣya* addition because knowing death from well-known signs cannot be called a *siddhi*. Angot mentions Bhoja's remark that *ayoginām apy ariṣṭebhyaḥ prāyeṇa tajjñānam utpadyate*, 'as a rule, also for the non-yogis the knowledge of that/that knowledge arises through the *ariṣṭa*s.'

> *śṛṇoti ity ekam ariṣṭam ādhyātmikam; avaṣṭabdhe'ṅgulyādinā bhrāmite cakṣuṣi vahnikaṇatulyaṃ jyotir na paśyati ity aparam; anyāny api vividhāny ariṣṭāni vasiṣṭhamārkaṇḍeyādibhir uktāni dinamāsasa[ṃ]vatsarādibhedaiḥ / mṛtyucihnāni saṃkṣepata āha - viparīta[ṃ] vā sarvam iti / sarvaṃ śvāsapraśvāsādikam iti...*
>
> This result is also [derived] from the knowledge of *ariṣṭa*s—[this] is told in the *sūtra* just due to the occasion, because it is the subject of the very *siddhi*s [acquired] by *saṃyama.* And the *ariṣṭa*s, the signs of death, should be determined by the yogi for the purpose of attention in *(savikalpa?) samādhi.* He introduces them: [they are] threefold. One *ariṣṭa* pertaining to the self is, [if] closing the ears, one does not hear the particular sound, a noise in one's own body, which is like the sound of the burning of fire. Another one, [if] one does not see the light like sparks of fire when one revolves the eye[s] with a finger pushed [into them]. Also various other *ariṣṭa*s are told by Vasiṣṭha, Mārkaṇḍeya etc. according to days, months, years [one will live]. He tells in short [further] signs of death: or everything as contrary. Everything [points to] ingoing and outgoing breath etc....

Mārkaṇḍeyapurāṇa 40.1ff contains a list of *ariṣṭa*s, which are in the beginning enumerated in descending order according to the time someone has to live, as in the *abhaṅga.*[9] It is mentioned that the nose becomes crooked (*vakratām eti*, 40.25), which also may be a reason that one cannot see its tip any more, and in 40.28 one reads: *pidhāya karṇau nighoṣaṃ na śṛṇoty ātmasambhavam / naśyate cakṣuṣor jyotir yasya so'pi na jīvati*, '[if] covering the ears he does not hear the noise that arises by itself, the light of whose eyes disappears, he, too, does not live.'

It seems it was a good old custom to hand down lists of *ariṣṭa*s also in other texts, which sometimes provide reasons why it is important to know them:

Mahābhārata 12.305

> *ariṣṭāni tu vakṣyāmi vihitāni manīṣibhiḥ /*
> *saṃvatsaraviyogasya sambhaveyuḥ śarīriṇaḥ // 8 //*
> *etāvanti ariṣṭāni viditvā mānavo 'tmavān /*
> *niśi cāhani cātmānaṃ yojayet paramātmani // 17 //*
> *pratīkṣamāṇas tatkālaṃ yatkālaṃ prati tad bhavet /*
> *athāsya neṣṭaṃ maraṇaṃ sthātum icched imāṃ kriyām // 18 //*
> *sarvagandhān rasāṃś caiva dhārayeta samāhitaḥ /*
> *tathā hi mṛtyuṃ jayati tatpareṇāntarātmanā // 19 //*
>
> But I shall tell the *ariṣṭa*s, expounded by the wise, [which] arise for an embodied being whose separation [from the body comes about after] a year

9. I could not identify 'Vasiṣṭha' so far: no *ariṣṭa*s can be located in the *Yogavāsiṣṭha*, nor in *Vāsiṣṭhadharmaśāstra.*

(8)... A human being endowed with [knowledge of] the self, after seeing so many *ariṣṭa*s should day and night connect the self to the highest self (17), expecting that time at which he becomes that. Now/if[10] his death is unwanted, [if] he should wish to remain [alive]..., he should, being absorbed, concentrate on all smells and tastes, because then he conquers death by his inner self which [is] absorbed in that [highest self] (18,19).

Mārkaṇḍeyapurāṇa 40

jñātvā kālaṃ ca taṃ samyag abhayasthānam āśritaḥ /
yuñjīta yogī kālo 'sau yathā nāsyāphalo bhavet // 40 //
dṛṣṭvāriṣṭaṃ tathā yogī tyaktvā maraṇajaṃ bhayam ...// 41 //
yuñjati yogam nirjitya trīn guṇān paramātmani /
tanmayaś cātmanā bhūtvā cidvṛtt[i]m api saṃtyajet // 45 //
tataḥ paramanirvāṇam atīndriyam agocaram /
yad buddher yan na cākhyātum śakyate tat samaśnute // 46 //

After knowing correctly the time, resorting to a place free of fear, the *yogi* should practice [*yoga*] so that that time should not be fruitless for him (40). Seeing an *ariṣṭa*, thus abandoning the fear resulting from death... (41) he practices *yoga* with respect to the highest self, after conquering the three *guṇa*s. After becoming identical with the self, he also abandons completely the fluctuation of the mind (45). Then he attains the highest *nirvāṇa*, which is above the senses and not an object of the intellect, which cannot be described (46).

In *Liṅgapurāṇa* 1.91.1, too, the *ariṣṭa*s are said to be *yena jñānaviśeṣeṇa mṛtyuṃ paśyanti yoginaḥ*, 'by which special kind of knowledge the yogis see death.' After a list similar to the one in the *Mārkaṇḍeyapurāṇa*, in stanza 30 two signs relevant for the *abhaṅga* are given: *ghoṣaṃ na śṛṇuyāt karṇe jyotir netre na paśyati,* 'he does not hear the sound in the ear, he does not see the light in the eye.' Then the author continues:

Liṅgapurāṇa 1.91

ariṣṭe sūcite dehe tasmin kāla upasthite /
tyaktvā khedaṃ viṣādaṃ ca upekṣed buddhimān naraḥ // 36 //
prācīṃ vā yadi vodīcīṃ diśaṃ niṣkramya vai śuciḥ /
sameti sthāvare deśe vivikte jaṃtuvarjite // 37 //
samakāyaśirogrīvo dhārayan nāvalokayet /
yathā dīpo nivātastho neṃgate sopamā smṛtā // 39 //
khinnasya dhāraṇāyogād vāyur ūrdhvaṃ pravartate /
tataś cāpūrayed deham oṃkāreṇa samanvitaḥ // 44 //
tathoṃkāramayo yogī akṣare tv akṣarībhavet ...// 45 //

When an *ariṣṭa* is revealed in the body [and] death near, the intelligent man should become indifferent, abandoning dejection and sorrow (36).

10. *yadi* instead of *atha* according to version Cv.

> Proceeding to the east or the north, the pure one goes to a stable, lonely place devoid of living beings (37). Keeping his body, head and neck even (in a straight line), he should not look down, as a lamp in a [place] sheltered from wind does not move—that is considered to be the comparison (39). [When] breath goes upwards of one who is exhausted due to yoga consisting in concentration, then he should fill [with it] the body, together with *oṃ* (44). Thus the yogi who is identical with *oṃ* becomes eternal in the syllable.

To die meditating on the *praṇava* is also recommended in the *Bhagavadgītā* (8.5-15), from where the comparison with the lamp in a place sheltered from wind is taken as well (6.19). The *Liṅgapurāṇa* adds the worship of Rudra (*rudranamaskāra*, 1.91.70), and offers the alternative of going to Varāṇasī, and there to *avimukta kṣetra*, or to Śrīparvata (1.91.73-5). The idea of resorting to spiritual aims before one's death is also expressed in a general way by Vāgbhaṭa in *Aṣṭāṅgasaṃgraha* 10.20 (here with respect to someone who emits cold sweat from neck, forehead and the heart region, while the other areas of the body are hot): *śaranaṃ tasya devatāḥ*, 'his refuge are the deities.' That remark may of course also indicate the resignation of a medico. In any case, in order to attain a perfect death in the sense of a *bhakta* and yogi, it is vital to know the time beforehand, and the little *abhaṅga* does not look so strange any more in the midst of songs on devotion and yoga.

Moreover, it also belongs to the commonplaces in hagiographies for yogis, *siddha*s, saints, *mahātmā*s etc. of any denomination to know the time of their death in advance. This was so in the case of the Buddha, and (to name some more recent personalities) Akkalkoṭ Svāmī, Rāmakṛṣṇa, Lahiri Mahāśaya, Nīb Karaurī Bābā.[11] Some are even said to have been able to fix the exact time themselves. The best-known case of that sort in the Hindu universe is Bhīṣma who waited for the sun to be on its northern path, and the best-known case from Maharashtra is Jñāndev himself, who is said to have taken his finals *samādhi* when he was twenty-one. Another one from the middle of the twentieth century is Śaṅkar Mahārāj of Poona who out of friendliness for his *bhakta*s added seventeen years to his appointed life-span.[12] Gaurībāī from Gujarat chose *rāmnavamī* for her death, and when Yamamoto Gempo Roshi decided to die, his disciples persuaded him to postpone it until the weather was warmer and the funeral less

11. For Rāmakṛṣṇa, see Christopher Isherwood, *Ramakrishna and His Disciples*, 1965, repr. London: Shepheard-Walwyn, 1986, p. 295; for the rest Sushila Blackman (ed.), *Graceful Exits. How Great Beings Die. Death Stories of Tibetan, Hindu and Zen Masters*, New York and Tokyo: Weatherhill, 1997, pp. 28, 36, 37, 83, 84.

12. J. Taṇḍle, *Śri Śaṅkarmahārāj*, Pune, 1985, pp. 155, 200, 202, 207.

uncomfortable.[13] When Daito Kokushi felt his end approaching, he broke his leg that had been crippled for a long time, sat down in lotus posture and died. The idea that saints should have this sort of knowledge inspired Bhīṣma Sāhnī to write the satire *Samādhi Bhāī Rāmsiṃh* in which one *sādhubābā* fails to live (or die) up to his announcement of taking final *samādhi*.[14] The disappointed devotees kill him, but afterwards build a nice shrine in his memory.

A question to be asked, but perhaps not to be answered, is the one about the author of the *abhaṅga*. The *mudrikā* line contains the name of Jñāndev, but as I have shown elsewhere, such attributions are not as straightforward as they seem to be.[15] Especially the sentence 'this is the sign/characteristic of a *sādhu*' might as well sum up songs describing a *sant*, which, in fact, are frequent in that kind of literature.[16] The *Jñāneśvarī* Jñāndev, though, cannot be completely excluded from the list of possible authors since he was not only a yogi, but also conversant with ayurvedic terms and concepts. In his *Bhagavadgītā* commentary he uses twice the word *cikitsā*, '(medical) treatment' (13.226, 227 Gov. ed., Rājvāḍe *cikitsikā* in 225), and once *nidāna* in the sense of aethiopathogenesis. In 13.224ff he discusses Āyurveda which he also calls by that name (in 13.832 of the Gov. ed. he speaks of *vaidyaka,* Rājvāḍe reads *vaidika*). He mentions several times the *doṣa*s, the humors, on which the system of Āyurveda is based, for example in *Jñāneśvarī* 16.42 together with *sadvaidya*, a good *vaidya*. Particular *doṣa*s appear in 8.215 *(śleṣma)*, 224 *(vāta śleṣma)*, which are said to press the heart and drown consciousness at the moment of death. He knows that the heat in the body increases when *pitta* predominates over *vāta* and *śleṣma* (14.195), or that a person may be overcome by *vātaśleṣma*, even though he eats his natural food (Gov. ed. 17.114, Rājvāḍe 113 *vāyu*). He considers the *tridoṣa*, 'the [group of the] three faults/humors,' the cause of death (Gov. ed. 16.255, Rājvāḍe 253), which they actually are when they are unbalanced *(asāmya)*. He obviously distinguishes the term *doṣa* from the term *dhātu*, which he uses quite rightly in the context of balanced humors (*dhātusāmya*, 6.351).[17] *Dhātu* in the sense of *doṣa* is also used in connection

---

13. For this and the following, see Sushila Blackman, *Graceful Exits*, pp. 33, 52, 53, 86, 87.
14. Bhīṣma Sāhnī, *Merī priya kahāniyāṁ*, Dillī, 1993, pp. 22ff.
15. Kiehnle, *Songs of Yoga*, 1997.1, pp. 38-41; 1997.2, pp. 38-57.
16. e.g. JñāndevGāthā *F*, pp. 123-34 (songs on the subject of *saṃtamahimā*); Vinobā [Bhave] (ed.), *Eknāthāṃcīṃ bhajaneṃ*, Pavnār, 1977, pp. 88-90 (Eknāth's songs on *santas*); id. (ed.), *Tukārāmācīṃ bhajaneṃ*, Pavnār, 1973.1, pp. 97-111 (songs by Tukārām on *satsaṅgati*); id. (ed.), Rāmdāsāṃcīṃ *bhajaneṃ*, Pavnār, 1973, pp. 21-4 (songs by Rāmdās on *satsaṃgati*); Rāmdās, *Saṭīpa Śridāsabhoda*, ed. Śaṃkar Śrīkṛṣṇa Dev, 10th ed., Mumbāī, 1978, 5.2 *gurulakṣaṇa*, 5.8-10 *mumukṣu-, sādhaka-, siddhalakṣaṇa,* 11.6 *mahantalakṣaṇa,* 12.3 *bhaktalakṣaṇa*, 12.10; 18.6 *uttama puruṣa*.
17. This information I owe to Dr. Hedwig Gupta, an ayurvedic doctor in Baden-Baden (February 2004).

of the influence of food on the humors, or of the humors on the mood (Gov. ed. 17. 116, 117, Rājvāḍe 115, 116). When there is mention of *saptadhātu* (Gov. ed. 12.50, Rājvāḍe *dhātu*), undoubtedly the seven bodily tissues are meant. In 13.80 (Rājvāḍe 81) it is unclear whether the fever is waiting for an unsuitable diet in the tissues or in the humors.

Jñāndev's ideas about food are not only based on the Gītā, which recommends it in restrained/measured quantity (*yuktāhāra*, BhG 6.17), they are also in accordance with ayurvedic principles: he knows that a restricted diet *(pathya)* is given to a patient (3.8, Gov. ed. 18.706, Rājvāḍe 703), and that someone who eats *apathya* will never be left by disease (Gov. ed. 18.757, Rājvāḍe 754). Moreover, Jñāndev distinguishes between dark and light meat (*kāḷeṃ goreṃ*, 18.554). In spite of his knowledge of the traditional Indian medicine, he was not enthusiastic about it. He resented *jīvāṃ kāraṇeṃ karāvā jīvāṃ ghātu*, the murder of living beings for the sake of living beings (13.224). He felt compassion not only for the animals whose bile is taken for the preparation of medicine (Gov. ed. 13. 230, Rājvāḍe 229), but also for the plants which are dug up, or whose roots, bark and centre are removed (Gov. ed. 13.227, 228, Rājvāḍe 226, 227) and who die in consequence (Gov. ed. 13.229, Rājvāḍe 228).

Death is mentioned in several passages of the *Gītā* and also in Jñāndev's commentary. In *Bhagavadgītā* 8.5-6, the moment of death is discussed during which one should remember the Lord. The inner and outer signs of death, however, that are described in that context in the *Jñāneśvarī* pertain only to the time when life departs, and when the senses loose their power for that very reason (Gov. ed. 8.121ff, Rājvāḍe 119ff), not to the time before that. When death comes, the effect of medicine is said to be nil (2.67), even if one seeks the protection of the creator (Gov. ed. 16.255, Rājvāḍe 253 *dhātreyā hī geliyāṃ śaraṇa*). Therefore, one learns that a noble soul is constantly remembering death, and that an ignorant one does not bother even if his body decays (Gov. ed. 13.545, 552, 732, 16.318, Rājvāḍe 13.543, 550, 730, 16.316). The thirteenth chapter contains a detailed description of old-age, which the wise contemplate in time: [18]

Jñāneśvarī 13

> *hmaṇe ājicāṃ avasareṃ / puṣṭi je he śarīriṃ /*
> *te pāhe hoīla kācarī / sijalī jaisī // 554 //*

18. I am using the text of the Rājvāḍe edition. Its readings look sometimes older than those of the Government edition. Lambert (*Jñāneshvarī: A song-sermon on the Bhagavadgītā*, trans. by V. G. Pradhan, ed. by H. M. Lambert, 2 vols. 1969, 2nd Ind. repr., Bombay, 1982) compared Rājvāḍe's readings with the translation by Pradhan, which, however, is not always very literal. The best rendering into a modern language is that by Maṃgrūḷkar (*Jñānadevī,* ed. by Arviṃd Maṃgrūḷkar [and] Vināyak Moreśvar Keḷkar, Mumbāī, 1994) into modern Marāṭhī. This publication also contains a reprint of the Rājvāḍe text.

padmadalemṣiṃ isālemṃ / bhāṃḍatāti he ḍole /
te hotīla paḍavalemṃ / pīkalīṃ taisīṃ // 558 //
bhavaiciṃ paḍalemṃ / vomathatī sinasālemṃ /
uru kuhijaila jalemṃ / āṃsuvāṃceni // 559 //
rāṃdhavaṇa voli puḍhemṃ / parhive vāhāti khātāḍem /
taisiṃ hoti nākāḍem / biḍibiḍitīla //561//
kulavāḍi jaisī kheṭalī / kāṃ vākaḍiyā ḍhoremṃ baiṭhali /
taisī nūṭhīla kāhiṃ kelī / jībha hemṃ // 564 //
vācesi apavāḍu / kānāsi anughāḍu /
piṃḍu garuvā māṃkaḍu / hoīla ha // 567 //
malamūtradvāremṃ / houni ṭhāṃti khoṃkaremṃ /
navasiyemṃ sūṃti yeremṃ / mājhāṃ nidhaniṃ // 570 //
dekhauni thūṃkīla jagu / maraṇācā paḍaila pāṃgu /
soiriyāṃ ubhagu / hoīla mājhā // 571 //
striyā hmaṇati viṃvaṃsī / bālemṃ jāti musiṃ /
kiṃbahunā cilasi / pātra hoina // 572 //
ubhalicā ujagarā / sejiyāṃ sāileyāṃ gharā /
siṇavī hmāṃtārā / bahutāṃtemṃ hā // 573 //

He says, the fleshiness that is in the body at today's time, see, it will be like a cooked slice of vegetable (554). The eyes [that now] rival jealously with lotus petals, will be like [over-] ripe snake-gourds (558). The screens of the brows hang down dry-skinned, [and] the chest will rot due to the water of tears (559). As from the gutter of the kitchen flows sewage water, oh, so the nose will be smeared (561). Like a low caste farmer pushed aside, or cattle sitting in the pouring rain, so this tongue will not rise, whatever one may do (564). In the speech helplessness, in the ear blockage, the body will be a big monkey (567). The doors of excrements and urine become leaky, [and] other people make vows concerning my death (570).[19] Seeing [me] the world will spit out [when] death comes [only] lamely, [and] the relatives will be disgusted with me (571). Women call [me] a demon/goblin, children faint [seeing me], in short, I shall be an object of nausea (672). Due to [my] consistent cough the sleeping neighbors of the house get a wakeful night [and they say] 'that old man troubles lots of people' (673).

Apart from the indications of old age in the above passage that show the grim humor of the author, some of them are close to the signs of the *abhaṅga*. In order to find them out, however, one need not be a medical doctor, nor a student of holy scriptures or of yoga, for they are more or less known to everyone. Thus they have only indirectly to do with the lists of Epics, Purāṇas, *Yogasūtras*, and the *abhaṅga* under discussion. So all one can say about the authorship of the little song is that it does indeed belong to

19. A *navas* is a sort of deal with a deity: one promises him/her something in case he/she sees to it that a certain event comes about—in this case the death of the old relative.

the tradition of classical culture and especially of *yoga sādhana*, which is the subject of many songs attributed to the great Jñāndev. He may have known models of the list, but that may have also been the case with many of his followers. The appearance of his name in the last line only indicates that the knowledge thus transmitted was considered to belong to the 'Jñāndev school,' as one might call the closer circle of Jñāndev devotees within the Vārkarī tradition. As to the *ariṣṭa*s in general, it would be worth-while to examine them in a more detailed fashion. The fact that elderly Indians still know some of them shows that they have become or have always been part of Indian folklore. Not seeing Arundhatī (a small star near Vasiṣṭha in the sign of the seven *ṛṣi*s in the zodiac), for instance, is usually mentioned by informants, and belongs to the best-known *ariṣṭa*s in literature. It occurs already in the *ariṣṭa* enumeration of *Mahābhārata* 12.305.9 (*yo 'rundhatīṃ na paśyeta dṛṣṭapūrvāṃ kadācana,* 'who does not see Arundhatī, which [he] saw at some time before...),' and at the beginning of a long list in *Liṅgapurāṇa* 1.91.1. Moreover, there is a verse of admonishment, said to be addressed by Vidura to Duryodhana: *dīpanirvāṇagandhaṃ ca suhṛtvākyam arundhatīm / na jighranti na śṛṇvanti na paśyanti gatāyuṣaḥ,* 'those whose life is [about to] expire do not smell, hear, see [respectively] the smell of the extinction of a lamp, the words of a friend, and Arundhatī.'[20] *Carakasaṃhitā*, 'Indriyasthāna' 11.5, too, contains a stanza about the star: *saptarṣīṇāṃ samīpasthāṃ yo na paśyaty arundhatīm / saṃvatsarānte jantuḥ sa saṃpaśyati mahat tamaḥ,* 'who does not see Arundhatī [which is] situated near the seven *ṛṣi*s, that living being sees the great darkness at the end of a year.' Just like Arundhatī's invisibility, the lack of sound in the ears and light in the eyes are two signs that occur in almost all the lists in Epics and Purāṇas. Such lists, in turn, are often incorporated into medical texts, so that there is ample scope for more research into the evolution of *ariṣṭa* lore.[21]

---

20. Oral communication by Prof. G.C. Tripathi (March 2004). The stanza is not included in the Poona edition of the *Mahābhārata*.

21. For the enumeration of *ariṣṭa*s in medical texts see G.J.Meulenbeld, *The Mādhavanidāna,* Leiden, 1974, p. 442.

Appendix

[...] conjectures or reconstructions
<...> words that may also belong to the next caraṇ
? orthographical difficulties in the mss
bold in the text: important variants of the jāṇā version; bold in the last column: faulty rhyme

stanza 1	a	b	c	d	syllables
			jāṇā version		
A 604.1	*kānī ghāluniyāṃ boṭeṃ*	*nāda je pāhāve*	*na disatāṃ jāṇāveṃ*	*naū divasa*	8+6+7+5
S 697.1	*kānī ghāḷunī boṭeṃ*	*nāda je pāhāvo?*	*na di(se?)satāṃ jāṇāve*	*nava đīvasa*	7+6+[7]+5
S 1510.1	*kāni ghāluniyā boṭe*	*nāda je uṭhati*	*teṇe jāṇāve āyuṣya*	*nava divasa*	8+6+8+5
S 1733.1	*kāṇī boṭa ghāluni*	*nāda te pāhāve*	*na disatā jāṇāve*	*nava dīna*	7+6+7+4
Bh 482.3	- - -	- - -	- - -	- - -	
S 217.1	*kāni ghālunīyā boṭa*	*nādā te pāhāve*	*nāīkatā jāṇāve*	*nava divasa*	8+6+6+5
S 1159.1	*kāni ghālūni boṭa*	*nāda je pāhāve*	*na disatā jaṇāve*	*nava divasa*	7+6+7+5
R 200.1	*kāni ghāloni boṭe*	*nāda pāhāvā*	*nāykatā jāṇāvā*	*nava divasa*	7+5+6+5
			nayanā version		
S 132.1	*kānī ghālunī boṭa*	*nādā ta pāhāve*	*nāykatā jāṇāve*	*navā đīva[sa]*	7+6+6+5
S 169.1	*kānī ghāloyā boṭa*	*nāde? jo p...[ā]vā*	*na aikātā jānāvā*	*nava đīvasa*	7+6+7+5
S 550.1	*kāni boṭa ghāluni*	*nādā te pāhāve*	*nā aikatā jāṇāve*	*nava divasa*	7+6+7+5
S 604.1	*kānī ghālunīyā boṭe*	*nāda aikāve*	*nā aikatā[ṃ] j[āṇā]ve*	*maraṇa nava đīvasa*	8+5+7+8
S 1254.1	*kāni ghāloniyā boṭeṃ*	*nāda jo aikāvā*	*nāīkatāṃ jāṇāvā*	*nava đīvasa*	8+6+6+5
S 1449.1	*kānīṃ deuni boṭeṃ*	*nāda jo aikaṇeṃ*	*na aike tari jāṇeṃ*	*nava divasāṃ*	7+6+7+5

stanza 1	a	b	c	d	syllables
S 2085.1	*kānī ghālunī boṭe*	*nādā te aikāve*	*na aikatā jāṇāve*	*nava dīvasa*	7+6+7+5

stanza 2	a	b	c	d	syllables
			jāṇā version		
A 604.2	*bhoṃvayā pāhātā*	*na dise jāṇā*	*āyuṣyācī gaṇanā*	*sāta divasa*	6+5+7+5
S 697.2	*bhovayā pāhātāṃ*	*na dīseti jāṇā*	*āyusyāśā?cī gaṇaṇā*	*sāta dīvasa*	6+6+8?+5
S 1510.2	*bhovayā*	*na disati jāṇā*	*tari āyuṣyāci gaṇanā*	*sāta divasa*	3+6+7+5
S 1733.2	*bhovayā pāhātā*	*na disati jāṇa*	*teci te gananā*	*sāta dīna*	6+6+6+4
Bh 482.3	*bhovayā pāhātā*	*na disati jāṇā*	*tethici gaṇanā*	*divasa sāta*	6+6+6+5
S 217.2	*bhovayā pāhatā*	*na dīsatī jāṇā*	*tyāci ti gaṇanā*	*dina sāta*	6+6+6+4
S 1159.2	*ḍoḷāyācyā bhovayā*	*na disatī jāṇā*	*tai āyuṣyācī gaṇanā*	*sāta divasa*	7+6+8+5
R 200.2	*ḍoḷayācyā bhovayā*	*na disatā jāṇāvā*	*āyuṣyācī gaṇanā*	*sāta divasa*	7+7+7+5
			nayanā version		
S 132.2	*ḍoḷayācyā bhovayā*	*na dīsa nayanā*	*tai[ṃ] ā[u]śācī gaṇanā*	*sa... ...vasa*	7+6+8+[5]
S 169	- - -	- - -	- - -	- - -	
S 550.2	*bhovayā pāhātā*	*na dise nayanā*	*teci te gaṇanā*	*divasa sāta*	6+6+6+5
S 604.2	*bhovaī pāhātā*	*na dīsatī nayanā*	*āyuśyācī gaṇanā*	*sāta dīvasa*	6+7+7+5
S 1254.2	*bhoṃvayā pāhatāṃ*	*na dīsatī nayanā*	*āyuṣyācī gaṇanā*	*sāta dīvasa*	6+7+7+5
S 1449.3	*bhoṃvayā pāhatāṃ*	*na disatī nayanā*	*āyuṣya gaṇanā*	*pāṃca divasa*	6+7+6+5
S 2085.2	*bhovayā pāhātā*	*na disatī nayanā*	*āśācī ganaṇā*	*sāta divasa*	6+7+6+5

stanza 3	a	b	c	d	syllables
			jāṇā version		
A 604.3	*ḍoḷā ghāloniyāṃ boṭa*	*cakra jeṃ pāhāve*	*na disatāṃ jāṇāveṃ*	*pāṃca divasa*	8+6+7+5
S 697.3	- - -	- - -	- - -	- - -	
S 1510.3	*ḍoḷāṃ ghāluniyā*	*cakre je pāhāve*	*te na dise teṇe jāṇāve*	*āyuṣya tīna divasa*	6+6+9+8
S 1733.3	*ḍoḷā ghālunī boṭe*	*cakrā- te pāhāve*	*nā disatā jānāve*	*pāca dīna*	7+6+7+4
Bh 482.1	*ḍoḷā ghāluniyā boṭe*	*cakrā te pāhāve*	*na disatā jāṇāve*	*nava divasa*	8+6+7+5
S 217.3	*ḍoḷā ghāluniyā boṭe*	*cakrā te pāhāve*	*na distā jāṇāve*	*pāca dina*	8+6+6+4
S 1159.3	*ḍoḷā ghāloni boṭe*	*cekra je pāhāve*	*na disatā jāṇāve*	*pāca divasa*	7+6+7+5
R 200.3	*ḍoḷā ghāluni boṭa*	*cakra je pāhave*	*na disatā jāṇāve*	*pāca divasa*	7+6+7+7
			nayanā version		
S 132.3	*ḍoḷā ghālaunī boṭa*	*cekre je pāhāvī/e*	*na dīsatā jāṇāve*	*p... dīvasa*	7+6+7+[5]
S 169.2	*ḍoḷā ghālunī boṭa*	*cakra jo pāhāve*	*na dīsatā jānāve*	*āṭa dīvasa*	7+6+7+5
S 550.3	*ḍoḷā ghāluni boṭa*	*cakrā te pāhāve*	*na disatā jāṇāve*	*divasa pāca*	7+6+7+5
S 604.3	*ḍoḷā ghālunīyā boṭe*	*cakra je pāhāṇe*	*na pāhātā jāṇāve*	*pāca dīvasa*	8+6+7+5
S 1254.3	*ḍoḷā ghāloniyā boṭeṃ*	*ceṃkra je pāhatī*	*na dīsatāṃ jāṇāveṃ*	*pāṃca dīvasa*	8+6+7+5
S 1449.2	*ḍoḷāṃ deuni boṭeṃ*	*cakreṃ jeṃ pāhavīṃ*	*na disatāṃ jāṇāvī*	*sāta divasa*	7+6+7+5
S 2085.3	*ḍoḷā ghāḷuniyā boṭe*	*cekre to pāhāve*	*na disatā jāṇāve*	*pāca divasa*	8+6+7+5

stanza 4	a	b	c	d	syllables
	jāṇā version				

stanza 4	a	b	c	d	syllables
A 604.4	*nāsāgrāceṃ agra*	*na dise nayanīṃ*	- - -	- - -	6+6+?+?
S 697.3	*nāśāgrāce āgra*	*na dise nayanā*	*traye dina*	*urale jāṇā*	6+6+4+5
S 1510.4	*nāsāgrāce agra*	*na dise nayanī*	*tari dona divasa*	*āyuṣyāce*	6+6+7+4
S 1733.4	*nāśāgrāce agra*	*na dīse nayani*	*tari traya dinī*	*urale jānā*	6+6+6+5
Bh 482.3.3	*nāsāgrācā agra*	*na dise nayanā*	*tari urale jāṇā*	*nava divasa*	6+6+7+5
S 217.4	*nāśikācā āgra*	*na dise nayanī*	*tari divasa tīnī*	*urale jāṇa**	6+6+7+5
S 1159.4	*nāśikāce agra*	*na disatā nayanī*	*t... te?... divasa tīnī*	*āyuṣyāśī*	6+7+[7]+4
R 200.4	*nāsikāce āgra*	*na disatā nayani*	*tai urale āyuṣya jāṇā*	*tina divasa*	6+7+9+5
			nayanā version		
S 132.4	*nāsīkāce [āgra]*	*na dīse nayenā*	*tai urala tina <dīvasa>*	*<>[ā]yuṣeṃ jāṇā*	[6]+6+9+5/[6]+6+6+8
S 169.4	*nāsikāce agra*	*na dīsatā nayanā*	*ayuṣyācī gananā*	*pāṃca dīvasa*	6+7+7+5
S 550.4	*nāsikāce āgra*	*na dise nayani*	*tai(?)ci traya dini*	*urale jāṇā*	6+6+6+5
S 604.4	*nāsikāce āgra*	*pāhātā na dīsa nayanā*	*tarī urale jāṇā*	*tīna dīvasa*	6+9+7+5
S 1254.4	*nāsīkāceṃ āgra*	*pāhatāṃ na dīse*	*tarī jāṇāve āyuṣya*	*donī dīvasa*	6+6+8+5
S 1449.4	*nāsikāceṃ agra*	*pāhatāṃ na dise*	*tari teṃ āyuṣya*	*doni divasa*	6+6+6+5
S 2085.4	*nāsikāce āgra*	*pāhatā dise nā*	*tarī urale jāṇā*	*tīna divasa*	6+6+7+5

*the ms adds here another stanza: *nakha kesa nayanā ' na disati jāṇā / toci divasa jāṇā ' prayāṇāca:* 7+6+7+4

stanza 5	a	b	c	d	syllables
			jāṇā version		
A 604.4	- - -	- - -	*tarī teṃcī dinīṃ hmaṇā*	*rāmakṛṣṇa*	?+?+8+4
S 697.4	*jivhece agraja*	*na dise nayanā*	*tarī tecī dīvasī*	*rāmakṛṣṇa mhaṇā*	6+6+7+6
S 1510.5	*jivhece je agra*	*na lāge ṭāḷusi*	*tari teci divasi*	*rāmakṛṣṇa*	6+6+7+4
S 1733.5	*jīvhece je agra*	*na dīse nayenā*	*teca divasī hmaṇā*	*rāmakṛṣṇa*	6+6+7+4

stanza 5	a	b	c	d	syllables
Bh 482.3.4	*jivhece te agra*	*na dise nayanā*	*teci divasī hmaṇā*	*rāmakṛṣṇa*	6+6+7+4
S 217.6	*jivhecā to agra*	*na dise nayanī*	*tari teca dini*	*rāmakṛṣṇa*	6+6+6+4
S 1159.5	*jivhecā saṇa?*	*na disatā nayanī*	*te kāḷī maraṇa*	*yeka divasa*	5+7+6+4
R 200.5	*jīvhece āgra*	*na disatā nayanā*	*teci kāḷī hmaṇā*	*rāmarāma*	5+7+6+4
			nayanā version		
S 132.5	*jīvheca āgra*	*na dīsa nayanā*	*tarī teca [d]īṇī ...nā*	*rāmarāma*	5+6+[8]+4
S 169.3	*jīṃvhece agra*	*na dīsatā nayanā*	*ayuṣyācī ganāṇā*	*sāta dīvasa*	5+7+7+5
S 550.5	*jivhece te āgra*	*na dise nayani*	*tari teci dini*	*rāmakṛṣṇa*	6+6+6+4
S 604.5	*jīvheca āgra*	*pāhātā dīse nā*	*tarī tecī dīvasī hmaṇā*	*rāmakṛṣṇa*	5+6+9+4
S 1254.5	*jīvheṃca āgra*	*na dīsatāṃ nayanā*	*tarī teca dīvasa hmaṇā*	*rāmakṛṣṇa*	5+7+9+4
S 1449.5	*jivheṃce paiṃ agra*	*na disatāṃ nayanā*	*teci divasīṃ jāṇā*	*rāmārāma*	6+7+7+4
S 2085.5	*jīvhece āgra*	*te pāhātā dise nā*	*teci divasī jāṇā*	*rāmarāma*	5+7+7+4

stanza 6	a	b	c	d	syllables
			jāṇā version		
A 604.5	*jñanadeva hmaṇe*	*heṃ sādhūceṃ lakṣaṇa*	*aṃtakāḷīṃ āpaṇa*	*pahā vegīṃ*	6+7+7+4
S 697.5	*jñānadeva mhaṇe*	*sādhucī lakṣaṇe*	*aṃtakāḷīṃ āpaṇa*	*pāhā vegī*	6+6+7+4
S 1510.6	*jñānadeva hmaṇe*	*he saṃtāce lakṣaṇa*	*hṛdayi ādaḷaliyā <maraṇa>*	*<> pāve*	6+7+11+2/ 6+7+8+5
S 1733.6	*jñānadeva hmane*	*he sādhucī lakṣane*	*aṃtakāḷī apane*	*pāhā vegī*	6+7+7+4

stanza 6	a	b	c	d	syllables
Bh 482.3.5	*jñānadeva hmaṇe*	*sādhakāce sādhana*	*aṃtakāḷī apaṇa*	*pāhāveṃ vegī*	6+7+7+5
S 217.7	*jñānadeva hmaṇe*	*he sādhuce lakṣaṇe*	*aṃtaḥkāḷi āpaṇe*	*pāhāviti*	6+7+7+4
S 1159.6	*jñānadeva hmaṇe*	*he saṃtācī lakṣaṇe*	*vicārūnī mane*	*hita karā*	6+7+6+4
R 200.6	*jñānadeva hmaṇe*	*hī sīdhāci lakṣaṇe*	*vīcārunī mana*	*hīta karā*	6+7+6+4
nayanā version					
S 132.6	*jñānadeva mhaṇe*	*sādhucī lakṣaṇe*	*āṃtakāḷī a...paṇa*	*pāhāve vegī*	6+6+[7]+5
S 169.6	*jñānadeva mhaṇe*	*dehabuddhīc e lakṣana*	*aṃtaḥkāḷī khuna*	*jānavītī*	6+8+6+4
S 550.6	*jñānadeva mhaṇe*	*sādhuci lakṣaṇa*	*āṃtakāḷi jāṇa <āpaṇā>*	*<>pāhāve*	6+6+9+3/ 6+6+6+6
S 604.6	*jñānadeva hmaṇe*	*he sādhucī lakṣaṇe*	*āṃtakāḷī āpaṇe*	*pāhāvī vegī*	6+7+7+5
S 1254.6	*jñānadeva hmaṇe*	*sīddhāceṃ lakṣaṇa*	*āṃtakāḷī āpaṇa*	*pāhā vegī*	6+6+7+4
S 1449.6	*jñānadeveṃ aisī*	*jāṇoniyāṃ khūṇa*	*nivṛtticeṃ caraṇa*	*dṛḍha dharile*	6+6+7+5
S 2085.6	*jñānadeva hmaṇe*	*sīddhāce lakṣaṇa*	*āṃtaḥkāḷī jāṇa*	*pāhā vegī*	6+6+6+4

Kanakadāsa: The Philosopher-Poet of the *Haridāsa* Tradition of Karnataka

Rohini Mokashi-Punekar

The Vaiṣṇava *bhakti* movement of Karnataka covers a period of over five hundred years beginning with Narahari Tirtha in mid-thirteenth century and extending to the late eighteenth century with Jagannātha Dāsa. The saint-poets of this tradition are known as *haridāsas*, servants of Hari, who wrote exquisite poetry that has had great influence on the development of the Kannada language and its literature, and Carnatic music, the southern branch of Indian classical music. Like the Vārkarī tradition of Maharashtra, the source of loving devotion for this *bhakti* movement too is the deity of Viṭṭhal at Pandharpur, though it is also associated with the Udipi Kṛṣṇa temple consecrated by Madhvācārya himself. Some of the *haridāsas*, like Kanaka, are associated with local manifestations of Viṣṇu. The sixteenth century is considered the golden age of the *haridāsas*; Purandaradāsa, the brahmin saint and founder of Carnatic music, and Kanakadāsa, the low-caste saint, who both belong to it, are the most well- known and loved poets of this literature.

Section one of this paper explores the legends surrounding Kanakadāsa's birth into the shepherd caste and his adventurous and colourful life as a warlord, a householder and a saint. It attempts to articulate the contradictions of Kanaka's position of power in his society as a military chieftain, a scholar, one of the greatest poets in Kannada language, and a person of wealth (note the name Kanaka, meaning 'gold') militating against the humiliating position he is reduced to when it comes to religious standing. Section two attempts to locate Kanaka within the *haridāsa* tradition. The last section enumerates the possible directions that this project hopes to take in the future.

I

As happens with most *bhakti* poets, the little knowledge that we have of their lives is hagiographic. Legends, folk-songs, fleeting references in his own poems and those of the other *haridāsas* form the basis of Kanakadāsa's life. The *Vādirāja caritāmṛta* (mid-seventeenth century) refers to Kanaka's visit to Udupi and the miracles that took place there.[1] Only two of Kanaka's own poems, and these are minor poems, are autobiographical and offer some meager personal information: his birth to a military chieftain, his own career as a warrior and a fairly influential man about the town, his close brush with death on the battlefield and the transformation in his personality which that effected, and his initiation into the *haridāsa* tradition. The *mudrikā*, or the iconic signature with which all *haridāsas* sign off their poems, in Kanaka's case is Ādikeśava of Kāginelle, and at times of Bada. A large majority of *haridāsas* use various names of Viṭṭhalā as their *aṅkita* or *mudrikā*, for instance Purandaradāsa calls upon *'Purandara Viṭṭhalā'* for his signature. Kanaka mentions Viṭṭhal of Pandharpur in two or three poems, but his intimate godhead is Ādikeśava of Kāginelle. Folklore says Kanaka was born at Bada village, near Dharwad in Karnataka, to Bīrappa and Bacamma. Bīrappa was a military chieftain and an administrator of seventy-eight villages, and there are ruins in old Bada of the home and fort of Kanaka's father, as well as of the original temple of Ādikeśava. His parents belonged to the *kuruba* (shepherd) caste, which is a Śūdra caste; Kanaka's poems reveal only too clearly how his caste determines his treatment by society. Legend has it that Kanaka's parents were childless and the child was born only after the fulfillment of a vow to go on pilgrimage to the Veṅkaṭeśvara temple at Tirupati. In fact, the baby was named Timma after the God; the name Kanaka comes from another legend that he discovered a buried cache of gold. When the boy was a little older it is said that he studied at the Śaiva *maṭh* (temple monastery) near Bada. There are some ruins of the *maṭh* and a figure on the wall is said to be that of Kanaka's. Kanaka's base in poetry, prosody, grammar, the epics and the *Bhāgavata-Purāṇa* is as wide as it is deep, as is his understanding of the scriptures and related fields such as astronomy and geography. His poetry reveals a capacity for logic, analysis and dialectics. Kanaka's wide range of poetic works and the density of complex allusions to the Upaniṣads and the Purāṇas testify to his sound education. His earliest extant work, one of the greatest descriptive epics of about three thousand verses in Kannada, *Mohana-taraṅgini* pays profuse tributes to the well-known Śrīvaiṣṇava guru Tirumale Tātācāri, the royal guru of the Vijayanagar court who had his *āśram* in Anegondi. It is reasonable to assume that Kanaka was educated here for some time. His physical training in martial arts and other skills was undertaken by his father. Kanaka lost his father early in life in one of the numerous battles with the Muslim forces of Adil Shah of Bijapur. This must have been in the first decade of the sixteenth century and Kanaka seems to have taken over the army chieftain or administrator's post after his father's death and lived on for several years at Bada. There are about sixteen poems addressed to Ādikeśava

1. *Śri Vādirāja caritāmṛtam*, Kannada script, Belgaum: Haṃsāvāhana Prakāśana, 1995.

of Bada which must have been written during this period. Later poems show Kanaka introspecting his life during this time when he was both raising his own family, and enjoying his power and privileges as a chief.

The battle that transformed his life took place near Bada somewhere between 1510 and 1512. Kanaka lost his family, his ancestral home, his chief-taincy, and was grievously wounded, saved only, as he believed, by the intervention of his God. Bada was razed to the ground and Kanaka fled south carrying with him his beloved idol of Ādikeśava, establishing it in Kāginelle. It appears he lived in Hampi, the prosperous capital of the Vijayanagar Empire and the seat of learning and culture between 1515 and 1545, drawn by the presence of the great Vaiṣṇava guru Vyāsa Rāya, and also Tātācāri in whose *āśram* he lived for some time. He seems to have moved away from Śrīvaiṣṇavism, and Tātācāri, to the Dvaita fold and Vyāsa Rāya, guru to Kṛṣṇadevarāya himself. It is around this time that he seems to have found some answers to his spiritual quest, he recognizes the bestowal of divine grace and is soon admitted into the fold of the *haridāsas*. Some of the more celebratory of his *bhakti* poems belong to this period as does *Rāma dhanya caritre*, a satire of a hundred and fifty-eight verses (the first satire, in fact, in the Kannada language). The satire must have been written during this period, since the description of the army at Ayodhya in the poem matches with threpresentation of Kṛṣṇadevarāya's review of troops in the Portugese traveler and chronicler Domingo Paes's accounts.[2]

Kṛṣṇadevarāya, the greatest of the Vijayanagar kings died in 1529, Vyāsarāya in 1539. With the political and spiritual pillars gone, the empire suffered slow attrition, and the end came with the battle of Tālikote in 1565 between the Vijayanagar king and the coalition Sultanate forces, and spelt the annihilation of a great empire and its temples, palaces and culture built over two hundred years. Kanaka seems to have spent a period of time after Vyāsarāya's death in Udipi in Vādirāja's *maṭh*. Though there are songs of the guru Vādirāja's warm welcome to Kanaka (the two must have known each other in Hampi), and his preference for Kanaka as a student-devotee (these are songs attributed to Purandaradāsa), the hostility of the temple priests seems to have made life in Udipi miserable. One of the most moving stories in Hindu theology, and perhaps the most incriminating against the caste structure, is the story of *Kanakanakhindi*: Kanaka's window. Kanaka, having been refused entry into the Kṛṣṇa temple at Udipi, stands in worship outside, to the west of the temple, yearning to see the image. Kṛṣṇa himself turns westwards, the walls of the temple crack, and He shows himself to his true devotee. People thronging the Udipi Kṛṣṇa temple today worship at this small window and glimpsing the image of Kṛṣṇa, forever turned to his *bhakt*,

---

2. Robert Sewell, *A Forgotten Empire: Vijayanagar*, London, 1900, 10th repr., New Delhi: Asian Educational Services, 2000.

marvel at the miracle, as do perhaps the Brahmin priests officiating at the temple since centuries. While the concept of divinity and *bhakti* gathers mysterious layers of significance in Hindu thought, lived structures seem to be able to only accommodate the complexity at a metaphysical level, unable to bring it down to any change in social praxis. There is a similar story about rice gruel. Once rice gruel started flowing down the little channel from the temple even before the priests had offered the customary daily rice to the Lord; Kanaka, who was in his usual position outside, picked up a handful of the gruel and offered it to Kṛṣṇa. When the news of this reached Vādirāj, he instantly realized what had transpired and ordered a fresh batch of the gruel to be made and offered to the Lord. The temple continues the practice of offering rice gruel to the deity, instead of rice, to this day in Kanaka's honour.

In spite of the genuine regard that the high priest Vādirāj seems to have had for him, Kanaka went away from Udipi. He seems to have lived for a while in Belur with Vaikuṇṭhadāsa, another well-known *haridāsa*, before coming back finally to Kaginelle where he lived till his death around 1575. Kanaka's *Nala caritre*, a lyrical work of around five hundred verses recounting the story of Nala and Damayanti, his more philosophical *bhakti* poems and *Hari bhakti sāra*, a work of a hundred and eight verses on mystic philosophy, seem to have been composed around this time. Nothing much is known about Kanaka in this final period when the Vijayanagar Empire was destroyed, Hampi a mass of ruins, the spiritual and cultural base of the kingdom in shambles, and the band of *haridāsas*: the *dāsakūta*, scattered.

II

The *haridāsas* are followers of Madhva, the philosopher who propounded the Dvaita interpretation of the Upaniṣads: Naraharitīrtha, the first of the *haridāsas*, who composed his devotional songs in Kannada is said to be a direct disciple of Madhva. *Bhakti* for a personal god is thus the central plank of the *haridāsa* philosophy. Traditionally the *haridāsas* are said to be of two kinds: the *vyāsakūta* and the *dāsakūta*. There is no doctrinal difference between the two, the difference is only in the mode and manner of their practice. The *vyāsakūta haridāsas* are ascetics and scholars interested in theological and metaphysical interpretations of the Vedas, Upaniṣads and the Purāṇas. They wrote their philosophical exegeses in Sanskrit and devotional songs in Kannada. Vyāsarāya, Vādirāja, Śripādarāya are some of the saints of this category. The *dāsakūta haridāsas*, on the other hand, composed their songs in Kannada, reaching out to the common man, content to leave philosophical argument to the ascetics. Purandaradāsa and Kanakadāsa belong to this kind. The *dāsakūta haridāsas* can be compared to the Vārkarī poet saints; both are devotees of Viṭṭhal at Pandharpur, and though householder saints, both evoke a sense of the mendicant-minstrel.

But even if there are similarities with the Vārkarī saint-poets, it seems quite clear that the *haridāsa* movement was not, at any point of time, a mass movement of the people. In his practice of devotion, the ordinary Vārkarī is not much different from the Vārkarī saint-poet. It is not difficult to see that the scriptural base, the rigorous polemic that characterizes the work of the *vyāsakūta* forms the fountainhead of inspiration for the poetry of the *dāsakūta*. While the *haridāsas* sang of *bhakti* through their immensely popular poetry in the common man's Kannada, the *bhakti* could never transform itself into a folk tradition like the Vārkarī cult.

Given this background, it is not surprising that all the saints of the *vyāsakūta* group, and almost the entire band of *dāsakūta*, are male Brahmins. Many *bhakti* songs speak of the absurdity of the caste system, but Kanakadāsa is only one of the two or three non-Brahmin *dāsas*. There is no untouchable in this group, nor is there any movement towards the reversal of caste hierarchy, or the more fundamental questioning of it that characterized the Vīraśaiva movement of the same region a few centuries earlier. While the neighbouring Vārkarī movement was and remains contained within the dominant religious structure, its disaffection with orthodoxy turned into a quietist, yet a longer lasting democratization: the brahmin saint-poets (Jñāneśvar, Eknāth) are fewer and more radical; the lower-caste saint-poets at various levels of the caste hierarchy are the majority; and more significantly it accommodated lower-caste women, a courtesan or prostitute, and the Mahār untouchable Cokhamelā and his family as legitimate saints. Symptomatically the Vārkarīs disavow the validity of the scriptures completely, focusing instead on the Name: the well-known story of Jñāneśvar making a buffalo recite the Vedas is a case in point.

However, assuming that the *haridāsa* tradition is securely lodged in Brahminical orthodoxy, a few contradictions vis-à-vis Kanakadāsa's caste and his position within the *dāsakūta* still remain. First, his obvious erudition. Kanaka was a *kuruba*: a member of the shepherd caste. If historical deductions from available sources are correct, then Kanaka, as shown in Section I, had an elementary education in a Śaiva *maṭh*, was accepted by a royal Śrīvaiṣṇava guru a little later, and then exposed to sophisticated systems of knowledge by the Dvaita guru to the king himself.[3] It shows a social mobility that is unusual; it is also a movement of religiously determined factional affiliations: the Śaiva, Śrīvaiṣṇava and Dvaita factions in Karnataka have bitter differences amongst themselves. Kanaka's poetry, however, reveals what is known *ubhaya bhakti*, *bhakti* of both Śiva and Viṣṇu, a result, one would presume, of his eclectic training. While there are

3. Basrur Subba Rao, *Kanaka Dasa,* Madras: East-West Books, 2001.

stories of his later humiliation by the Brahmins of the Udipi Kṛṣṇa temple, there are none pertaining to his earlier life even on his visits to the bigger temples: we know that he went several times to the Veṅkateśvara temple at Tirupati and offered services there. The only explanation to these puzzling questions may lie in the nature and kind of political economy that prevailed in the Vijayanagar Empire, the peak of whose power and prosperity coincides with Kanaka's times. The following passage from a history of the Vijayanagar kingdom throws some light on Kanaka's caste status in view of the social, economic and military conditions of those times,

> Vijayanagar was perhaps the nearest approach to a war state ever made by a Hindu Kingdom; and its political organization was dominated by its military needs. The emperor maintained a large standing army consisting of an elephant corps, cavalry and infantry… In addition, military fiefs studded the whole length and breadth of the empire, each under a *nayak* or military leader authorized to collect revenue and to administer a specified area provided he maintained an agreed number of elephants, horses and troops ever ready to join the imperial forces in war. Fernao Nuniz counted more than two hundred such *nayaks*.[4]

Kanaka's father Bīrappa, and then he himself were administrators and military chieftains of considerable power. Such officials, known as *dannayakās,* not only administered the villages under them and collected revenue, but were also entrusted with raising and managing a specified number of troops and horses. Also, the fact that the family had a fort, *durga*, in Bada suggests high status: the *durga dannayakās* of the empire had status equivalent to provincial governors.[5] It is possible that Kanaka managed to procure an education in the scriptures and arts because of his father's, and then his own, position within the empire. Folktales narrate stories of Kanaka riding on an elephant to Hampi as a special honour conferred by Kṛṣṇadevarāya. His stay at Udipi at a later point of his life is painful, fraught as it is with caste restrictions. Why do these restrictions surface in Udipi, and not earlier in Tātācāri's *āśram*, or as a student of the famed Vyāsarāya? Is it because Udipi was removed from the hub of the military and political affairs of the empire that was so much a part of the capital Hampi? Did Hampi allow for some erasures of caste identities that were impossible in the Brahminical orthodox set up at Udipi? In spite of Vādirāja's love and respect for Kanaka, he is not allowed in the *āśram,* but forced to stay elsewhere. Kanaka at this point, one must remember, had lost not only his chieftaincy (that had gone long before), but also the support of Vyāsarāya after the latter's death. It seems strange that Kanaka should set up the Ādikeśava

4. K.A. Nilakanta Sastry, *A History of South India,* 4th ed., New Delhi: OUP, 1975, p. 307.
5. Basrur Subba Rao, *Kanaka Dasa*, p. 360.

temple at Kaginelle, have it consecrated by Vyāsa (as the legend goes), look after the running of the temple, and yet face restrictions at Udipi. This is the anomaly that crops up whenever the little or, *deśī,* traditions clash with the *mārga* tradition. Kanaka is caught between the two: a powerful soldier-poet in one; a low-caste shepherd in the other.

III

The two foregoing sections present only a cursory summary of the life and location of Kanakadāsa within the *bhakti* tradition. While there are a few excellent works in Kannada on the poet, extensive work needs to be done on the editing and compilation of Kanaka's poetry. The existing compilations are based on various sources, including private collections.[6] As far as studies in English are concerned, Basrur Subba Rao's meticulously researched and substantial *Kanaka Dasa,* published by East West Books in 2001 from Madras is indispensable; the translation of his poetry that the writer has attempted does give a glimpse of the vigour, the intellectual depth and the emotional charge of the Kannada original. Kanakadāsa, however, merits separate studies on various aspects of his work, perhaps more translations, and research on his social and historical position. An analysis of his poetry alone would be immensely fruitful, as would be his contribution to Carnatic music: all the poems of Purandaradāsa and Kanaka are set to different *rāgas*, and the two together are credited with systematizing and founding Carnatic music, a task that Tyāgarāja further contributed to later. I hope to work on a comparative study of the *haridāsas* and the Vārkarīs, with specific focus on Cokhamelā and Kanakadāsa, which I feel, would be rewarding work.

6. One of the most comprehensive compilations is Krishna Sharma Betigeri and Hutcharao Benigeri (ed.), *Kanakadāsara Hādugalu*, Dharwad: Samāja Pustakālaya, 1992.

Bājir as a Lover and a Yogi

Shyam Manohar Pandey

In Maulānā Dāūd's *Candāyan*,[1] Bājir is an interesting character who comes from Ujjain to Govargaṛh, the city of the heroine Candā and her father, King Sahdev, and sings the song of *vihāg*.[2] He is a mendicant who wanders around the city asking for alms and food (*bhuguti*).[3] Time and again he goes to the palace of the king and looks towards the window. One day, he looks at Candā watching through her window and, struck by her beauty, he falls on the ground and loses his senses. Candā closes her window.

---

1. References in this paper are given from the text *Cāndāyan* edited by Mātā Prasād Gupta, Agra: Prāmāṇik Prakāśan, 1967, unless otherwise quoted. Mātā Prasād Gupta calls his text *Cāndāyan,* but the title given to the text is not attested by the medieval Persian texts. Perhaps *Candāyan* is the correct title and not *Cāndāyan. Candāyan* was composed in 1379.
2. The original word in *Cāndayan* is *vihāū* which means *vihāg* or *bihāg*. This is one of the musical modes (*rāga*) which is sung during the night, generally after midnight. *Candāyan*, 54-1.
3. *Cāndāyan*, ibid., 54-2; *bhuguti* is used several times in Hindi Sufi texts. One simple meaning of the word is 'food.' This word has been used as the supreme love in the Sufi texts also. In Malik Muhammad Jāyasī's *Padmāvat* (1540), *bhuguti* has been used denoting 'the supreme love' in the following verse:

> *tab candan ākhar hiyeṃ likhe*
> *bhīkh leī tuiṃ jogi na sikhe*
> *bār āī tab gā taiṃ soī*
> *kaise bhuguti parāpati hoī* (V.S. Agravāl [ed.], *Padmāvat*, Cirgāṃv, Jhansi: Sāhitya Sadan, V.S. 2018, verse 195.3-5).

> Then Padmāvati inscribed in Ratnasen's heart with the sandal paste,
> 'you have not gained the ability of begging.
> When the opportunity came, you fell asleep.
> How can you obtain *bhuguti*, your objective (supreme love)?

This word *bhuguti* has been used together with *juguti* also. '*Bhuguti* and *juguti*' means the objective of love and the effort made for it. The Sanskrit word *bhukti* is found in many inscriptions in the classical period where it means enjoyment. A detailed study has been made by the historian R. S. Sharma. It appears that *bhukti* has become *bhuguti* and its original meaning is retained in it. For a detailed historical study of this term, see R. S. Sharma, *Indian Feudalism (A.D. 300-1200)*, New Delhi: Macmillan India Limited, 1990 [1st ed., 1965], pp. 12-15.

Bājir was unconscious and lifeless. He stopped breathing and people gathered around him and started sprinkling water on his face to revive him. They said 'perhaps a serpent has bitten him and so he cannot get up. His hands, feet and head, all are cold and he is in a precarious condition. Some said that he was struck by something and had collapsed (*sannipāt*) (55.4). Maybe he had a fit of epilepsy (*mirgī*). Other people said he was suffering from the disturbance of the wind in his body (*vāt rog*) (55.2). A few said he had been grabbed by a devil. His head was very dusty. He had become pale; his body had become yellow like turmeric. After a long time he gained his consciousness and was awake. He looked around him and then fixed his eyes at the window where he had seen Candā. His heart was broken—burnt with the fire of love. He was speechless. He could not utter a word. People asked him questions, but he did not answer them. He was silent all the time.[4]

(2)

Seeing him in this situation, wise people asked him:

> O Bājir, what was your pain; why were you suffering? Tell us, then we will bring medicine for you. O innocent and ignorant one (*binānī*), have you got a high fever from a cold? Are you suffering from stomach pain or a headache which has left you in this condition? Has some insect bite caused this swoon, or is it that you drank water after sun-stroke, and you fainted? Or is it that you are immersed in love for someone which has made you forgetful of yourself? Tell us, have you lost your wealth? Has some robber or bandit robbed you? O rustic and ignorant one, tell us who has wrought this havoc?[5]

(3)

Later, in a verse, Bājir replies in a symbolic way and expresses his love for Candā in a metaphor:

> People call me a fool and ignorant, but I want to tell you the sufferings of my heart. There is a tall tree and its fruits are hanging in the sky. I do not hope to get those fruits. Who has the capacity to stretch his arms long enough to pick them? Nobody can reach the twigs of that tree.

4. *Cāndāyan*, verse 52.
5. Ibid., verse 56.

Bājir says: I saw serpents on the twigs and the fruits and I was frightened. My heart was anguished and dried up. I was frustrated. The tempest of my sufferings in love shattered completely the leaves of my senses.[6]

Obviously, this is a metaphor in which Bājir wants to indicate that Candā was like a tree. Her breasts were fruits. Her arms were the branches of that tree. Leaves were the parts of her body. This verse in its Persian translation is preserved in the biography of Hazrat Quddus Gangohī (d.1456), *Lataif-i-Quddusī*, written by his son Ruknuddīn who completed the book two months after his father's death. The translation of *Candāyan* made by Quddus Gangohī was destroyed during the battle between Bahlol Lodī and Hussain Shāh Sharqī (A.D. 1458-1505), the king of Jaunpur.[7]

(4)

Bājir tells people:

I have been killed here in your city. She has struck me with the poisonous arrows of her eyes. You cannot see my wounds. There is no blood streaming out. The pain of my heart is acute, but nobody can see it. The woman who was standing in the upper room of the palace has entered my heart and cannot come out of it. What is this? I did not gain any profit, and lost my capital as well. I cannot tell you who has killed me. Nobody will know it, I assure you. The pain which has made me suffer so intensely cannot be expressed in words. Only I know it, and the one who has given me this pain knows it.[8]

Just as the other lovers in Hindi Sufi poetry, Bājir also expresses his sufferings in love. He says:

My death has approached and I shall leave Govargaṛh. I have seen here something that keeps me from sleeping. I cannot sleep day or night. Now I do not like food and water. Bājir expresses his fear that Mahar would have him killed if he knew the secret of his love. Noble men have said, 'We can live long if we protect ourselves from the extremes.'[9]

---

6. *Cāndāyan*, verse 57.
7. For details, see Shyam Manohar Pandey, '*Nakh-śikh* in *Candāyan*,' in *The Banyan Tree: Essays on Early Literature in New Indo Aryan Languages,* ed. by Mariola Offredi, New Delhi: Manohar, 2000, pp. 27-59. See also Simon Digby, 'Abd al Quddus Gangohī (A.D. 1456-1537). The Personality and the Attitude of a Medieval Indian Sūfī,' *Medieval India: A Miscellany* 3 (1975), p. 55.
8. *Cāndāyan*, verse 58.
9. Ibid., verse 59.

(5)

Bājir then leaves Govargaṛh, remembering Candā constantly and with a heavy heart. Passing from one place to another he reaches a city, Rajpur, which is ruled by the king Rūpcand and protected by sentinels and guards (*pauriyā*). He tells a watchman of the palace that he is a mendicant and lives by begging. He settles down in the city. During the day he wanders around and at night he sings the Candrāvali songs so beautifully that the whole city is amazed. He becomes very popular in the city.

(6)

Later, one night when Bājir sang the songs of Candrāvali in his sweet voice, the king's heart was moved. The songs and the sweet voice captivated his heart so much that he could not sleep that night. The next morning, he immediately called his minister Bāṃṭhā and ordered him to search for the singer who sang the previous night in such an enchanting manner. Bāṃṭhā brought Bājir before the king. Bājir sang the *nakhśikh* (head-to-foot description) of Candā. Rūpcand then cherished an intense desire to possess Candā. He attacked Govargaṛh. Candā's father Sahdev fought a fierce battle with the help of the valiant Lorik. Rūpcand was defeated. This event is crucial in the text. Had this battle not taken place, Lorik would not have proved his valour and the story of *Candāyan* would not have developed further. Candā's love for Lorik sprouts soon after this. Lorik also falls in love with Candā, who is the symbol of superb divine beauty on earth. In this way Bājir's role in the text cannot be underestimated. Had he not described Candā's beauty, the divine significance of Candā would not have been clear. I have already published a long paper on '*Nakh-śikh* in *Candāyan*' and explained the implicit symbolism in Candā's beauty, which attracts everyone.[10] Bājir and Rūpcand, both are struck by that beauty in different ways.

Who is this Bājir? The fact this figure has been created by the poet Maulānā Dāūd deserves special attention. He appears as a mendicant and as a beggar who is an expert musician. When he looks at Candā he becomes immersed in love for her at first sight. Her beauty strikes him hard. His ecstasy, his unconsciousness, his agony and people's reactions to his condition have already been described in some detail. Almost all the lovers in Hindi Sufi romances have been described going through the same state of mind. No character is spared and all are struck by divine light and beauty.

10. See Shyam Manohar Pandey, '*Nakh-śikh* in *Candāyan*,' op. cit.

Lorik falls in love with Candā, and at first sight he loses his consciousness as Bājir does. Lorik stops eating and can no longer sleep. His face fades and his brightness disappears. He loses consciousness. People put him in a bed to rest. His eyes are filled with tears. His family members, friends and neighbours come and then physicians and magicians are called to cure him.[11] Physicians say his pulse is working normally and his arteries are clear. The wind in his body (*vāt*) and his bile (*pitta*) are normal. He has neither a cold nor a fever. They say his blood is flowing normally. He is mentally alert. He has not been tricked by a devil or demon or by a male cat. They say that it is bad Kām-ras (sensual love) that has struck him. It is clear from this description that Bājir has the same condition as Lorik in the first instance.

Bājir's condition is very much like that of Lorik and other lovers in Sufi texts. But Bājir has fear, so his love fades. He runs away from Govargaṛh. Lorik's love for Candā matures with the help of Vṛhaspati, a girlfriend of Candā. In the case of Lorik, Candā, the divine beauty, also reciprocates his love. When Bājir looks at Candā, she shuts her window. Rūpcand is also attracted to Candā and he wants to take her by force, but he is defeated completely.

In *Mirgāvati*,[12] Manohar has the same condition after the sprouting of love for Mirgāvati in his heart. In verse 57 of *Mirgāvati*, Manohar loses consciousness after having seen Mirgāvati. Arrows from Mirgāvati's eyes wound the prince and he becomes unconscious (47.1-2). In one verse he is described as shedding tears continuously (30.2). He becomes pale and his body fades. Mirgāvati takes away his life and his body becomes lifeless (41.7). The prince is immersed in love and he does not like food or drink now (32.4).

In *Mirgāvati*, the prince Manohar himself describes the *nakhśikh* of Mirgāvati to his maidservant. Mirgāvati is a fairy, who first appears before the prince in the guise of a beautiful female deer. Later she appears in the form of a beautiful moon-like maiden along with her girlfriends who are like stars.

tāranh māṃjh cāṃd jo ahī
teī ek bāt āp seī kahī.[13]

Among the stars there was a moon
who herself said something.

---

11. *Cāndāyan*, verse 54.
12. Kutuban's *Mṛgāvati*, ed. by Mātā Prasād Gupta, Agra: Prāmāṇik Prakāśan, 1968.
13. *Mṛgāvati*, verse 45.1.

Fairies have the capacity to change their form at will. It is interesting to see that both Candā and Mirgāvati have been compared to the moon as far as their beauty is concerned. In *Candāyan* Candā is a symbol of the moon, Mirgāvati also looks like the moon (*cāṃd*) in her beauty (45.1). In Malik Muhammad Jāyasī's *Padmāvat*,[14] Padmāvati's forehead is more beautiful than the moon (*cāṃd*). Jāyasī's Padmāvati is more beautiful than the moon because she does not have stains in her beauty as the moon has. The moon is grabbed by Rāhu, but Padmāvati is always intact and perfect. Although *Padmāvat*'s imagery is a bit different, there is no doubt that the standard imagery of the moon was commonly used by Sufis in Persian and Hindi Sufi poetry.[15] Sanskrit literature is also filled with moon-faced heroines.[16]

In *Madhumālati*[17] the hero prince Manohar has the same condition after having the first glimpse of Madhumālati. When he saw Madhumālati, he fainted and then recovered (76.1). He had fallen in love and become lifeless as the leaves fallen from the tree (46.5). Elsewhere in *Madhumālati*, physicians come to see his condition but they are unable to tell what illness he actually has. In the end they declare that he is suffering from love. His fainting is due to this illness (154.6). Nobody knew the medicine for this.[18]

Obviously, Bājir does not look like a real lover in the style of the other lovers of the Hindi Sufi romances, but the beauty of Candā and its light strike him hard. Anyone struck by the divine light faces the same situation.

(7)

The identity of Bājir is a problem in *Candāyan*. Is he a Yogī or a singer with a musical instrument? This is not very clear from the text. Parameśvarī Lāl Gupta in his edition of *Candāyan* gives the meaning of the term as 'Vajrayānī Yogī' (verse 66).

14. Malik Muhammad Jāyasī, *Padmāvat*, ed. by Mātā Prasād Gupta, Allahabad: Bhāratī Bhaṇḍār, 1963, verse 101.

15. For the moon imagery in Persian literature, see Shyam Manohar Pandey, 'Love Symbolism in *Candāyan*,' in *Bhakti in Current Research*, ed. by Monika Thiel-Horstmann, Berlin: Dietrich Reimer Verlag,1983, pp. 269-93.

16. For moon imagery in Sanskrit literature, see Subandhu, *Vāsavadattā*, ed. by Śaṅkaradeva Śāstrī, Varanasi: Caukhambā Vidyā Bhavan, 1954, pp. 44-5. Subandhu lived in the seventh century A.D. See also *Bhartrihari: Poems*, transl. by Barbara Stoler Miller, New York and London: University of Columbia Press, 1967, pp. 68-9. According to Siegfried Lienhard, Bhartṛhari can be 'cautionally date[d] to about 400. A.D.,' see his *History of Classical Poetry: Sanskrit-Pali-Prakrit*, Wiesbaden: Otto Harrassowitz, 1984, p. 88. The Chinese traveller I-tsing refers to the grammarian Bhartṛhari as having died in 650. He is hardly identical with the author of the *Śatakas*.

17. Manjhan, *Madhumālati*, ed. by Mātā Prasād Gupta, Allahabad: Mitra Prakāśan, 1961.

18. *Madhumālati*, ibid. For details, see verses 153-5.

Mātā Prasād Gupta seems to be uncertain about the meaning of this word. In the main text he gives the word 'Bājur' and not 'Bājir.' In the modern Hindi commentary of the text he explains him as a player of a musical instrument and a beggar (54.1). In the glossary he gives the meaning of the term as 'player of a musical instrument:' '*bājir: vādyakār = bājā bajānevālā* (that is, player of a musical instrument).' In his commentary in modern Hindi, he mostly uses the word 'Bājir' and not 'Bājur,' which he himself has reconstructed.[19] It seems he was not very certain about the word and its meaning.

Bājir has two characteristics. As already mentioned above, (1) he sings Candrāvali songs which have penetrated the heart of Rūpcand, (2) he is a great singer and his melodic songs pierce King Rūpcand's heart and he calls him through his minister Bāṃṭhā and assigns him the job of singing songs, reciting poetry (*kavitta*), narrating tales (*kahānī*) and narratives (*kathā*), and he seems to be an expert in lyrics (*gīt*) and melody (*nād*). Maulānā Dāūd calls Bājir a *gāvanhār* (singer):

> *gīt nād ras kavit kahāni kathā kahi gāvanihār*
> *mor man raini divas sukhi rakhahiṃ bhuṃjasi gāṃv kuṭhār* [20]
>
> O singer, sing melodious songs and lyrics, poetry, tales and narratives.
> Give me happiness day and night and enjoy yourself with the wealth of this city.

King Rūpcand praises his sweet voice. Bājir seems to be an expert of *vihāg* songs which are sung in the late night. These songs are mostly filled with sentiments of love and eroticism.

Bājir may be a Yogī but it is not stated in the text. At the margin of the one verse in the Agra manuscript, a title is given '*Bājur amad jegī.*' Perhaps this *jegī* is a scribal error for *jogī* (Yogī). The name Bājir may have some connection with *vajrayāna*, but it does not seem likely that this singer of Candrāvali songs may have been a Vajrayānī Sādhu. *Candāyan* clearly suggests that Bājir sang *kavitta, kahanī, kathā* etc.

The word 'Bājir' seems to be derived from the *vajra* which means 'thunderbolt, diamond, hard, Indra's bow' etc. This *vajra* becomes *vajir* in Pali and *vajja* in Prakrit, thus *vajra* (OIA)>*vajir* (Pali)>*vajja, vair* (Prakrit). In the various dialects of Hindi *bajjar, bajar* etc. are used for thunderbolt or lightning. In Sanskrit dictionaries *vajra* and its several meanings have been listed.[21] They are 'hard and mighty one,' 'thunderbolt,' especially that of Indra, said to have been formed out of the bones of the sage (*ṛṣi)* Dadhīci.

---

19. *Cāndāyan*, cf. Mātā Prasād Gupta's commentary on the verses 59, 60, and 61.
20. Ibid., verse 61.6-7.
21. Monier Monier-Williams, *Sanskrit-English Dictionary*, Oxford: Oxford University Press, 1964 [1st rev. ed., 1899], p. 912.

Other meanings have been given as 'diamond,' 'a kind of penance' etc. In Rhys Davids' and Stede's *Pali-English Dictionary, vajira* has been rendered as 'thunderbolt,' in the sense of Indra's weapon, along with another meaning, 'diamond'.[22] In Edgerton's *Buddhist Hybrid Sanskrit Dictionary, vajira* has been listed as equal to *vajra. Vajira kāya* and *vajira sāra* are also found in the Hybrid Sanskrit texts.[23] In Prakrit and Apabhraṃśa *vajja, vair* and *vajra* have been derived from Sanskrit *vajra*. From *vajra* both words, *bājil* and *bājul*, can be derived. Sukumar Sen has listed both these terms in his *Etymological Dictionary of Bengali.*[24] Bājul is the supreme deity of the cult of the thunderbolt in the tantric tradition, i.e., he is Vajradhara, Vajril, Heruk. Bājul is a master of the cult of the thunderbolt (Vajrayāna). In *Caryāpada* texts, there is a reference to Bājil.

> *nācanti bājila gānti debī*
> *buddha nāṭaka bisamā hoi*[25]
>
> Bājil dances, and the goddess sings.
> The drama of Buddha is difficult (to understand).

The whole imagery of singing and dancing is present in the poem. In *Caryāpada* the word Bājul also appears as a deity.[26] In all these references it appears that Bājir or Bājur of *Candāyan* are much nearer to the *Caryāpada* texts, at least semantically. 'R' and 'l' are easily interchangeable. It is possible that Bājir or Bājur may have appeared in the guise of Vajrayānī Sādhu but there are no traces of a Vajrayānī character in him. Sufis normally borrowed many elements from the current Indian traditions but they transformed them to suit their own Sufi background.

Mātā Prasād Gupta has reconstructed the reading *Bājur* on the basis of the Agra manuscript which was bought by him for the K. M. Institute of Agra from Jaipur. This manuscipt was originally prepared in Samvat 1673 (A.D. 1616) in Devanāgarī. It seems the scribe of this manuscript preferred the word Bājur over Bājir. In many verses of this Agra manuscript Bājur is found, such as *bājur ek katahuṃ hut āvā* (a *bājur* came from somewhere). In the manuscripts found in Persian characters, Bājir and Bājur are written in

---

22. T.W. Rhys Davids and W. Stede, *Pali-English Dictionary*, London: Luzac and Company, 1966, p. 593.

23. Franklin Edgerton, *Buddhist Hybrid Sanskrit Dictionary*, repr., Delhi: Motilal Banarsidass, 1972 [1st ed., New Haven: Yale University Press, 1953], p. 467.

24. Sukumar Sen, *The Etymological Dictionary of Bengali (1000-1800)*, 2 vols., Calcutta: Eastern Publishers, 1971, p. 631.

25. Tarapada Mukherji, *The Old Bengali Language and Text*, Calcutta: University of Calcutta, 1963, pada 17. Bājila and Bājula, both the words, are found in the *Caryāpadas* (verses 17.35) having the same meaning.

26. Tarapada Mukherji, o.c., *pada* 35.

the same way. It is most likely that the Agra manuscript has been transcribed into Devanāgarī from a Persian manuscript. Many errors of the transcription and the colophon *nuskha Candāyan guftar Maulānā Dāūd Dalmaī* (the manuscript of *Candāyan* composed by Maulānā Dāūd of Dalmau), all suggest this.

Mātā Prasād Gupta, as I said uncertain about his reading, in his modern Hindi commentary uses the word Bājir ignoring his own reading Bājur. He gives the meaning of Bājir as *vādya bajākar māṁgne khāne vālā* 'some one who plays a musical instrument and begs for food.' Sanskrit *vādya* is a musical instrument. In Pali *vajja* is a drum. In Panjabi *vajja* and in Bhojpuri *bājā*, for a musical instrument is very common. But as far as I know there is no word like Bājir or Bājur found in local dialects. *Bajavaiyā, bajaniyā, bajāvanhār* are the words which are used for the Sanskrit word *vādyakāra* ('a player of musical instruments'). It is unlikely that Bājir can be derived from *vādyakāra*. Bājir has of course many qualities. He is a singer and a player of musical instruments. He is also a storyteller, and a reciter of poetry. In Apabhraṃśa *vajjir* is found but it means 'that which rings' or 'produces sound'. It does not mean *vādyakāra*.

Bājir as a Vajrayānī Yogī does not fit in the Sufi scheme of thought. In Hindi Sufi romances almost all the heroes set out for their journeys as Nāthpanthī Yogīs but in their hearts they are *prem yogīs* (lovers). In other words they were Sufis in disguise. The same applied to Bājir. He was most probably a Sufi character. Miniature paintings in two different manuscripts depict Bājir in two different ways. The picture in the Manchester manuscript portrays him as a Sādhu or Faqir who plays small cymbals while singing. He has matted hair on his head and a bag on his shoulder. In the Berlin manuscript he wears a special kind of shirt and holds a musical instrument on his shoulder. It seems both artists have different imaginations of Bājir. Perhaps the Sufi poet also wished to maintain the ambiguity of this character Bājir. Medieval scribes of the manuscripts of *Candāyan* also seemed to be in doubt about the personality of Bājir or Bājur as are the modern Hindi scholars.

The Candrāvali *gīt* which Bājur sings needs some thorough investigation. Mātā Prasād Gupta is of the opinion that it was a tale of love which was very popular in Bengal. In the introduction of his edition of the *Mṛgāvati* he discusses various versions of Candrāvali-*kathā* and suggests that perhaps Bājir's Candrāvali songs were current in his days and the author of *Mṛgāvati,* Kutuban, borrowed his story from Candrāvali songs.[27]

A kind of pathetic Candrāvali songs are still current in some parts of Northern India, particularly in Hariyana. Rāhul Sāṃkrityāyan says that Candrāvali songs were sung in the rainy season and were filled with *karuṇa*

---

27. *Mṛgāvati*, Introduction, pp. 19-20.

rasa (pathetic sentiments). An example has also been given by him in his book *Ādi hindī kī kahāniyāṃ aur lokgīt.*

In my opinion Candrāvali songs sung by Bājir or Bājur in *Candāyan* were simply the narratives or tales of Lorik and Candā which were current during Maulānā Dāūd's time. I have already published five complete volumes of the Lorik Candā tale. Perhaps Bājir was singing only a part of it. Later in the text he describes Candā's *nakhśikh* (head-to-foot description) which prepares a background for the battle between Rūpcand and Sahdev, the father of Candā. Valiant hero Lorik brings victory to Sahdev through his bravery and valour. Later Lorik and Candā develop love for each other. It is most likely that Bājir was singing the tale of Candā's love rather than anything else.

Bājir describing Candā's beauty to Rūpcand
(Berlin Manuscript)

Bājir describing Candā's beauty to Rūpcand
(Manchester Manuscript)

Bājir running away from Govargaṛh out of fear
(Manchester Manuscript)

Hagiography and Reception History: The Case of Mīrā's *Padas* in Nāgrīdās's *Pada-prasaṅga-mālā* [1]

Heidi R. M. Pauwels

In this paper, I raise the issue of the interconnection of hagiography and reception history of bhakti poems. Editions of bhakti poems are often primarily based on manuscripts of collections of the poems themselves, with references to commentaries of the text, if existent. I argue that it is important also to collate versions of the poems as preserved in hagiographies. They are useful, not only as testimonia, but also to trace the reception history of the songs. By looking at their contextualization in hagiographies, we can reconstruct which songs were popular and how they were understood by the author(s) of the hagiography. A particularly interesting document for studying this is the mid-eighteenth-century *Pada-prasaṅga-mālā*, attributed to Nāgrīdās. I hope to work on an edition and translation of this text for my future research. For the purpose of this paper, I concentrate on one case study: the *padas* of Mīrābāī.

Introduction

When we work on editions of early bhakta poets, we start mostly by busily doing manuscript research, collating collections of poetry by our poet, and locating songs in early anthologies. If extant, we also study the commentaries, which provide both evidence of the text of the poems, as well as a glimpse of the way they were interpreted by the tradition. This research is demanding enough in itself. Yet, we should not neglect to take a next step and look at the poetry preserved in hagiographies about our poets. These texts are often only mined as sources for biographical information. It has been stressed less that they can contain alternative versions of the poetry (which can serve as testimonia in our editions), and also information of their

1. This paper is based on a graduate paper that I wrote in 1992 for the late Prof. Alan Entwistle. I am grateful to him for his comments on the paper and help with the translation of the text. Some parts of the paper are an updated version of material I presented first at the conference: 'Celebrating Mīrābāī: Hindu Saint for a Global World' held at UCLA, Oct. 3-6, 2002.

reception history. They are rich sources for mapping the popularity of our poets in a particular period and by their contextualization, also in the way their poetry was understood.[2]

One wonderful source for such a study is the mid-eighteenth-century *Pada-prasaṅga-mālā,* 'Garland of stories about songs,' attributed to the poet-king Nāgrīdās. This prose hagiography, in which several great *bhakta*s, or more precisely, their compositions or *pada*s are praised, is exactly what the title promises: the stories are organized around the author's favorite devotional songs. This hagiography is very interesting in its own right, and I will have more to say about it elsewhere, but suffice here to zoom in on one example related to Mīrābāī.

Mīrābāī may well be one of the most-studied *bhakti* saints, yet her case is maybe also the most difficult because of the absence of early evidence for a corpus of songs by her and the instability of the text of the individual songs. It seems that the songs entered late into the scribal tradition and were instead transmitted orally early on. This has led to all kinds of speculation, including the proposition that Mīrā's songs were the property of illiterate women, and/or that she was discriminated against because she was a woman, or because she took up the case of low-castes.

As it turns out, Mīrā figures prominently in the mid-eighteenth-century *Pada-prasaṅga-mālā (PPM):* No less than five chapters are devoted to her, quoting a total of six of her *padas* (for the full translation, see the appendix). So far, these chapters have been treated mostly as part of the growing hagiographic corpus on Mīrā. In another paper, I have discussed how these chapters provide evidence of a positive Rajput (Rāṭhaur) evaluation of Mīrā.3 This paper's contribution is to uncover their significance for the textual and reception history of Mīrā's songs.

1. Some Caveats Regarding Nāgrīdās's Hagiography *Pada-prasaṅga-mālā*

Nāgrīdās is the pen name of Sāvant Singh of Kishangarh (1699-1764). This romantic figure is best known for the impact he had on the visual arts. When he was the crown prince of Kishangarh, in the thirties and forties of the eighteenth century (1735-48), he inspired the local painters to develop a new style of miniature painting. The new style showed a preponderance of

2. J. S. Hawley brings this to bear marvelously on the case of Sūrdās; see John Stratton Hawley, *Sūr Dās: Poet, Singer, Saint*, Seattle and London: University of Washington Press, 1986.

3. Heidi Pauwels, 'Rāṭhaurī Mīrā: Two Neglected Rāṭhauṛ Connections of Mīrā, Jaimal Meṛtīyo and Nāgrīdās,' in *Proceedings of the Mīrābāī Conference in Los Angeles* (provisional title), October 2002, ed. by Nancy Martin [forthcoming].

depictions of the Rādhā-Kṛṣṇa theme and was characterized by elongated eyes of the personages depicted.

The prince was an ardent Kṛṣṇa devotee, he visited the Braj area several times, and was a prolific poet in Braj Bhāṣā. In fact, several of the paintings produced by the Kishangarh atelier were directly inspired by Nāgrīdās's own devotional poetry. He was also an avid composer of anthologies, including poems of his famous and less famous contemporaries and predecessors, including Mīrā.

The work that is the focus of this study, the aforementioned prose hagiography *Pada-prasaṅga-mālā,* is not dated. A conservative estimate would place it either shortly before or after the middle of the eighteenth century. A turning point in Sāvant Singh's life was 1748, the year of the death of his father. Shortly after, his half-brother Bahādur Singh usurped the throne.[4] Unable to regain his throne, Sāvant Singh seems to have made the Braj area his new home. When eventually he managed to recover part of his kingdom, the area around Rūpnagar, he placed his son, Sardār Singh, on the throne and retired to Vrindāban, where he died in 1764. Whether the hagiography was written before or after Nāgrīdās lost his kingdom is unclear. Nāgrīdās's interest in devotional songs long predates his retirement to Vrindāban, but the frequent reference to Rūpnagar in the last verses of the work may indicate that it was towards the end of his life. In any case, 1764 is a firm *terminus ad quem.*

The attribution of *Pada-prasaṅga-mālā* to Nāgrīdās could be debated. The work is not really signed, though the final *pada*s are all with *chāpa* 'Nāgar.' Towards the end of the work, the author frequently praises *pada*s by Nāgrīdās, which may indicate that these passages were composed for Nāgrīdās, rather than by him. Whatever may be the case, the work clearly is to be attributed, if not to the prince himself, at least to his close entourage. It is with this caveat that I will refer to Nāgrīdās as author in the rest of the paper. The Kishangarhi connection is reinforced by the fact that there are miniature paintings from Kishangarh that seem to be illustrations of this work, in particular the meeting of Haridās, Tānsen and Akbar.[5] This seems to confirm an attribution to the prince himself, who is known to have commissioned paintings for his own poetry.

As regards the chapters on Mīrābāī, there is another major caveat, that has not been sufficiently appreciated so far by authors on Mīrā who quote Nāgrīdās. *Pada-prasaṅga-mālā* is usually consulted in the edition of

4. Vijay Kumar Mathur, *Marvels of Kishangarh Paintings: From the Collection of the National Museum, New Delhi*, Delhi: Bharatiya Kala Prakashan, 2000, p. 11.
5. Ibid., pp. 98-9, plate 31.

the prestigious Nāgrīpracāriṇī Sabhā series by Kiśorīlāl Gupta.[6] Upon investigation, it appears that the text of this *Pada-prasaṅga-mālā* is based on that of an earlier edition of Nāgrī's works, *Nāgar samuccay,* published in Bombay in 1898. Still, Gupta consulted also one undated manuscript from the Nāgrīpracāriṇī Sabhā collection.[7] It has often been overlooked that Gupta reports in his introduction that the latter manuscript does not include any of the chapters devoted to Mīrā. In that manuscript, then, Mīrā does not figure at all. There is another, lesser-known edition of Nāgrī's works by a Kishangarh-based scholar, Faiyāz Alī Khān.[8] In this edition too, the chapters on Mīrā are included, but as it turns out, it is also based on the same 1898 edition that Gupta based his on. However, Khān has carried out a fuller manuscript study (unfortunately, he gives no details, but refers to his unpublished Ph.D. thesis from Jaipur University from 1962) and he claims to have used authoritative manuscripts from the royal collection. Unfortunately, it is not clear whether the Mīrā chapters are in the manuscripts or not. One suspects not, because it is reported elsewhere that the oldest manuscript he used (dated VS 1805) is substantially shorter than his edition (48 *prasaṅgas* as opposed to 68).[9] Should we cast doubt on the authenticity of the Mīrā chapters in *Pada-prasaṅga-mālā?* Are they an innovation, added by the editor of the 1898 edition? Have we been merely going around in circles, back to the nineteenth century after all?

The picture is further complicated by the fact that there is substantial debate about the text of other works of Nāgrīdās. As so often is the case for *bhakti* poets, the crux of the arguments of textual authenticity revolves around a dispute of sectarian allegiance. In this case, the Vallabha- and Nimbārka-sampradāya both claim that Nāgrīdās was initiated in their sect. The Vallabhan claim is put forward in the aforementioned Bombay edition, and both Khān and Gupta accept this claim that Nāgrīdās was a Vallabhan. However, there is Vrajvallabhśaraṇ's rival edition sponsored by the Vrindāban-based Nimbārkan Śrīsarveśvar Press.[10] In the foreword, the Vallabhan claim is refuted and the late-nineteenth-century editor in Bombay accused of tampering with the evidence.[11] A Nimbārkan claim is staked and a connection is made between the royal court of Kishangarh and the nearby Nimbārkan seat of Salemabad. Evidence is cited for documentary evidence

6. Kiśorīlāl Gupta, *Nāgrīdās,* 2 vols. (Ākar Granthmālā 8), Benares: Nāgrīpracāriṇī Sabhā, 1965.

7. Ibid., vol. 2, p. 1.

8. Faiyāz Alī Khān, *Nāgrīdās granthāvalī,* New Delhi: Kendrīya Hindī Nideśālay, 1974.

9. See Vrajvallabhśaraṇ, *Śrī Nāgrīdāsjī kī vāṇī: Nāgrīdāsjī ke jīvanvṛtta evaṃ vāṇiyoṃ kā saṃśodhit saṃskaraṇ,* Vrindāvan: Śrī Sarveśvar Press, 1966, p. 26, quoting Khān's unpublished dissertation.

10. See preceding note.

11. Ibid., pp. 25-33.

in the royal registers (*bahī*) regarding the initiation of Nāgrī's mother, stepmother and stepsister, as well as Nāgrīdās himself.[12] Unfortunately, *Pada-prasaṅga-mālā* is not part of the discussion, and the whole work is omitted from the Śrīsarveśvar edition for reasons unstated. One may well speculate that its failure to include the great saints of the Nimbārka-sampradāya may have something to do with it.

If we are to regard the whole *Pada-prasaṅga-mālā* as inauthentic, or even just the Mīrā chapters as an interpolation, the question is when this attribution/ interpolation took place. One possibility is that it happened early on, still in the eighteenth century. We know of other cases where manuscripts from Kishangarh's ateliers were 'corrected.' The same has been claimed to be the case for manuscripts copied in Rūpnagar in 1727 and 1729 containing the poetry of Ānandghan.[13] It appears that some revisionist project went on in the twenties. Another hypothesis is that it happened about twenty years later, under influence of the usurper Bahādur Singh. The Nimbārkans allege that he converted to the Vallabha-sampradāya after a quarrel about the succession of the Salemabad Nimbārka *pīṭha*.[14] They claim that this caused a substantial revision of court documents as well as of manuscripts of Nāgrī's works.

This raises the question whether *Pada-prasaṅga-mālā* betrays a Vallabhan agenda, or whether the longer redaction is Vallabhan. However, neither the long nor the short version betrays partiality for the Vallabha-sampradāya. While several of the stories told—most of which are also reported to be included in the Nāgrīpracāriṇī Sabhā manuscript—are reminiscent of the influential Vallabhan *Vārtā* literature, that is not the case for the majority of the chapters. The text starts with the Sanskrit poet Jayadeva, includes the great Sants (Nāmdev, Kabīr and Raidās), several Rāma-devotees, as well as Rādhāvallabhan and Gauḍīya *bhaktas*.[15] Thus *Pada-prasaṅga-mālā* cannot be said to be an exclusively Vallabhan document. If we make a list of the stories that are included in the editions but not in the manuscript, consulted by Gupta, we find that the saints added in the edition, and the stories added for the other saints, do not particularly betray Vallabhan sensitivities. One would actually be more inclined to see the revision going the other way around, and postulate that the Vallabhan redaction excised the original Mīrā chapters because of sectarian sensitivities

12. Ibid., pp. 11-12 and 17.

13. Imre Bangha, 'Mundane and Divine Love in Anandghan's Poetry: An Eighteenth Century Literary Debate,' in *The Banyan Tree: Essays on Early Literature in New Indo-Aryan Languages,* ed. by Mariola Offredi, vol. 2, New Delhi: Manohar, pp. 523-7, 532-3.

14. Vrajvallabhśaraṇ, *Śrī Nāgrīdāsjī,* pp. 17-18.

15. It has to be pointed out, though, that Nāgrīdās shows remarkably little awareness of the sectarian identity of the Gauḍīyas he mentions, thus, for instance, the story on Gadādhar Bhaṭṭ (*PPM* 45) does not mention his presumed guru Jīva Gosvāmī.

and the enmity towards her in the *Vārtā* literature. If the chapters are part of a Vallabhan redaction they represent an unusual Vallabhan perspective that evaluates Mīrā positively.[16]

Another possible scenario is that the interpolations happened as late as at the end of the nineteenth century. The 1898 edition is said to be based mainly on a manuscript predating it by only about fifteen years (dated VS 1940), which was preserved in the so-called Sarasvatī Bhaṇḍār of the royal library in Kishangarh.[17] The manuscript and the edition date thus from exactly the period that the academic construction of Mīrā began, the period that Śyāmaldās was compiling his *Vīrvinod* in Mewar. The date of the edition is exactly the same as the publication of the first academic work, *Mīrābāī kā jīvancaritra* by Munśī Devīprasād. This may lead us to suspect that the chapters are part of the active Rajputization and reintegration project of Mīrā that Martin has so nicely laid out for us.[18] Further manuscript research of *Pada-prasaṅga-mālā* will have to help clarify whether the Mīrā *prasaṅgas* surface only late in the manuscripts and whether they are linked to a Vallabhan redaction or not.

2. The Mīrā *Padas* in *Pada-prasaṅga-mālā*

Thus, it may be the case that Nāgrīdās's Mīrā *prasaṅgas* are interpolations. However, there is another *prasaṅga* in *Pada-prasaṅga-mālā* in which a *pada* of Mīrā is quoted. This has been overlooked in research so far, because the *prasaṅga* praises an obscure *bhakta* by the name of Nāgrīdās Naṭvā (*PPM* 58, translated in the appendix). Interestingly, this chapter is included in the manuscript consulted by Gupta.

There is then evidence of at least one of Mīrā's songs in *Pada-prasaṅga-mālā,* that is with more certainty attributable to the mid-eighteenth century. If the other songs are also authentic, Nāgrīdās's testimony provides us with a little Mīrā core corpus of a total of seven *padas*, apparently prevalent in Kṛṣṇa devotional circles in Rājasthān and Braj in the mid-eighteenth century. If the chapters on Mīrā are not authentic, they remain

16. One wonders about the origin and extent of the *Vārtā*'s enmity towards Mīrā. It may have been inspired by a contemporary power struggle with the *pujārīs* of the Raṇachoḍ temple in Ḍākor and the subsequent Vallabhan take-over; see Françoise Mallison, 'Lorsque Raṇachoḍarāya quitte Dwarka pour Dakor, ou comment Dvārakānātha prit la succession de Daṅkanātha,' in *Devotion Divine: Bhakti Traditions from the Regions of India*, ed. by Diana L. Eck and Françoise Mallison, Groningen: Egbert Forsten, 1991, pp. 197-207.

17. Vrajvallabhśaraṇ, *Śrī Nāgrīdāsjī,* p. 26.

18. Nancy M. Martin-Kershaw, 'Mīrābāī in the Academy and the Politics of Identity,' in *Faces of the Feminine in Ancient, Medieval, and Modern India*, ed. by Mandakranta Bose, New York: Oxford University Press, pp. 162-82.

interesting for the reception history of her songs in Rājasthān, but for later, possibly as late as the end of the nineteenth century.

The following analysis will first focus on the contextualization of the songs and what that tells us about their reception history. Then I will turn to the songs themselves.

2.1. Nāgrīdās's Contextualization of Mīrā *Padas*

The most interesting contribution of *Pada-prasaṅga-mālā* is that it provides us with a glimpse of the reception history of Mīrā's songs. Whether the stories date from the eighteenth or the nineteenth century, they give us an idea of how the songs were understood in Rajput circles. Their contextualization is interesting in several respects.

The first song is portrayed as Mīrā's answer to a specific challenge of the Rāṇā: his urging her to become a *satī* after her husband's death. The poem fits well in that several lines address the Rāṇā directly. However, the address to the Rāṇā is frequently hypermetrical. Judging from the refrain and the majority of the lines, the song seems to have been composed in a very popular *bhajana* meter of sixteen *mātrās* before the caesura and twelve or fourteen afterwards. Wherever it occurs, the address *Rāṇājī* renders the line metrically irregular. It seems to come from a sung tradition, in which such interjections are frequent, maybe a folk tradition from Rājasthān. However, if we strip the poem from these terms of address, it becomes more ambiguous. To demonstrate this, I give the translation of the metrically 'corrected' version below (full translation with notes is in the appendix):

> Mīrā('s heart) is colored with passion for the Lord, all other passion is blocked.
> I will sing (praise) of Giridhara, I will not become a sati, my heart is enchanted by the one named 'Raincloud.'
> The relation of elder brother and sister-in-law (does) not (matter): I am a servant, (but) He is (my) Lord.
> [My] bracelets are *dūrva* grass, *tilak* and *mālā*. (My) adornments are moral rectitude and fasting.
> No other adornments please me, [just] so much as the knowledge of the guru.
> Some will curse me, some will bow before me. I will just sing the praise of Gobinda.
> The path by which the holy men reached (their goal), is the one on which I will go.
> Neither by robbing (me) nor by tormenting (my) soul will anyone do anything to me.
> When mounted on an elephant, one does not ride a donkey, that just doesn't happen.

> By being a king, you will fall into the hell: merry-makers are Yama's to take.
> By being devoted, you reach freedom, by practising yoga, you live.
> Girdhara is (my) Lord. Girdhara is (my) family, mother, father, son, brother.
> Yours to you and mine to me. That is Mīrābāī 's message.

If read thus, the poem can take on different meanings. For one, it may be directed to anyone, including the women of her family. The latter option seems likely in the light of the references to jewelry. Mīrā's defiance then becomes more general, not just against the outrageous request of sati, but stressing her preference of the path of devotion in contrast with that of *strīdharma.* This poem seems to have undergone an interpretative process before it reached Nāgrī's ear. Likely, a folk tradition interpreted it as directed to the Rāṇā, and Nāgrīdās adds the specifics of circumstance, no doubt inspired by the reference to sati in the second line and the one to the *jeṭh-bahū* relation in the third.

The next poem is contextualized with the most famous Mīrā story: her drinking the poison cup without harm. Nāgrī's story stresses the Rāṇā's evil intent and also that Mīrā was not fooled by his trick of presenting the poison as *caraṇāmṛta.* Mīrā's poem triumphantly declares she was not harmed by the poison, but it centralizes God throughout the poem, postulating a divine intervention. The triumph is not hers over the Rāṇā, but God's over a mere king. There is thus a certain tension between the song and the contextualization.

The most interesting contextualization is that of the poem about Dvārkā. The introduction to the *pada* hardly gives any detail: most of this chapter is on Vrindāban. The poem is an appeal for shelter, hinting that Mīrā has burned all bridges with her 'kingdom' where she belongs. She describes herself as being without male protector and appeals to Kṛṣṇa to take on that role. Nāgrī's story does not comment on Mīrā's vulnerability. In fact, he makes it seem as if Mīrā was properly escorted by Brahmins from Mewar in the next story:

> Voicing her desire in this way, singing this song, she arrived in Dvārkā. She stayed there for several days. After that, the *purohit* and other servants of the Rānā *who had accompanied* Mīrā said that many days had passed now and that she should return to (her own) land (as) the king had commanded. They insisted on this for a few days. Then they started pressing Mīrābāī (*PPM* 17, italics mine).

While Nāgrīdās has preserved the vulnerable tone of the *pada* he quotes, he downplays Mīrā's vulnerability in the contextualization. This seems to be a case of irenic reinterpretation.

The two songs that appear in *prasaṅga* 16 are also appeals to Kṛṣṇa. The first is the more formulaic blackmail of the *bhakta,* asking to be delivered, citing mythological precedent. The second is a similar appeal, but cast in the more erotic language of *viraha.* Both receive extra poignancy by Nāgrīdās's contextualization as Mīrā's last poems. Special power is ascribed to these poems, because they finally convinced Kṛṣṇa to transfer Mīrā to his heaven.

The last poem in the Mīrā chapters too is a poem of *viraha,* this time addressed to the female companion. Nāgrīdās has made it fit with the hagiography by transforming the sympathetic friend into a spy. Again, he stresses the special power of the song that moves the spy such that she is spontaneously converted and stays with Mīrā as the friend the song was intended to be directed to.

Finally, there is the song in the *prasaṅga* of Nārāyaṇdās to consider (*PPM* 58). He was a dancer performing the song of Mīrā with refrain *sācau prīta hī ko nātau* 'The only true bond is that of love.' When he mimed the line *madanamohana raṃga rāta,* 'Colored in the color of the enchanter,' he took on a *tribhaṅga* pose, and froze for ever in that position. He blissfully passed away, instantly reaching paradise. There is even precise geographical information: the incident is set in Haṇḍiyā Sarāy, near Allahabad. The context is a performance for a *navāb*, but the singer is stressed to have turned the performance into a sacred one by dancing in front of a *tulsīmālā.*

This contextualization is typical for Nāgrīdās, who often ascribes to the songs he quotes special powers of instilling feelings of devotion, and indeed the capacity to bring about the performer's blissful death, which leads them straight to Kṛṣṇa's heaven. To some extent that was the case with Mīrā's 'disappearance.'

Thus, Nāgrīdās, in his contextualizations has added new aspects to the interpretation of the songs. In some cases, these elements may have predated him, and he may simply be representing an existing oral tradition. In other cases he seems more creative and actively linking hagiographic tradition with specific songs he liked. Sometimes there is a tension between the contextualization and the song and Nāgrīdās's commentary serves as an irenic reinterpretation.

2.2. Nāgrī's Testimony for an Early Corpus of Mīrā *Padas*

Let us now turn to the songs themselves. First, there is Nāgrīdās's evidence of a new song of Mīrā in the chapter on Nāgrīdās. This song is nowadays relatively 'forgotten,' that is, it does not figure in most of the anthologies (I have found only one alternate version: in the *Mīrā bṛhatpadāvalī* 1.261, no. 603, where the source is given as Nāgrīdās). But there is more, Nāgrīdās sets us on an interesting track towards yet earlier evidence of the reception of this Mīrā song in Allahabad. The same story, as it turns out, is narrated in Nābhādās's *Bhaktamāla* (*chappāī* 145). As usual, Nābhādās is extremely brief:

Nṛtaka Nārāyanadāsa kau premapuṃja[19] *āge baṛhyau*
Pada līnau parasiddha prīti jāmeṃ dṛḍha nāto
Akṣara tanamaya bhayau madanamohana raṃga rāto
Nācata saba kou āhi kāhi pai yaha bani āvai
Citra likhita so rahyau tribhaṃga[20] *desī ju dikhāvai*
Haṃḍiyā sarāya dekhata dunī haripura padavī ko caṛhyau

The dancer Nārāyaṇdās expanded his wealth of love.
He took the famous song in which love is (declared) a strong bond.
He became engrossed in the words 'dyed in Kṛṣṇa's passion.'
Everyone can do some dancing, but who can manage this?
He remained frozen when he showed the thrice-bent Deśī position.
While people looked on in Haṇḍiyā Sarāy, he obtained a spot in heaven.

Clearly, 'the famous song in which love is (declared) a strong bond' which contains the words 'dyed in Kṛṣṇa's passion' is understood by Nāgrīdās as authored by Mīrābāī. While Nābhādās unfortunately does not say the song is Mīrā's, still he paraphrases the refrain and quotes one rhyme. There is no doubt about the authenticity of this *chappāī* as belonging to *Bhaktamāla.* It is included in the critical edition based on early manuscript evidence. This pushes the date for early evidence for one of Mīrā's songs (though not with certainty of *chāpa*) back close to 1600, or if you want to be really strict, 1647, the earliest manuscript attestation of *Bhaktamāla.* Thus, the evidence from hagiographies has led to the discovery of a new song, that actually seems to be one of early attribution to Mīrābāī.

At this point, we can turn to the text of the other songs. Not surprisingly, none corresponds exactly to today's Mīrā anthologies. Out of the six songs, two are quite different from their published counterparts, only the refrain and rhyme are similar. I provide in the appendix to this paper the text of all the songs as it appears in the Gupta edition[21] and provide a comparison to the text of the closest variant versions I could detect.[22] There

---

19. The critical edition by Jhā gives a variant: *premapāvaka.*

20. The critical edition by Jhā leaves out *tribhaṃga,* and gives variants: *sabha bhayau sugandha* and *jo tribhaṃga desīju.*

21. There are some slight variants as compared with the text published by Khān. Interestingly, both authors worked on the basis of the same published text, but still have different interpretations of the characters.

22. I have highlighted in bold the most salient variants, including dialectical variants but not spelling differences.

is, as expected, a fair amount of dialectical variance, some scribal errors, some oral variants, but also some significant difference in meaning. I provide the translation of the text of Nāgrīdās and give the meaning of the variants in the notes. In several cases, the reading from Nāgrīdās seems preferable (*PPM* 17a, refrain and last line, 17b second line). Thus, the hagiographic testimony adds to our understanding of the songs. Also, the 'Vulgate' version of the first song (variant 2) does not contain the reference to sati. Even so, it remains interesting to take into account the variants, which add nuances, such as a possible reference to *jauhar* (in the variant to 14), and the Rāṇā's offer to make Mīrā his first queen (in the first variant to 15). Also, whereas in Nāgrīdās Mīrā says she prefers God to the Rāṇā, in the variants she prefers holy men (variants to 15). As usual, the multiplicity of variants renders the most interesting and rich understandings of the poems.

Further, it is interesting to consider the range of topics covered in the *pada*s quoted. Mīrā's enmity with the Rāṇā figures importantly in two of the songs, one is defiantly addressed to him, in the other one she describes her reaction to the poison cup he sent her. The Rāṇā figures also in a third song, where Mīrā only mentions him to say she has left him: the focus here is rather her devotion for Raṇachoḍ of Dvārkā. In this, as in the two next poems, she directly addresses Hari. One poem is a plea for protecting her honor (*lāja*) and the other for ending the torment of separation (*viraha*). Separation is also the theme of the last song in the Mīrā chapters, but this one is addressed to a sympathetic friend. The theme of the song in the Nāgrīdās chapter is the strength of the bond of true love. This is pretty much the range of Mīrā themes most popular today, with the exception that it stresses Mīrā's Dvārkā connection over the one with Vrindāban. That is surprising given that the author, Nāgrīdās, had strong connections with Vrindāban. In terms of the significance of range of topics, one can argue that this is limited by the biographical context. Still, in the light of Nāgrīdās's general 'favorite songs' approach in the rest of the work, the ones he picks seem to be indicative of what he and his milieu evaluated as being Mīrā's best.

This brings us to a related question of how Nāgrī's testimony functions in the context of the manuscript material available for Mīrā's songs. We find that the first two of the songs quoted by Nāgrīdās occur also in Rājasthānī anthologies, in particular one dated 1783 and preserved in the Rajasthan Oriental Research Institute in Jodhpur (manuscript 12590, folios 35-7).[23] Nancy Martin has discussed the variants of the manuscript and

23. See Nancy M. Martin-Kershaw, 'Dyed in the Color of Her Lord: Multiple Representations in the Mīrābāī Tradition,' Ph.D. Dissertation for Faculty of the Graduate Theological Union, Berkeley, California, 1995, pp. 145-6.

hagiographic version in translation.[24] Most notable is the omission in the anthology of the reference to Mīrā's refusal to become a sati. This may be attributed to the fact that the anthology was presumably royally commissioned. The manuscript resembles the Nāgrī selection of Mīrā *padas* also in one other respect: it has a lot of references to the Rāṇā (it contains a total of eighteen songs, one third of which reportedly refer to the Rāṇā).[25] It is tempting to theorize that the two songs in particular, and the Rāṇā songs in general, were popular in Rāṭhaur circles in the second half of the eighteenth century. This would be an interesting case of royal commission allowing the defiant voice of Mīrā challenging Rājput ideals to be heard. Further detailed manuscript research of Mīrā's *padas* in Jodhpur anthologies is needed to confirm or discredit this hypothesis.

We find overlap with some Mīrā songs quoted by Nāgrīdās also in the devotional milieu in Vrindāban. Three of these songs are quoted in the roughly contemporary *Bhaktmāl dṛṣṭānt,* a commentary on Priyādās's famous work by his grandson, Vaiṣṇavdās.[26] The work is unpublished, but the section on Mīrā is quoted by Prabhāt.[27] He does so on the basis of a manuscript preserved in Prācya Vidyā Mandir in Baroda that was written in Benares in 1767 CE (1824 VS).[28] Prabhāt suggests that Vaiṣṇavdās copied the songs from Nāgrīdās.[29] The two last songs of Mīrā are indeed quoted in exactly the same context as in *Pada-prasaṅga-mālā,* namely Mīrā's plea to the Kṛṣṇa image in Dvārkā to end her worldly suffering. However, Vaiṣṇavdās places also the song about Dvārkā in that context, which is different from Nāgrīdās, and in general, Vaiṣṇavdās's commentary stresses different elements than Nāgrī's text. Still, it is remarkable that not only the same songs are quoted, but that the text of the three songs is practically identical, with very minor variants (see notes in the appendix). At the very least we can say that these were indeed the versions of all three songs by Mīrā that were

24. Unfortunately she does not give the Braj manuscript version.

25. Martin, 'Dyed in the Color,' p. 145.

26. Given that he is Priyādās's grandson, he is usually reckoned to be Gauḍīya, for which see Prabhudayāl Mītal, *Braj ke dharm sampradāyoṃ kā itihās,* Delhi: National Publishing House, 1968, p. 534. This is confirmed by his quoting his predecessor in his line of descendants from Gopāl Bhaṭṭ, Vallabh Rasik, earlier in his commentary on the Mīrā story; see C. L. Prabhāt, *Mīrā: jīvan aur kāvya,* 2 vols., Jodhpur: Rājasthānī Granthāgār, 1999: 1.41-2. It is not clear to me why Prabhāt (ibid., 1.41) says he is Nimbārkīya.

27. Ibid., 1.44.

28. It is laudable and refreshing that Prabhāt has chosen not to correct any perceived mistakes, but that he has reproduced the commentary 'as is' in the manuscript; ibid., 1.44, n. 1.

29. Though the manuscript date of course is after Nāgrīdās's death, it is not strictly speaking necessary that Vaiṣṇavdās's work postdates Nāgrīdās's. Two other works ascribed to Vaiṣṇavdās are dated 1750 (1807 VS) and 1757 (1814 VS, see Mītal, *Braj ke dharm sampradāyoṃ kā itihās,* p. 534). Priyādās's grandson and Nāgrīdās seem to have been roughly contemporary.

popular in mid-eighteenth-century Vrindāban. Significantly, the songs quoted in the devotional milieu are directly addressed to God and stress Mīrā's vulnerability, whereas the court milieu is more preoccupied with her defiance to Rajput ethos.

The overlap of the songs quoted by Nāgrīdās in other milieus seems to be an argument in favor of their authenticity. Still, one cannot exclude the alternative, more cynical interpretation, that the interpolator used exactly these sources to concoct his chapters on Mīrā.

Conclusion

At the end of this investigation I feel cautiously optimistic that Nāgrīdās himself was positively inclined towards Mīrābāī. Assuming that *Pada-prasaṅga-mālā* was indeed authored or commissioned by him, which seems very likely, there is at least one song of her that Nāgrīdās approved of. Nowadays, the major Vallabhan temple within the Kishangarh fort, the Kalyāṇ Rāi Havelī, appears not to feature any of her songs in *samāja*.[30] On the other hand, there is an image of Mīrā in the royal collection, likely commissioned by Nāgrīdās.[31] Navina Haidar in her dissertation points out that this was an unusual choice of subject matter that was never repeated in Kishangarh.[32] This state of affairs seems to point to an inclusion of Mīrā at the time of Nāgrīdās and a subsequent excision of her during his successors. This may account for the instability of the Mīrā chapters in the manuscripts, but again, further investigation is necessary.

The study of the hagiography has proven to be interesting for textual studies of Mīrā's poetry in several respects. We have found evidence for a small corpus of Mīrā *pada*s as early as 1750. For one song, or at least fragments of it, we find pointers to even earlier evidence, possibly 1600. We have located variant readings for the text of these songs, that show interesting shifts in meaning. Finally, we have found clues for the reception of these songs in the mid-eighteenth century in a Rāṭhaur milieu with close connections to Vrindāban.

As a follow-up for this study, I am planning a critical edition and translation of this interesting work of Nāgrīdās (and others). I hope that this will inspire others too to include the study of hagiographical material in their editions of Bhakti poets.

---

30. Navina Najat Haidar, 'The Kishangarh School of Painting c. 1680-1850,' 2 vols., unpublished Ph.D. dissertation, University of Oxford, UK, 1995, p. 10.
31. Ibid., fig. 125.
32. Ibid., p. 139.

Abbreviations

BBSK	Gupta, Dīndayāl and Premnarārāyaṇ Ṭaṇḍan (ed.). *Brajbhāṣā Sūrkoś*, Lucknow: Viśvavidyālay Hindī Prakāśan, 1974 (VS 2031).
Caturvedī 1983	Caturvedī, Paraśurām, *Mīrābāī kī padāvalī*, Prayāg: Hindī Sāhitya Sammelan, [1972] 1983.
MBP	*Mīrā bṛhatpadāvalī*, vol. 1 ed. Purohit, Harinārāyaṇjī, vol. 2, ed. Śekhāvat, Kalyāṇsiṃh (Rājasthān Purātan Granthmālā 96, 120), Jodhpur: RORI, 1968, 1975.
RSK	Lāḷas, Sītārām, ed. 1962-78, *Rājasthānī sabad kos*, 4 vols. Caupāsnī Jodhpur: Rājasthānī Śodh Saṃsthān.
Śekhāvat 1984	Śekhāvat, Kalyāṇsiṃh (ed.), *Mīrāvāṇī*, Jodhpur: Garg, 1984.

Appendix

Translation of Nāgrīdās's *prasaṅgas* related to Mīrā, with comparative charts for variants of the *padas*

14

In Meḍtā [lived] Mīrābāī. She was married off to the younger brother of the Rāṇā, as is known world-wide. So, after some days this brother of the king passed away, and the Rāṇā himself was troubled by Mīrābāī. She stayed in the company of the Vaiṣṇavas, that's why. At that time she was informed by the Rāṇā that this was an auspicious occasion, and she should become a sati at the side of her husband. Then the passion for the Lord, which Mīrābāī had previously experienced, continued to affect her in the same way [as before]. At that time, she did not consider there to be any sorrow, and in answer to [his] command, she composed a new *viṣṇupada*, wrote it down and sent it to the Rāṇā. That *pada* became very famous. It was the following *pada*:

PPM 14	Variant 1 (Śekhāvat 1984: 35, no. 9)
Mīrā ke raṃga lagyo harī kau,	Mīrā raṃga lāgyo syāṃmma hari,
aura raṃga saba aṭaka parī	ora raṃga paṭaka parī
Giridhara gāsyāṃ satī na hosyāṃ,	Giridhara gāsyāṃ satī na hosyāṃ,
mana mohyo ghana nāmī	mhai vara pāyo ghaṇanāmī
jeṭha bahū ko nāto nahīṃ rāṇājī,	jeṭha bahū ko nāto nahīṃ rāṇājī,
hūṃ sevaga ye syāmī	the sevaga mhai syāṃmmī
cūḍo dobaḍo tilaka ju mālā,	gehaṇo mharai dovaḍī mālā,
sīla barta siṃgāra	sīla vrata siṇagāra
aura siṃgāra bhāvaiṃ nahīṃ rāṇā jī,	ora gehaṇo nahīṃ pairāṃ rāṇājī,
yauṃ gura gyāna hamāra	vo guragyāṃna hai mhārai
koī nidoṃ koī biṃdo,	johara karāṃ na jīva satāvāṃ,
guṇa gobinda rā gāsyām	guṇa jo govinda kā gāsyāṃ
jiṇa māraga vaiṃ saṃta pahūṃtā,	jiṇa māraga vesa pahuṃtā,
tiṇa māraga mhe jāsyāṃ	uṇa māraga mhai jāsyāṃ
corī karāṃ na jīva saṃtāvāṃ,	hari ko bhajana mhai nisa dina karasāṃ,
kāṃī karasī mhāro koī	kāṃī karasī mhāro koī
hasatī caḍhi gadhaiṃ na caḍhā,	hasatī caḍh kara khara nahīṃ caḍhasāṃ,
yā to bāta na hoī	ā to vāta nahī hoī
rāja karaṃtā naraka paḍesī,	rāja karatāṃ naraka paḍatāṃ,
bhogīḍā jama kaiṃ līyā	bhogīḍā jama kaiṃ līyā
bhagata karaṃtā mukta pahūṃtā,	bhagatī karatā mugata na pahuṃtā,
joga karaṃtā jīyā	joga karatā jīyā
Giradhara dhaṇī kaḍūṃbo Giradhara,	
māta pitā suta bhāī	
the thāre mhe mhāre ho rāṇājī,	
yauṃ kahai Mīrābāī	

Variant 2 (Caturvedī 1983: 107, no. 25)

Mīrāṃ lāgau raṃga harī, aurana aṃṭaka parī
Cūḍau mhāṃra tilaka aru mālā, sīsa barata siṃṇagāro
Aura siṃgāra mhāṃra dāya na āvai, yoṃ guru gyāna hamāro
Koī nindo koī bindo, mheṃ to guṇa govinda kā gāsyāṃ
Jiṇa māraga mhāṃrā sādha padhārai, uṇa māraga mhe jāsyāṃ
Corī na karasyāṃ jiva na satāsyāṃ, koī karasī mhāṃro koī
Gaja se utara ke khara nahiṃ caḍhasyāṃ ye to bāta na hoī

Mīrā('s heart) is colored with passion for the Lord,[33] all other passion is blocked.[34]
I will praise Giridhara, I won't become a sati, my heart is enchanted[35] by the one named 'Raincloud.'
The relation of elder brother- and sister-in-law (does) not (matter), Rāṇā. I am a servant, (but) He is (my) Lord.[36]
[My] bracelets are *dūrva* grass,[37] *tilak* and *mālā*. (My) jewelry is moral rectitude and fasting.
No other adornments please me, Rāṇā, [just] so much as the knowledge of the guru.[38]
Some will curse me, some will bow before me.[39] I will just sing the praise of Gobinda.
The path by which the holy men reached (their goal), is the one on which I will go.
Neither by robbing (me) nor by tormenting (my) soul[40] will anyone do anything to me.
When mounted on an elephant, one does not ride a donkey,[41] that just doesn't happen.

33. The Braj text uses the term *ramga,* which can mean 'passion' as well as 'color.' The word *harī* can mean 'green,' as well as be a spelling variant of Hari, 'the Lord.' The variant reading makes the second meaning explicit by adding 'the dark one.'
34. The variant reading is less satisfactory: 'is overthrown.'
35. In the variant: 'I have obtained for groom.'
36. The variant is more radical, and reverses the worldly roles: 'you are the servant, I am the master.' This is incidentally also the reading provided in *PPM* as edited by Khān.
37. *RSK* gives for *dobaḍo* the synonymous *dob*, meaning *durvā*, 'a kind of auspicious grass.' The variant reads: 'My jewelry is *durvā* grass and *mālā*.'
38. The variant reads: 'No other jewelry, knowledge at the feet of the guru is mine.'
39. The variant seems to have switched this line with 8a. It seems to read: 'neither by doing suicide (*jauhar*), nor tormenting (my) soul.' Does this reflect an understanding of Mīrā escaping the sack of Cittorgaṛh? Interestingly, this reading is closer to the variant provided by Khān: *jorā karāṃ,* which however simply means 'with joined hands,' implying 'even if one begs me (to stop).'
40. The variant seems to have switched this line with 6a. It reads: 'I will sing the Lord's praise day and night.'
41. An alternative meaning of *hastī* is 'throne' (*BBSK*). The variant has a future: 'I will not mount a donkey.'

By being a king, you will fall into the hell: merry-makers are Yama's to take.
By being devoted, you reach freedom,[42] by practising yoga, you live.
Girdhara is (my) Lord. Girdhara is (my) family, mother, father, son, brother.
Yours to you and mine to me, Rāṇā. That is Mīrābāī's message.[43]

15

The Rāṇā kept getting troubled by Mīrā. Her ways differed from the family tradition of the Rāṇā. In particular, she associated with pious people (with connection to the Lord). She did not respect etiquette with people related to her physically at all. The Rāṇā kept trying to make her see. In the end he sent her a cup with poison, telling (the servant) to give [it to her], pretending it was *caraṇāmṛta* (water used to bathe the deity's feet). She had a vow. Through the name of *caraṇāmṛta* she would definitely drink it. And that is what happened. [But] she drank it fully aware [that it was poison].The Rāṇā kept waiting for her death, but she took her cymbals and drums and, in utter ecstasy, composed a new song, which she sang in front of the Lord. The song became very famous. This was the following song:

	Variant (Śekhāvat 1984: 23)
rānaiṃ jū viṣa dīnau hama jānī	rānau jī zer diyau maiṃ jāṇī
jāna būjhi caranāmṛta suni piyo, nahiṃ baurī bhau rānī	
kaṃcana kasata kasauṭī jaisaiṃ, tana rahyo bāraha bānī	kaṃcana jharai agana meṃ ḍāro, nikasauṃ bāri bānī
āpuna giradhara nyāva kiyo yaha, chāṃnyau dūdha ru pānī	rānāujī bisa ko pyālo melyo, jhelo mīrāṃ rāṇī
	rānāujī mīrāṃ kahai sādhāṃ rau saṃga parau nivārau to thānai karūṃ paṭarāṇī
rānā koṭaka vārau jihiṃ para, hauṃ tihiṃ hātha bikānī	koṭa bhūpa vārūṃ sādhana tai, sādhāṃ hātha bikānī
	hathalevo rāṇājī joḍyau, giradhara kī paṭarāṇī
	choḍyau muradhara mevāḍa meḍto, choḍī kuḷa rī kānī
Mīrāṃ prabhu Giradhara nāgara kaiṃ, carana kamala lapaṭānī	Mīrāṃ ke prabhu Giradhara nāgara caraṇa kamala lapaṭānī

42. The variant seems to say: 'you will not reach liberation.'

43. Caturvedī reads: 'I won't dismount the elephant to ride a donkey, that is just not done,' which is a variant of line 9 in the other versions.

rānaiṃ jū viṣa dīnau hama jānī
jāna būjhi caranāmṛta suni piyo,
  nahiṃ baurī bhaurānī
kaṃcana **kasata kasauṭī jaisaiṃ,**
  tana rahyo bāraha bānī
āpuna giradhara nyāva kiyo yaha,
  chāṃnyau dūdha ru pānī

rāṇā koṭaka vārau **jihiṃ para,**
  hauṃ tihiṃ hātha bikānī
Mīrāṃ prabhu Giradhara nāgara kaiṃ
  carana kamala lapaṭānī

Variant (Caturvedī 1983: III, no. 38)
rāṇojī **the zahar** diyau mhe jāṇī
apaṇe ghara kā paradā kara le,
  maiṃ abalā baurānī (l. 4)
jaise kaṃcana **dahata agani meṃ,**
  nikasata vārāvānī
lokalāja kula kāṇa jagata kī,
  dai bahāya jasa pāṇī
tarakasa tīra lagyo mere hiyare,
  garaka gayo sanakāṇī
saba saṃtana para tana mana vāraum,
  caraṇa kamala lapaṭāṇī
Mīrāṃ **ke** prabhu **rāṇi laī hai,**
  dāsī apaṇī jāṇī

The Rānā has given me poison, I know.
Fully aware, I drank it hearing (it called) 'sacred water,' I'm not crazy or deluded.[44]
Like gold tested on the touchstone, my body remained intact.[45]
Giridhara himself has settled the matter: he has separated milk from water.[46]
I give up thousands of Rānās for him, I am sold in his hands.[47]
Mīrā clings to the lotus feet of her Lord, clever Giridhara.[48]

16

The Rānā's younger brother may have been Mīrā's husband as far as physical existence is concerned. But he died. From then on Mīrābāī was on pilgrimages to the Ganges and so on, and she also came to Vrindāvan. There

44. I have interpreted *bhaurānī* as one word, as a feminine perfective participle of a causative derived from the verb *bhor-* 'to delude' (*RSK*). A literal translation would be 'caused to be deluded.' This line is not in any of the parallel versions, but the fourth line of the second variant has a similar rhyme. It reads: '"Keep purdah in your house." "I am weak and crazy."' This seems to represent the Rāṇā's command to Mīrā, and her answer.
45. The variants read: 'Like gold burning in the fire, comes out complete.'
46. The first variant reads instead: 'The king gave Mīrā a cup with poison, Queen Mīrā suffered it.' This variant goes on 'The king said (to) Mīrā: "Ward off the company of holy men, I will make you (my) foremost queen."' Interestingly, this seems to assume that the Rāṇā made a pass at Mīrā, trying to get her married to himself. The second variant reads: 'Propriety, honor of family and the whole world, I've let it slip like water' (the use of 'water' in the context of honor is common). It goes on: 'Quiver and arrow have hit my heart, startled, I became crazy.'
47. In both variant readings, it is the holy men whom Mīrā prefers to kings. In the second version she says: 'I surrender myself body and soul to all holy men, clinging to their lotus feet.' The first variant adds the lines: 'The king joined our hands (in the marriage ceremony), but I'm Giridhara's Queen. I've given up Mārvāṛ, Mevāṛ, and Meṛtā, I've given up my family's name.'
48. The second variant had 'lotus feet' in the previous line and substitutes here: 'Mīrā 's Lord has taken the queen, she considers herself (His) servant.'

she made Jīu Gusāī give up his vow of not looking at any woman. She honored all as guru Govinda and stayed in their company. She left for Dvārikā in order to make it her residence. On the way there she composed a new song. It became very famous. This was the following song:

	Variant (*MBP* I, no. 543)
Rāya śrī Ranachoḍa dījyo,[49]	Rāya śrī Raṇachoḍa dīje,
Dvārikā ko bāsa	Dvārakā ko bāsa
saṃkha cakra gadā padma[50] darasaiṃ,	saṃkha cakra gadā padma darase,
miṭai jama kī trāsa	miṭe jagata kī trāsa
sakala tīratha Gomatī ke,	sakala tīratha Gomatī ke,
rahata nitta[51] nivāsa	rahata nitta nivāsa
saṃkha jhālara jhāṃjha[52] bājaiṃ,	saṃkha jhālara jhāṃjha bāje,
sadā sukha kī rāsa	sadā sukha kī rāsa
tajyo desa ru besahū taji,	tajyo desa ru besa pati graha,
tajyo rānā rāja	tajyo rānāṃ-rāja
dāsi[53] Mīrāṃ sarana āvata[54]	dāsī Mīrāṃ sarana āvata,
tumhaiṃ aba saba lāja	tumheṃ aba saba lāja

King Śrī Raṇachoḍ, please let me stay in Dvārkā.
One glimpse of (your) conch, disc, club, and lotus, and fear of Death is obliterated.[55]
On all the shrines (*tīrtha*) of the Gomatī river, dwelling for ever,
Conch, bells and cymbals resound, the eternal Round Dance (*rāsa*) of bliss.
(I)'ve given up country and also identity, (I)'ve given up king and kingdom.[56]
Mīrā, (like a) servant, seeks shelter: on you now (depends) all (my) honor.

17

Voicing her desire in this way, singing this song, she arrived in Dvārkā. She stayed there for several days. After that, the *purohit* and other servants of the Rānā who had accompanied Mīrā said that many days had passed now and that she should return to (her own) land (as) the king had commanded. They insisted on this for a few days. Then they started pressing Mīrābāī. Then Mīrābāī, under the pretense of bidding farewell to Ranachoḍ, went alone

49. *Bhaktamāl dṛṣṭānt* has *dījai.*
50. *Bhaktamāl dṛṣṭānt* has *paduma.*
51. *Bhaktamāl dṛṣṭānt* has *nitya.*
52. The editor of this part of *Bhaktamāl dṛṣṭānt* has misinterpreted the last two words in the manuscript as *māla rimāṃmī.*
53. *Bhaktamāl dṛṣṭānt* has *dāsa.*
54. *Bhaktamāl dṛṣṭānt* has *sarana giridhara.*
55. The variant reads: 'Fear of the world.'
56. The variant reads: 'husband and house.'

inside the temple. In a grandiose *āratī* she sung a newly-composed song. That was the following song:

	Variant (Caturvedī 1983: 118, no. 61)
Hari kariho jana kī bhīra[57]	Hari theṃ haryā aṇa ro bhīra
Dropadā kī lāja rākhī,	Dropatā rī lāja rākhyāṃ,
tuma baḍhāyo cīra	the baḍhāyāṃ cīra
bhakti[58] kārana rūpa narasiṃgha,[59]	bhagata kārana rūpa narahari,
dharyo āpa[60] sarīra	dharyāṃ āpa sarīra
Harinakasyapa māri līnauṃ,	Harinakasyapa māri līnauṃ,
dharyo nāhina dhīra	dharyo nāhina dhīra
būḍhataiṃ gaja grāha tāryo,	būḍhatāṃ gaja rājarākhyāṃ,
kiyo bāhira nīra	kaṭyāṃ kuṃjara bhīra
dāsi[61] Mīrāṃ lāla Giridhara	dāsi Mīrāṃ lāla Giridhara,
dukha jahāṃ tahāṃ pīra	harāṃ mhārī pīra

Lord, help your servant.[62]
Draupadī's honor was protected when you lengthened her garments.
For the sake of a devotee,[63] you came down yourself in the body of a lion-man,
You killed Hiraṇyakaśipu, refusing to put up with him.
You grabbed the drowning elephant and saved him,[64] lifted him out of the water.[65]
Mīrā is your servant, dear Giridhara, when (she) suffers, (you) are pained.[66]

Even by singing this song, (she) did not stir from there. Then she composed another song and sang it in a surge of love in the grandiose *āratī*. Only then

57. Khān reads: *hari hariho jana kī pīra,* which looks like a *lectio facilior* and is also inferior in that the same rhyme word occurs in the last line of the *pada*. The reading as it stands in Gupta is confirmed in its rhyme word by the variant, which is also the reading in *Bhaktamāl dṛṣṭānt: he hari harahu janakī bhīra.*
58. *Bhaktamāl dṛṣṭānt* has *bhakta.*
59. *Bhaktamāl dṛṣṭānt* has *narahari.*
60. *Bhaktamāl dṛṣṭānt* has *āya,* which may just be a misreading of the editor.
61. *Bhaktamāl dṛṣṭānt* has *dāsa.*
62. This is a lesser-known meaning of *bhīṛa,* attested in *RSK* (third meaning glossed as *madad*). The reading *pīra* of Khān translates as: 'Lord, end (your) servant's torment.' In the variant *bhīra* (irregularly masculine) has a different meaning (the second in *RSK*, glossed as *saṃkaṭ)*: 'God has relieved the torment of other (devotees).'
63. Literally: 'of devotion.'
64. Or: 'You saved the drowning elephant and the crocodile' (*grāha* can mean 'crocodile' as well as 'seizing.' The variant has 'kept (safe) the elephant king.'
65. The variant reads: 'You saved the elephant who was drowning, the frightened elephant cut free.'
66. The meaning seems clear from the parallellism of the two names in the previous line. Note how the variant dumbs it down: 'You have ended my sorrow.'

the Lord took her, absorbing her from her earthly body into himself. Not even a corpse remained. The song she sang when she became absorbed was the following song:

	Variant (Caturvedī 1983: 131, no. 107)
sajana sudhi jyauṃ jāṃnaiṃ jyauṃ[67] lījaiṃ	sajaṇa sudha jyūṃ jāne tyūṃ lījai ho
tuma bina meraiṃ aura na koī,	tuma viṇa mhāre avara na koī,
kṛpā rāvarī kījaiṃ	kryā rāvaro kījai ho
dyausa[68] na bhūkha raiṃna nahiṃ nidrā,	dina nahiṃ bhūkha raiṇa nahiṃ nidarā,
yaha tana pala pala chījaiṃ	yūṃ taṇa pala pala chījai ho
Mīrāṃ prabhu[69] Giradhara nāgara aba,	Mīrāṃ ke prabhu giradhara nāgara,
mili bichurani nahiṃ kījaiṃ	mila bichaḍana mata kījai ho

	Variant (Śekhāvat 1984: 20)
sajana sudhi jyauṃ jāṃnaiṃ jyauṃ lījaiṃ	sājana sudhi jyauṃ jānauṃ jyauṃ lījyau jī
tuma bina meraiṃ aura na koī,	uṭhata baiṭhata jāgata sovata,
kṛpā rāvarī kījaiṃ	kabahuka yādi karījyau jī
	āvata jāvata jīvata pīvata,
	supanai surati dharijyau jī
	hama pativaratā nārī binā prabhu,
	kāhūsauṃ na patījyau jī
	sāco prema prīti ro nāto
	tāhī sauṃ tuma rījhajyau jī
dyausa na bhūkha raiṃna nahiṃ nidrā,	rāti divasa mohi dhyāna tihārau,
yaha tana pala pala chījaiṃ	āpahī darasana dījyau jī
Mīrāṃ prabhu Giradhara nāgara aba,	Mīrāṃ prabhu Giradhara nāgara aba,
mili bichurani nahiṃ kījaiṃ	mili bicharana mati kījyau jī

My love, as soon as (this) comes to your attention, take it to heart.[70]
Without you, I have no one else, bestow (your) grace.[71]

---

67. *Bhaktamāl dṛṣṭānt* has *tyauṃ*.
68. *Bhaktamāl dṛṣṭānt* has *divasa*.
69. *Bhaktamāl dṛṣṭānt* has *lāla*.
70. The word *sudhi* qualifies both *jāṃnaiṃ* and *lījaiṃ*. With the first it means 'to find out,' with the second 'to take to thought of.'
71. The reading *kryā* in the first variant seems a misreading, but it would translate as: 'Do your act.' The second variant has a totally different line, 'When standing or sitting, waking or sleeping, some time, please remember (me),' and goes on in that vein with one more line: 'When coming or going, living or drinking, or in a dream, please keep the memory.' The next two lines add a remarkable reversal of roles: 'Except for me, a loyal woman, do not put faith in anyone else, Lord. True love, a bond of love, be pleased with that alone.'

> No hunger by day, no sleep at night: this body wears out every second.[72]
> Mīrā's Lord, the clever Giridhara, now that we've met, don't leave.

So these two *pada*s were memorized and written down by her very clever Vaiṣṇava girlfriends who were standing nearby in the porch. These became famous.

18

Some backbiting people started to repeatedly make all kinds of innuendos about Mīrābāī in front of the king. So one day, the Rāṇā sent word to a woman from his own harem to follow her wherever she went after midnight. She should not let anyone stop her.[73]

And thus she did. Mīrābāī simply had the habit of sleeping on the roof (of the palace) and remaining awake. Staring intently at the moon above, she suffered from separation in being obstructed [in meeting her] beloved. Desiring him evermore, she fell down, hardly breathing. When she (the spy) came and stood (near her), Mīrābāī asked her to sit down a little while and to listen to her sorrow: 'This time, I have found a sympathetic ear in you.' Never mind that she was from a different caste. When someone is impatient with love, she does not distinguish between own and another's caste. Someone who wants to speak out her mind, will simply tell what she has to say. Hence, at that time, in front of this (woman), she started to sing a song and went on composing. When the girl who had come heard the song and saw her condition, she fainted in utter love. She became her close friend and a devout Vaiṣṇava. She never returned to the harem of the Rāṇā. Afterwards the Rāṇā sent some other women to (spy on) her. They shrunk back (from doing so), saying that those who spy on her lose their mind and that that was the reason why they would not go. This matter has become very famous. So the song that the previous night had rendered the Rāṇā's girl ecstatic upon mere hearing it, was the following:

	Variant (Caturvedī 1983: 126, no. 87)
sakhī merī nīṃda nasānī ho	sakhī myārī nīṃda nasāṇī ho
piya ko paṃtha nihāratāṃ,	piya ro paṃtha nihāratā,
saba raina bihāṃnī	saba raiṇa bihāṇī ho
sakhiyani mili sīkha daī,	sakhiyana saba mila sīkha dayāṃ,
mana eka na māṃnī	maṇa eka ṇā mānī ho
bina dekhaiṃ kala nā parai,	bina dekhyāṃ kala nā paḍāṃ maṇa,
jiya aisī ṭhāṃnī	rosa nā ṭhānī ho

72. The first variant reads: 'Thus, (my) body wears out…' The second variant reads: 'Day and night, I am absorbed in you, now do your part, and please give me a glimpse.'
73. *BBSK* gives for *harak-* the meaning *rok-* and *haṭā-*.

aṃga chīna vyākula bhaī,	aṃga khīṇa vyākula bhayāṃ,
mukha piya piya bāṃnī	mukha piya piya bāṇī ho
aṃtara bedana biraha kī,	aṃtara vedana biraha rī,
vahi pīra na jānī	mhārī pīḍa ṇā jāṇī ho
jyauṃ cātaka ghana kauṃ raṭai,	jyūṃ cātaka ghaṇa kūṃ raṭai,
macharī bina pānī	macharī jyūṃ pāṇī ho
Mīrāṃ vyākula birahanī,	Mīrāṃ vyākula birahaṇī,
sudhi budhi bisarānī	sudha budha bisarāṇī ho

O friend, my slumber is disturbed.
I spend the whole night waiting for my lover.
My friends ganged up to lecture me, but my heart did not listen.
Without seeing him, I do not find rest, that's what my heart is set on.[74]
My body is exhausted, I am restless. On my lips the words 'my love, my love.'
The pangs of separation inside, such a torment no one knows.[75]
Like a *cātak* crying for the cloud. Like a fish without water.[76]
Mīrā is desperate in separation. She has forgotten mind and soul.

58. The Chapter on Nāgrīdās Naṭavā

There once was a Nāgrīdās, a dancer. He was very fond of Vaiṣṇavas. So wherever there was a good Vaiṣṇava public that would listen, he would go and dance without greed (for a fee). So one time, some Navāb in Haṇḍiyā Sarāy insisted much on making him dance. He placed a *tulsī*-garland in front and danced in front of it. The Navāb too remained spellbound. Many were delighted. The song he was singing had a rhyme 'dyed in Kṛṣṇa's passion.' He was showing its meaning by taking on (Kṛṣṇa's) thrice-bent position. But he remained in that position. In a flurry of great love he left his body. That was the following song:

	Variant (*MBP* I no. 603)
sācau prīta hī ko nātau	sāṃco prīti (prema) hī ko nāto
kai jānaiṃ vṛṣabhāna naṃdinī,	kai jāne vṛṣabhāna naṃdinī,
kai madanamohana raṃga rātau	kai (madana)mohana raṃga rāto
yahaiṃ saṃkhalā ati balavaṃtī,	yahai sṛṃkhalā ati bala-vaṃti,
baṃdhyo prema gaja mātau	baṃdhyo prema gaja māto

74. The variant reads: 'Without seeing him, my heart finds no peace, it is not set on anger.'
75. Alternatively: 'Outside, the pain is not (known) apparent.' The variant reads: 'My sorrow is not understood.'
76. The variant reads: 'Like (to) a fish water (he is to me).'

Mīrāṃ ke prabhu Giradhara nāgara,	Mīrāṃ ke prabhu Giradhara nāgara,
kuṃja mahala basā tau	kuṃjani mahala basā to

The only true bond is that of love.
This knows Vṛṣabhānu's daughter, or (one) dyed in Kṛṣṇa's passion.[77]
That is the strongest chain: a mad elephant is restrained by love.
Mīrā's Lord, Mountain-holder, make (me) dwell in the palatial groves (of Braj).

77. Alternatively: 'or Kṛṣṇa, dyed in passion.'

Bhakti Texts in the *Khyāl* Songs of North India

Lalita du Perron

My task in the four-year project 'Songs of North Indian Art Music,' funded by the Arts and Humanities Research Board (Britain), is—at least on paper—straightforward: to transcribe the lyrics of some three hundred of the 'classics' of *khyāl*, mainly taken from vinyl recordings from the first half of the twentieth century. With my colleague Nicolas Magriel working on the musical side of things, the aim is to present a collection of song transcriptions with the actual recordings present on a CD. Although many volumes of musical transcriptions have been published in the last seventy years or so, these transcriptions rarely if ever mention what performance of the *rāg* they are based on. It is therefore impossible to put music and transcription together. Our final output, accompanied by the CD, will finally allow the reader and listener respectively, to marry up the musical transcriptions with the actual aural evidence. Furthermore, as our project involves a language-dedicated person there will be a substantial linguistic analysis, which is usually lacking in musicological works.

In reality my task is of course not quite as straightforward as may seem, as transcribing the song texts poses a number of problems. First of all there is the issue of sound quality. Even with modern technology at my disposal, it seems to be impossible to clean up particularly fuzzy recordings. There are also certain philosophical concerns to do with 'correcting mistakes'. There is no doubt that a lot of distortion goes on and has been going on since recording began, and so even in those instances where I may be able to surmise what the actual 'original' text may have been, it is not my role as transcriber to do anything other than transcribe, i.e. to note down, what is going on. My musicologist colleague faces similar dilemmas of transcription when he finds that one of the acclaimed greats of the twentieth century regularly sings in his 16-beat *tīntāl* compositions cycles of only 12 or 13 beats, with the onus on the *tablā* player to somehow pull the whole thing back together. In these situations where we feel some explanatory comment is required, we are grateful for the existence of that much-maligned feature of academic scholarship, the footnote.

Without a doubt the grandfather of published musical transcription in India is the Maharashtrian lawyer and music lover, Vishnu Narayan

Bhatkhande, who in the 1920s and 1930s published a six-volume collection of musical transcriptions *Kramik pustak mālikā*. In this work, Bhatkhande did not separate the words out from the musical transcriptions and so does not give the reader any clues as to where one word ends and another one begins. In a famous example of potential confusion, the line in *rāg* Malkauṃs *paga lāgan de mahārāj* is often quoted ('Let me touch your hem, great king', i.e. 'Let me be your servant'). Without discreet song texts the same text could in theory be read as *paglā gande mahārāj* ('Crazy dirty king'). In spite of this potential scope for error (and I think it is largely potential although the texts can certainly present a challenge), there is evidence that Bhatkhande did tidy up the songtexts he transcribed so they would make more sense or become more poetic. In other words, he was engaged with the lyrics, but he did not consider them entities separate from the music. Whatever criticism may validly be directed towards Bhatkhande, there is no doubt that he was one of the front-runners in revolutionizing the milieu of North Indian art music, and making it accessible to non-hereditary musicians.

I would now like to turn to two texts I have recently been working on. The first text is a song by the somewhat eclectic performer Onkar Nath Thakur. The recording stems from 1948. The lyrics are clearly based on the Mirabai poem that is also included below. The Onkar Nath recording is odd in that it appears to consist of the same song twice, first sung with the first *antarā* and secondly with the second. One would normally expect a singer to progress organically from the first to the second *antarā*, without a break. Having said that, it is also actually quite unusual to have a second *antarā* at all. Most <u>*kh*</u>*yāl* lyrics follow the *sthāī-antarā* model, and can sometimes even omit the *antarā* altogether.

Rāg Malkauṃs, tīntāl, sung by Onkar Nath Thakur:

पग घूँघर बाँध कर नाची ।
बाप कहे मीरा भई बावरी
लोग कहें कुल नासी ॥
मीरा के प्रभु गिरिधर नागर
मैं तो तोरी दासी ॥

paga ghūṁghara bāṁdha kara nācī.
bāpa kahe mīrā bhaī bāvarī
loga kaheṁ kula nāsī.
mīrā ke prabhu giridhara nāgara
maiṁ to torī dāsī.

Tying her ankebells on her feet she danced.
Her father said: Mira has gone mad.
People will say: she destroys the (honour of the) family.
Mira's Lord is the courtly mountain-holder
I am at your command.

Mīrābāī poem:

पग घूँघरू बांध मीरा नाची रे ।
मैं तो मेरे नारायण की, आपही हो गयी रे ।
लोग कहैं मीरा भई बावरी, न्यात कहै कुलनासी।
विष का प्याला राणा जी भेज्या पीवत मीरा दासी रे ।
मीरा के प्रभु गिरिधर नागर, सहज मिले अविनासी रे ।[1]

paga ghūṁgharū bāṁdha mīrā nācī re.
maiṁ to mere nārāyaṇa kī, āpahī ho gayī dāsī re.
loga kahaiṁ mīrā bhaī bāvarī, nyāta kahai kulanāsī.
viṣa kā pyālā rāṇā jī bhejyā pīvata mīrā dāsī re.
mīrā ke prabhu giridhara nāgara, sahaja mile avināsī re.

We can contrast this composition, which clearly draws on the bhakti corpus, with the following khyāl text:

Rāg Alhaiyā Bilāval, tīntāl, sung by Vilayat Hussain Khan:

मैं तोहे देता हूँ अपनी मौज सों
हाथ लगी मेरी ये पचतन सों
महम्मद अलि फातिमा हुसैन हसन ॥

maiṁ tohe detā hūṁ apanī mauja soṁ
hātha lagī merī ye pacatana soṁ
mahammad ali fātimā husain hasan

These lines are taken from the *antarā*, and from the last line it is quite clear that we are in an Islamic idiom. It is not entirely clear what the implications of this idiom may be—evidence suggests that most of the Islamic or Muslim compositions have been written in response to modern tendencies towards 'Hinduization.' The trend by which lyrics performed in khyāl are taken from existing sources such as Mīrā's poetry or the *Rāmcaritmānas* in an effort to locate the genre in a more traditional or specifically Hindu framework, is

1. As quoted in Padmāvatī, *Mīrā vyaktitva aur kṛtitva*, Vārāṇasī, Hindī Pracārak Saṃsthān, 1973. There are many other but similar versions of this poem.

recent. Manuscript evidence from the late eighteenth century indicates that at that time *khyāl* bandishes were relatively uniform, and described the standard motifs of the lovelorn heroine's struggles with her mother-in-law, or her agony at being left behind by her husband.

The song in Alhaiyā Bilāval we just looked at was recorded in 1935, suggesting that already at that time a response to the inclusion of bhakti texts in *khyāl* was taking place. Although no purpose is served by polarizing the lyrics of *khyāl* along religious lines, it is nevertheless important to observe that the variety of topics as presented in modern *khyāl* are most likely to be the result of twentieth-century innovations. Many texts in *khyāl* do follow the somewhat stereotyped and predictable Krishnaite idiom, but if one is prepared to spend a bit of time on the poetry and eke out incongruities, one may well run into a few surprises.

Kiśangaṛh Rādhā: A Textual and a Visual Profile

Ileana Cornelia Popescu

The subject of my presentation is a most felicitous example of the perfect blending between poetry and painting in the cultural context of the eighteenth-century small Rajput kingdom of Kiśangaṛh.[1] Here, during the life (A.D. 1699-1764) and reign (A.D. 1748-1757), and direct patronage, of Sāvant Siṃh,[2] has briefly, but spectacularly, flourished, with an unprecedented lyrical force, the Kishangarh style of miniature painting. As you well know, Maharaja Sāvant Siṃh is known in literary history as a Vallabhan devotee and poet, Nāgarīdās.[3]

1. Kiśangaṛh/Kisangarh and Kṛṣṇagaṛh—adapted to fit the desired etymology, are free variations of this toponym; I have kept the already established transliteration Kishangarh for the school and style of painting, as customary.

2. Sāvant (e.g. *Nāgarīdās granthāvalī*, ed. Kiśorīlāl Gupta, Varanasi, 1965)/Sāmant (e.g. *Nāgarīdās granthāvalī*, ed. Faiyaz Alī Khān, New Delhi, 1974) variants seem to originate from a different interpretation of the nasalization, cf. Samvat (e.g. M. V. Pandia, 'The Antiquity of the poet Nāgarī Dās and his concubine Rasik Bihārī alias Baṇī Ṭhaṇī,' *Journal of the Asiatic Society of Bengal*, vol. LXVI, part I (1897), pp. 63-75); also cf. *editio princeps*, *Nagar samuccay*, ed. Jayalāl, Bombay, 1898; I have used Siṃh, instead of the more common Singh, which is the transliteration required by the Hindi name, as in both, Gupta's and Khān's, editions.

3. See the contribution of Heidi Pauwels in this volume.

Fig. I

1. Portrait of Rādhā
Kiśangaṛh, A.D. 1735-1757 (Dickinson and Khandalavala, *Kishangarh Painting*) / *c.* A.D. 1760 (Craven, *Indian Art*)
Artist: Nihāl Cand
Paint on paper
19 x 14 in. (48.2 x 35.3 cm)
Kiśangaṛh Darbār, Rajasthan
Bibliography: Eric Dickinson and Karl Khandalavala, *Kishangarh Painting* (Lalit Kala Series of Indian Art 4), New Delhi: Lalit Kala Akademi, 1959, pl. IV; Roy C. Craven, *Indian Art*, rev. ed., London: Thames and Hudson, 1997, ill. 189; Usha Bhatia (ed.), *Kishangarh Painting*, [text by Karl Khandalavala] (Lalit Kala Series Portfolio 43), New Delhi: Lalit Kala Akademi, 1998, pl. I.

2. Rādhā and Kṛṣṇa / Tāmbūla Sevā
Kiśangaṛh, *c.* A.D. 1775
Artist: attributed to Nihāl Cand
Opaque watercolour with gold on cotton
40 ¾ x 37 in. (103.5 x 94 cm)
Philadelphia Museum of Art. Purchased with the Edith H. Bell Fund, 1984
1984-72-1
Bibliography: Stella Kramrisch, *Painted Delight*: *Indian Paintings from Philadelphia Collections*, Philadelphia: Philadelphia Museum of Art, 1986, pl. 75.

There are several distinctive features that define the Kishangarh *qalam,*[4] but the most striking of them is the female facial type: an elongated face, with high arched eyebrows, large and decoratively designed eyes, a nose with a thrusting end, and a sharp chin.[5] This type differs categorically

4. Its heyday period was *c.* A.D. 1735-70; for a comprehensive analysis of this style, see Krishna Chaitanya, *Rajasthani Traditions*, vol. 3 of *A History of Indian Painting,* New Delhi: Abhinav Publications, 1982, pp. 126-30, as well as Adris Banerji, 'Kishengarh Paintings,' *Roop-Lekha*, vol. XXV, 1 (1954), pp. 22-5.

5. See descriptions in Eric Dickinson, 'The Way of Pleasure: The Kishangarh Paintings,' *Marg*, vol. III. 4 (1950), p. 36; Adris Banerji, 'Kishengarh Paintings,' pp. 23-4; Eric Dickinson and Karl Khandalavala, *Kishangarh Painting* (Lalit Kala Series of Indian Art 4), New

from any other example of feminine beauty in Indian painting, beginning with those of the Mughal school, from where most of the artists at the court of Kiśangaṛh originated, including Nihāl Cand (A.D. 1710?-1780?), the best known and also the most accomplished among them. This is the facial type used for the portrayal of Rādhā, and, as by reflection in a mirror, gradually transposed into the masculine prototype used for the image of Kṛṣṇa. The portrayal of the divine lovers, in painting as in poetry, reached in those days, at Kiśangaṛh, its peak, and we find it to be a favourite topic with the Kishangarh artists, the couple being represented not only in the customary genre scenes of the various *Kṛṣṇa līlās*, but also in the simple and direct manner of what we might call portraits (fig. I, ills. 1 and 2; fig. II, ills. 3-6).[6]

Fig. II

3. Portraits of Rādhā and Kṛṣṇa, by the artist Nihāl Cand
Kiśangaṛh, *c.* A.D. 1750
Collection of Maharaja Braj Raj Singh of Kiśangaṛh
Bibliography: Mohinder Singh Randhawa and Doris Schreier Randhawa, *Kishangarh Painting*, Bombay: Vakils, Feffer & Simons Ltd., pl. II.

Delhi: Lalit Kala Akademi, 1959, p. 10; Usha Bhatia (ed.), [text by Karl Khandalavala] (Lalit Kala Series Portfolio 43), New Delhi: Lalit Kala Akademi, 1998, p. 3; Mohinder Singh Randhawa and Doris Schreier Randhawa, *Kishangarh Painting*, Bombay: Vakils, Feffer & Simons Ltd., 1980, p. 10; Chaitanya, *Rajasthani Traditions*, pp. 126-7.

6. As a general idea, it is considered to be a portrait the rendering of the likeness of a human being as bearer of its own character, individuality, uniqueness, and not so, the use of individual features in order to create an ideal type. The art of portraiture—mostly illustrated by historical portraits of emperors, courtiers, etc. has evolved in the Mughal imperial studios since the time of Akbar (A.D. 1556-1605) and its naturalistic touch was elaborated through contact with European painting. It gradually became a fashion with the local Rajput courts also. However, even in Mughal painting, there are few instances of women 'portraits,' obviously due to their seclusion, but we can safely maintain that not all women painted in those times were merely examples of the ideal feminine beauty, as it is generally considered. One such example is *Lady Holding the Portrait of Jahangir*; that she holds this portrait implies her high status in the imperial family. See Milo Cleveland Beach, *The Grand Mogul. Imperial Painting in India. 1600-1660*, Williamstown, Massachusetts: Sterling and Francine Clark Art Institute, 1978, ill. 57, pp. 158-9.

4. Rādhā
Kiśangaṛh, mid-18th century
Private collection
Bibliography: Hilde Bach, *Indian Love Paintings*, New York: Crescent Books, 1985, pl. 40.

5. Portrait of Kṛṣṇa
Kiśangaṛh, *c.* A.D. 1800
50.5 x 38 cm (21 ¾ x 15 in.)
National Museum, New Delhi
Bibliography: Vijay Kumar Mathur, *Marvels of Kishangarh Paintings: From the Collection of the National Museum, New Delhi*, Delhi: Bharatiya Kala Prakashan, 2000, pl. 40.

6. Portrait of Rādhā
Kiśangaṛh, *c.* A.D. 1800
50.5 x 38 cm (21 ¾ x 15 in.)
National Museum, New Delhi
Bibliography: Mathur, *Marvels of Kishangarh Paintings. From the Collection of the National Museum, New Delhi*, pl. 39.

Underlying these 'portraits,' we learn about the story of the love of Sāvant Siṃh for his favourite, a *baṇī-ṭhaṇī*, a poetess herself under the pen-name of Rasikā Bihārī.[7] They are, supposedly, depicted in some of these paintings and said to have been the models, real life models, for the two divine characters. This, precisely, is one of the most controversial issues, in regard to the Kishangarh miniature paintings: were these, and Baṇī-Ṭhaṇī in particular, real-life, historical characters, the models for the divine lovers?

Fig. III

7. Baṇī Ṭhaṇī
Kiśangaṛh, *c.* A.D. 1775
18 x 13 cm (7 x 5 ¼ in.)
National Museum, New Delhi
Bibliography: Mathur, *Marvels of Kishangarh Paintings*, pl. 33.

8. Portrait of Sāvant Siṃh of Kiśangaṛh
Kiśangaṛh, *dated* A.D. 1745
Private collection, USA
Bibliography: Randhawa and Randhawa, *Kishangarh Painting*, pl. I.

---

7. The earliest mention of her life (A.D. 1717?-65) and work is in Pandia, 'The Antiquity of Nagari Das,' pp. 63-75; she was then rediscovered by Adris Banerji, 'Kishengarh Historical Portraits,' *Roop-Lekha*, vol. XXV. 2 (1954), p. 12; Dickinson, 'The Way of Pleasure,' p. 34, also refers to 'a very astonishing and romantic story' behind the facts of Kishangarh painting, although he does not consider it 'relevant' enough to be told at the moment.

9. The Red Canoe (Dickinson and Khandalavala, *Kishangarh Painting*) / **Sawant Singh and Bani-Thani in a Mango Grove** (Mathur, *Marvels of Kishangarh Paintings*)
Kiśangaṛh, A.D. 1735-1757 (Dickinson and Khandalavala, *Kishangarh Painting*) / A.D. 1735-50 (Mathur, *Marvels of Kishangarh Paintings*)
16 ¾ x 10 in. (26 x 18.5 cm)
National Museum, New Delhi
Bibliography: Dickinson and Khandalavala, *Kishangarh Painting*, pl. XII; Mathur, *Marvels of Kishangarh Paintings*, pl. 8.

In the selection I have prepared, the 'portraits' are grouped under three categories: (a) first, a series of Rādhā and Kṛṣṇa profiles, having the distinct facial type of the Kishangarh school, gradually growing into mannerism (fig. I, ills. 1 and 2; fig. II, ills. 3-6); (b) next, the alleged portraits of Sāvant Siṃh and Baṇī-Ṭhaṇī (fig. III, ills. 7 and 8); (c) and last, a painting, *The Red Canoe* (fig. III, ill. 9), which combines the typical feminine profile with a masculine, yet undefined one, bearing more or less a resemblance to the profile of Sāvant Siṃh, as we know him from his portrait.

Among the commentators of Kishangarh painting, Faiyaz Alī Khān has definitely rejected the possibility that Baṇī-Ṭhaṇī, with all her charismatic appearance, may have 'posed' for *Rādhā*[8]—and I am deliberately using this term with the meaning it has in the Western art history. Karl Khandalavala, instead, was keen on the idea that it was her face that was used for painting *Rādhā* (fig. I, ill. 1).[9] Again, there is the general opinion that Rādhā was painted under the influence of Nāgarīdās, therefore using not

8. For his arguments, see Faiyaz Alī Khān, 'Kishangarh Painting and Bani Thani,' *Roop-Lekha*, vol. XL.1 (1975), pp. 83-8; Randhawa and Randhawa, *Kishangarh Painting*, pp. 9-10.

9. First mention of this theory appears in Banerji, 'Kishengarh Historical Portraits,' pp. 11-12. See also Dickinson and Khandalavala, *Kishangarh Painting*, p. 26; Chaitanya, *Rajasthani Traditions*, p. 126; Vijay Kumar Mathur, *Marvels of Kishangarh Paintings: From the Collection of the National Museum, New Delhi*, Delhi: Bharatiya Kala Prakashan, 2000, p. 22. Khandala-vala, cautiously, proposes the accompanying concept of 'a process of idealization' undergone by the profile inspired by Baṇī Ṭhaṇī, and everybody else after him agrees with this notion.

a real life model, but an ideal, textual one.[10] And this may well be true, as far as it was said about this famous profile that no real woman could look like this.[11]

I have tried to follow into the steps of Eric Dickinson,[12] who discovered the Kishangarh miniature paintings in 1943, by putting together textual and visual representations, in order to set off the correspondences between the textual and the visual registers, and to understand how the communication between textuality and vision works.

Before proceeding, we should keep in mind that, far from being realistic, in the thorough manner of the Mughal historical portraits, this profile (fig. I, ill. 1),[13] with its highly emphasized features and produced in a manner that resembles the technique of caricature, that is graphically accentuated, could be considered a portrait, from the point of view of an Indian artist.[14] A tendency towards symbolic representation, and towards types,[15] rather than individuals, usually dominates the vision of an Indian artist. But not this time, in my opinion. Here, Nihāl Cand seems to be fascinated with certain individual facial features, and almost obsessed with rendering them in an emphatic manner, the result being the striking impres-

---

10. See Dickinson, 'The Way of Pleasure,' pp. 30-6; Randhawa and Randhawa, *Kishangarh Painting*, p. 10; Roy C. Craven, *Indian Art*, rev. Ed., London: Thames and Hudson, 1997, p. 229; Mathur, *Marvels of Kishangarh Paintings*, p. 22. This theory is clearly rejected by [Dickin-son and] Khandalavala, *Kishangarh Painting*, p. 9, and Chaitanya, *Rajasthani Traditions*, p. 126. A distinction should be made between a textual model that descends from the entire tradition of Sanskrit and Brajbhasha poetics, and the more pointed reference to the lyrics of Nāgarīdās, as originally made by Dickinson. The argument in the first case, basically, revolves around the eye, shaped like a lotus petal—*padma-palāśa locana*, which is the main attribute of the 'Sanskrit ideal of feminine beauty,' *i.e. padmākṣī, kamalākṣī.*

11. *Ad litteram,* 'for no woman could have such eyes,' in Randhawa and Randhawa, *Kishangarh Painting*, p. 9.

12. Dickinson, 'The Way of Pleasure,' pp. 28 and 35; also Dickinson and Khandalavala, *Kishangarh Painting*, pp. 9 and 44.

13. See Jeremiah P. Losty, *The Art of the Book in India*, London: The British Library, 1982, pp. 43-4, for a discussion on the evolution of the Indian portrait from the three-quarter profile to the typical strict profile.

14. An eloquent apology of the legitimate existence of an Indian painter's point of view, by contrast with that of the European one, in portraiture in particular, can be found in Joachim K. Bautze, 'India and the West: the Interaction of Artists,' in *Indian and Western Painting: 1780-1910. The Ehrenfeld Collection*, ed. Joachim K. Bautze, Alexandria, Virginia: Art Services International, 1998, p. 19.

15. The portrait has been designated, as early as Dickinson, 'The Way of Pleasure,' p. 35, as an instance of the *vāsaksajjā nāyikā*, i.e. 'the adorned heroine in expectation of her lover', according to *nāyikā-bhed* classifications; she might even be a *padminī*, i.e. 'the lotus-woman,' according to *kāma-śāstra* taxonomies, especially if we interpret the lotus buds in her hand.

sion of a strong, fascinating personality.[16] And does one need to add that, in Western art, individuality, personality, and the shades of inner life are the basic requirements for the modern art of portraiture, starting with Renaissance painting! Therefore, even at first glance, the visual representation should impress as far more individualized than the usual, conventional literary depiction of feminine beauty, as in *rīti* poetry the *nakha-śikha varṇan,* for example.

To resume my evocation of Eric Dickinson's inspired discovery and inspired commentaries on the paintings, I have identified the sources of two of the quotes from Nāgarīdās, translated by him with the help of an Indian pandit.[17] They come from the *udāharaṇs* quatrains nos. 31 and 33 in *Vraj Sār,*[18] a small work in *dohās* and *kavittas.*[19]

A Portrait of Rādhā

sārī kī kinārī girda kañcana divāra mañjha,
dṛga dvaiṃ sabhā sara praphulla kaula sauṃ bhare/

bhauhaiṃ madhupāvalī, siṃgāra latā alakani,
phabe karnaphūla phūla, phūle chabi sauṃ khare//

nāsikā sirūṃ ke ḍhiga, lālā gula kyārī bālā,
'nāgarī' adhara raṃga, cita bita kauṃ hare/

rādhā-mukha-bāga bīca khañjana gupāla naiṃna,
bhūle āja cañcalatā ika ṭaka hvai pare //33//[20]

[Clad] in a falling-to-earth sari bordered with gold all around,
her two eyes are full of words [and promises],
like a pond crowded with flowers.

Her eyebrows, rows of black bees, her finery of tresses, like creepers,
and [her ears] adorned with earrings in shape of flowers,
she radiates with extreme beauty.

16. Banerji, 'Kishengarh Paintings,' pp.17 and 21-2, speaks of 'psychological intensity' (*Pavilion in the Grove*) and 'extreme mastery of the facial expression' (*Rādhā*).
17. Pandit Bala Sahai Shastri of the Punjab University. See Dickinson and Khandalavala, *Kishangarh Painting*, p. 4.
18. Dated V.S. 1799 (A.D. 1742), in the colophon, *Vraj Sār* consists of 41 *dohā* couplets and 22 *kavitta* quatrains, dealing with Braj and *Kṛṣṇa līlās* themes.
19. Considering some of the differences in translation, the quatrain no. 33 might not be the precise quote selected by Dickinson.
20. *Nāgarīdās granthāvalī*, Gupta ed., vol. II, p. 239.

With her nose equal [in beauty] to the cypress tree,
and lips red-coloured like beds of tulips and roses,
she would steal away one's heart and thought.

On Rādhā's garden like face, the eyes of Gopāl, a wagtail,
would rest now, staring, forgetting all their playfulness.[21]

Contemplating the painting (fig. I, ill.1) after we have read the poem, we can easily see how almost every facial trait described in the poem, by way of comparison, corresponds to an accentuated facial trait in the portrait. We might say that what the painter did, was to put special care in drawing those very features that are eulogized in the poem: the eyes, the eyebrows, the nose in particular, which resembles the cypress plant. I must admit to not having yet established if this analogy with the *saru* plant is commonplace or not.[22] Her ornaments are also mentioned in the text, and this detail may not be as significant in the literary portrait as it is in the painting.[23] Therefore, I would assume that the textual portrait played an important role in the making of the visual Rādhā. If this is true when we refer to the prototype—this famous *Rādhā*, discovered by Dickinson—it would be even truer in the case of later versions. We can see how the original *Rādhā* gradually attenuates

---

21. Her face is gleaming like the brightness of the sun.
High-arched, twin pencilled eyebrows hover on her brow
like black bees over a lily pond,
And her dark tresses fall here and there
like the curling tendrils of a creeper.
Bejewelled is her nose, curved and sharp
like the thrusting *saru* (cypress) plant,
And her lips have formed a gracious bow
parting into a queenly smile,
Lips red as poppy flowers glowing in the scorching sun
Of June's long stagnant afternoon—what time
the amorous dove complains.

In Dickinson and Khandalavala, *Kishangarh Painting*, p. 9. This version differs from the original translation published by Dickinson in 1950, p. 35.

22. Rather unexpected, and probably idiosyncratic, this comparison might relate to the frequent use of the cypress (*Cupressus sempervirens,* fam. *Cupressaceae*) motive in Persian poetry, where it is mainly associated with the handsome silhouette of the beloved. The cypress tree is frequently encountered in the backgrounds not only of Persian (see Alexandra Beldescu, *Manuscrise persane în colecții din România* [Persian Manuscripts from Romanian Collections], Bucharest: Editura Meridiane, 1987, p. 24), but also of Mughal, as well as Rajput miniature paintings. That Sāvant Siṃh must have been conversant with Persian poetry, too, can be corroborated with his lyrics in Persian style, i.e. *Iśk ciman*, see Gupta ed., vol. I, pp. 63-4; also Khān ed., 'Bhūmikā', pp. 23-4.

23. Lavish ornamentation of this kind is one of the marks by which Kishangarh style can be recognized; and it could be taken as an allusion to the *baṇī-ṭhaṇī*, i.e. 'adorned,' heroine.

her mysterious charm and the force of her personality under a more flat and decorative portrayal of her features.[24]

Fig. IV

10. The Pavilion in the Grove
Kiśangaṛh, *c*. A.D. 1742-57
Artist: Nihāl Cand
16 ¾ x 10 in. (42.5 x 25.5 cm)
National Museum, New Delhi
Bibliography: Dickinson and Khandalavala, *Kishangarh Painting*, pl. XIII.

24. This can be clearly seen in the last two profiles in the series: fig. II, ills.7 and 8. As for those from ills. 5 and 6, it seems that the artist strove to reach the resemblance of the famous prototype, and also to obey directions in the poem. As one can easily see, both pairs convey different physiognomies altogether, as well as different psychological messages: in one case (ills. 5 and 6), a sort of a denser majestic quality, in the other (ills. 7 and 8), just another kind of gracefulness somewhat superficial.

11. Tāmbūla Sevā
Kiśangaṛh, *c.* A.D. 1760 (Dickinson and Khandalavala, *Kishangarh Painting*) / *c.* A.D. 1735-50 (Mathur, *Marvels of Kishangarh Paintings*)
Artist: other than Nihāl Cand (Dickinson and Khandalavala, *Kishangarh Painting*) / attributed to Nihāl Cand (Mathur, *Marvels of Kishangarh Paintings*)
9 ¼ x 10 in. (42 x 25 cm)
National Museum, New Delhi
Bibliography: Dickinson and Khandalavala, *Kishangarh Painting*, pl. VI; Mathur, *Marvels of Kishangarh Paintings*, pl. 5.

12. Rādhā offering beetle leaves to Kṛṣṇa
Kiśangaṛh, *c.* A.D. 1800
35.5 x 24 cm (14 x 9.5 in.)
National Museum, New Delhi
Bibliography: Mathur, *Marvels of Kishangarh Paintings*, pl. 38.

Let us now proceed to quatrain no. 31, which describes the offering of betel to the beloved Rādhā. This was obviously a favourite theme of the Kishangarh painters. Several versions of it exist, starting with Nihāl Cand's *Pavilion in the Grove* (fig. IV, ill.12), which Dickinson saw as a representation of this poem. I would rather associate with it another painting, from the Philadelphia Museum of Art (fig. I, ill. 2).[25] In this painting, the

25. For the relationship between this painting and *Rādhā*, see Stella Kramrisch, *Painted Delight. Indian Paintings from Philadelphia Collections*, Philadelphia: Philadelphia Museum of Art, 1986, p. 173.

elaborate background of the others[26] is reduced, I would say, to a minimum, and the observer is compelled to concentrate on the gesture—the gesture of offering of the betel leaf, on its purity, a perfect support for *śṛngāra rasa*. The painting catches that very moment when *śṛngāra* is transfigured into *bhakti*. And this is exactly the meaning conveyed by the lyrics: the transformation of the ephemeral, human, gesture into the eternity of love. Enveloped in *rasa* here there is this double 'portrait' of Rādhā and Kṛṣṇa.

Tāmbūla Sevā

nāgarī navala guna āgarī raṃgīlī, jāko
bāṛhyo haiṃ prakāsa mukha-canda kuñja-bhauṃna maiṃ/

baṃkī bhauṃ haiṃ, baṛe naina, kahata banai na chabi,
rahyo haiṃ sarasa raṃga barasa citauna maiṃ//

cahaiṃ sukhadaina mukha daiṃna bīrī pyārī jū kaiṃ,
pai na calaiṃ kara uta rūpa sarasauṃna maiṃ/

saki jāta, caki jāta, chaki chaki jāta lāla,
sithala hvai gāta jāta bhauṃha bhaṃga hauṃna maiṃ //31//[27]

[She] is the accomplished one of immaculate virtue, whose brilliant face has filled,
the house and grove, with light, as the [full] moon.

With arched eyebrows and large eyes, whose likeness cannot be rendered into words,
her charming beauty dwells in her radiant glance.

[He] would put a betel leaf into the happiness-bestowing mouth of this most beloved one,
but his hand would not move thither, enchanted by her beauty as he is.

Seeming able to do so, Lāl moves [his hand] towards her, in amazement he tries again,
and then, again and again, he keeps trying in astonishment, shivering with cold, his body moves as if under the heavy spell of her eyebrows.[28]

26. I have selected three more paintings on the subject of *tāmbūla sevā*, including the well-known *Pavilion in the Grove*. See fig. IV, ills. 10, 11 and 12.
27. *Nāgarīdās granthāvalī*, Gupta ed., vol. II, p. 238.
28. She is full of all good qualities. The brilliance of her face has filled the house and bower with light,

By the definition we are bound to follow, none of the above profiles[29] could be accepted into the genre of portraiture. They represent ideal types, and not intentional imitations of life as such. Though the likeness to the features of a certain historical character might have stood at their origin, they have undergone a 'process of idealization' that altered not only the shape but also the meaning they convey. Briefly, this would be the generally credited theory for the Kishangarh profiles.

In spite of all the consistent arguments in favour of this view, all of them of a sensible nature, I want to claim on behalf of the famous *Rādhā* profile the status of the portrait, that is, a portrait of Baṇī Ṭhaṇī in the guise of Rādhā. In doing so, I am aware not only of the risks I take, but also of the fact that the line of research that would produce evidence in support of this thesis is just at the beginning. This line of research, initiated by Dickinson himself, would require (a) an *extensive* textual analysis of the work of Nāgarīdās, to be associated with (b) an unbiased visual analysis focussing on Nihāl Cand's technique.

Hopefully, the compendious textual analysis attempted here may have succeeded in suggesting that Nāgarīdās has created a literary portrait of Rādhā somewhat idiosyncratic in its relation with the current aesthetic convention and the larger frame of an entire tradition of Sanskrit and Brajbhāṣā poetics; that this literary portrait could have and did function as a guideline for the painter, Nihāl Cand, and also for his epigoni. The literary portrait acted as a *catalyst* in the process of *individuation* of Rādhā, enabling the particular to surface, and not to be homogenized into the utter conventional and ideal.

Arched are her eyebrows and large her lovely eyes,
and indescribable her charm and grace.
Oh she, whose glances are like fleeting moonbeams
showering their loveliness through cloud dappled skies.
And he, the bestower of all pleasure, with soft caress now seeks to give
This one so loved the scented betel leaf. But blinded by her beauty sighs
And his quivering hand moves not, and he knows not
where to turn his face.
So helpless is his hand to place the shiny leaf into her parted lips.
Intoxicated with her fair form his body quivers as he vainly tries
To break the spell of glances cast'neath eyebrows arched aright.

In Dickinson and Khandalavala, *Kishangarh Painting*, p. 44. In Dickinson, 'The Way of Pleasure,' p. 28, this translation appears only in the form of a prose description accompanying the painting *Pavilion in the Grove*, an interpretation that was obviously suggested by his knowledge of these lines.

29. Except for the 'historical' portraits of Baṇī Ṭhaṇī and Sāvant Siṃh (fig. III, ills. 7 and 9), of course.

If we try to grasp this elusive notion of the 'process of idealization' that was made responsible for the highly stylized profile—and we do this not at the reception end, be it filtered through one aesthetic convention or another, but at that of its production—we may see how this is the result of a stylistic choice made by the painter: it is the very technique of a Rajasthani painter, in the following of a great tradition, distinct from that of a Mughal, or, at the opposite pole so to speak, of an European one. This technique bears all the marks of the great tradition that has generated it,[30] but does not avoid the particular, the individual, it interprets it in an emphatic, hyperbolic manner that does certainly *allude* to the archetype of feminine beauty, but does not limit itself to it. At the same time, being concerned with the rendering of emotions, *bhāva,* and *rasas*, it does concentrate on the inner life, discovering novel ways to express it outwardly throughout the physical realm.

Notwithstanding how thorough our analysis be, in the end the masterpiece will continue to baffle our perception. This *Rādhā* cannot be held prisoner of any one man's idea of her. The language she speaks is an universal language, therefore she epitomizes the tradition that has generated it, she also transcends its boundaries, of place and of time.

30. For example, the eyes like lotus petals found in 'the images of Buddha and Boddhisattva in Gandhara, Mathura, Banaras, Central Indian school of Malwa in the 5th century A.D.,' see Banerji, 'Kishengarh Paintings,' pp. 23-4.

The Exchange of Services and Gifts at the Birth of Hindu Boys as Described in Hindi Bhakti Literature and Folk Songs

Teiji Sakata

I. The Scope and the Source Material of this Study

The birth of a child is celebrated all over the world. The birth of a boy is especially welcome in Hindu families, as most of these must have a male heir to continue the patrilineage. On the auspicious occasion of the birth of a boy in a Hindu family, family members and relatives offer services and gifts to the child and its parents. The people advising and serving the family, including Brahmans, carpenters, and blacksmiths of the community also offer services and gifts. In return for the services and gifts, the head of the family celebrating the birth of a son will offer generous gifts to the relatives and to the servers. This kind of exchange is based on affection and the role expectations in the traditional Hindu society. This practice seems to be still observed in present-day villages. We will find some description of this practice in Hindi Bhakti literature and folksongs. This paper is based on the following sources:

A. *Sūrsāgar*, attributed to Sūrdās,
B. *Rāmcaritmānas* by Tulsīdās,
C. Hindi folksongs sung in Avadhi, Braj and Bhojpuri dialects.

II. The Exchange of Services and Gifts at the Birth of Hindu Boys in Literature and Folk Songs

Ravindra Bhramar offers us detailed information on the relevant bhakti literature concerning the birth ceremonies and the customs related to them.[1] The excerpts below have been chosen on the basis of that information.

1. Ravīndra Bhramar, *Hindī bhakti sāhitya meṁ lok-tattva*, Dillī: Bhāratī Sāhitya Mandir, 1965, ch. 7, pp. 214-15.

A. The Exchange of Services and Gifts at the Birth of Hindu Boys as Described in the *Sūrsāgar*

Given below is a tentative summary by the present author of the portions from *Sūrsāgar* related to the subject. Serial numbers are those of the edition of the Nāgarīpracāriṇī Sabhā.[2]

1. The midwife takes advantage of the occasion of the child birth
When the midwife said, 'I am not ready to cut the umbilical cord of your child. I will take the bejeweled necklace you wear [,when you give it to me, then I will serve you as a midwife], because I have been looking forward to this occasion so long a time, and I, the quarrelsome midwife, have been quarreling with others to work for you.' Queen Yaśodā smiled, took her bejeweled necklace off and gave it to the midwife. (633, lines 1-6)

2. Many people including cowherds and brahmans came to celebrate the birth of Nanda's son
Nanda came to receive them, and gave clothes to the Brahmans. After throwing himself to the feet of the brahmans [to pay respect and thank them for the blessings], Nanda presented cows to many of them. (642, lines 37-40)

3. People come to congratulate King Nanda and receive gifts from him
There is a big crowd today at the gate of King Nanda. One comes to congratulate King Nanda on the birth of his son, and another takes leave of him. King Nanda gives a cow to one person, to another person some diamonds and jewels. (643, lines 1-5)

4. Some people are eager only to watch the celebrated newborn baby. They are not interested in gifts from the king
One *ḍhāṛhī*, 'singer or dancer,' came a long way to congratulate King Nanda. He just wants to watch the baby walk on his feet and smile. (654, lines 1-4)

5. Various people serve according to their special skills and receive gifts in return
The *magadh-sūts* or bards in and out of the courtyard describe the scene. The *mālins* or women gardeners are decorating the arched gateway with flowers. The *sunār* or goldsmith made necklaces spotted with jewels and brought them for the lovely Nanda's son. The *nāin* or barber's wife brought red dye and she received one lakh rupees and the ear-rings for her service as Yaśodā's midwife. (658, lines 4-16)

2. *Sūrsāgar*, ed. by Nandadulāre Vājpeyī, 2 vols., Varanasi: Nāgarīpracāriṇī Sabhā, 1958-61.

6. The carpenter received an enormous amount of money for building a splendid cradle for the newborn baby

> Kanha's cradle, *re*!
> He built it and brought it, the carpenter, *re*!
> and set it to swing for you the baby's cradle *re*!
> He asked for a fortune [Rupees one hundred thousand], the carpenter (*barhai*), *re*!
> Father [King Nanda] gave him two; the baby's cradle, *re*! (665, lines 1-2; tr. by Kenneth Bryant[3])

7. The role of the astrologer

> A great astrologer (*jotiśī*) has come to your house, hearing of the birth of your son. He has drawn up a most thorough horoscope, and would tell you about it. (704, lines 1-2; tr. by Kenneth Bryant[4])

As we have seen above, the people of the community, including brahmans, astrologers, bards, women gardeners, goldsmiths, carpenters, barber's wives, offer advice and the services with their knowledge and skill, and in return they often receive gifts in money and kind.

B. The Exchange of Services and Gifts at the Birth of Hindu Boys as Described in the *Rāmcaritmānas*

Given below are relevant portions from the *Rāmcaritmānas* by Tulsīdās. The basic text for this section is the English translation by R. C. Prasad with occasional revision by the present author.[5] All citations are from Chapter 1, numbers being given according to the Prasad version by *caupāīs* and *dohās*.

1. The services by the brahmans rewarded by the king with gold, jewels and cows etc.

After performing the Nandīmukha Śrāddha, assisted by Guru Vasiṣtha and other brahmans, and all the ceremonies connected with the birth of a child, the king made gifts of gold, cows, raiment and jewels to the brahmans. (193)

---

3. Kenneth Bryant, *Poems to the Child-God: Structures and Strategies in the Poetry of Sūrdās*, Berkeley: University of California Press, 1978, pp. 152, 211.
4. Ibid., 158-9, 213-14.
5. Tulsīdās, *Shriramacharitamanasa*, tr. by R. C. Prasad, Delhi: Motilal Banarsidass, 1990.

2. Affectionate gifts and services by the people rewarded with whatever the king possessed

> Women streamed forth in crowds; they came running just as they were. Carrying vessels of gold and platters full of auspicious articles, they entered the portals of the royal palace, singing as they went along.
> After waving the lights round and round over the child's head, they cast their gifts before him and time after time threw themselves at the infant's feet. Bards (*magadhs*), minstrels (*sūts*), panegyrists (*bandīgan*) and songsters (*gāyak*) chanted solemn praises of Raghunayaka.
> The king gave everyone whatever he possessed; and he who received from the king did not keep it for himself. (194.2-4)

3. All the people who came to celebrate the birth of the sons of the king received generous gifts from the king

On that occasion [of the birth of the sons] the king granted the desire of everyone's heart, in whatever manner one came. He bestowed elephants, chariots, horses, gold, cows, diamonds and all kind of raiment. (196.4)

Noteworthy here is that in these limited citations, brahmans and bards are mentioned to bear the role of praising King Daśaratha and Prince Rāma, whereas the artisans such as goldsmiths and carpenters are not referred to at all, although they are expected to supply necessary goods for bringing up the newborn baby.

C. The Exchange of Services and Gifts at the Birth of Hindu Boys as Described in Hindi Folksongs

Relevant portions from folksongs of the Hindi region will be cited here from the following three collections, (1) Upādhyāy's collection of Bhojpuri folksongs, (2) Pāṇḍey's, of Avadhi folksongs, and (3) Satyendra's, of Braj folksongs.[6]

1. Extracts from Bhojpuri folksongs

1.1. *Description of gifts presented on the occasion of the birth of Rāma (Bhojpuri; Upādhyāy no. 20, p. 86 pass.)*

> Queen Kauśalyā asked King Daśaratha , 'On this auspicious occasion of the birth of Rāma, what should be given to the people serving us?'

6. (1) Kṛṣṇadev Upādhyāy, ed., *Bhojpurī lok-gīt*, vol. 1, Prayāg: Hindī Sāhitya Sammelan, 1990, (2) *Avadhī lok-gīt aur paramparā*, ed. by Induprakāś Pāṇḍey, Prayāg: Rāmnārāyaṇ Lāl, 1958, (3) Gaurīśaṅkar Satyendra, 'Braj aur lok sāhitya,' in *Sāhitya Vācaspati Seṭh Kanhaiyālāl Poddār abhinandan granth*, ed. by Vāsudevśaraṇ Agravāl, Mathura: Akhil Bhāratīy Sāhitya Maṇḍal, 1953.

King Daśaratha said, 'I will offer gold to the brahman, silver to the bard (*bhāṭ*) and garments to the midwife (*dhagrinī*).'
The midwife received splendid garments and wore them. She, standing in the middle of the courtyard, prayed to the Sun God to bless King Daśaratha's his extensive offspring.

Midwife will be either a barber's wife or a water-drawer's wife:

Nauniyā (the barber' wife) and *bariniyā* (the water-drawer's wife) visit people, and each of them says,' On the occasion of the birth of Rāma and Bharata, I myself will work as the midwife.' They are quarreling on this matter. (Bhojpuri; Upādhyāy, no. 9, p. 76)

2. Extracts from Avadhi folksongs

2.1. Description of gifts presented on the occasion of the birth of a boy (Avadhi, Pānḍey, nos. 3.-15, pp. 54-55)

People blessed the woman who had just given birth to a boy: 'Long live your baby!'
The woman just blessed with a boy said: 'Oh, my dear boy! I presented my mother-in-law a fine bracelet, a necklace to my sister-in-law and an auspicious garland to the wife of my husband's elder brother.
I gave a beautifully dyed cloth to the *nāin* (barber's wife), a cotton sari to the *bārin* (torch-bearer's wife) and a sari to *teliniyā* (the wife of the oil-seller[7]).
I presented the brahman with an elephant, the bard with a horse and the brother-in-law with a ring.'
Her husband says to his wife: 'That's fine, you presented every one with splendid gifts. And I want to ask you what have you presented me ?'
The wife answered in this manner: 'Oh, I presented you everything: the son. Our son will keep our lineage going forever.'

2.2. The scene of the birth of Nand's son Kṛṣṇa (Avadhi; Pāṇḍey, no. 9.1, p. 85)

Watch! The people of the Braj area are celebrating [the birth of Lord Kṛṣṇa].
In what manner was the umbilical cord of the boy cut, in what manner was the boy bathed?
His umbilical cord was cut with the knife made of gold, and he took his first bath in the sacred water of the river Yamuna.
Who gave birth to the boy? And whose boy is he to be called?
He was born from Queen Devakī and he is to be brought up by Queen Yaśodā .

7. Pāṇḍey understands the *teliniyā* as a *camārin*, the wife of a leather-worker.

3. Extracts from Braj folksongs

3.1. The expectant mother requests everyone in the family to pepare for the childbirth (Braj; Satyendra, no. 1, lines 1-5, p. 913)

The expectant mother caused uproar today, oh, please come my mother-in-law,
and prepare the place for my child.
Oh, please come my midwife, and cut the umbilical cord of your child..
Oh, please come my sister-in-law, and draw the auspicious mark at the corner of the room.
Oh, please come, wife of the husband's elder brother, and prepare a bed for my child.
Oh, please come my sister-in-law,
and draw the auspicious mark at the corner of the room.

The exchange of services and gifts between the happy family and the surrounding community groups is described in some of the folksongs cited here: King Daśaratha offers gold to the brahman, silver to the bard as shown in 1.1. The exchange of services and gifts among the family member is also minutely described in 2.1 and 3.1. These particular customs seem to be given little place in the bhakti literature including the *Sūrsāgar* and the *Rāmcaritmānas.* Thus, the description in Hindi folksongs covers family affairs and supplements the description of bhakti literature. Community affairs as described by bhakti literature and family affairs as described by folksongs, for both of these the two kinds of sources offer vivid pictures of the customs concerning childbirth in the sixteenth century, the era of Sūrdās and Tulsīdās.

It should also be noted that 2.1 describes the list of gifts to the family members and the relatives from the husband or the wife, while 3.1 shows the list of services extended or expected from the family members. Thus, these two, sung in different areas, make a set of gifts and services. The chart given below shows the services and gifts exchanged at the birth of a boy in the *Sūrsāgar*, the *Rāmcaritmānas* and in Hindi folksongs. It is clear from the chart that the *Sūrsāgar*, as compared to the *Rāmcaritmānas*, covers a wide range of exchange. It is also clear that the exchange among family members is referred to in folksongs, not in the bhakti literature.

Chart: *Exchange of Services and Gifts on the Occasion of the Birth of a Boy as Described in* Sūrsāgar, Rāmcaritmānas *and Hindi Folksongs*

Notes:

1. Citations in the chart identical with those of the main body of the paper.
2. Arrangement of the caste status and order based on Oscar Lewis, *Village Life in Northern India.*, New York: Random House, 1958, p. 68, with some additions by the present author.
3. Abbreviations: S = services offered, G = gifts received.

Castes, family/ relatives	***Sūrsāgar***	***Rāmcaritmānas***	**Hindi folksongs**
Brahmans	G: cloths, cows: 642.	S: perform ceremony G: gold, cows: 193	G: gold: Bhojpuri 1 G: an elephant: Avadhi 1
Astrologers	S: draw a horoscope: 704		
Rich farmers in the villages and kings in literature	Receive various services from the people of the community and offer them gifts as given in each column		
Bards, minstrels	S: describe the scene: 658	S: praise the prince G: everything: 194	G: silver: Bhojpuri 1 G: a horse: Avadhi 1
Carpenter	S: builds a cradle G: Rs. two lakhs: 665		
Goldsmiths	S: necklaces: 658		
Woman gardeners	S: decorate a gate: 658		
Midwife	S: helps with delivery G: a necklace: 633		S: helps with delivery G: garments: Bhojpuri 1
Midwife (barber's wife)	S: helps with delivery G: Rs. one lakh and ear-rings: 658		G: a dyed cloth: Avadhi 1
Mothers-in-law			S: prepare

Castes, family/ relatives	***Sūrsāgar***	***Rāmcaritmānas***	**Hindi folksongs**
			place for the child: Braj 1 G: a bracelet: Avadhi 2
Sisters-in-law			S: draw an auspicious mark: Braj 1 G: a necklace: Avadhi 2
Wives of husband's elder brothers			S: prepare a bed for the child: Braj 1 G: a garland: Avadhi 2

III. The Exchange of Services and Gifts at the Birth of Hindu Boys in Anthropological Studies

D.N. Majumdar provides a splendid description of the customs observed on the birth of a child in a village near Lakhnau, with a sociogram on the pattern of inter-caste relations on the birth of a *ṭhākur* (headman) child and related explanations of services offered by the serving people and the gifts given to them in return by the *ṭhākur* of the village.[8] *Ṭhākurs* form the dominant caste group in the village. They are leaders both politically and economically. Their status reminds us of the kings in the bhakti literature including *Sūrsāgar* and *Rāmcaritmānas*. The 'kings' in the bhakti literature are often chieftains of the clans or the localities, rather than paramount kings or emperors.

The sociogram prepared by Majumdar

1. The brahman prepares a detailed horoscope for the child and receives cash payment from the *ṭhākur*.

2. The *lohār* or ironsmith makes a knife and a bangle to receive grains.

3. The *nāī* or barber serves at the feast offered to the villagers and receives food.

8. D. N. Majumdar, *Caste and Communication in an Indian Village,* Bombay: Asia Publishing House, 1958, pp. 37-40.

4. The *nāin* or the wife of the barber attends upon the expectant mother and massages her to receive grains.

5. The *pāsī* or toddy extractor carries the news and receives food.

6. The *bhaksorin* or basket maker's wife serves the mother and helps her in delivery to receive grains.

7. The *dhobī* or the washerman washes the clothes of the mother and the baby to receive grains.

The sociogram prepared by Majumdar and the related explanations by him correspond to the descriptions in the bhakti literature and Hindi folksongs. Services and gifts were exchanged in an elaborate way in the days of bhakti literature. Exchange of services and gifts was still in practice in the twentieth century. This fact suggests that the customs and social relations concerning childbirth in the sixteenth century survived in the twentieth-century villages of India. Then we have a question here: Is this limited to village India only? Probably not! Some of the customs may be practiced in the present-day megalopolises in a slightly modified way.

One question seems pertinent here. The midwife occupies a very important place in childbirth. She must be a community member, intimate to the expectant mother, be she a villager or a queen. From which caste is the midwife recruited? This is an interesting issue. The role of the midwife is performed, in the above sociogram, by the *bhaksorin* or basket-maker's wife. A later study led by Majumdar himself in a village of District Mirzapur, Uttar Pradesh reveals that the role is performed by a *camārin*, the wife of a leather-worker.[9] In the case of the village near to Delhi studied by Lewis, the role of the midwife is performed by the *bhangin*, the wife of sweeper.[10] Reports by social anthropologists thus tell us that the role is performed variously by women of different castes.

In the bhakti literature cited above, the only mention is made in II. A. 5 of the *nāin* or barber's wife as serving as Yaśodā's midwife. Among the folksongs translated above, the role of midwife seems to be fulfilled by *nāin* (barber's wife), *bārin* (torchbearer's wife), *and teliniyā* (the wife of an oil-seller or the wife of a leather-worker).

Keeping all these cases in mind, we can say that the role of midwife is performed by women of different castes. It is also obvious that any of the castes given above is deemed to form the people at the bottom of the community. Women of bottom status serve as midwife and help mothers to deliver children—this should be an issue to be noted and studied in social contexts.

---

9. Dhīrendranāth Majumdār, *Chor kā ek gāṁv*. A Fringe Village, Bombay: Asia Publishing House, 1960, p. 131.

10. Oscar Lewis, *Village Life in Northern India*, New York: Random House, 1958, p. 47.

IV. Conclusion and Discussion

We conclude from this study that

1. traditional exchange of services and gifts on the child birth is described in bhakti literature and folksongs,
2. the two sources complement each other, and community affairs are minutely described in bhakti literature and family affairs are vividly sung in folksongs,
3. the pictures drawn in bhakti literature and folksongs correspond to the practice observed in twentieth-century village India. This fact suggests that the customs and social relations concerning childbirth in the sixteenth century, the days of Sūrdās and Tulsīdās, have survived.

As to the *Rāmcaritmānas* by Tulsīdās, its authenticity is undoubted, with its edition based on many old manuscripts. The case of the *Sūrsāgar* attributed to the blind poet Sūrdās is quite different. In its present form, the *Sūrsāgar* is a huge compilation. The Nāgarīpracāriṇī Sabhā edition, which is currently widely accepted, contains upward of five thousand poems, while the Fatehpur manuscript of 1582, now in Jaipur, contains only 270 poems.[11] After a minute and joint study with Kenneth Bryant, John Stratton Hawley comes to the conclusion that the poems in circulation in the sixteenth century, when the original Sūrdās quite probably lived, should be either 428 or 430.[12] Among seven poems cited in this paper from the *Sūrsāgar*, only no. 642 of the Nāgarīpracāriṇī Sabhā edition, which corresponds to No. 221 of the Fatehpur manuscript and starts with *braja bhayau mahara kaiṃ pūta*, 'A son was born to the King of Vraj,' is among those testified to in the sixteenth-century-manuscript. The seven poems cited above from *Sūrsāgar* give us vivid pictures of the customs related to childbirth, but we must keep in mind that many of these poems may be of a later date.

---

11. See John Stratton Hawley, *Sūr Dās: Poet, Singer, Saint*, Seattle: University of Washington Press, 1984, p. 35, and for the Fatehpur MS, *Pad Sūrdāsjī kā/ The Padas of Surdas*, ed. by Gopal Narayan Bahura, with an essay by Ken Bryant, Jaipur: Maharaja Sawai Man Singh II Museum, City Palace, 1984.

12. 'Report on Bhakti Research,' in *Devotional Literature in South Asia: Current Research 1997-2000*, ed. by Winand M. Callewaert et al., New Delhi: Manohar, 2002, pp. 67-8.

The Cosmic Journey through the Body: Dādū's *Kāyābelī* and Its Commentary*

Ingrid Schuhmann

The *Kāyābelī* is a text by Dādū (1554-1603) and forms part of his *padas*. *Sākhīs* and *padas*, distichs and songs, respectively, by Dādū have been handed down in *Dādūvāṇī* manuscripts in which the distichs are organised in thematic chapters and the songs in chapters devoted to one *rāga* each. The *Kāyābelī* forms part of the *padabhāga* and falls under 'Rāga Sūhau,' although in structure and content it differs from all other songs. This paper discusses the *Kāyābelī graṃtha arthabhāva* which handles the *Kāyābelī* like a theological treatise. The expression *arthabhāva* finds parallels in the Dādūpanthi tradition itself and in other Bhakti traditions where the spiritual interpretation is called the *bhāva* (*artha*) (such as in the *Caurāsī vaiṣṇavan kī vārtā*). The author of the commentary is anonymous. Its *terminus ad quem* is the first generation of Dādū's disciples, of whom several are quoted, and its *terminus ante quem* is the mid-eighteenth century, for dated copies of the text come from the period prior to that. Dādū's Muslim disciples and distinguished poets Bakhanā and Rajab being cited quite often, this may indicate the constituency where it was written. Contemporary commentators, such as Svāmī Maṃgaldās[1] and Svāmī Nārāyaṇdās,[2] have been intrigued by the text and supply us with an abundance of information. Svāmī Mangaldās draws heavily on the *Arthabhāva* in his own commentary. My study of the text is based on an undated MS from the Dādūdvārā at Naraiṇā (Rajasthan). The MS owes its origin to a doctrinal confluence typical of north-west India (roughly, the northern parts of Rajasthan, the Panjab and Hariyana), for besides the Dādūvāṇī it also contains the *Pārasbhāg*, the Indic version of Al-Gazzālī's *Kīmiyā-e saʿādat*, which was propagated by the Aḍḍan-Śāhī-Sikhs. The mansucript contains a third text, namely, the *Dvijakanyāsaṃvāda* by Khemdās, a disciple of Rajab. After my edition of the text, an edition of the

---

* This paper is based on research carried out for the author's M.A. thesis (University of Heidelberg, 2004; unpublished).

1. Swāmī Maṃgaldās (ed.), *Bakhanājī kī vāṇī*, Jaypur: Premprakāś Mudrālay, 1937; *Śrī Dayāljī kī vāṇī*, Jaypur: Śrī Svāmī Lakṣmīrām Cikitsālay, 1951.

2. Swāmī Nārāyaṇdās (ed.), *Śrī Dādū vāṇī, Śrī Dādū girārtha prakāśikā ṭīkā sahita*, Puṣkara, 1969.

Kāyābelī commentary was published by Brajendra Kumār Siṃhal.[3] It is based on a manuscript also held in the library of the Dādūpanth in Naraiṇā but, as shown by textual variants, not identical with the one on which I based my study.

Structure of the Text

The language is the eastern Rājasthānī variant of Braj Bhāṣā. The *Kāyābelī* consists of eight *caraṇas*. Quotations from this original text are tagged as *tuka*, which is the equivalent of *mūlapāṭha*, 'basic text.' Each half line of the original verse is followed by the *artha*. Verses which appear as one line in modern editions are split into halves which are treated separately, although contextually they still belong together. Each half of a line is followed by its exegesis. This may be given in prose and/or by giving illustrative verses composed in *dohā*. Except for prose explanations there are a host of *sākhīs* and *padas* from Dādū, his disciple Rajab or Kabīr and some other authors like Dādū's disciples Bakhanājī, Sundardās and, outside the Dādūpanth, Nāmdev. Besides *sākhīs* and *padas* there are some occasional *saloku*, *ramāī*, *kavitta* and *caupaī* scattered over the text.

Ṭeka, refrain, and concluding verse frame each *caraṇa* of the *Kāyābelī*. Within this frame, each line opens with *kāyā māṃhaiṃ* followed by a microscopic item in the human body. The stanzas end with a final verse by proclaiming the importance of the guru for acquiring knowledge, and thereby resume the topic of the *ṭeka*. It is the guru who shows everything in the body. The *satguru*, that is God, is the one who gives insight into this along with all spiritual achievements. Divine grace experienced by the Sant will open the way to wisdom and enlightenment.

Punctuation is another important aspect of structure in the manuscript, providing the reader or listener with a clear marking of the different elements (*tuka*, *artha*, *sākhī*, *pada*, *ṭeka*, *dūjā artha*, *praśna*, *uttara*, *caupāī*, *śloka*, numbering). These elements create the exegetical body of the *pada*. In the following example, *caraṇa* 1.1a, this structure is demonstrated.

> *tuka // kāyā māṃhaiṃ sirajanahāra // artha // sirajanahāra pramesvara kāyā maiṃ kahyā // so kaisaiṃ jāṃṇiyeṃ //* ***sākhī*** *// dādū jala maiṃ gagana gagana maiṃ jala hai // phunavai gagana nirālaṃ // brahmajīva ihi bidhi rahai, aisā bheda bicāraṃ // 1 // jyauṃ drapana maiṃ mukha dekhiye // pāṃṇī maiṃ pratibyaṃba // 2 // jīmyeṃ teṃla tilana maiṃ // jīyeṃ gaṃdha phulaṃna // jīye maṣaṇa ṣīra maiṃ // īyeṃ [ra]bu rūhaṃni maiṃ // 3 / /īyeṃ rabu rūhaṃni maiṃ // jīye rūha raṃgani // jīyeṃ jerau*

3. Published in *Saṃt Śiromaṇi Śrī Dādū Dayāl jī Mahārāj caturśatī nirvāṇ viśeṣāṅk*, Delhi: Akhil Bhāratīy Śrī Dādū Sevak Samāj, 2003, pp. 50-77.

*sūra maiṃ // cantau camdra basamni // **4** // **pa[da]** // āpa āpaṇa maiṃ khojau re bhāī // basta āgocara gurū lakhāī // **5** // **śloka** // tila madhe jāthā telaṃ // kāṣṭa madhe huttāsnaṃ // pai maṃdhe jathā dhanaṃ // dehī maṃdhe tathā devatā // **6** // **sākhī kabīr** // jyauṃ naiṃnāṃ maiṃ pūtalī // tyau ṣālika ghaṭa māṃhi // mūriṣa loga na jāmnahī // bāhari ṭūṭaṇa jāṃhi //*

Text. Inside the body is the creator. **Meaning**. The creator inside the body is called God. How [is one] to imagine that? **Verse**. [Dādū *vicāra kā aṃga*] Dādū, like the sky in water and water in the sky, while the wind blows lonely, similarly, the imagination of the soul being part of Brahma is a mystery. **1**. [Dādū *vicāra kā aṃga*] As one sees the face in the mirror and reflection in the water, [Thus the soul is part of Rām, Dādū, in complete oneness.] **2**. [Dādū *vicāra kā aṃga*] Like oil in sesame seeds, like scent in flowers, like butter in curd, so God is in the soul. **3**. [Dādū *vicāra kā aṃga*] God is inside the soul like the soul is in the canals of the body, like the heat is in the sun, and the coolness inherent in the moon. **Song**. [Pada Dādū *rāga bhairūṃ*, ṭeka] Brother, seek yourself inside of you. The guru will show you the object you are not able to recognize. **Śloka**. [not idenitified] Like oil in sesame, like fire in wood, like wealth in the earth, the deity dwells inside the incarnated soul. **Sākhī Kabīr**. [Kabīr *piu pahicānibe kau aṃga*] Like the pupil in the eyes, the creator is in the body, simple people orientated to the outside won't recognize this.

The example demonstrates the structure and hierarchical organisation of citations. First, the words of the line are identified with synonyms. Sometimes this is followed by an additional explanation. The author continues by quoting one or more *sākhīs* of Dādū or other Sants. In general, the *sākhīs* of Dādū are cited by their first line, while the Kabīr *sākhīs* are almost always fully cited. From this we can conclude that the Dādū *sākhīs* were familiar to the contemporary readers, whereas the Kabīr *sākhīs* had to be fully brought to memory. Usually, if a *sākhī* by Kabīr is cited it follows a *sākhī* by Dādū. In some cases, where several *sākhīs* of Dādū are cited, they are used for explaining a wider context and are listed in one of the *sākhī-aṃgas* in that very sequence. The contemporary commentary of Svāmī Nārāyaṇdās arranges the verses in this contextual sequence. The author of the *Arthabhāva* made sure to pick those *sākhīs* and *padas* for illustration that were to the point of the text commented. All this reveals a tradition thoughtfully taken care of and expanded.

The next example shows a sequence of *sākhīs* and *padas*. Whereas the *sākhī* of Dādū is given by its first line, the *pada*, here as most often a composition of Dādū, is always cited by its *ṭeka*. This means that the reader is supposed to know Dādū's *Vāṇī* by heart. The structure of the *Arthabhāva* suggests that it was used for preaching. The *sākhīs* and *padas* interspersed were perhaps meant for congregational recitation or served the preacher as a guide for his own homily on the *Kāyābelī*. The example represents *caraṇa* 6.5a.

> *tuka // kāyā māṃhaiṃ lāgai raṃga // artha // raṃga pramesvara kī bhagati raṃga // jaisaiṃ majīṭha raṃga kapaḍā saṃgi lāgai // taisaiṃ prāṃṇa pramesvara saṃgi lāgai // sākhī // dādū je jana hari ke raṃga raṃme // so raṃga kade na jāi // 1 // dādū rātā rāṃma kā // abināsī raṃga māṃhi // 2 // sāhiba kīyā so kyūṃ miṭai // suṃdara sobhā raṃga // 3 // pada // raṃga lāgau re rāṃma kau // so raṃga kade na jāi re // hari raṃga mero mana raṃgyau // aura na raṃga suhāi re // ṭeka // 4 // soī raṃga //*

> Text. Inside the body [the soul] is dyed. Meaning. The colour is the colour of devotion to god. Like the madder colouring the fabric, the breath takes hold of god. Verse. [Dādū *sādha kā aṃga*, cited several times] Dādū, if his servant is dyed in the colour of Hari that colour never faints, [Followers of the Sants will eternally be dyed in the colour of oneness with God.] 1. [Dādū *sādha kā aṃga*] Dādū, dyed in the colour of Rām, dyed in the colour undestructible, [In this world being dipped in the washerman's basin again and again, this dye will not be removed.] 2. [Dādū *sādha kā aṃga*] Dādū, how can that which the Lord made be destroyed, that beautiful shining colour? [Dādū, instead of the washer man's basin his colour resists successfully day by day.] 3 Song. [Dādū *rāga dhanāśrī*, Ṭeka]. Dyed with Rām, this colour will never faint, Hari's colour dyed my mind, no other colour will ever again please me. 4. Ṭeka. This is [the meaning of] colour.

The Cosmic Journey through the Body According to Dādū

Each of the eight *caraṇas* in the *Kāyābelī* dwells on one particular topic. These topics may be described as follows:

Caraṇa 1–universe and creation or evolution of *prakṛti*
Caraṇa 2–body as residence
Caraṇa 3–water and flow
Caraṇa 4–wealth, treasury, city, palace, pathway
Caraṇa 5–religion and God
Caraṇa 6–love and experience of God
Caraṇa 7–deliverance
Caraṇa 8–light, enlightenment, joy, celebration

Caraṇa 1–Universe and Creation

Importance of the guru who imparts all knowledge relating to this world; the basic notion *jo brahmaṇḍe so pyaṇḍe*, 'all that is in the cosmos is in the body,' is illustrated by numerous examples. *Ūṃkāra* causes creation. Knowledge of the Sant is the light in the world of dumbness, which destroys the tree of religion (*dharma*). Theory of *sasihara sūra*, of moon and sun. Enumeration of the sixteen digits of the moon and the twelve digits of the sun. Explanation of the *anāhada śabda*. Conceptual categories, namely, the three gods, the four Vedas, the four languages, the four kinds of living beings, and their respective place in the body. Circle of life, death and rebirth. Speculation about the *nirguṇa* character of God. In contrast to the following *caraṇa* less citation from *sākhīs*. The example represents *caraṇa* 1.4a.

> *tuka // kāyā māṃhaiṃ sasihara sūra // artha // sasihara mana // sūra pavana // doū netra bhī sasi sūra kahiaiṃ // bāṃvāṃ netra sasi // dāṃhiṇāṃ netra sūra // e aṣṭāṃgajo[ga] maiṃ kahe haiṃ // uhāṃ caṃda sūra prakāsaiṃ // ihāṃ netra prakāsika // uhāṃ sītala tapati kiraṇi // ihāṃ svāti diṣṭi sasi kalā // krodha diṣṭi sūra kiraṇi // uhāṃ solā caṃdramāṃ kī // bāraha kalā sūra kī // ihāṃ solaha kalā mana kī // caṃdramāṃ kī ghaṭa maiṃ te kauṃṇa // svāṃti //1// nrivarati //2// ṣīmāṃ //3// nrimala //4// nihacala //5// gyāṃṇa //6// sarūpa //7// pada //8// nribāṃṇa //9// nribiṣa //10// niraṃjana //11// nirāsa //12// nrilobha //13// niciṃta //14// nrimoha //15// nihaprapaṃca //16// bāraha kalā sūra kī ghaṭa maiṃ te kauṃṇa // ciṃtā //1// tara[ṃ]ga //2// ḍiṃbha //3// māyā //4// pragraha //5// prapaṃca //6// heta //7// budhi //8// kāma //9// krodha //10// lobha //11// driṣṭi //12//*
>
> Text. Inside the body there are the moon and the sun. Meaning. The moon is the mind. The sun is the breath. The two eyes are also called moon and sun. The left eye is the moon. The right eye is the sun. They are named in the eightfold yoga (*aṣṭāṃgajo*[*ga*]). There (in the world) moon and sun are shining. Here (inside the body) the eyes are shining. There are cool and hot rays. Here the digits of the moon with its [soothing] *svāti*-gaze, the sun with its wrathful gaze. There the sixteen [digits] of the moon [and] the twelve discs of the sun. Here the sixteen digits of the mind. Which are [the digits] of the moon in the body? Calmness (1), renunciation (2), forgiveness (3), purity (4), stillness (5), knowledge (6), veracity (7), discretion [8], deliverance (9), kindness (10), immaculate (11), humility (12), modesty (13), faith (14), objectivity (15), inaffectedness (16). Which are the twelve digits of the sun in the body? Anxiety (1), uneasiness (2), fighting (3), illusion (4), occupation (5), subjectivity (6), attachment (7), intellect (8), passion (9), anger (10), greed (11), conceit (12).

Caraṇa 2–Body as Residence

Explanation of *jo brahmaṇḍe soī pyaṃḍe* as beyond and here, outside and inside the body. Explanation of the *prāṇa* as the fundament of life, but only when connected with love of *rāma* and *paramesvara*. Display of *prakṛti* and consequent illusion in the body. Beginning and end of creation. Breath and coolness of a quiet mind. King of the three worlds. The fourteen worlds in Bhakti and yoga. The continents and islands of Sumer. The eighteen continents. The heart as home. Body as the location of Kailāśa and in the sense of the 'tenth door' of yogic micro-cosmology. Enumeration of the fourteen worlds in bhakti and *aṣṭāṅgayoga* and the respective parts of the world in the body. Enumeration of the twenty-one heavens and islands of Sumer. Enumeration of the nine places of pilgrimage. Enumeration and explanation of the nine doors of *aṣṭāṅgayoga*, that is, the nine continents of Jambūdvīpa in the cosmos and the nine *cakras* in the body. Three worlds explained. Various yogic and puranic topics. No *sākhīs*.

Caraṇa 3–Water and Flow
The seven seas and the seven isles in bhakti and their location in the body. The *navadhā bhakti*. Flowing water, Gaṅgā, Yamunā and Sarasvatī and their waters and waves as the flowing love in the heart of the *bhakta*. Kāśī as the lotus of the soul where the *bhakta* is staying quietly in love. Enumeration of the five holy *tīrthas* and their location in the body. Inside the body one practises *pūjā*, *snāna*, *japa*. Inside the body one is united with one's own self. The body is a city of wealth. The wealth consists of fourteen items. In the body man is attracted for whatever manifestation of experience. Topic of this *caraṇa* is a discussion of sacred items, such as Banaras, holy rivers, bathing, pilgrims. The wealth of the soul, innate interest in it, the experience of non-dual identity inside the body. Lotus of the soul, breath, metaphors of water, the flow of cooling rivers and floating love and soul.

Caraṇa 4–Wealth, Treasury, Palace, City, Urbanity
In the body there is the difficult path which can be walked by controlling breath, *prakṛti* and her implications, and leads to union with *brahma*. The highest place in the body is the lotos of the heart, where the *bhakta* experiences highest bliss and love in union with the supreme self. This is the wealth to be found by the *bhakta* in his heart, here the footsteps of Prameśvara are found. The heart is the treasurehouse of the body and one's abode. Enumeration of the nine *nāṛīs* as treasuries and their location in the body, in yogic and bhakti terms. Enumeration of the eight *siddhi*s with explanation, in yogic and bhakti terms.

Caraṇa 5–Religion and Pathway to God
Everything in the body is Parameśvara, *pūjā* for him is a spiritual act, and all utensils are at hand in the body. The meeting with God takes place inside the body. Here he is met, here is the *brahma*, here it is recognized, here the Sant is born by practising remembrance of Prameśvara's name. In this *caraṇa* we find all sorts of terms describing God and his existence inside the human body as *agama agādha, vāra pāra, caraṇa, pūjā, bīnatī, pracai, bharapūra, bistāra, unamāna, anaṃta apāra, dekhnā, hairāṃna, bicāra, pīva, agocara, sahaja, samādhi, sādhana, sumiraṇa, ciṃtāmaṇi, amṛtabāṇī, darsana, ādhāra, nirādhāra, aparaṃpāra, aṃtara niraṃtara*, terms often juxtaposed

to indicate a *coincidentia oppositorum.* The term missing here is *mana*, mind, sometimes more appropriately rendered by heart. The mind is the force that is susceptible to involvement in the world and therefore to alienation from God and therefore needs to be constantly disciplined and brought back to God. In striving after God the antagonist power of the mind is subdued.

Caraṇa 6–Love and Experience of God
In the body the communion with God is experienced in the lotos of the heart. The colour of the divine is produced by the love of God and colours the whole body. In the act of breathing the divine conquers the body. Bhakti terms are *mana* and *prāṇa*, *prīti*, *saneha*, *prema*, *rāṃma rasa*, *anāhata śabda*.

Caraṇa 7–Deliverance
The topic of this *caraṇa* is reaching the shore of salvation, phrased in the appropriate vocabulary from the semantic field of swimming, crossing, passing, such as the verbs *utarṇo*, *tirṇo*, *tajṇo*, *tārṇo*, *ūbārṇo*. God's grace is shown in salvation. When the door opens there occur merging, vanishing of *māyā*, perception of the divine, colour, praise, the experience of *so'ham*, bliss of the Sant. Joy is expressed in beautiful lively poetry.

Caraṇa 8–Light, Enlightenment, Joy, Celebration
The light appearing in the state of union with God is the topic of the last *caraṇa*. The divine quality as expressed in *caraṇa* 5 is connected with attributes of light. Whereas the fifth chapter demonstrates the theological climax of the text, the climax of bhakti takes place in *caraṇa* 8. Here it is expressed by metaphors of jewels, light, holy men, eternity, rejoicing, rain, spring, music. Through grace the self recognizes its divine quality. Only the one *agamāgādhā* and *anāhata śabda* prevails eternally.

Conclusion

The title *Kāyābelī* means 'body creeper,' which indicates the *kuṇḍalinī*—but why then *Kāyābelī*, if the contents deal with yoga? The snake of Śakti arising from the lowest *cakra* winds up to the top. The creeper is a metaphor for the loving soul wound around God, its consubstantial supportless support. These two concepts merge in the text. By the term and the composition of *Kāyābelī* Dādū transports the yogic concepts into his own concept of bhakti.

Both in the original *pada* and in the *Arthabhāva*, beginning with its fifth chapter, there is a clear tendency towards spirituality free from implication of matter which culminates in transcendence at the end of the text.

While *caraṇas* 1 to 4 enumerate puranic and yogic details, *caraṇas* 5 to 6 introduce the reader to matters of *nirguṇa* bhakti. So this part of the *Kāyābelī* refers especially to the advanced spirituality of the *bhakta*, whereas the first chapters explain the material basis and also provide the cosmological basis of bhakti, that is, the human body as instrument for gaining union in bhakti with God. It seems that reading the manuscript was intended to be itself for the *bhakta* a rehearsal of the pathway to the *sahaja*, the spontaneous union with God. Reading, reciting and singing divine knowledge were the ways of acquiring the *bhāva*, the interior meaning and mood of the text.

The fourth *cakra* is the *anāhada cakra* or *hṛdaya cakra*, where the union of the *bhakta*'s absolute devotion and God's grace takes place. By way of a pun, the chapters are called *caraṇa*, denoting at the same time Prameśvara's feet located in the *hṛdaya kaṃvala*. Walking *caraṇa* by *caraṇa*, step by step and stanza by stanza, one reaches the place of the *caraṇa* of the Supreme. The spiritual process is thus reflected in the contents matter of the text as much as in its structure. Similar to the *Rāmcaritmānas*, where the seven chapters are considered as *ghāṭs* leading to the shore of deliverance and thus named *sopāna*, the *Kāyābelī* is a representative of an Indian literary genre of religious texts in which structure, framing and content meet on a symbolic level.[4]

Another important aspect of the text is his positive attitude towards the human body as a unique instrument of bhakti. The texts attunes to asceticism and a yogic view according to which the cosmos is transported into, and identified with, the human body. bhakti here is built on the worldview of yoga, however much yoga be recast in bhakti concepts. The *asthāṃnas*, the halts on the spiritual path in the body, as given in the first chapters were perhaps also taught as part of practical yogic training. Yogic postures, breath control, singing in praise of God and listing to the words of Dādū and other saints—all these are not mere theory, but essentially practice. This is why the *Arthabhāva-ṭīkā* can be regarded a vehicle designed for carrying to *bhagatiyogabhāva*, 'inner realisation of the yoga of bhakti.'

---

[4] Lutgendorf Philip, *The Life of a Text: Performing the* Rāmcaritmānas *of Tulsidās*, New Delhi: Oxford University Press, 1994, p. 18.

The Seat of Love and Service: *Dhyānalīlā* of Gadādhara Bhaṭṭa

Swapna Sharma

The context of my ongoing research is the Caitanya *sampradāya* within which I focus on the esoteric tradition of spiritual discipline as taught by Gadādhara Bhaṭṭa. Caitanya Mahāprabhu (1486-1533)[1] emphasized the path of *bhakti* or loving service. The system or the path of learning is called *upāsanā* which basically involves sitting near a teacher. The teachings and injunctions of a teacher discipline us as to what is to be done and what is not to be done. The path of *bhakti* which generally consists of nine steps is called *vaidhī bhakti,* but a seeker is not to stop by merely receiving the injunctions and acting upon them. The discipline of *vaidhī bhakti* is like learning the grammar of *bhakti* which will allow us to freely, but correctly use *bhakti* as a means of highest realization.

The Caitanya tradition accepts Śrī Kṛṣṇa of Vraja as *ārādhya* whose *dhāma* is Vṛndāvan, while the best path of *upāsanā* is the one practiced by the *gopīs*. The authority is *Bhāgavata Purāṇa* and loving service (*prema bhakti*) is the ultimate *puruṣārtha* , goal of human life.[2]

The name, the form, the *līlā* and the *dhāma* of the object of devotion is the framework of the Caitanyite spirituality. But the Absolute and Eternal Being cannot fit in the human experience which is mundane and limited. Therefore, the absolute divinity becomes meaningful to the limited humanity by descending in human history and space. This manifestation of divine interaction with the human is called *līlā*.

The Caitanya tradition emphasizes the path of *bhakti* which is imperative to begin with, but culminates in the spontaneous and loving service (*rāgānugā*). The object of *bhakti* is Śrī Kṛṣṇa in the company of Śrī Rādhā. All these principles are received in the *śruta-paramparā* of the Vedas evolving fully in the *Bhāgavata Purāṇa*. The name and form of that ultimate reality is *sacchidānanda vigraha* or Śrī Kṛṣṇa along with his *hlādinī śaktī*,

---

1. For a standard biography, see *Caitanya Caritāmṛta of Kṛṣṇadāsa Kavirāja*: *A Translation and Commentary* by Edward C. Dimock, ed. by Tony Stewart (Harvard Oriental Series 56), Cambridge, MA: Harvard University Press, 1999.

2. Śrīnātha Cakravartī, *Śrīcaitanyamatamañjūṣā,* ed. by Purīdāsa, Vṛndāvana: Haridāsa Śarmā, 1955, p. 1, *maṅgala* verse 1.

Śrī Rādhā. The *līlā* needs a locale which means *dhāma*. What I am trying to describe is a moment or stage in the path of meditation in the higher spontaneous journey of the seeker in the Caitanyaite tradition.

Gadādhara Bhaṭṭa, scholar, saint and a poet, living in Vṛndāvan in the sixteenth century, was a follower of Śrī Caitanya. He emphasized the role of the divine *loka* in the mundane world. Vṛndāvan is that holy *dhāma*. A *bhakta* is required to meditate or visualize in memory the secret geography where Śrī Rādhā and Śrī Kṛṣṇa manifested their *līlā* or divine play. For him, *dhāma sevā* and *dhāma upāsanā* is primarily for sustaining the *nāma, rūpa* and *līlā* of the *upāsya tattva*. In this meditative *bhakti* the seeker participates in the divine play which is taking place eternally in the seeker's theatre of memory. All memory is always of some thing or an event, which in this case is the *līlā* of Śrī Rādhā and Śrī Kṛṣṇa which took place in Vraja. A seeker has not physically seen it but it is received through a guru. The guru in turn has received it from his or her guru. The first guru who had really seen or participated in the original *līlā* are the *sakhīs* or *gopīs*. In the Caitanyaite tradition, the guru is essentially a *sakhī* who draws upon her own memory to create and enrich the memory of a seeker.

The primary textual support for the *mānasī upāsanā* is the *Bhāgavata Purāṇa*, but it is a general framework. Rūpa Gosvāmī in his eight-verse *Smaraṇamaṅgalastotram*[3] provides the data for memory in which the daily schedule of Śrī Rādhā and Śrī Kṛṣṇa—from waking up in the early morning till retiring late at night, a typical day—is divided into eight periods, *aṣṭayāma*. In the loving relationship between human and divine a time comes when for a lover, a seeker, time and space are fully taken over by the remembered time and space of the beloved, Śrī Rādhā and Śrī Kṛṣṇa, and in this theatre of memory a devotee is day and night mentally serving the divine couple. Rūpa Gosvāmī's scheme was given an elaborate textual body by Kṛṣṇadāsa Kavirāja in the 23 chapters of his *magnum opus Śrī Govindalīlāmṛtam.*[4]

The seventh period of meditation is described in detail in the twenty-first chapter of *Govindalīlāmṛtam.* Śrī Rādhā and Śrī Kṛṣṇa arrive in Vṛndāvan in the evening to enjoy their daily night-time *rāsa līlā*. When the *rāsa* is over and the divine lovers are aesthetically tired, the *sakhīs* make them rest on the seat of union *(yogapīṭha)*. The place where they finally meet

3. Ed. and publ. by Bābā Kṛṣṇadāsa, Govardhana, n.d.

4. Ed. and transl. into Hindi by Śyāmadāsa, Vṛndāvana: Śrīharināma Saṃkīrtana Maṇḍala, 1999. See also Neal Delmonico, 'How to Partake in the Love of Kṛṣṇa,' in *Religions of India in Practice*, ed. by Donald S. Lopez Jr., Princeton: Princeton University Press, 1994, pp. 244-68.

and rest is presently called Govinda Mandir.[5] While the couple is resting the *sakhīs* are attending on them, each *sakhī* has her unique role of service.

For the convenience of devotees, Śrī Gadādhara Bhaṭṭa has beautifully summarized the description of *yogapīṭha* in a long Brajbhāṣā poem.[6] This poem, written in *rolā and chaupāī* metre, he appropriately entitled *Dhyānalīlā* or *Yogapīṭha*.

After worshipping the feet of Govinda, he describes the glory of Śrī Vṛndāvan which is a natural forest, rich in flora and fauna situated on the banks of the Yamunā. In the centre of Vṛndāvan, the shade of the wish-fulfilling tree is a shiny great edifice in which there is a lotus-shaped seat of divine meeting.

> Only the fortunate ones are able to visualize that. The seat is within thousands of petals and like the crystals, the pearls and jewels glitter and the *karṇikā* is made of sapphire like a ten-syllable *mantra*. In that temple there are infinite *gopikā*s, who are more beautiful than Rati, Rambhā, Umā, and Ramā. They are attending the seated handsome prince of Vraja, who has a dark complexion and is adorned in *pītāmbara* and a peacock-feather crown. He is wearing all sort of beautiful ornaments and through his flute is showering the nectar of melodies.
>
> To his left is seated his most fortunate darling, Śrī Rādhā, draped in a blue sari, her fair body glows, every limb and every ornament is beyond description. These two beautiful adolescent youths are sitting there, lost in each other. Gadādhara says, the mind of those who meditate upon them with the feeling of love and devotion will not waver in worldly lust. Day and night, walking or seated, will be cured of all malice the mind of those who contemplate the *yogapīṭha*. Those who drink the nectar of this meditation will not be affected by worldly suffering.[7]

Meditating upon the lotus-seat is a common religious practice in the Indian tradition. In Buddhist, tantric and Shaiva traditions this divine seat is taken as the seat of micro-creation. All these traditions have practiced the *yogapīṭha* which is most commonly depicted as the Śrī Yantra. In the Caitanyaite tradition the science of meditation on the *yogapīṭha* has been elaborated in *Haribhaktivilāsa*[8] and *Śrī-Kṛṣṇasandarbha*,[9] which draw from several pauranic, tantric and agamic texts.

---

5. Margaret H. Case (ed.), *Govindadeva: A Dialogue in Stone,* New Delhi: Indira Gandhi National Centre for the Arts, 1996.

6. *Śrī Gadādhara Bhaṭṭa kī vāṇī*, ed. and publ. by Bābā Kṛṣṇadāsa, Kusumasarovara, Vṛndāvana: Rādhe Śyām bookseller, [Samvat] 2015, pp. 1-6. For a critical edition of the text see Svapnā Śarmā, 'Gadādhara Bhaṭṭa: paramparā aura sāhitya' (Hindi), unpublished doctoral dissertation, University of Agra, 1991, pp. 269-94.

7. Translation by Swapna Sharma.

8. Gopāla Bhaṭṭa Gosvāmī, *Śrī Haribhaktivilāsa*, ed. by Purīdāsa Dāsa, Mymensingh: Śrī Sacīnātha Rāyacaudhurī, 1946, Chapter 17, pp. 548-67.

The *Yogapīṭha* or the *Dhyānalīlā* of Gadādhara Bhaṭṭa was to be sung by a devotee properly initiated in this esoteric tradition. Previously esoteric poems like this were meant for oral transmission only, but its preservation in manuscript form and my ongoing research on the literary works of Gadādhara Bhaṭṭa have made accessible this so far unknown ritualistic poetry to the academic world, especially outside the Hindi speaking area. My research project has the following main aspects:

(1) I wish to establish the definitive texts of Gadādhara Bhaṭṭa's writings with critical readings from various manuscripts and published editions and anthologies.

(2) The Caitanya Sampradāya emphasizes the role of musical offerings to God, the *kīrtana*, specially the *samāja kīrtana* where a ritualistic group singing in the temple courtyard is the most important offering. I shall document and analyse the musical dimension of this living literary heritage.

(3) From within the Caitanyaite tradition, I wish to make a contribution to understanding its religion and philosophy.

9. Jīva Gosvāmī, *Śrī-Kṛṣṇasandarbha,* ed. by Purīdāsa, Vṛndāvana: Haridāsa Śarmā, 1951, pp. 83-96.

Ethical Implications of the *Mahāvākyas* in the Literature of the Cānd Bodhale Circle (Marāṭhvāḍā, 1550-1650)

Hugh van Skyhawk

In his introduction to the confrontational philology of Paul Hacker (1913-79) the late Wilhelm Halbfass (1940-2000) emphasizes the importance of Hacker's encounter with the so-called *'tat tvam asi*-ethics' of Neo-Hinduism. For Hacker, the position that altruism logically follows from the realisation of the unity of being[1] was a by-product of the dialogue with Christianity. Within the cognitive system that underlies the 'Great Sayings' (*mahāvākyas*) of Indian radical non-dualism (*advaita-vedānta*) altruism, according to Hacker, was logically impossible, even 'monstrous'.[2]

When Paul Hacker expanded his assertion to medieval Hinduism and the ethics of the *Bhagavadgītā* (hereafter: *BhG*) he ignored the fact that a crucial change in textual context had taken place.[3] Though the *BhG* as one of the three scriptures of the canonical *prasthāna-traya* of the *advaitin* ('radical non-dualist') has been commented upon by famous *ācāryas* (Śaṅkara, Rāmānuja, Abhinavagupta, etc.), it has had a far greater influence on the shaping of ethics in Hinduism via the commentaries on it in the regional languages of India and the transmission of its teachings in the *Purāṇas*, especially, in the *Bhāgavata-purāṇa* (hereafter BhP). I have twice called attention to this fact at some length in previous publications.[4]

---

1. Held most notably by Swami Vivekananda and, later, by Sarvepalli Radhakrishnan. Cf. Paul Hacker, 'Schopenhauer und die Ethik des Hinduismus,' in *Saeculum* 4 (1961), pp. 365-99; repr. in Paul Hacker, *Kleine Schriften*, ed. by Lambert Schmithausen (Glasenapp-Stiftung 15), Wiesbaden: Franz Steiner Verlag, 1978, pp. 531-64; now available in English in *Philology and Confrontation. Paul Hacker on Traditional and Modern Vedanta*, ed. by Wilhelm Halbfass, Albany, NY: State University of New York Press, 1995, pp. 273-318.

2. Halbfass, Philology, pp. 8ff.

3. Hacker, 'Schopenhauer,' pp. 365ff.; Schmithausen, Paul Hacker, *Kleine Schriften*, pp. 531f. and Halbfass, *Philology and Confrontation*, pp. 273f. The English translation '...probably not...' (p. 274, line 15) for Hacker's '...höchstwahrscheinlich nicht...' is not emphatic enough. More appropriate would be '...highly unlikely...'.

4. Hugh van Skyhawk, *Bhakti und Bhakta. Religionsgeschichtliche Untersuchungen zum Heilsbegriff und zur religiösen Umwelt des Śrī Sant Ekanāth* (Beiträge zur Südasienforschung 132), Stuttgart: Franz Steiner Verlag Wiesbaden, 1990, pp. 107-11; id., 'Perceptions of Hindu Ethics in German Indology,' *Annals of the Bhandarkar Oriental*

Criticism of my position and defense of Paul Hacker's perception of Hindu ethics have not been wanting. In this connexion I refer to Peter Gaeffke:

> The basic 'good' action of a *sant* consists, however, in teaching *bhakti* and by doing so he helps others to reach liberation. This is something very different from the Muslim injunction to pay *zakāt* for the poor and missionary work in hospitals and with untouchables. (...) This is surely a different sort of *'Nächstenliebe'* ['altruism'] and one of the reasons why, until today, the Hindu society has not been able to solve the social problem of the 'scheduled castes.' I think Hacker put his finger on one of the most sensitive spots in Hindu attitudes and gave a very convincing account of it.[5]

In the present paper I intend to show that the perception of the unity of being (*advaita*) contained in the teachings of the bhakti *sant* of sixteenth-century Maharashtra Śrī Sant Ekanāth, which ultimately derive from the *BhG* 13.27f.,[6] was similar to perceptions of the unity of being (*waḥdat al-wujūd*) prevalent among the *Qādirī-šaix* of the fifteenth and sixteenth centuries, such as among the followers of Śāh Niᶜmatullāh Walī of Kirmān (d. 1431).[7] Moreover, both the bhakti and Sufi traditions of the unity of being later found expression in the *Yogasaṃgrāma* (hereafter: *YS*) of the *Qādirī-šaix* Śekh Mahaṃmadbābā Śrīgondekar (1560-1650), who was the disciple of the mysterious 'Cānd Bodhale,' who himself had been the disciple of Śekh Mahaṃmad's own father, Rāje Mahaṃmad. Śekh Mahaṃmadbābā was thus the *guru-bandhu* (co-disciple) of Janārdana-svāmī, *killedār*[8] of Daulatābād and guru of Śrī Sant Ekanāth of Pratiṣṭhān (Paiṭhaṇ) (1533-99),[9] the author of the influential Old Marāṭhi commentary on the eleventh book of the BhP, the *Ekākārā-ṭīkā* or, as it is popularly known, the *Śrī Ekanāthī Bhāgavat*

Research Institute LXXIV (1993), *Amṛtamahotsava Supplementary Volume*, ed. by R. N. Dandekar and S. D. Laddu, Poona: Bhandarkar Oriental Research Institute, 1994, pp. 85-9.

5. Peter Gaeffke, 'Review of Hugh van Skyhawk, *Bhakti und Bhakta. Religionsgeschichtliche Untersuchungen zum Heilsbegriff und zur religiösen Umwelt des Śrī Sant Ekanāth*,' *Journal of the American Oriental Society* 118.4 (October-December 1998), pp. 560ff.

6. Cf. van Skyhawk, 'Perceptions of Hindu Ethics,' pp. 85-9.

7. The most notable of whom was the ninth ruler of the Bahmanī sultanate, Aḥmad āh Walī, d. 1436.

8. Marāṭhī (from Persian) 'commander'.

9. Tulpule, Shankar Gopal, *Classical Marāṭhi Literature. From the beginning to A.D. 1818*, (*A History of Indian Literature*, ed. by Jan Gonda, vol. IX.4), Wiesbaden: Otto Harrassowitz Verlag, 1979, pp. 356. Up to the present day there is no scholarly consensus concerning the dates of the birth and death of Janārdana-svāmī.

(hereafter: *EBh*).[10] It is to this closely connected group of bhakti *sants* that I have given the name the 'Cānd Bodhale Circle.'

I will now present new material drawn from the *EBh* of Śrī Sant Ekanāth, the *YS* of Śekh Mahaṃmadbābā Śrīgondekar, and the *Dīvān* of Śāh Niᶜmatullāh of Kirmān and Aḥmad Śāh Walī Bahmanī. First, the famous passage of the *BhG* (13.27f.) cited by Hacker in his discussion of the *'tat tvam asi*-ethics' of Neo-Hinduism:

> He who sees the same Highest Lord abiding in all beings, not perishing when they perish, he (truly) sees. Seeing the same Lord abiding equally everywhere, he does not injure the Self by means of the Self. Thus, he advances to the highest path.[11]

In his final words in the final verses of his *magnum opus* of 18,810 *ovīs* ('quatrains') Ekanāth emphasizes just this, the core of the ethics of Hinduism:

> Janārdana has taught me just this:
> 'See only me in all beings.
> Do not consider the characteristics of *prakṛti* ('matter') at all.'[12]
> (*EBh* 31.519)

> 'Seeing the *prakṛti-guṇa* ("characteristics of matter") of others the *mana* ("organ of thinking") becomes irritated. But that should be ignored. One should see the *caitanya* ("consciousness-substance") abiding equally in all beings.'[13] (*EBh* 31.521)

---

10. Cf. van Skyhawk, *Bhakti und Bhakta*, 1990, pp. 310-25 and Hugh van Skyhawk, 'Der muslimische Beitrag zur religiösen Dichtung Marāṭhi-sprechender Hindus,' *Zeitschrift der Deutschen Morgenländischen Gesellschaft* 153.1 1(2003), p. 91f.

11. *samaṁ sarveṣu bhūteṣu tiṣṭhantaṁ Parameśvaram*
vinaśyatsv avinaśyantaṁ yah paśyati sa paśyati
samaṁ paśyan hi sarvatra samavasthitam Īśvaram
na hinasty ātmanātmanaṁ tato yāti parām gatim.
The Mahābhārata, ed. by Shripad Krishna Belvalkar, volume seven, *The Bhīṣmaparvan. Being the sixth book of the Mahābhārata, the great epic of India*, Poona: Bhandarkar Oriental Research Institute, 1947, p. 169. All text passages from the *EBh* cited in this paper refer to *Śrī Ekanāthī Bhāgavata*, ed. by G. R. Somana, parts one and two, Sātārā: Śrī Ekanātha Maṇḍaḷa Sātārā, 1973. All references to the text of the *Yogasaṃgrāma* of Śekh Mahaṃmadbābā Śrīgondekar refer to *Śekha Mahaṃmadabābā Śrīgondekara kṛta* Yogasaṃgrāma, ed. by Vāsudeva Sītārāma Bendre, Muṃbai: Pī. Pī. Eca. Bukasṭāla, 1959.

12. *heṃciśi kavileṃ Janārdaneṃ// sarva bhūtīṃ majaci pāhaṇeṃ// prakṛtiguṇāṃcī lakṣaṇeṃ// sarvathā āpaṇeṃna mānāvīṃ.*

13. *evaṃ parāce prakṛtiguṇa// pāhatāṃ sarvathā kṣobhe mana// te na pahāve āpaṇa// sarvabhūtīṃ caitanya samatveṃ pahāveṃ.*

> Janārdana has greatly stressed this teaching. Otherwise no Man of Knowledge can cross the Ocean of Reincarnation.[14] (*EBh* 31.522)
>
> Man and God are one. Knowing this one is liberated completely. But not recognising this many have drowned in the confusion of their own Self.[15] (*EBh* 31.562)

Let us now turn to some passages in the *EBh* in which Ekanāth describes in detail the conduct of those who have attained the realisation of the unity of being. Concerning the conduct of the yogi we learn:

> Nothing but altruism emerges from the mountain. It simply does not know any other attitude than doing good for others.[16] (*EBh* 7.384)
>
> Verily, the *sādhaka* should be generous like the mountain in body, words, and thoughts. He is happy when he can give everything to others.[17] (*EBh* 7.385)
>
> In all his actions he should always do good for all (of mankind). Kicking in scorn at the possession of crores (of rupees) he should always be ready to do good for others.[18] (*EBh* 7.386)
>
> His desire is for the highest goal (enlightenment and liberation from suffering and re-birth). He immediately gives up his own material interests and ventures into difficulties for the sake of others.[19] (*EBh* 7.387)
>
> Hear me! Just as the sugarcane does good deeds through its sweetness, so also does the yogi practice altruism in the world through his sweetness.[20] (*EBh* 7.389)

For the bhakti *sant*s virtuous conduct was the distinguishing mark of those who had realised the unity of being, while those who clung to dualities were

---

14. *yeci upadeśīṃ atyādara// Janārdeṃ kelā thora// yavegaḷā bhavābdhipāra// sajñāna nara pāvoṃ na śake.*

15. *jana Janārdana eka// jāṇe to suṭalā niḥśekha heṃci neṇoniyāṃ loka// guṃtale aneka nijātmabhrameṃ.*

16. *evaṃ parvatācī je utattī// te paropakārārtha ekāṃtīṃ// upskārāvāṃcūni cittīṃ// dujī vṛtti jāṇenā.*

17. *tyā parvatāaiśī tattvatāṃ// asāvī sādgakāsī udāratā// kāyā vācā āṇī cittā// sarvasva detā ulhāsu.*

18. *ceṣṭāmātreṃ paropakāratā// sarvadā karāvī samastāṃ// koṭilābhā hāṇoni lātā// upakārī tattvatāṃ.*

19. *paramārthāciyā cāḍā// svārtha sāṃḍoni rokaḍā// paropakārārtha avaghaḍā// righe sāṃkaḍā parārtheṃ.*

20. *ūṃsu jaisā avaghārīṃ// sarvāṃsī goḍapaṇeṃ upakārī// taisāci yogiyā saṃsārīṃ// paropakārī madhuratveṃ.*

at best spiritually benighted and, more often than not, morally flawed. By juxtaposing virtuous and immoral figures from the colourful medieval society in which he lived his long life, Śekh Mahaṃmadbābā Śrīgondekar—not unlike Geoffrey Chaucer—shows the link between transcendental vision and ethical conduct with striking imagery and earthy humour:

> The virtuous conduct of those of true mystical vision will I describe to you through the liberating knowledge of the Self. When all the saintly beings have heard this they will rejoice with the bliss of the Self.[21] (*YS* 5.78)
>
> The *kājī*[22] is he who knows without being told. When judging the *mansubī*[23] ('legal disputes') his *citta* ('mind') does not waver. He strives assiduously to find the balance of the equal and the odd. He does not take bribes.[24] (*YS* 5.79)
>
> Thus, he awards (punishments) only according to virtues and vices. His *mana* ('mind') is engrossed in the worship of God. Having first cleansed himself within he then shows (outward purity). Know ye that he is the true *kājī*.[25] (*YS* 5.80)
>
> The *mulāṇā*[26] is he who knows his *mūḷā* ('origin').[27] He considers the suffering of others to be his own (suffering). The inexpressable crowing of the Egg of Brahmā thunders 'I am He'[28] as he turns the *tasbī* ('rosary').[29] (*YS* 5.81)

---

21. *sāhī darśanāṃce ācāra saguṇa// ātmajñānem̐ sāṃgena tyāṃcem̐ lakṣaṇa// teṃ aikona sakaḷa sādhujana// svānaṃdem̐ mānavatī.*

22. Arabic (hereafter: Ar.) *qāẓī*.

23. Ar. *Masubah*.

24. *kājī to jyāsa sāṃgitlyāviṇa kaḷe// manasubī karitāṃ citta nā caḷe// sama viṣama tuḷadhāra nyāhāḷe// lāṃca neghe mhaṇūnī.*

25. *jyācem̐ bhūṣana dūṣaṇa tyāsīca lāvī// Īśvarabhajanīṃ āpulem̐ mana govīṃ// aṃtara dhuvaṭa karonī bāhera dāvī// to jāṇā satya kājī.*

26. Persian *maulānā* ('Our Lord'), a title of judges and heads of religious orders. Often used as an honorific title when mentioning Jalāl ud-Dīn Rūmī (d. 1273).

27. A pun is intended here despite the difference in pronunciation of *l* and *ḷ*.

28. Though strictly speaking not one of the four classical *mahākāvyas* of *advaita-vedānta*, the saying *so'ham* 'I am He,' that is, 'I am (the transcendental) *puruṣa*' or 'I am that (supreme) deity' (*Bṛhadāraṇyaka-Upaniṣad*, V.15.2) has essentially the same meaning as *aham brahmāsmī* ('I am the *brahman*') or *ayam ātma brahma* ('The Self is the Absolute') and is very close in meaning to the 'Great Saying' of the Sufi tradition on the doctrine of the unity of being (*waḥdat al-wujūd*) '*hama ūst*' 'Everything is He,' that is, 'Everything is 'Allāh, the Absolute.' Śekh Mahaṃmad clearly perceives in this venerable upanishadic expression of the identity of the individual self with the transcendental Self not only a metaphysical axiom but an ethical truth of great significance. For those of true mystical vision the suffering of others is their own suffering.

29. *mulāṇā to jo āpulem̐ mūḷa jānem̐// āpulem̐ duhkha taise parāvem̐ māne// anirvācya bāṃga brahmāṃḍa daṇāṇe// so'hama tasabī pherī.*

With *viveka*[30] he slaughters the water-buffalo of *ahamkāra*[31] using the knife of *akkal*[32] ('wisdom', 'good sense') and feasts upon it. He deposits his prayers in the Mosque of *unmanī*.[33] He it is who is called *mulāṇā*.[34]

(*YS* 5.82)

The *phakīr*[35] is he who has relinquished attachment to the objects of sense. When inhaling and exhaling he always remembers Allāh. Having seen loose behaviour and confusion he flees and enjoys bliss in solitude.[36] (*YS* 5.83)

He is not ostentatious of the status of being a *phakīr*. He himself teaches the ways of the twenty-three and thirteen.[37] He is moved by the intoxication of divine love through the nature of the Self. Verily, he is the devout *phakīr*.[38]

(*YS* 5.84)

The *ācāryā* ('spiritual teachers') of the *Yavana* ('Muslims') are the *mulla* ('doctor of theology') and the *kājī* ('Islamic judge'). They throw out all the

---

30. The power of separating the eternal Self from the world of appearances, or spirit from matter, truth from falsehood, reality from illusion.
31. Literally: the 'I-maker,' i.e. the mistaken identification of the eternal, unchanging Self with the incarnated individual.
32. Ar. '*aql*'.
33. The fifth and highest state of human consciousness, the final union of Śiva and Śakti in the teachings of the *Nātha-siddhas (Kānphaṭā-yogīs)*, in which human consciousness is completly liberated from the *māyā* ('illusion'). The frequency of similar terminology in the *YS* confirms Śekh Mahaṃmad's familiarity with the practice of *Haṭha-yoga* and tantric *sādhana* ('method,"practice').
34. *ahaṃkāra ṭoṇagā akkala surī// vivekeṃ kāpūna bhakṣana karī// unmānī maśidīṃta nimāja gujarī// to bolije mulāṇā.*
35. Ar. *faqīr.*
36. *phakīra to jo rāga viṣayīṃ sāṃḍavalā// śvāsa ucchvāseṃ nitya āṭhavī Allā// dekhoni paḷeṃ bāṣkaḷa galabalā// ekāṃta sukha bhogī.*
37. As in the poetry of Śrī Sant Ekānth (cf. van Skyhawk, *Bhakti und Bhakta*, pp. 24-30 and passim) mystical numbers play an important role in the *YS* of Śekh Mahaṃmad Śrīgondekar. The mystical meaning of the numerals 23 and 13 mentioned above can be obtained by using the system of *abjad*, also known as the fourteen *Nūrānī* letters, the total numerical value of which is 693. By further addition of the digits 6+9+3=18 and 1+8=9 the mystical numeral 9 is obtained which stands for Haẓrat ʿAlī ibn Abī Ṭālib' (d. A.D. 661), the son-in-law of the Holy Prophet [S.], husband of Fāṭima, father of Imān Ḥasan and Imām Ḥusain, the fourth *xalīfah* of Islam, first *imām* of the Shias and first *pīr* of all Sufi orders with the exception of the Naqbandiyya. According to Sufi tradition Haẓrat ʿAlī was chosen by the Holy Prophet [S.] to receive the inner meaning of the Holy *Qurʿān*, the '*ilm-i-bāṭin*. As a *Qādirī-šaix* Śekh Mahaṃmed would have every reason to teach the esoteric knowledge of the 23 and 13, that is, of Haẓrat ʿAlī (2+3+1+3=9). (On the system of *Nūrānī* letters see e.g. 'Allāmah Naṣīr al-Dīn Hunzāī, *Nuqūs-i ḥikmat* ('Diagrams of Wisdom'), Karachi: Khānah-i Hikmat Idārah-i ʿĀrif, 1998, pp. 58 and 81.
38. *phakīrapaṇācā dāvī nā torā// svayeṃ vāṭā bujavilyā tevisa terā// premācā aṃmala lāgalī sahaja mudrā// satya to phakīra jiṃdā.*

irreligious people. They who rule over the (practices in) the family and the worship of God are the true *ācāryā*.[39] (*YS* 5.99)

The true Sufi is the *ācāryā* of fourteen *panth*s ('spiritual lineages').[40] The one who says that only his way is good, scorns the others, and puffs himself up with pride, his *jñāna* is false.[41] (*YS* 5.100)

The *jaṅgama*[42] is one who knows the *āgamas*.[43] He causes the comings and goings (i.e. the cycle of births and deaths) to cease forever.[44] When *jīva* ('the unreleased soul') and Śiva became one he gave up trouble and care, as when bitter becomes sweet.[45] (*YS* 5.89)

The *jaṅgamas* themselves name five *panth*s. They become intensely involved with others. They are like *Īśvara* himself in their experience (of the Divine) through their condition of strong spiritual knowledge.[46] (*YS* 5.103)

Know ye that the guru of the *śūdra-varṇa* is the *brāhmaṇa*. These clever ones say: "There is pollution everywhere!" They do not recognise that the mark of *brahmaṇ*-ness and full divinity is (to be found) equally everywhere (i.e. in all beings).[47] (*YS* 5.104)

---

39. *Yavanāṃcā ācaryā mullā kājī// sakaḷa adharmāṃsī dyāvīṃ bājī// gotrāsa karāveṃ bhaktisā rājī// to ācāryā kharā.*

40. The tradition of the *čaudah xānvādah* ('fourteen households') attributed to the third (9) and fourth (5) of the original *cār pīr* ('four guides'), Haẓrat ᶜAlī ibn Abī Ṭālib (d. A.D. 661), Hasan Basrī (d. A.D. 728), Ḥabīb ᶜAjamī (d. A.D. 738), 'Abdu-l Wāhid bin Zaid Kūfī (d. ??) is alluded here. Cf. Jaᶜfar arīf, *Qānūn-i-Islām*, translated by G. A. Herklots and revised and annotated by William Crooke, Oxford: Oxford University Press, 1921; repr. New Delhi: Oriental Books Reprint Corporation, 1972, p. 287f.

41.*caudā paṃthāṃcā ācāryā sophī kharā// āpalyāca mārgāsa barā// āṇikāṃteṃ nikhaṃdūni karī torā// tyāceṃ jñāna mithyā aseṃ.*

42. The entry under *jaṃgama* in James Thomas Molesworth's *A Dictionary, Marṟthḥ and English*, Bombay 1831, reprinted there in 1857, is still unequalled for its brevity and marksmanship: 'An individual of a particular sect [*Vīraśaiva, Liṅgāīt*]. They follow *Śiva*, worship the lingam and hate the Brāhman. 2. A *guru* amongst the people.'

43. The body of Sanskrit texts that teach the nature and worship of Śiva from within the *Vīraśaiva, Liṅgāīt* tradition are meant in this context.

44. There is a good-natured pun on the five repetitions of verbal roots of motion (Sanskrit *gam-, yā-*) in the first two *caraṇas* of the *ovī*. See the Marāṭhī text below.

45. *jaṃgama to jyāsa kaḷe āgama// āyāgamanācā karī nirgama//jiva Śiva hoūni sāṃḍī śrama// kaḍū goḍa taiseṃ jāleṃ.*

46. *jaṃgama svayeṃ pāṃca paṃthī mhaṇavī// āpaṇa guṃtalā āṇikāṃteṃ goṃvī// Īśvarā-sārikhā hoya anubhavī// prabaḷa jñātpaṇeṃ.*

47. *śūdra varṇācā brāhmaṇa guru jāṇā// sarvata aśuca mhanavī śāhāṇā//sarvatrīṃ sama neṇeṃ brahmatvācyā khuṇā// purate Īśvaratvapaneṃ.*

> Īśvara always sees (only) one. Behold! The *ācāryā* ignores the consciousness of dualities. In this way he does not get mixed up and cools (others) down. The *sadguru* is like sandalwood paste.[48] (*YS* 107)

> Though the *sadguru* abides in the true mystical vision, his grace can illuminate certain people. But others, adhering to the consciousness of dualities and the evils of life in the world die completely in vain.[49] (*YS* 5.108)

On the southern wall of the *dargāh* of Aḥmad Śāh Walī Bahmanī at Bidar the following inscription taken from the *Dīvān* of Śāh Niᶜmatullāh Walī bears witness to the devotion of the ninth Bahmanī sultan for the great *šaix* of Kirmān. The core statement in this context is Aḥmad Śāh Walī's avowal:

> I have found Niᶜmat Ullāh ('Divine Bounty') in every form of existence, for I have noticed love and infatuation in all.
> Nim'at Ullāh is One in the entire universe; thou shalt not find any one like me, nor one like me can be found (by others).[50]

The spiritual phenomenon of seeing the guru in all beings and, thus, seeing him as a divine being, is well known in the bhakti traditions of Maharashtra. Indeed, it is the most familiar teaching of Śrī Sant Ekanāth whom we have quoted above in this connexion.[51] On the left side of the western wall an extensive tract of Niᶜmatullāh's teachings on the unity of being and the ethical implications derived from this vision of the Divine have survived up to the present day. The similarity to the teachings of Śrī Sant Ekanāth and Śekh Mahaṃmadbābā Śrīgondekar is particularly striking:

> Thou shouldst consider His multiplicity always like the bubble transitory,
> His unity like the ocean, and the source thus established. (line 11)

> Thou shouldst regard Unity and Multiplicity as hypothetical,
> And read the book of wisdom in that way. (12)

> I notice the picture of the universe as imaginary,
> And in that imaginary picture I see His beauty. (13)

---

48. *Īśvareṃ sarvadā eka dekhileṃ// ācāryeṃ pahā bhāvitāṃ vaṃcale// parī miśrita hoūni nāhīṃ nivāle// sadguru caṃdana jaisā.*
49. *sāhī darśanamadhyeṃ sadguru ase// parī tyācī kṛpā koṇī ekāsa prakaśe// yera ghetātī dvaita prapaṃcāceṃ jhāṃse// udaṃda vzartha mele.*
50. Yazdani,Ghulam, *Bidar. Its History and Monuments*, London: Oxford University Press, 1947: 127.
51. Cf. van Skyhawk, *Bhakti and Bhakta*, 1990, pp. 83-95, 294-9.

He is the quintessence pervading all;
The water of Life flowing in our stream (existence). (14)

Whoever talks of knowledge (Truth),
He speaks of himself, if he were to understand that. (16)

'Thou are I, and I am Thou', thou shouldst leave duality;
Ego does not survive, hence give up (the idea of separate entities of) 'me' and 'thee'. (17)

Thou; and not 'thou and I' except He;
He, and there is no god but He. (18)

None remains in the house but He;
According to me, any one but He is the thief (deception). (19)

The shadow and the person appear two;
But really they are one, without 'I' and 'Thou'. (23)

O my friend and the apple of my eye, I am thy vision,
And (to say that) Thy existence is my existence undoubtedly means the same. (25)

In manifestation duality emanated from unity,
The eye which see one as two is squint. (26)

The (squint) eyed perceives two when he perceives;
He does not hear the single note. (27)

The false echo is true;
Thou shouldst not communicate the secret truth to the liar. (28)

The (wise people) consider God and His attributes (both united) as one;
They call the Divine Being without His attributes single. (29)

The Divine Being can be ascertained through His attributes:
Whoever has perceived Him, he has perceived Him thus. (30)

Lovers who represent each other's existence,
They perceive their own existence from the existence of each other. (33)

Apparently, although they are several in number;
But in reality they are (one), neither of them being a commoner or distinguished. (34)

They are all sympathetic to each other;
Whatever happens, they stand by each other. (35)

Whoever is not sympathetic to the afflicted,
Thou mightst say that he is not from the group of manly (persons). (36)

... as I am initiated into the secret of Existence,
I know the secret of Niʿmat Ullāh also. (39)

The love of Majnūn and the beauty of Laila;
Have been described amply and heard of amply.[52] (40)

The conversation of lovers, come and listen;
Do not listen to 'We' and 'Thou', but listen to God. (41)

Delightful life is flowing in the stream,
Thou shouldst seek the source of the stream and seek it from the waters. (42)

Praise be unto (God) Who is the Praiser and the Praised,
All that which exists is His gift.[53] (43)

---

52. I.e. Majnūn's love for Laila was so great that in his rapture he exclaimed: 'I am Laila!,' that is, Majnūn merged with Laila completly. Niʿmatullāh and Aḥmad āh Walī are drawing an analogy here to the merger of the *murīd* with his *šaix* in the spiritual practice of *fanā fi-š-šaix* ('extinction of individual personhood of the *šaix*'). Cf. Annemarie Schimmel, *Pain and Grace: A Study of Two Mystical Writers of Eighteenth-Century Muslim India* (*Studies in the History of Religions* [Supplements to *Numen*]), Leiden: E. J. Brill, 1976, p. 157. This practice is also the most important *sādhana* ('spiritual practices') in the bhakti of Śrī Sant Ekanāth. Cf. van Skyhawk , *Bhakti and* Bhakta, pp. 82f., 87ff., 95, 192, 294.
53. Yazdani, *Bidar,* pp. 122f.

God's Anger: Notes on the Nature of Tulsīdās's Rām*

Danuta Stasik

The story of Rām's life and deeds has been popular in India for over two thousand years. In its oldest extant form—the *Rāmāyaṇa* the great Sanskrit epic ascribed to the sage Vālmīki (*VR*),[1] Rām figured not only as the ideal man, but also, what seems even more important in this context, as the very epitome of kingly virtues. With the passage of time the divinity of Rām was becoming more and more prominent and finally he was equated with the absolute being—God who is always content and infinite in his love and mercy.[2]

One of the best expressions of this attitude is found in the sixteenth-century Hindi epic, the *Rāmcaritmānas* of Tulsīdās. Considered to be the greatest achievement of Hindi literature, it is undoubtedly the quintessence of its own times' spirituality, and at the same time it has also exerted an immensely strong influence upon the religious life in North India. Put it differently, Tulsīdās's *Rāmcaritmānas* not only gave fresh impetus to both strengthen and promote the new religion, i.e. *Rām-bhakti*, but has also had a decisive impact on the sociocultural life of North India, having become an important component of North Indian ethos. Drawing upon the most important traditions, the poem has become the embodiment of an ideal of society, state and its ruler. Describing the story of Rām's deeds, the poet set a

---

* An earlier version of this paper was published in Polish as: 'Gniew boży w hinduizmie—na przykładzie poematu *Ramćaritmanas*,' in: Anna Duszak, Nina Pawlak (ed.), *Anatomia gniewu. Emocje negatywne w językach i kulturach świata*, Warszawa: Wydawnictwa Uniwersytetu Warszawskiego 2003, pp. 75-83.

1. The now extant version of *Vālmīki-Rāmāyaṇa* was undoubtedly composed over several centuries perhaps between 500 B.C. and A.D. 300; J. L. Brockington, *Righteous Rāma: The Evolution of an Epic*, New Delhi: Oxford University Press, 1984, p. 1.

2. For more on the Rāmāyaṇa tradition and the significance of the figure of Rām, see e.g. Brockington, op. cit.; Frank Whaling, *The Rise of the Religious Significance of Rama*. Delhi: Motilal Banarsidass, 1980; Philip Lutgendorf, *The Life of a Text. Performing the Rāmcaritmānas of Tulsidas*, Berkeley: University of California Press, 1991; Sheldon I. Pollock, 'Rāmāyaṇa and Political Imagination in India,' *The Journal of Asian Studies* 52.2 (May 1993), pp. 261-97; Kāmil Būlke, *Rāmkathā: utpatti aur vikās*, Ilāhābād: Hindī Pariṣad, 1999, and Danuta Stasik, *Opowieść o prawym królu. Tradycja Ramajany w literaturze hindi*. (*The Story of the Righteous King. The Rāmāyaṇa Tradition in Hindi Literature*), Warszawa: Wydawnictwo Akademickie DIALOG, 2000.

pattern of behaviour for every Hindu, and because his vision has perfectly met the needs of Hindu society, the poem, being a clear exposition of rules governing different spheres of life, has become an authority.

Some authors (like Kapur)[3] maintain that in recent times the above-mentioned image of Rām has undergone a radical transformation—from compassionate, benign, and graceful into angry and fierce God. And they view it as a result of the Hindu-Muslim conflict in Ayodhyā over his legendary birthplace. No matter how justified such observations on the contemporary image of Rām are, one should not overlook the evidence of such a text as the *Rāmcaritmānas*, as well as of other texts belonging to the Rāmāyaṇa tradition. They prove that Rām's anger forms an integral feature of his nature, and should not be viewed as a contemporary addition to it.

The present paper thus seeks to explore this evidently less known—but by no means less important—feature of Rām's character by analysing different contexts in which it is manifested and by discussing the implications of Rām's anger for the social and religious life of Hindus.

Let us first have a look at the most important features of Rām's nature as presented in the tradition preceding the *Rāmcaritmānas* and in the *Rāmcaritmānas* itself.

2. Essential Features of Rām's Nature

2.1. The Figure of Rām in the Tradition Preceding Tulsīdās[4]

Rām, the son who without slightest hesitation acquiesces to his father's will and at the same time is a paragon of brotherly and marital love, has become known in the world as the 'best of men' (*puruṣottama*).[5] His steadfastness in striving for his people's well-being, true concern for their opinion, as well as his just rule till today are famous and serve as an example of a state in which all goes according to a prescribed order. Rām is an ideal character, one feels tempted to say, so ideally balanced that in India he has become the most important and at the same time the most definite example of a perfect human being.

His perfection lies in the fact that he emotionally and morally surpasses an average mortal. Almost in all situations he is characterized by

3. Anuradha Kapur, 'Deity to Crusader: The Changing Iconography of Ram,' in *Hindus and Others: The Question of Identity in India Today,* ed. by Gyanendra Pandey, New Delhi: Viking, 1993, pp. 74-107. See also Dāmodar Agarvāl, 1993. 'Sattā kī rājnīti meṃ Rām kā badaltā svarūp,' *Dharmyug*, 1.01.1993, pp. 32-3.

4. For more on this subject, see Whaling, *Rise of the Religious Significance* and Stasik, *Opowieść o prawym królu*, pp. 41-8 and 121-2.

5. See Sheldon I. Pollock, 'The Divine King in the Indian Epic,' *Journal of American Oriental Society*, vol. 104.3 (1984), p. 516 and Stasik, *Opowieść o prawym królu*, p. 42.

His perfection lies in the fact that he emotionally and morally surpasses an average mortal. Almost in all situations he is characterized by tranquility, restraint and the absolute esteem for the rules of *dharma*.[6] His real nature is best exemplified in two situations. Firstly, acquiescence to the fourteen-year exile depriving him of the right for the throne of Ayodhyā. Secondly, his abstention from defending his beloved wife, Sītā, against slanderous gossip which spread among his subjects after his triumphant return from the exile and his enthronement as the rightful king of Ayodhyā. These moments graphically describe his character: In the name of the prescribed rules, which are aimed at maintaining law and order, he is capable of renouncing his own rights and suppressing his emotions. It is worth noting that in the first of these cases he explains to his brother that 'angered' (*kruddha*) he could subjugate the [whole] world, but does not want to bring *adharma* to it by force (*VR*, II.47.25-6). As far as the second case is concerned, it should be noted that, although Rām after the fire ordeal does not himself question Sītā's chastity, as a king he can let no one raise any doubts concerning his person, and therefore has to banish her.[7] Of interest here is the fact that in both these situations he is true to the traditional concept of *puruṣārtha*: He subjugates emotions (*kāma*) to righteousness (*dharma*), which ranks higher.[8]

Rām's consistent line of conduct and perfect control of emotions are the basic reason for the enormous esteem in which he is held in India,[9] and all that despite certain situations, or maybe thanks to them (?!), in which he seems to lose control over himself, having thus become a character so humanly ambivalent that countless generations of Indians, for different reasons, refer to the story of his life and deeds.

Three such episodes should be noted. The first of them comes from Book 3 of Vālmīki's *Rāmāyaṇa* (*Araṇyakāṇḍa*) after Rāvaṇ, the king of Laṅkā and the main antagonist of Rām, has abducted Sītā. Rām's profound grief and the feeling of helplessness drive him to the verge of madness (*śokād unmatta*; *VR*, III.58.10), which then transforms into fierce anger, so that he is ready to annihilate the universe (*VR*, III.50-62, esp. 58-62).[10] He utters very symptomatic words:

> The thirty gods themselves must surely think me powerless, because I have been mild, compassionate, and self-restrained, striving for the welfare of the

6. For more on this subject, see Stasik, 2000, *Opowieść o prawym królu*, pp. 42-3.
7. Cp. ibid., pp. 43 and 46-7.
8. See Veena Das, 'Kāma in the Scheme of Puruṣārthas: the Story of Rāma,' *Contributions to Indian Sociology* n.s. 1-2 (1981), pp. 183-203.
9. Cp. Robert P. Goldman (trans., intr.), *The Rāmāyaṇa of Vālmīki: An Epic of Ancient India,* Princeton: Princeton University Press, 1984, pp. 49-50.
10. See Sheldon I. Pollock (transl.), *The Rāmāyaṇa of Vālmīki: An Epic of Ancient India*, vol. 3, Princeton: Princeton University Press, 1991, pp. 55-67.

> world. Look how in my case, Lakṣmaṇa, a good has become an evil. But now I will efface it (...) in order to exterminate the rākṣasas and all living things. (...) Watch now, Lakṣmaṇa, as I fill the sky with missiles and darts, leaving no space whatever for creatures that move about the three worlds. I will bring the host of planets to a standstill, darken the moon that brings the night, paralyze both fire and wind, blot out the light of the sun (...). Now the gods shall witness the power of my shafts when I ply them in anger; they shall see how far they carry when, my patience exhausted, I release them. (...) Like old age or death or time or fate, which no creature has ever defied, Lakṣmaṇa, so in my rage I cannot be withstood; let no one doubt it. (*VR*, III.60.38-51)[11]

Although, thanks to Lakṣmaṇ who mitigates Rām's anger, these words remain an unfulfilled threat, they should be paid special attention, because here Rām in an extremely straightforward way, alludes to the reason of his anger; and what is more, we also learn how it is manifested to the world. Thus Rām under the influence of a painful experience (i.e. the loss of Sītā), first—as has already been mentioned—sinks into despair, which is then transformed into anger. He wants to make the whole world know that his feelings must not be ignored and whoever does so will be punished. He intends to demonstrate his power, and that, not only in this case, is synonymous with reaching for his bow, serving him as the ultimate instrument of exercising authority.[12] Luckily for the world Rām's anger is appeased by Lakṣmaṇ's entreaties. Had it not been for his mediation, Rām could have put to death every living creature and could have annihilated the entire universe, as such is the power of his arrows released in anger.

We deal with a similar sequence of events in the second episode, coming from Book 6 (*VR*, *Yuddhakāṇḍā* VI.14). Here Rām wants the ocean to give passage to his army across its restless, dangerous waters. He tries first to persuade the unwilling ocean, but seeing no result, after three days he finally loses his temper and threatens it to shoot his arrow and dry up its waters. Almost immediately he achieves his aim—the ocean helps Rām (*VR*, VI.14).

Yet another similar sequence occurs in the third episode, which we encounter in the culminating moments of Rām's war with Rāvaṇ (*VR*, VI.83-97). But here, unlike in the two preceding cases, Rām does not confine himself to mere threatening, but time after time uses his weapon, putting to death everyone at whom his arrow is pointed.

As we can see, in all these scenes Rām manifests the angry aspect of his nature which figures as quite an important feature inVālmīki's *Rāmāyaṇa*.

---

11. Translation by Sheldon I. Pollock; ibid., pp. 220-1.
12. As a well-known fact it may be noted here that in iconography the bow has become an inseparable attribute of Rām.

2.2. Tulsīdās's Rām[13]

Putting to death his opponent, i.e. Rāvaṇ, Rām did what for certain reasons neither gods nor humans were able to do. He thus proved his true nature, the nature of man-god, or more precisely of a divine king,[14] who is a real support to his subjects, saves them from any imminent danger, and at the same time is the embodiment of virtues essential for the harmonious existence of any society. These features of Rām's nature, and especially his divinity, portrayed by Vālmīki rather symbolically,[15] were taken up and developed in the later Rāmāyaṇa tradition. The culmination of this process was the rise and lively growth of Rām's cult (*Rām-bhakti*), in which an important role was played by the *Rāmcaritmānas*.

Without going into too many details of theological and philosophical nature,[16] we may say that the poem portrays Rām as the Supreme Being, infinite in his mercy, and regards as the Ultimate Well-Being (*parama hita*; II.298).[17] Thanks to the devotion of his worshippers and out of love for them (the bond of bhakti) the 'Ocean of Mercy assumes body for the well-being of people' (*kṛpa sindhu jana hita tanu dharahīṃ*; *RCM*, I.122.1). Therefore he is simultaneously a human being, who–tested in times of adversities–remains the epitome of virtuous nature; he is the 'Ocean of Virtue' (*sīlasindhu*; *RCM*, II.243.1) and sets the best example for others. Like in the case of Vālmīki's hero, Tulsīdās's Rām is characterized by righteousness–his steadfast devotion to truth and *dharma* are testified to in a number of passages and one of the most telling of them is formed of Rām's own words:

> There is no dharma equal to truth,
> so preach the Āgamas, Nigamas and Purāṇas
> I have acquired it naturally,
> had I abandoned it, the three worlds would have been disgraced.

---

13. For more on this subject, see Stasik, *Opowieść o prawym królu*, pp. 276-91 and, 'On the Nature of Rāma in Tulsīdās's *Rāmcaritmānas,*' *Toḥfa-e-Dil: Festschrift Helmut Nespital*, ed. by Dirk W. Lönne, Reinbek: Dr. Inge Wezler Verlag für Orientalistische Fachpublikationen, 2001, pp. 487-500.

14. For more on this subject, see Pollock, 'The Divine King,' and Sh. Pollock (transl.), *The Rāmāyaṇa of Vālmīki: An Epic of Ancient India*, vol. 2, Princeton: Princeton University Press, 1986, pp. 15-54.

15. Cp. Whaling, *The Rise of the Religious Significance*, p. 92.

16. For more on this subject, see Stasik 2000, *Opowieść o prawym królu*, pp. 131-44 and Stasik, 'On the Nature of Ram.'

17. All quotations according to the edition: Tulsīdās, *Rāmcaritmānas*, Gorakhpur: Gītā Pres, 1972 (V.S. 2029); hereafter *RCM*.

[And] disgrace to a man of honour
is like a fearful fire of myriads of deaths. (II.95.3-4)[18]

It should be also remembered that from the perspective of Rām as God his mundane life is a play or *līlā*, in which he himself participates both as an actor (*naṭa iva kapaṭa carita kara nānā*; VI.73.6), and as a spectator (*jagu pekhana tumha dekhanihāre*; II.127.1). Thus it can be assumed that even if Rām just plays his role of a man, he has not only to play it accordingly to the expectations of the people who surround him but also, most probably, not against their nature.[19]

3. Angry Rām
3.1. Notes on the Vocabulary

In modern standard Hindi, which is known for its lexicon of diversified origin, the most frequently used words denoting 'anger' are: Sanskrit *krodh* belonging to the higher register of Hindi, and more colloquial Arabic *ġussā*. Apart from them we should also note Persian *nārāzgī*, Sanskrit *kopa* and *roṣa* or New Indo-Aryan *riṣ* (f.; S.),[20] but these words, except for the first of them, do not belong to the basic lexis of Hindi. In this context it may seem interesting to note that Hindi speakers talking about 'God's anger' have at their disposal two phrases, most commonly used in such contexts, which contain nouns yet different from those that we have just mentioned. One of them is composed of Sanskrit words, and it is *daivī prakop*, and the other one—*xudā kā ġazab*—uses Perso-Arabic vocabulary. In the first of them, an earlier mentioned noun *kop* has been modified with a prefix *pra*, reinforcing its basic meaning; thus *prakop* signifies, among other things, 'violent anger, rage, wrath, fury.'[21] It is also worth mentioning that the phrase *daivī prakop* has been lexicalized with the meaning 'cataclysm, natural catastrophe.' Taking into consideration the scope of meaning of the noun *ġazab* ('anger, outrage'; 'calamity, disaster') one cannot exclude the possibility of *daivī prakop* being a calque.

---

18. *dharamu na dūsara satya samānā; āgama nigama purāna bakhānā./ maiṃ soi dharamu sulabha kari pāva; tajeṃ tihūṃ pura apajasu chāvā./ saṃbhāvita kahuṃ apajasa lāhū; marana koṭi sama dāruna dāhū.*

19. Interesting remarks concerning this thesis can be found in Pollock, *The Rāmāyaṇa*, pp. 63-4.

20. R. S. McGregor, *The Oxford-Hindi-Dictionary*, New Delhi: Oxford UniversityPress, 1993, p. 865; Baccūlāl Anvasthī, *Tulsī śabd-koś*, Dillī: Buks en' buks, 1991, p. 926.

21. Cp. e.g. R. S. McGregor, *The Oxford-Hindi Dictionary*; John T. Platts, *A Dictionary of Urdū, Classical Hindī and English*, New Delhi: Oriental Books Reprint, 1977, and Kālikā Prasād et al. (eds.), *Bṛhat hindī koś*, Vārāṇasī: Jñānmaṇḍal Limiṭeḍ, 1984.

Some of these words, functioning in modern standard Hindi, can be also found in the sixteenth-century Avadhi of the *Rāmcaritmānas*.[22] The most common word for 'anger' in the poem is a Sanskrit noun *krodha*, which together with its phonetical variants (*krodhī*, *krodhu*), has been used 51 times on its own and 4 times in compounds (*krodhātura* and *krodhānala*), and an adjective *kruddha*, which together with its variants (*kruddhā*, *kruddhe*) has been used 16 times.[23] We should also mention a New Indo-Aryan noun *koha*, etymologically connected with *krodha*, that together with its variants (*kohā*, *kohu*, *kohū*) and an adjective *kohī* have been used 17 times.[24] From the point of view of its frequency, slightly behind *krodha* come a new Indo-Aryan *risa*, which has been used 35 times, and verbal forms derived form it, used 18 times;[25] Sanskrit *kopa*, with variants (*kopā*, *kopu*), used 23 times, and new Indo-Aryan verbal forms derived form it (*kopahi*, *kopi*, *kopihi*, *kope*, *kopeu*, *kopyo*), used 26 times, and, finally, also Sanskrit *roṣa*, with its variants (*roṣā*, *roṣu*, *roṣū*), used 21 times, and, connected with it, a new Indo-Aryan form *rosā* with variants (*rosu*, *rosū*) used 6 times.[26]

It may be noted here that *ġazab*, *ġussā* and *nārāzgī*, mentioned earlier, are not used in the poem, although some examples of Perso-Arabic vocabulary can be found in it.[27]

An important observation about the word *roṣa* should be made. When used with the name of Rām (e.g. *RCM* II.218.3. III.29.9 and VII.66 kha) it points vividly to this feature of his nature, which the tradition does not seem to much emphasize, and which is simply disclaimed by some contemporary authors.[28] (An entirely different matter is the fact that for most of his followers, Bhaktas, he is one who never grows angry!)

Let us thus examine in which contexts the word 'anger,' and words related to it, appear in the *Rāmcaritmānas* in connection with the figure of Rām.

---

22. For more about the language of Tulsīdās, see Devakīnandan Śrīvāstav, *Tulsīdās kī bhāṣā*, Lakhnaū: Lakhnaū viśvavidyālay, 1957 (V.S. 2014).
23. Winand M. Callewaert and Philip Lutgendorf, *Rāmcaritmānas Word Index,* New Delhi: Manohar, 1997, p. 75.
24. Ibid., p. 74
25. *risāi, risāī, risāte, risāna, risāni, risānī, risāne, risāhiṃ, risauhaiṃ*; ibid., p. 273.
26. Ibid., pp. 74, 273 and 275.
27. For more, see Śrīvāstav, *Tulsīdās kī bhāṣā*, pp. 205-13.
28. E.g. Dhirendra Narain, quoted by Goldman, *The Rāmāyaṇa,* p. 50.

3.2. Rām and Anger

We have mentioned earlier that Vālmīki pictured Rām's anger in three different situations. Tulsīdās slightly departs from this tradition and depicts the angry countenance of his hero only in the two of them.

Thus we see Rām trying to persuade the ocean to subdue its waters and let his army cross over to Laṅkā. The ocean, however, does not give in to his persuasion. Finally, Rām concludes angrily that the ocean will not be of help to him until it experiences the feeling of fear (*bole rāmu sakopa taba bhaya binu hoi na prīti*; *RCM* V.57). Therefore he takes his bow and fits to it a frightful arrow of fire, which—still on the bowstring—emits blazing fire straight onto the ocean. This poses a terrible threat to its existence, so the frightened ocean asks Rām to forgive him. Rām, himself the Ocean of Mercy, smiles, as if nothing has happened, and wants to learn about the way in which the monkey host could cross over to Laṅkā. (*RCM* V.51.3-4, 56.1-3, 57-60.4).

Angry Rām is also portrayed in battle scenes, i.e. in a few interventions during the war on Laṅkā, and when it comes to its climax, i.e. in his duel with Rāvaṇ (*RCM* VI.69.3, 71.2, 87.4, 91.4, 91 *chand*, 92.3, 93.3 and 101 *chand*). It is of importance to note here that in these scenes comments on Rām's emotions are limited to, so to say, a symbolic minimum. And whenever his anger is referred to, it is synonymous with the uplifting of his bow ready for a shot (cp. e.g. *RCM* VI.71.2, 87.4, 91.3 and 101 *chand*); sometimes it is accompanied with his smile or laugh. It is so, because these terrifying moments are a real threat but for others, not for him, because it is them and not him who are filled with fear; and fear, as should be noted, is familiar not only to the soldiers of the two armies, but also to the gods observing the battle (cp. e.g. *RCM* VI.71.2).

The third situation, which chronologically is the first one in Tulsīdās's poem, takes an entirely different course. The despair of Rām after the abduction of Sītā has no single climax in the form of an outburst of uncontrolled anger, as in Vālmīki. It subsides and returns, inflaming his pain, being followed by an unexpected finale. It takes the form of a dialogue between Rām and the sage Nārad, dealing with the imperfect human nature and a disgraceful role played by women in leading this world astray (*RCM* III.38.6-46B). It is very symptomatic, as if Tulsīdās expressed the conviction that Rām's anger would not be proper in such a situation (i.e. because of the loss of his woman) which seems to be corroborated by those moments of this episode in which Rām, or more precisely his name, is presented as the destroyer of sin (*agaha khaga gana badhikā*; *RCM* III.42.4); and sin is the cause of anger (*krodhu pāpa kara mūla*; *RCM* I.277), as well as of, among other things, desire (*kāma*), greed (*lobha*), intoxication (*mada*), delusion (*moha*) and pride (*māna*) (*RCM* III.43, 44.2, 45.4; cp. e.g. I.43.3, II. 130.1, III.39.2, III.43, V.38 and VII.73A).

Rām is pictured in such a way almost in the whole poem—he is the one who eradicates every fault (*doṣa*/*dosā*) and sin (*pāpa*). Thus in this context a question essential for the understanding of Rām's nature arises. How to reconcile his anger, anger which annihilates *dharma* (*RCM* IV.15.2), with the fact that Rām is the one who upholds *dharma*?

3.3. Conclusions

From the foregoing analysis it is evident that in the *Rāmcaritmānas* Rām's behaviour, reduced almost to a symbol, sets the standard of the modes of conduct that are culturally best justified and thus most acceptable.

The poem clearly indicates that anger as such is not proper, that it is an emotion which should earnestly be avoided, because unrestrained it leads almost straight to violence, and as a result of it may lead to annihilation. What is very symptomatic is that Rām never grows angry if someone opposes only him, if he intends to harm only him.[29] His high morals, praised and admired by all, and his power cause that there is no need for him to resort to violence in such situations. However, in certain circumstances Rām grows angry and his anger can be justified by the fact that it appears in situations in which the well-being of persons dear to him—his relatives, devotees and subjects—has been threatened in the course of someone's vicious, hostile doings. In such circumstances Rām has to intervene, and this can take a form of either his direct persuasion or a mediation on his behalf. But if such efforts fail, anger accumulates in him and is demonstrated in order to evoke fear in the person concerned. This fear makes an evildoer either withdraw from his course of action, which means his pleading with Rām for his forgiveness that is instantly granted, or a flight, i.e. a physical withdrawal. However, if such a demonstration of his anger does not bring the desired effect, then the whole situation results in an outburst of Rām's anger accompanied by violence, ending with the death of everyone infatuated with conceit and stubbornness. They have to end their lives in such a way, because being elements of chaos and anarchy they pose a threat to society. And because from the very beginnings of the *Rāmāyaṇa* tradition it is known that Rām, in the name of *dharma*, is able to subdue his emotions, his outbursts of anger can only signify that maintaining order or upholding *dharma* is otherwise impossible. Using Sheldon Pollock's words, they can be understood as 'a "natural" manifestation of those violent and destructive

---

29. *RCM* II.218.3: *suni suresa raghunāthasubhāū; nija aparādha risāhiṃ na kāū. jo aparādhu bhagata kara karaī; rāma roṣa pāvaka so jaraī.*

capacities inherent in him as king, which have hitherto lain dormant and (...) are above (or a part of superordinate) *dharma*.'[30]

In such a way the divine king Rām teaches his subject-devotees what *dharma* is, as he knows very well that

> Lamentable is a king, who does not understand statecraft,
> and to whom his subjects [are] not as dear as his life. (*RCM*, II.172.2)[31]

30. *The Rāmāyaṇa*, p. 66.

31. *socia nṛpati jo nīti na jānā; jehi na prajā prana samāna*.

Contributors

IMRE BANGHA is Head of the Alexander Cosma de Körös Centre of Oriental Studies at the Hungarian University of Transylvania (M. Ciuc, Romania) and Lecturer in Hindi at the University of Oxford. At present he is working on the critical edition of the *Kavitāvalī* of Tulsīdās as well as the poetry of Ṭhākur and Bājid. His publications include *Saneh ko mārag* on Ānandghan (in Hindi) and *The First Published Anthology of Hindi Poets: Thomas Duer Broughton's Selections from the Popular Poetry of the Hindoos, 1814*.

MAREN BELLWINKEL-SCHEMPP is an anthropologist and independent scholar with a long-standing interest and expertise in north Indian Dalit culture.

ALLISON BUSCH is Assistant Professor in the Department of Middle Eastern and Asian Languages and Civilizations at Columbia University. Her research interests include courtly poetry in Hindi and the intellectual history of early-modern India.

WINAND M. CALLEWAERT teaches Sanskrit and Indian Religions at the Department of Asian Studies, Katholieke Universiteit Leuven. Currently he is working on the project 'Dictionary of Bhakti literature' (translating into modern Hindi and English).

VASUDHA DALMIA is Professor of Hindi, Department of South & Southeast Asian Studies, University of California, Berkeley. Her research foci are Hindi literature and Modeṛn Hinduism. Her most recent monograph *Poetics, Plays and Performances: The Politics of Modern Indian Theatre* will be published in 2006.

BALWANT SINGH DHILLON is Head, Department of Guru Nanak Studies at Guru Nanak Dev University, Amritsar. He is the author of *Early Sikh Scriptural Tradition: Myth and Reality* (1999). Another major work, *Rājasthānī Sources on the Sikh History and Religion*, is forthcoming.

DANIEL GOLD is Professor of South Asian Religions at Cornell University, Ithaca, NY. He has most recently published *Aesthetics and Analysis in Writing on Religion* (2003) and is currently studying problems of urban religion in Gwalior, M.P.

JOHN STRATTON HAWLEY (a.k.a. Jack Hawley) is Ann Whitney Olin Professor of Religion at Barnard College, Columbia University. His most recently published book on India is *Three Bhakti Voices: Mirabai, Surdas, and Kabir in Their Time and Ours* (Oxford, 2005).

MONIKA HORSTMANN is Professor at the Department of Modern South Asian Studies (Languages and Literatures), South Asia Institute, University of Heidelberg, Germany. She is the author of *In Favour of Govinddevjī* (1999) and is currently studying early-eighteenth-century religious debates at the court of Jaipur.

CATHARINA KIEHNLE is Professor of Indology at the University of Leipzig. Among her research foci is the Bhakti tradition of Maharashtra.

ROHINI MOKASHI-PUNEKAR teaches at the Department of Humanities and Social Sciences, Indian Institute of Technology, Guwahati, Assam, India. A new world edition of her translations of the poetry of Cokhamela, *On the Threshold: Songs of Chokhamela*, was published by the International Sacred Literature Trust in December 2004. *Untouchable Saints: An Indian Phenomenon*, co-edited with Eleanor Zelliot was published by Manohar in August 2005.

SHYAM MANOHAR PANDEY is Professor of Hindi Language and Literature in the Department of South Asian Studies (Università degli Studi di Napoli 'L'Orientale'). His main interest is Oral Epics in Northern India and Hindi Sufi Literature. He has already published five volumes based on the *Lorik and Candā* tale and numerous articles on medieval Hindi Literature and *Candāyan*.

HEIDI R. M. PAUWELS is Associate Professor at the University of Washington, Department of Asian Languages and Literature, Seattle. Her research foci are Braj, Avadhi, Sant Bhasha, Rajasthani; Krishna, Rama, and Nirguna Bhakti (esp. 16th and 18th Century); Hagiography; Hindu goddesses as role models for women; contemporary film and television versions of Rama and Krishna mythology and of saints; confluence of temple and court, Mughal and Rajput milieus.

LALITA DU PERRON, Ph.D. She is Researcher in the project 'The Songs of North Indian Art Music,' Department of Music, School of Oriental and African Studies, University of London. Her main research interests are Hindi song texts, performance and patronage in North India, representation of the female voice, Hindi dialects. Her book *Thumri: Hindi Song and the Courtesan Legacy* is forthcoming.

ILEANA CORNELIA POPESCU is Research Assistant in South Asian Studies at The Sergiu Al-George Institute of Oriental Studies, Bucharest, Romania. Her research foci are Krishnaite Bhakti; the feminine divine in Hinduism; Indian art, especially Rajasthani and Pahari miniature painting, and Indian aesthetics.

TEIJI SAKATA is Professor of Hindi at the Takushoku University, Tokyo. He is interested in the study of Hindi Bhakti literature and Hindi folktales. At present he is translating the *Rāmcaritmānas* of Tulsidās into Japanese (about a quarter of the whole work). He also plans to translate some lyrics by Sūrdas into Japanese.

INGRID SCHUHMANN, M.A., is presently member of the Hindi-Database Project at the Department of Modern South Asian Studies, South Asia Institute, University of Heidelberg. She has studied Sanskrit, Hindi and Tamil and anthropology. Her research has focused on Sant literature and preaching in the Caitanya tradition.

SWAPNA SHARMA holds a Ph.D. from Agra University. She is currently working on the Dictionary of Bhakti Literature Project, conducted by W. M. Callewaert at the Katholieke Universiteit Leuven. Her current research focus is on the Caitanya tradition.

HUGH VAN SKYHAWK is Associate Professor of Indology and South Asian Religions at the University of Mainz (Germany). His research foci are Bhakti literature in Old Marathi, folk religion of the Deccan, the cults and literature of Hindu-Muslim saints; oral traditions of the Burusho, oral traditions of the Ḍóma in Hunza and Nager (Karakoram).

DANUTA STASIK is Professor in the Department of South Asian Studies, Institute of Oriental Studies, University of Warsaw, where she teaches modern and old Hindi languages and literature. Her main research interests are the Rāmāyaṇa tradition in Hindi literature, Rām Bhakti in North India and the Indian diaspora in the West (particularly as represented in Hindi writing). Recently she co-edited with John Brockington *Indian Epic Traditions—Past and Present*, Warsaw 2002.

Index